CONTENTS

List of Illustrations vii
List of Abbreviations viii

1 Historicizing Consumer Culture 1

PART ONE A New World of Goods: 1800–1870

Preface 19

2 Producing Consumers: Consumption Practices 21

3 Alternative Paths: The Politics of Consumption 41

PART TWO Making a Mass Market: 1870–1920

Preface 63

4 Image Worlds: The Rise of Modern Advertising 65

5 Shopping as Pleasure: Department Stores 87

6 Co-op Commonwealth: Consumer Organizing 109

PART THREE A Consumers' Democracy: 1920–2000

Preface 133

7 Ideal Home: The Growth of the New Consumerism 135

8 Mass Consumerism: From Austerity to Affluence 157

9 Consumer Culture: The Hegemony of Choice 179

Epilogue: Satisfaction Guaranteed? 201

Notes 211
Select Bibliography 263
Index 269

ILLUSTRATIONS

Figure 1	George Cruikshank, 'The Dispersion of the Works of All Nations from the Great Exhibition of 1851', in Henry Mayhew, *1851: Or, the Adventures of Mr and Mrs Sandboys and Family* (1851). 29
Figure 2	George Cruikshank, 'Alarming Sacrifice', *Comic Almanack* (1851). 38
Figure 3	Anti-Corn Law League membership card, 1839. 44
Figure 4	C. J. Grant, 'The Modern Nero', *Penny Satirist*, 30 October 1841. 54
Figure 5	'The Age of Advertising', *Fun*, 21 January 1885. 77
Figure 6	'The Greedy Soap Trust', *Daily Mirror*, 22 October 1906. 79
Figure 7	'Selling off Winter Stock', *Snap-Shots: Humorous Pictures and Amusing Reading*, 19 January 1895. 95
Figure 8	Fred Pegram, 'The Dedication of a Great House', 1909. 105
Figure 9	Liberal postcard, 1905. 126
Figure 10	Conservative Party leaflet, 1910. 128
Figure 11	Advertisement for opening of Marks & Spencer store, November 1936. 139
Figure 12	Fred Hayward, *The Co-operative Boycott and Its Political Implications* (1930). 151
Figure 13	George Chrystal, *News of the World*, 27 May 1962. 171
Figure 14	David Low, *Guardian*, 10 June 1960. 176
Figure 15	Charles Griffin, *Daily Mirror*, 12 May 1988. 186
Figure 16	Martin Rowson, *Guardian*, 28 September 1998. 199

ABBREVIATIONS

BMA	British Medical Association
BMP	Boase, Massimi, Pollitt
CPS	Centre for Policy Studies
CA	Consumers' Association
CAI	Council for Art and Industry
CIC	Co-operative Independent Commission
CWS	Co-operative Wholesale Society
EMB	Empire Marketing Board
ILP	Independent Labour Party
IEA	Institute of Economic Affairs
JWT	J. Walter Thompson
NCC	National Consumer Council
NFTL	National Fair Trade League
NUWSS	National Union of Women's Suffrage Societies
OPEC	Organization of Petroleum Exporting Countries
RPM	Resale Price Mechanism
SCA	Shadow Communications Agency
SCAPA	Society for Checking the Abuses of Public Advertising
SDF	Social Democratic Federation
WCG	Women's Co-operative Guild
WSOC	Wider Share Ownership Council
WSPU	Women's Social and Political Union

1

Historicizing Consumer Culture

In early August 2011, serious riots broke out on the streets of London. Triggered by the shooting of an alleged criminal by the Metropolitan Police, they soon spread to other cities across England. Five people died in the disturbances and about 2,500 shops were looted in total, rioters helping themselves to designer clothing, flat screen televisions and other expensive consumer durables. Police reported that nearly 3,300 offences were committed in London, more than a third of which involved looting. The cost of damage to property was estimated at upwards of £200 million; a Miss Selfridge store was set alight in the centre of Manchester causing £500,000 worth of damage alone. For Prime Minister David Cameron the riots were evidence of a more general moral malaise – a sign of a 'broken Britain' – while the head of research for a leading City broker blamed the unrest on the 'consumerist ethos, in which a materialist vision is both peddled and, for the vast majority, simultaneously ruled out by exclusion', with damaging social and economic consequences.[1] In a similar vein, the Marxist sociologist Zygmunt Bauman contended that these riots were the actions of 'defective and disqualified consumers'. The problem of absolute scarcity may have been solved, Bauman observed – rioters were not stealing bread after all – but those who were denied the good things in life felt isolated and, as 'defective consumers', they were frequently shut out from shops and shopping, which had acquired a 'truly eschatological dimension' in modern society, lending meaning to people's lives.[2] Criminologists later supported this interpretation, coining the memorable phrase 'aggravated shopping' to describe the looting that had occurred. Denied a formal political voice or institutional power, the mainly young men and women who took part in the unrest had 'nowhere to take their anger and resentment but the shops'.[3] There were other motives behind the riots besides thwarted consumerism, as more recent academic studies have shown.[4] Nevertheless, these motives were certainly important and it is also significant that this aspect was what attracted most attention at the time, across the ideological spectrum. The riots of 2011 undoubtedly exposed deep-rooted anxieties about modern consumer culture, anxieties that had been pushed conveniently to one side during the good times but which had gradually come more to the fore since the financial crisis began in 2008.

No one could deny that the language of consumption is now ubiquitous. Our 'consumer choice' rather than our productive activity is widely regarded as *the* source of self-definition and identity: 'I shop therefore I am', as the American artist Barbara Kruger wryly observed. We are constantly addressed as consumers and the virtues of consumption are regularly proclaimed, not only by advertisers and entrepreneurs but also by politicians and commentators of all kinds. No mainstream political party would dare tell 'citizen-consumers' that they ought to significantly lower their material expectations, except to meet the exigencies of a short-term emergency. Admittedly, discordant notes are sounded quite frequently nowadays, by religious leaders concerned about rampant materialism or by environmentalists understandably worried about the effects of our seemingly insatiable appetite for things on the natural world. The onset of the 'credit crisis' prompted the Bishop of Liverpool, James Jones, to link these anxieties on BBC Radio 4 in 2009. 'We call ourselves "consumers" and fail to see the irony. To consume is to devour and to destroy', Jones noted, and he continued, 'I imagine that historians of the twenty-second century might look back with incredulity that we could have called ourselves so comfortably "the consumer society", plundering and consuming the earth as if it were some limitless larder. If you couple our cavalier attitude to consumption to the reality of the debt we are now in both nationally and, for many of us, personally, you begin to realise just how much more serious the situation really is.'[5] This powerful argument for personal and social reflection on the meaning of consumption gained a hearing for a short while, when it seemed as if our economic system was on the brink of collapse. But such voices were soon drowned out amid the general chorus of approval, as commercial and political elites looked eagerly for signs of rising 'consumer confidence' that would portend a return of plenty.[6]

When did consumerism assume this central position in British life? Recalling their own experiences, some scholars have suggested that an important turning point occurred towards the end of the twentieth century. The literary critic Rachel Bowlby, for example, has observed that until the 1960s and 1970s the phrase 'consumer society' carried largely pejorative connotations, referring to a deluded, usually female population – easy prey for manipulative advertisers. By the turn of the century, however, 'a remarkable rhetorical turnabout' had taken place, whereby 'the consumer has been elevated to a status of exemplary good sense in areas extending far beyond shopping itself'.[7] Similarly, Avner Offer, retired Chichele Professor of Economic History at the University of Oxford, pinpoints the late Thatcher years as a key moment of change, remembering that 'no longer did notices and loudspeakers speak to travellers as "passengers", or to sick people as "patients". They were now addressed as "customers".' Musing on the significance of this linguistic shift, Offer suggests that 'it appears almost as the ideological mirror image of the use of the term "comrade" in the Soviet Union. Customers were supposed to be "empowered" by "choice".'[8] The view that profound change occurred in the late twentieth century has a lot to recommend it, though the roots go back a very long way indeed. Consequently, this book explores how our consumption habits have changed over the past two hundred years, particularly our consumption of consumer goods. Some major omissions have had to be made, primarily for reasons of space. Little is said in the pages that follow about housing, for instance – the cost of which represented a large percentage of private expenditure, particularly for working-class consumers throughout the nineteenth century and well beyond – or leisure, sport and tourism, areas of social life which also came to be thoroughly commercialized during the period covered by this book.[9] The focus here is mainly on the sphere of retailing and the practice of shopping for everyday goods, the most immediate and quotidian signs of modern consumer culture.

The generally positive contemporary dominance of 'consumer' and 'consumption' as descriptive nouns for the use of all kinds of goods and services tells us a great deal about the kind of society we now live in. 'Consume' dates back to the fourteenth century and was originally almost always used in a negative sense, meaning to use up or waste, as the Bishop of Liverpool reminded listeners. This negative sense can still be found in 'consumed by fire' and consumption as a popular description of tuberculosis that caused people to literally waste away. Similarly, 'consumer' was negatively freighted when it entered the language in the sixteenth century. From the mid-eighteenth century, however, this word began to be used in a more neutral sense within the emergent discipline of political economy and, as the capitalist market extended its reach, spheres of human activity began to be conceived more abstractly in terms of production and consumption, with corresponding identities defined increasingly as producer and consumer. Negative connotations of consumer were remarkably persistent though, continuing until the late nineteenth century at least.[10] 'Consumerism' was used during the interwar period in America but only appeared in Britain after the Second World War. It carried two distinct meanings, referring to movements of organized consumers that had developed to protect consumer interests between the wars, but also conveying a more general sense of a growing propensity to consume. Some tried to give the term a positive spin early on. In 1955 the *Daily Express* quoted the vice president of Ford who proposed that '"consumerism" be substituted for "capitalism"' owing to the fact that the 'consumer is the real boss and beneficiary' of the economic system.[11] But opprobrium stubbornly clung to the term, which only increased following the publication in the late 1950s of books by American intellectuals such as J. K. Galbraith and Vance Packard that were critical of the 'affluent society' (another neologism) and its methods.[12] Both 'consumer society' and 'consumer culture' also tended to be used pejoratively from about this time, usually to condemn the supposed shallowness and moral vacuity of a commercialized 'mass culture'.[13] Talking about George Lichtenstein's graphic art in 1964, for example, a correspondent writing in *The Times* spoke about how it captured 'the utter banality of mass consumer culture'.[14] Clearly, then, these concepts are highly complex and come loaded with a great deal of historical baggage.[15]

This complexity has led some historians to deny the usefulness of terms such as 'consumerism', 'consumer society' and 'consumer culture' altogether.[16] We need to be wary of over-generalized, imprecise concepts, certainly, and we ought to be careful of moralistic attacks on people's consumer practices in the past. Middle-class intellectuals have often been too quick to denounce the materialistic 'consumerism' of the 'masses', easy to do when one has enough of the good things in life oneself.[17] Nevertheless, there is no need surely to reject these terms out of hand so long as we are aware of their problematic and changing meanings – after all, we need concepts to think with and help make sense of the past and present. The concept of a 'consumer culture', for instance, helps us to grasp the fact that a whole way of life has been constructed around the consumer and to realize how consumption now figures as a motivating centre around which other aspects of social life revolve. This is not to suggest that every aspect of our lives have been commoditized or that consumption is now the only source of identity; work remains an important source of meaning for many people and some simple pleasures are still free, but the reach of consumer culture seems clear enough. Its eventual hegemony depended on the agency of numerous manufacturers, retailers, advertisers, newspaper proprietors, publishers and politicians as well as countless numbers of men, women and children whose day-to-day purchasing decisions made modern consumer culture possible. When and why did people want more goods and how did they acquire them? What did commentators say about the transformations that this widening market entailed and how did they evaluate these changes?

The answer to why people desired more things has often been regarded by historians as self-evident, particularly as far as working-class consumers are concerned; they wanted more 'comforts' in order to 'ameliorate' lives that were frequently impoverished by material scarcity.[18] Of course, there is some truth in this argument but it is seriously flawed. It underestimates the way different groups in society had competing visions of consumption and sought to organize consumers to make those visions real. It ignores the way consumer culture was shaped by government policy, sometimes restrained or channelled in certain ways, at other times encouraged and celebrated. In short, instinctivist explanations for the emergence and generalization of consumer culture ignore questions of power – how the making of consumer culture was necessarily a political process that involved the triumph of particular historical alternatives and the suppression of others. This study of the making of consumer culture in Britain over the past two centuries explores such issues, presenting an overview of and a route through a vibrant field of inquiry. It argues that the consumer culture which emerged during this period was shaped as much by political relationships as it was by economic and social factors.

Some theoretical perspectives

Historical understanding of this subject has perhaps been hindered as much as helped by the work of earlier social theorists who tended to share the generally negative stance towards consumption traditionally adopted by many intellectuals. It is not the intention here to discuss theoretical perspectives in detail, though a brief consideration might be useful. Karl Marx may have accompanied his wife, Jenny, on shopping trips and been obsessed with the burgeoning world of goods on the streets of mid-Victorian London, but his analysis of capitalism focused squarely on production and he had remarkably little to say about consumption. Classes, for Marx, were formed by virtue of their relationship to the means of production and the majority, the working class, who had nothing to sell but their labour power, were alienated both from the products of their labour, which were taken from them by the owners of capital, and from the wider society, over which they had little or no control. He prophesied that finding their exploitation increasingly unbearable, organized producers would eventually rise up to overthrow the dominant economic system and replace it with socialism.

Although Marx tended to ignore the specificities of Victorian consumerism – including the opportunities it afforded for organized consumer action – a relatively minor aspect of his analysis of the commodity form in the first volume of *Capital* (1867) has subsequently been highly suggestive: the idea of 'commodity fetishism'. Marx argued that as commodities were torn from the social and historical relationships that had brought them into existence, they took on the properties of a religious fetish. As totemic objects of worship, commodities appeared to have fallen from the skies and presented themselves not as products of labour but as endowed with lives of their own, seemingly able to bring themselves to market. The exchange of the products of labour in the capitalist market created ideological mystification, turning everything on its head and making the social world appear topsy-turvy. Relations between people thus took on the quality of relations between things or were reified, while things were typically personified, taking on characters of their own. Marx wrote:

> The mysterious character of the commodity-form consists therefore simply in the fact that the commodity reflects the social characteristics of men's own labour as objective characteristics of the products of labour themselves, as the socio-natural properties of these things. Hence it also reflects the social relation of the producers to the sum total of labour as a social relation between objects, a relation which exists apart from

> and outside the producers. Through this substitution, the products of labour become commodities, sensuous things which are at the same time supra-sensible or social … It is nothing but the definite social relation between men themselves which assumes here, for them, the fantastic form of a relation between things. In order, therefore, to find an analogy we must take flight into the misty realm of religion. There the products of the human brain appear as autonomous figures endowed with a life of their own, which enter into relations both with each other and with the human race. So it is in the world of commodities with the products of men's hands. I call this the fetishism which attaches itself to the products of labour as soon as they are produced as commodities, and is therefore inseparable from the production of commodities.[19]

Although somewhat tangential to Marx's theoretical project and highly speculative, many literary and cultural critics have found the notion of 'commodity fetishism' very useful, helping them to better understand the transformation of the role of advertising, for instance, as advertisers, it is thought, implicitly grasped the mystical or 'phantasmagorical' nature of the commodity and used it to their advantage.

More influential, as far as historians of consumption are concerned, have been the ideas of the late nineteenth century American sociologist, Thorstein Veblen. The son of Norwegian immigrants, Veblen's Lutheran religious background no doubt shaped his views, as did his fraught relationship with the academy and his outsider persona. In his caustic analysis of the plutocracy, *The Theory of the Leisure Class* (1899), Veblen argued that consumer goods did not merely fulfil material needs but were complex, highly symbolic phenomena. In an increasingly urbanized, anonymous modern society, Veblen believed, people used dress and other commodities to say things about themselves, particularly their status. The rich displayed their wealth and asserted their power by means of wasteful 'conspicuous consumption', often showing off their possessions in a highly ritualistic, even theatrical manner. However, it was not just the idle rich who acted in this way; all groups were affected, including the middle classes with more disposable income and also artisans and workers. Moreover, Veblen emphasized that consumption practices were frequently gendered and that men and women had access to different kinds of goods. This had been the case in pre-capitalist, 'traditional' societies, but differences persisted in the modern world; women were generally prohibited from consuming narcotics such as tobacco and spirits, for example. Finally, and most importantly, Veblen suggested that peoples' consumption habits could best be explained in terms of 'social emulation'; whenever possible, individuals copied the consumption practices of their superiors, were forever craning their necks and looking upwards, taking their consumption cues from those above them in the social and economic hierarchy.[20] Veblen expressed these ideas with venomous wit, deflating the pretentions of the super-rich of his time such as the Vanderbilts, and attacking their wasteful expenditure as immoral. His emphasis on the symbolic meanings of goods and the gendered nature of consumption was valuable but other aspects of his work have attracted much criticism, especially the notion of social emulation as an explanation for why people want goods. As many scholars have pointed out, most consumers are not forever looking upwards and desiring goods always out of reach. Instead, they seek to consume goods that enable them to better fit in and identify with the socio-economic group to which they belong, rather than that to which they aspire. Thus, consumption practices are more often about maintaining one's position in the race rather than winning, looking sideways rather than above.[21]

Whereas Marx's sense of the 'fetishism' of commodities was influenced by the shopping streets of Victorian London, and Veblen's views on 'conspicuous consumption' were shaped by the showy excesses of American plutocrats during the fin de siècle, the critique of consumer society produced by the French intellectual Jean Baudrillard was grounded in the post–Second World War shopping mall. In *La Société de Consummation* (1970), Baudrillard brought the developing study of semiotics to the analysis of consumer culture. In this work, Baudrillard rejected Marx's overriding emphasis on production, arguing that modern capitalism was best understood from the perspective of consumption. He contested the idea that people were simply duped into wanting more things by canny advertisers who created 'false' needs, as liberal thinkers like the American economist J. K. Galbraith had maintained. Baudrillard questioned the instinctivist basis of this argument, suggesting that the definition of needs was far more complex than moralistic critics of modern consumerism allowed; the boundary between wasteful 'luxury' and basic 'necessity', for instance, was historically contingent and therefore constantly changing. Like Marx and Veblen, Baudrillard stressed that commodities were complex things, which carried symbolic meanings and functioned as signifiers. Understood as a totality, consumer goods constituted a kind of language through which buyers articulated both their real and imagined desires. Linked together in the mail-order catalogue or in displays behind plate-glass windows in department stores, the desire for particular commodities was part of what he called a 'general hysteria', which Baudrillard likened to the pathology of this mental illness – the desire for particular goods was analogous to the way in which various symptoms paraded themselves in patients suffering from hysteria. The quintessential space where this disease of modern capitalism could be found was the shopping mall. The implications were grim. For Baudrillard, Western consumers strolling through these climate-controlled utopias were unwitting inhabitants of a new kind of prison, akin to Max Weber's bureaucratic iron cage but constructed instead from their own insatiable desires. Feeding off 'general hysteria', contemporary consumer society according to Baudrillard was nothing other than a form of 'social control', and he argued that 'the current training in systematic, organized consumption is the equivalent and extension, in the twentieth century, of the great nineteenth-century-long process of the training of rural populations for industrial work'. Attempts by consumers to reform this system were destined to fail because they lacked agency and were necessarily divided rather than united by their practices and identities as consumers.[22]

The eighteenth-century context

These key thinkers analysed consumption as either 'fetishism', 'emulation' or 'hysteria'. They not only shared a highly negative outlook, their theories also lacked historical specificity and failed to explain precisely when and how modern consumerism had emerged or how it had contributed to the enormous changes that had taken place since industrialization.[23] With these questions in mind, a number of historians have traced the roots of consumer society in Britain back to the seventeenth century and earlier.[24] The most ambitious (or foolhardy) have sought to construct an even wider frame, narrating the ineluctable global march of the 'empire of things' across more than half a millennia.[25] Many historians, however, look for origins in the eighteenth century. The enormously rich historical work in this field that has appeared over the last three decades or so employed some of the theoretical insights that have been briefly discussed. Neil McKendrick's path-breaking work leans heavily on Veblen's notion of social emulation, for example. According to McKendrick, the eighteenth century witnessed nothing less than a 'consumer revolution' – a transformation as profound as the revolution in production – as growing numbers of consumers eagerly bought the latest china, furniture and furnishings, clothing, and imported slave-produced foodstuffs such as sugar, tea, and coffee. Evidence of this new material culture was obvious to foreign observers, who drew contrasts with the relative lack of consumer goods elsewhere in Europe. A combination of factors accounted for this British peculiarity: the growth and increasing prosperity of the 'middling ranks' of society; the size and importance of London as a commercial centre; the overturning of the economic doctrine of mercantilism, which aimed at achieving a balanced rather than an expanding economy and which denigrated imported foreign 'luxuries' as morally dubious and enervating; and the spread of fashion consciousness among all levels of society, including among the large class of domestic servants that provided a vital link in the chain of consumption, as even the lower orders had an eye for the latest bonnet, taking their cues from their social superiors. The notion that an increasing propensity to consume was the motor of economic advance slowly spread before 1776 when Adam Smith could state in the *Wealth of Nations* that 'consumption is the sole end and purpose of all production; and the interest of the producer ought to be attended to, only so far as it may be necessary for promoting that of the consumer. The maxim is … perfectly self-evident.'[26]

In McKendrick's account, fashion was no longer regarded as a trivial phenomenon, best left to amateur (and frequently female) historians, but featured instead as a motor of economic change. Its influence was spread by the production of cheap fashion dolls and numerous periodicals such as the *Lady's Magazine*, which published the first colour fashion print in 1771. The industrial revolution depended on the sale of humble products like beer, buckles and buttons, knives and forks, cups and saucers and cheap cottons, and contemporary commentators often remarked how all ranks participated in the new consumerism; the *London Magazine* in 1772 complaining that 'the lower orders of the people (if there are any, for distinctions are now confounded) are equally emerged in their fashionable vices'. Although London set the pace, 'Scotch drapers' and other itinerant traders brought goods within reach of provincial consumers and shops such as Browns of Chester also catered for the expanding wants of genteel consumers far from the metropolis.[27] Entrepreneurs like Josiah Wedgwood played a vanguard role in stimulating consumer desire. The Staffordshire potter was a major promoter of the 'china mania' that gripped Europe's rich during the last third of the eighteenth century. His astonishing success was due not to pricing (his goods were actually more expensive than most of his rivals'), nor to draconian methods of labour control, though these were employed at his factory at Etruria, but owed more to Wedgwood's astute marketing strategy: 'One of the most brilliant and sustained campaigns in the history of consumer exploitation'. Wedgwood went to great lengths to ensure that his goods were judged fashionable, securing the patronage of royalty, nobility and gentry, and he made extensive use of warehouses and showrooms not only in London but also in Bath, Liverpool, Dublin and elsewhere, as well as pushing his products nationwide through exhibitions, trademarks, press advertisements and travelling salesmen. When he died a very wealthy man in 1795, people no longer spoke of 'common pewter' but of 'common Wedgwood'.[28]

A generation of scholars have fleshed out these insights. The sociologist Colin Campbell, for example, argued that romanticism provided the ideological underpinnings of modern consumerism in the eighteenth century, encouraging greater reflection on the self and a quest for hedonistic pleasure, which, like romantic love, could never be fully satisfied. As such, it complemented the discipline of the Protestant work ethic that Max Weber famously suggested had made possible the rise of capitalism during the preceding century.[29] Unsurprisingly, historians tended to take a less speculative approach to the subject. One of the most useful studies to appear was Lorna Weatherill's monograph based on a national sample of about 3,000 probate inventories that listed household goods of deceased persons from the middle ranks between 1675 and 1725. From this kind of evidence, one is able to gain a less impressionistic picture of the spread of material possessions, the kinds of goods people purchased and the kinds of people who bought them. Weatherill concluded that those engaged in trade, commerce, and professional occupations were more likely to own fashionable domestic goods than those engaged in agricultural occupations, underlining the importance of urban consumption, as did research by other scholars.[30] She found that despite their higher social standing, the lesser gentry were less likely to own most kinds of goods than commercial and professional people and contested earlier explanations that relied on Veblen and the idea of social emulation to explain consumer practice. Importantly, Weatherill also stressed that 'we should be very cautious about accepting that the market extended as far down the social hierarchy' as McKendrick had maintained, as the middle ranks – between the upper gentry and labourers – constituted the most important consumer markets. Although admitting the relationship between status and ownership of goods, she helpfully observed that 'the theory of emulation, while applicable in some cases, can easily be overstated with little regard for the practical and social situations of people's lives or the exact nature of the social hierarchy'.[31]

Other historians have used qualitative sources to explore the social life of goods more deeply. Using letters and diaries of provincial women in Georgian Lancashire, Amanda Vickery has researched genteel consumption in meticulous detail, allowing greater understanding of how goods were appropriated by their owners and the meanings that were assigned to them. She shows how genteel women used material culture to construct their social identities and assert their status: 'Mahogany, silver, porcelain and silk all announced the wealth and taste of the privileged. A shared material culture united polite families.' Metropolitan gentlefolk may have regarded themselves as cutting edge with their Chippendale furniture but North-West elites were not in their shadow, actively preferring the productions of Gillows of Lancaster as less showy, better lasting. The world of goods was gendered of course; a gentlewomen and housekeeper like Elizabeth Shackleton was the main household consumer but husband John bought big ticket items like their mahogany dining table. Consumption was not only about keeping up appearances either, as women invariably expressed their personalities by means of their possessions, especially dress. Again, evidence suggests that although they were often very fashion conscious, they did not simply follow the dictates of high fashion or mimic the styles of their economic and social superiors.[32] Early taste professionals advised them on the right things to buy in order to appear respectable rather than flashy.[33] Elizabeth Shackleton used goods to help maintain barriers between social groups but she also frequently endowed her things with emotional meaning and freighted them with family memories. Gift giving played an important role here. Shackleton sometimes gave cast-offs and small trinkets to her servants, hoping to strengthen bonds of obligation and deference thereby. However, she made servants in her employ no allowance for 'luxuries' such as tea, coffee and sugar, and keenly asserted her property rights when insubordinate servants helped themselves. In the late 1770s, Shackleton recorded in her diary that she was 'much vexed' when she discovered that her cook was drinking full-cream milk, and fiercely contested the expropriation of what seemed to her to be illegitimate perquisites, indignantly complaining about how 'servants come to a high hand indeed'.[34]

We now know a great deal about many aspects of eighteenth-century consumerism. Detailed studies of colonial goods such as sugar, coffee and tea that were being transformed into everyday luxuries craved by both rich and poor – much to Shackleton's dismay – have deepened our understanding of both the local and global impact of commodity flows. Tea and coffee drinking became important rituals requiring a panoply of material accoutrements, which helped to cement gendered spheres of private and public life, frequently bridging both.[35] Clothing and footwear have also attracted historians, who have sometimes lent support – often on the basis of rather flimsy evidence – to the argument for an extension of demand down the social scale to plebeian consumers.[36] Unsurprisingly, the place where people purchased goods has also attracted attention and the subject of shops and shopping has been thoroughly re-evaluated.[37] Numbers of fixed shops increased across the century, though fairs, markets and hawkers continued to be important, especially for poorer consumers. Those towards the bottom of the social hierarchy no doubt benefited from the growth in fashion consciousness, which meant goods were passed down the chain more quickly to be resold by second-hand dealers, whose numbers grew in London and elsewhere.[38] For those who could afford it, shopping became a leisure pursuit in itself, approved practice bound up with the etiquette of politeness.[39] A contemporary source from 1764 was typically condemnatory, interpreting it as a symptom of lassitude and referring to the way in which 'Ladies are said to go a *Shopping*, when, in the Forenoon, *sick of themselves*, they order the Coach, and driving from Shop to Shop, without the slightest Intention of purchasing any thing, they *pester* the Tradesman, by requiring him to show them his Goods, at a great Expence of Time and Trouble.'[40]

A generally optimistic picture emerges from this literature of a dynamic commercial society, gradually improving the lives of the majority of the population.[41] The influential work of the economic historian Jan de Vries, who has described how an 'industrious revolution' took off in Britain during this period based on a relatively high wage economy compared to its European counterparts, lends support to this roseate view. According to de Vries, women and children as well as men were sucked into wage labour and they worked hard to better themselves and buy more goods – it was their 'industriousness' that depended intimately on new consumer desires which drove modern capitalism forward.[42] Despite the undoubted strengths of such arguments they are partial, as they tend to marginalize the existence of widespread scarcity and the prevalence of social and economic protest that regularly punctuated the polite veneer of Georgian society. As we have seen, evidence from probate inventories opens a window onto the consuming habits of the middle ranks but they tell us nothing about the relationship between the labouring poor and the world of goods. This is not to say that the latter did not benefit sometimes from the greater amount and diversity of things in circulation – the odd second-hand coat or dress, a cotton frock, more sugar, tea, coffee and tobacco – but they remained poor relatively speaking, often went hungry, and resorted to direct action to vent their feelings. The historiographical trend has been to ignore the people whose lives were consumed by the growth of a consumer society, among historians of eighteenth century consumerism at least, or else to assure us on the basis of inconclusive evidence that they must have been benefiting from material advance.

The insights of E. P. Thompson still have much to offer here. In a famous article, Thompson reconstructed the workings of what he called the 'moral economy' that, he maintained, was eroded over the course of the eighteenth century. Labouring families were dependent on bread above all else, spending over half of their weekly income on it when prices were high. What Thompson termed the 'bread-nexus' was therefore intensely political, analogous to the 'cash nexus' of the nineteenth century, and generating a 'highly-sensitive consumer-consciousness'. Buyers and sellers met together in real markets – not the abstraction imagined by Adam Smith – and the bargains they struck were saturated with values and not determined by economic rationality alone. A paternalist model existing in eroded statute law, common law and custom condemned 'immoral' market practices such as forestalling, engrossing and regrating, which were used by avaricious millers and dealers to magnify their profits. This 'moral economy' commanded a good deal of assent across social groups and when that model was tested in times of dearth, plebeian consumers sprang to its defence. In bad years, when harvests failed or supplies were interrupted by war, the threat of starvation was very real indeed and well-disciplined crowds often forcibly seized corn and other goods, 'set the price' and distributed it to those in need in a ritualized, disciplined manner, action that frequently provoked sympathy from members of local elites who had not yet fully internalized the 'truths' of political economy like the 'law' of supply and demand. Increasingly, the model drifted away from reality as political economy grew stronger towards the end of the century and the spheres of morality and economics became more completely disaggregated in both theory and practice.[43]

Modern scholarship is divided on the usefulness of the idea of 'moral economy'. Some deny that it ever existed, pointing out that all economic systems are shot through with morality and that capitalism therefore cannot be accused of 'demoralizing' the economic sphere. At the moment this side seems to have the advantage.[44] It might be worth pausing, however, to consider what may be lost if the concept is thrown overboard too readily. Critics like Thompson are seeking to understand how the transition to industrial capitalism happened, and the idea that economics became 'disinfested of intrusive moral imperatives' is one way of grasping that transition.[45]

Interestingly, one well-known contemporary observer provides support for this approach, albeit rather tangentially. The doggerel poem and extended polemical commentary, *The Fable of the Bees*, which began life in 1714, has often been referred to by historians of eighteenth-century consumerism, for its author Bernard Mandeville emphasized the progressive stimulus of fashion that he believed affected all consumers, the poor emulating the rich whenever they could. For Mandeville, fashion and emulation were not trivial and suspect but were instead the mainsprings of economic growth. He wrote: 'To this Emulation and continual striving to outdo one another, it is owing, that after so many Shiftings and Changing of Modes, in trumping up new ones and renewing of old ones, there is still a *plus ultra* left for the Ingenious; it is this, or at least the consequence of it, that sets the Poor to Work, adds Spurs to Industry, and encourages the skilful Artificer to search after Improvements.'[46] But there was more to Mandeville than this. The book provoked a scandal when an enlarged edition was published in 1723 that lasted, remarkably, for the rest of the century; the Dutch-born London physician who pared the flesh of the body politic was called a 'MAN-DEVIL' and his book presented as a public nuisance by the grand jury of Middlesex. Mandeville's error was to tear back the polite skin of Georgian society to reveal the vices that propelled it forward. The bees in the allegorical poem that prefaced the work cleaned up their flourishing hive, denounced the sins of avarice, prodigality, pride, vanity and luxury that created insatiable wants, and drove these vices out. The hive soon collapsed, falling prey to rival hives that had no such scruples. Mandeville was suggesting that, to be successful, capitalist modernity had necessarily to be, if not immoral, then certainly amoral, hence the work's subtitle – *Private Vices, Publick Benefits*. Morality and commercial progress were incompatible, he thought – the notion of a moral capitalism simply absurd – and that was why his book was attacked so vehemently.[47] Adam Smith was still troubled by it in *The Theory of Moral Sentiments* (1759) and it was not until the 1930s that John Maynard Keynes sought to resuscitate Mandeville as an early exponent of under consumptionist theory.[48]

Structure and argument

Focusing mostly on retailing and shopping, in this book I tell the story of how forms and relations of consumption have changed over the past two centuries in Britain. Although many vital developments certainly took place in the eighteenth century and continuities were therefore important, the market for consumer goods did not expand to encompass the majority fully until the nineteenth century. Employed in ever-expanding numbers in workshops, factories and mines – as well as in the home – working people were increasingly dependent on the market for their everyday needs, while those further up the ladder enjoyed greater choice than ever before. The growth of the 'mass market' was made possible by a combination of structural factors. The population of Britain expanded from nearly 11 million in 1801, to about 21 million in 1851, rising to over 37 million by 1901. People migrated to towns and cities looking for work and new urban centres like Merthyr Tydfil in South Wales sprang up almost overnight, sucking workers in from rural districts, while London continued to mushroom. Incomes also increased, for the middle but also for the working class, meaning that there was more money to spend in the shops and markets that boomed in tandem with the expansion of production. Technological and social change made it possible to produce more goods than ever before and more were consumed. The exact timing of the rise in real wages enjoyed by working people has been the subject of intense debate among historians for generations, 'pessimists' maintaining that the standard of living for the majority did not improve significantly until after mid-century, 'optimists' arguing for improvement decades earlier. This is a vast subject which is not only beyond the scope of the present book, it is also somewhat irrelevant to it.[49] One or two comments are necessary, however, especially as the 'dark satanic mills' view of the industrial revolution has been recently criticized as both misleading and outdated in a work that alternatively stresses the increased scope for individual advancement made possible by the new economy.[50] One might point to the expanding retailing sector and the burgeoning world of goods to buttress this argument, though it is a simplistic view which ignores the fact that a great many people protested against industrial capitalism in its early stages and sought to reform or replace it with more humane, democratic ways of consuming as well as producing goods. Many workers no doubt had a bit more cash in their pockets, even before mid-century, and they often spent it on 'luxuries' like tea and sugar as we shall see. But this did not mean that they were content with their lot or with their society, especially when those better off – who generally ignored their protests – enjoyed plenty as never before, while in bad years they still suffered from want of the necessities of life.

A major argument running through this book is that it is impossible to understand the making of consumer culture in modern Britain without placing power at the heart of things.[51] Like production, consumption is an intensely political sphere: the distribution, exchange and circulation of the products of social labour necessarily raise questions of power. Anthropologist Mary Douglas has put the point well. Goods, she observes, are arranged in 'vistas and hierarchies' that are neither fixed nor randomly arranged but under gird structures, 'anchored to human social purposes … [which] may well deserve all the criticism and moralizing that is generally given simply to the consumer's choice of goods', and she goes on to insist that there is 'no serious consumption theory possible that avoids some responsibility for social criticism. Ultimately, consumption is about power'.[52] Although historians of modern Britain were relatively slow to appreciate fully the importance of the politics of consumption, historians of the United States were rather less tardy, publishing studies which explored key phases from the American Revolution to post–Second World War.[53] This may perhaps have something to do with the fact that intellectuals in the United States have often been less coy to admit the interpenetration of commercial and political domains than they have traditionally been in Britain. The influential American conservative historian Daniel Boorstin, for example, argued for an intimate connection between mass consumption and democracy; indeed he once defined the latter as no more than 'a set of institutions which aim to make everything available to everybody'.[54] Richard Cobden, leader of the Anti-Corn Law League that mobilized middle-class consumers behind the cause of free trade in Britain in the 1840s, would have heartily agreed with this crudely instrumentalist view.[55] However, citizenship and consumption have not usually been conflated so absolutely on this side of the Atlantic, where greater diffusion of goods has caused deep anxiety, for various reasons, across different social groups, as we shall see in the chapters that follow.

Although the present book focuses on Britain, this is not to deny the fact that consumerism was a global phenomenon. As has already been noted, some of the earliest commodities that fuelled growing and more widely diffused consumption were colonial goods – sugar, coffee and tea especially. From the outset, empire was inextricably bound up with the making of consumer culture in modern Britain and its continuing influence is easily demonstrated. A national focus remains useful, however, as consumer culture not only emerged at a very early stage in Britain, it also had different characteristics to those observable in other countries. A number of studies have appeared in recent years that have considerably deepened our understanding of these different paths of development as far as the consumer is concerned, including studies of the United States, France and East and West Germany,[56] and also Asia and Africa.[57] The notion that countries outside northern Europe and the United States were stagnant for consumers clearly no longer holds water. Moreover, desiring consumers have been found in various times as well as places, including Renaissance Italy, late Ming China and the Dutch Republic of the seventeenth century. Just as one can find examples of capitalist social and economic relations before the industrial revolution took off in eighteenth-century Britain, then, so too can one discern acquisitive consumers in very different contexts. One must be careful, however, not to draw simplistic conclusions from this and flatten out historical change to argue that things have ever been thus.[58] What made Britain distinctive from the late eighteenth century onwards was that the capitalist market widened inexorably and that governments as well as entrepreneurs endeavoured to create conditions that encouraged its continued expansion in the belief that the spread of material 'comforts' among consumers was a necessary sign of economic progress and national greatness.

Adopting a chronological framework, this book considers how a consumer culture was constructed in Britain from the beginning of the nineteenth century until the end of the twentieth. We can usefully divide these two centuries into three major phases and isolate three alternative 'consumption regimes' which existed and overlapped within these phases.[59] In the first phase, discussed in Chapters 2 and 3 and covering the period from the beginning of the nineteenth century until around 1870, industrial advances facilitated the mass production of more and cheaper goods. New ways of selling and marketing these goods stimulated consumption among all classes. Branding started to spread, the number and size of shops increased and advertising was better organized. Changes in representation also occurred, including a more positive identity for the consumer and a more elaborated language of goods. Alternative politics of consumption vied with one another. Chartists contended for a democratic consumerism that emphasized control and regulation of the emergent capitalist market to protect poor consumers and spread the benefits of industrialization more evenly. Conversely, middle-class radicals trumpeted a distinctive liberal consumerism, which emphasized the progressive effects of free markets and free trade that, it was thought, would maximize material improvement, which would eventually trickle down to the majority. Although anxieties continued to be generated by consumption, this latter creed enabled the middle classes to 'make peace with indulgence'.[60]

During the second phase discussed in Chapters 4–6, stretching from the onset of what historians used to call the 'Great Depression' in the late nineteenth century until just after the First World War, important quantitative but also qualitative changes occurred as the 'mass market' was enlarged and reimagined, notwithstanding the persistence of poverty revealed by social investigators. Major shifts took place during this phase as a number of factors came together to create a visibly different kind of economy and society. Advertising became increasingly sophisticated and extended its reach across both society and polity in conditions of growing industrial concentration and monopoly power; huge department stores emerged as temples to modern consumerism that spun fantasies or 'dream worlds' for large numbers of female but also male shoppers. Liberal consumerism and the hegemony of free trade came under pressure from other groups that purported to speak for the consumer during the fin de siècle, including 'fair traders' and socialists. A specifically imperial consumerism, backed by sections of the Conservative Party, gained a great deal of popular support from the turn of the century, as did a reinvigorated democratic consumerism articulated by the co-operative movement, the leaders of which believed that it was possible for working people to build a radical alternative to capitalism by means of the collective organization of their consumption practices.

The final phase discussed in Chapters 7–9 – the short twentieth century – witnessed the consolidation and full extension of the 'mass market' for consumer goods, increasingly produced by large multinational firms and sold by multiple shops and department stores, in the context of mass democratization. The spread of cheap luxuries was aided by new developments in leisure and entertainment, most especially the cinema but also the mass press. Free trade was abandoned finally and imperial consumerism came more to the fore between the wars, though democratic consumerism continued to grow stronger. The policy of 'fair shares for all' pursued during the Second World War gave the latter a major fillip, though it soon faced pressure from a more confident capitalist consumerism, reinvigorated by a strident ideology of 'consumer sovereignty'. The ability of social democracy to effect thorough economic and social transformation was seriously undermined by its failure to treat the consumer seriously; historically, both Liberals and Conservatives had more time for consumer interests than Labour, and the latter squandered the opportunities afforded by the co-operative movement, which went into inexorable decline after it lost 'the battle of the consumer' during the 1950s. Liberal consumerism was reconfigured by neo-liberalism, which championed the consumer when the golden age of capitalism eventually ended in the early 1970s. Trading on the language of 'choice' and placing the individual consumer at the heart of culture as well as economic and political life, the neo-liberal model became hegemonic during the last two decades of the twentieth century, gaining continuing momentum thereafter and leading to the seemingly inexorable erosion of social provision. The epilogue says something about how these changes have played out in more recent years, emphasizing the way in which a consumer culture that prioritizes 'freedom of choice' continues to generate not only satisfaction but also deep anxiety.

PART ONE

A New World of Goods: 1800–1870

Preface

During the first three quarters of the nineteenth century, Britain became not only the 'workshop of the world' but also the world's leading shopping nation. No longer was the consumption of a proliferating range of goods confined to the elite and the 'middling orders', as it largely had been in the eighteenth century. Now both an expanding middle class and working class bought and enjoyed goods more than they ever did before. Colonial expansion and involvement in the slave trade facilitated flows of goods such as coffee, tea and sugar back to the metropole, where they were transformed from luxuries into necessities consumed by all social groups. People used goods to meet their daily needs and to fashion individual and collective identities. Indeed, classes were defined to a major extent by what people consumed and where they purchased their food, clothes, furniture and other belongings. Countless retailing outlets sprang up in urban centres to meet growing demand. Old forms were developed and new ones appeared: arcades and bazaars heightened the pleasures of just looking; drapers' shops mushroomed into emporia and early department stores; street-sellers and shops of all kinds swelled in number and urban markets were redeveloped; while 'Scotch drapers' and packmen hawked goods throughout the country. Concrete transformations like these were accompanied by changes in representation and language. A new discourse was elaborated by the advertising industry, which trumpeted the emergent consumer culture on the walls of towns and cities and in the cheap newspapers read by their inhabitants. Wedded traditionally to the fundamental role of labour, political economists were generally reluctant to join in the chorus of praise to the desire for material things. But by around 1870, the consumer was no longer regarded as necessarily wasteful and therefore less important than the producer, while shopping was no longer dismissed as morally dubious and quintessentially feminine. Instead, they were now seen as motive forces of a whole economic and moral order, as generators of 'Progress'.

Such momentous economic and social changes sparked friction and political responses. The new world of goods was simultaneously a source of utopian imagining and seething discontent, during the first half of the nineteenth century especially. Many middle-class politicians and intellectuals looked forward to a time when goods would trickle down to the poor at home and abroad, civilizing them in the process. They hoped free trade would bring the good life to more and more people and they organized a popular campaign to press government to abolish tariffs, which they believed were holding back the tide of general improvement. All groups in society were consumers, they maintained, and their interests were therefore universal and above the sectional interests of class. On the other hand, the working class were often adversely affected by the spread of capitalist consumerism, losing what remained of their traditional means of subsistence. Dependent on the market for their everyday needs, they could no longer 'gnaw it out' during the bad times and were increasingly vulnerable to exploitation by middlemen. Plebeian radicals argued that markets needed to be regulated to protect poor consumers against rapacious capitalists who fleeced them and they sought to mobilize working-class consumers for political change. These alternative visions of consumption clashed violently in the early Victorian period. They blurred after mid-century, however, when a specifically liberal consumerism effectively appeased ordinary consumers and rising living standards seemed to prove that the confidence of free traders had indeed been well placed.

2

Producing Consumers: Consumption Practices

Forms of consumption

Writing in his autobiography in 1872, William Ablett, who described himself as 'the oldest draper now living in London', recorded the profound changes in retailing and the shopping habits of the people that he had witnessed since the early nineteenth century. Apprenticed to a 'low' draper in Whitechapel in London's East End at the age of thirteen following the death of his father (who had been a modest provincial draper), Ablett arrived in the city around 1810. He found a thriving and expanding shopping centre; a few years later Oxford Street alone included 153 shops catering solely for 'the whim-whams and fribble-frabble of fashion' according to a contemporary source, and the trade was changing fast.[1] Department stores were yet to appear but haggling over price was on the way out and the practice of 'ticketing' goods, that is, selling them at fixed prices, was gradually being adopted. Retailing was becoming much more artful and window dressing was being transformed. In this environment pushy salesmen could make their mark and Ablett took full advantage of the opportunities on offer, making a name for himself by selling slow-moving stock at inflated prices, for which he was paid handsome bonuses or 'tinges'. He worked his way up the haberdashery department, becoming a 'fancy buyer'. Aspiring to be a 'City shawl man' in upmarket stores, Ablett moved on, first to Waithman's at the corner of Fleet Street, then to Everington's on Ludgate Hill. He was keen on self-improvement, prided himself on clean living and read Ovid in his spare time, unlike the majority of his peers whose dissolute habits he abhorred. Ablett also worked hard to look the part – understanding very well that dress was 'the great secret of address' as the essayist William Hazlitt put it – and he spent much of his wages on clothes, in fact becoming a dandy, strolling regularly in Kensington Gardens 'in top-boots and white corduroy "smalls", with a slight riding cane'. Ablett's fashionable clothes no doubt boosted his popularity with female shoppers and by the age of sixteen he was earning about £100 a year.[2]

Ablett eventually saved enough money to open his own shop in Holborn but as the London drapery trade drifted west in the first half of the nineteenth century – a trend which accelerated after the construction of Regent Street in the decade following the end of the Napoleonic Wars – Ablett moved with it, purchasing an establishment in the West End. He noted in his autobiography how 'the migration of people westward had a wonderful effect at the time I am speaking about, and the construction of Regent Street was quite an event, although the majority of people who first opened shops there could not make them answer, let them try never so hard'. Ablett represented himself as 'the connecting link which united the old style of doing business with the new'. Looking back from a prosperous old age, he was keen to construct a progressive narrative and make amends for earlier wrongdoing, admitting 'I do not pretend to have passed on in my career blameless; on the contrary, I have done many foolish things which I have since sincerely regretted ... but I hope the excuse will be made for me that I was exposed to a good deal of temptation'.[3]

According to Ablett, shopkeeping had become much more sophisticated, well-ordered and rational during his lifetime. Silk was now supplied in reels rather than in skeins which had to be laid out singly in sheets. Most important, departments now had their own buyers and new departments had emerged for readymade articles such as women's petticoats and men's neck-ties. Shopkeeping, Ablett maintained, was also much more honest than it had been in his youth, a claim which proved harder to substantiate. He foregrounded the workings and decline of the so-called selling off system, which had been rife by the 1820s. This referred to the mode of whipping up custom by pretending that goods had been damaged in some way – usually by fire – therefore leading to massive reductions in price. Many shoppers were frequently intoxicated by the promise of a bargain, even usually careful buyers 'bought the goods, right and left, using but little judgement, and appearing to care only for being served with something or other'. However, such immoral tactics, Ablett asserted, had been rejected by modern drapery firms such as Harvey, Nichols and Company of Knightsbridge, Shoolbred's of Tottenham Court Road and Whiteley's of Westbourne Grove, which operated on 'fair and honourable principles'. Ablett reassured his readers that 'the trickery and cheating that was often prevalent in the trade, which sprung up as it were upon the birth of the *pushing system* which marked my young days ... may be said to have subsided'.[4] Reviewers of the text were not as sanguine; a writer in the *Spectator*, for example, remarked that if these specific immoral practices had died away, 'they have left a goodly crop of successors'.[5]

Ablett's fascinating autobiography sheds light on many of the themes of this chapter. His progress was made easier by the fact that the metropolis was in the vanguard of a burgeoning consumer culture that had fortuitously taken off following the end of the Napoleonic Wars. London had been a major shopping centre for decades as we have seen, but important changes occurred at this time. Elite consumers were catered for by newly emergent retailing outlets like arcades – covered passages containing shops – that were imported from Paris and which allowed buyers to shop in a dry, clean environment. Specialising in luxury goods and services, they housed fashionable bootmakers, hosiers, milliners, hairdressers, booksellers, jewellers and watchmakers, among other trades. The first London arcade, the Royal Opera Arcade, opened in 1817, followed by the Burlington Arcade the year after.[6] The spread of bazaars also fuelled a heightened propensity to consume among a wider public. Combining charitable and commercial functions, they were started by entrepreneurs who rented out counters. Specializing in 'fancy' goods such as china, perfume, shoes, guns, toys, artificial flowers and so on, they also invariably featured paintings and exhibitions, thus combining recreation with shopping. John Trotter's in Soho Square opened in 1816 and many others followed; indeed there was almost a craze for bazaars from this time. These new forms soon appeared in other cities too: by 1840, arcades had opened in Bath, Bristol, Glasgow, Ryde and Glossop, though they did not appear in the industrial north and midlands until the last third of the century; while bazaars sprang up in Manchester, Brighton, Bath, Norwich and elsewhere. The Albion Bazaar in Manchester, for instance, which featured a diorama and an art gallery, was welcomed by the editor of the *Manchester Times* as combining a sound business proposition with 'an exceedingly pleasant place of resort to its genteel inhabitants'.[7]

Widely known by the 1840s and 1850s as 'emporiums', it is the large London drapery shops rather than bazaars or arcades which can properly be regarded as proto-department stores, though origins are sometimes intertwined. Many had numerous departments under the same roof and catered for men, women and children. Their roots can be traced back to the late eighteenth century; Harding and Howell's established in Pall Mall in 1796, for instance, had five separate departments.[8] However, the pace of change accelerated in the second quarter of the nineteenth century and a qualitative as well as a quantitative shift can be discerned and not only in London. Certainly, some cities lagged behind. As a young man, Ablett worked for a draper in Bristol for a while, which he considered backward compared with the more competitive and innovative retailing culture found in the metropolis, and he did what he could to change things.[9] However, although developments in the capital were most often remarked by contemporary observers and were no doubt crucial, other towns and cities were pushing hard. As early as 1831, Jolly & Son opened the 'Bath Emporium' that insisted on ready-money transactions and fixed or ticketed prices, which took a good deal of the anxiety out of shopping for consumers of more slender means. Kendal Milne of Manchester began trading in 1836 on a site previously occupied by a bazaar established four years earlier by John Watts, who had also picked up the idea of fixed prices. The new owners realized the commercial potential of this practice and set up a large drapery shop that soon became very successful. The chief mover of the new venture, Thomas Kendal, had learnt his trade as a draper's assistant in London. Emerson Bainbridge, a Methodist lay preacher eager to lay up riches in this world, opened a store in Newcastle in 1838 which soon boasted twenty-three departments. Like Kendal, Bainbridge had also learnt his trade in London, at a silk and shawl warehouse in Regent Street.[10] Within a couple of decades most major northern cities had expanding draper's shops or 'emporiums', which were almost as important signifiers of urban status and middle-class civic power as the town hall.

New technologies, especially plate glass and gas lighting, encouraged increasing consumerism, and heightened the visual pleasure of the urban shopping experience: the early nineteenth century witnessed the conflation of shopping and spectacle that was to become a defining feature of modern consumer culture. Window glass was very expensive until the introduction of plate glass, the price of which fell dramatically after war with France. The introduction of sheet glass in the early 1830s accelerated the trend for larger shop fronts and more elaborate displays.[11] Not just arcades, many drapery shops were also affected. In his early work *Sketches by Boz* (1836), Dickens poked fun at the 'inordinate love of plate-glass, and a passion for gas-lights and gilding' that assumed 'epidemic' proportions among drapers and haberdashers, the 'disease' spreading inexorably until, 'dusty old shops in different parts of town, were pulled down; spacious premises with stuccoed fronts and gold letters, were erected instead; floors were covered with Turkey carpets; roofs supported by massive pillars; doors knocked into windows; a dozen squares of glass into one; one shopman into a dozen'.[12] The disease did not abate. Writing almost three decades later, Anthony Trollope pointed to the scopophilic possibilities of these new shopping spaces in a novel that gently ridiculed thrusting drapers who were always thinking up new ways of advertising their wares. In *The Struggles of Brown, Jones and Robinson* (1862) the protagonist, George Robinson, eulogizes plate glass as nothing less than a wonder of the modern world: 'To that which is ordinary it lends a grace; and to that which is graceful it gives a double lustre. Like a good advertisement, it multiplies your stock tenfold, and like a good servant, it is always eloquent in praise of its owner. I look upon plate glass, sir, as the most glorious product of the age.' William Ablett also drew attention to these transformations, noting how such displays of luxury that seemed 'almost unbecoming when applied to the every-day routine of buying and selling', drew visitors to the metropolis in greater numbers than ever before. Shop windows gradually became glittering showcases for the goods on sale and Ablett and his peers learnt through trial and error the new art of window dressing. Hitherto, goods were generally laid flat in drapers' windows but the technological changes now encouraged the improvization of more dynamic, eye-catching displays that showed off goods to their best advantage and brought them to life.[13]

Large drapers sometimes attracted aristocratic 'carriage trade' customers looking for a bargain but they mostly catered for middle-class shoppers. Their growth and evolution was undoubtedly the most immediately striking aspect of the changing retailing culture in this period. However, although we can discern a kind of watershed around mid-century with the spread of emergent forms such as arcades, bazaars and proto-department stores that constituted the most spectacular aspects of early Victorian consumerism, older forms of buying and selling continued to be vital. Indeed, more important for the daily needs of the mass of ordinary consumers were grocery or general provision shops, and these proliferated. Historians once thought that shops mainly served a better class of customer until the late nineteenth century, while public markets served the majority.[14] This view is no longer accepted, modified by the more recent work of historical geographers and economic and social historians. Industrialization and urbanization meant that the gap between producer and consumer increasingly widened. Market functions became separated into wholesaling and retailing for many goods before mid-century and this process accelerated over time. Scarcity of land in rapidly expanding towns meant that the vast majority of workers could not grow anywhere near enough food for their own requirements and therefore became more or less completely dependent on the market for their everyday needs. It is true that grocers had traditionally catered for wealthier consumers dealing in dried fruit, spices, teas, coffee and sugar, but stores selling a wide range of basic goods soon developed to meet working-class demand. In Sheffield, for example, their number grew from about 200 in the 1830s to over 1,000 in 1861. By mid-century they were the major source of food for most of the city's population. Not surprisingly, enterprizing individuals took advantage of these new opportunities, men like John Tuckwood of Sheffield, who owned several shops in the city centre and surrounding districts. By the late 1850s these were selling groceries, including articles that had either been processed or previously made at home including dried peas, oatmeal, biscuits, Cadbury's cocoa, Colman's mustard, jams and pickles; but they also stocked general household goods such as patent cleaners, soap, starch and washing powders.[15]

Evidence from Manchester and Salford tells a similar story, where groceries and provisions were already largely supplied by shops in the first half of the nineteenth century, numbers of which grew sixfold between 1800 and 1871. Despite the myth of home baking, bakers' shops sprang up to meet the demand of hard-pressed factory workers; numbers grew from 58 in 1800 to 293 in 1850. Many shops could be found in back streets (what we would now call 'convenience stores') – a necessity when the working day could be twelve hours long or more. James Bentley's shop in Minshull Street, for instance, which made little profit, sold goods in daily use such as tea, sugar, treacle, bread, flour, butter, eggs, potatoes, bacon and cheese.[16] In Elizabeth Gaskell's great 'Condition of England' novel of

1848, the eponymous heroine Mary Barton ran errands for her mother to a shop like Bentley's: 'Run, Mary dear, just round the corner, and get some fresh eggs at Tipping's ... and see if he has any nice ham cut, that he would let us have a pound of ... And get it Cumberland ham ... and Mary ... you must get a pennyworth of milk and a loaf of bread – mind you get it fresh and new.'[17] Detailed empirical studies of other industrial areas reinforce this picture of the spread and popularity of fixed shops. Between 1830 and 1853, for example, the number of shops listed in trade directories for the mostly working-class Halifax-Calder Valley area in West Yorkshire more than doubled, rising from 865 to 1,775. Most of these shops sold foodstuffs, though clothing and footwear made up almost a third of the total.[18]

Notwithstanding the undeniable hegemony of shops, markets continued to play an important role, particularly in the supply of perishable foodstuffs such as meat, cheese, fish and fruit and vegetables. Indeed, Sheffield market expanded during the 1840s because of increased demand to comprise hundreds of stalls that could be rented out on a weekly basis. Changes in supply encouraged growth. The distance between producer and consumer lengthened as farmers who used to sell a lot of meat themselves frequently devolved the trade to butchers who acted as middlemen. Consequently, numbers of butchers rapidly increased, from 148 in 1825 to 358 in 1861 according to local trade directories, and they dominated the public market in Sheffield and other cities including Manchester. As land was bought up for development in city centres, workers found it impossible to grow their own fruit and vegetables, so trade in these perishables also became largely dependent on cash. Local market gardeners sold their produce directly to these markets but fruit and vegetable production was also becoming dominated by operations of middlemen who could buy stocks of perishable goods from afar and ship them in by train.[19] Striking evidence of the continuing vitality of these forms from the 1830s onwards were the elaborate market halls constructed in many towns and cities as statements of civic pride. They were especially popular in Wales, north-west England and the midlands, and they were sometimes remarkably grandiose. At 9,000 square feet, Grainger market that opened in Newcastle-upon-Tyne in 1835 was probably the largest in Europe at the time; it housed a total of 166 butchers' shops and 54 vegetable shops. The Birmingham market that opened the same year was only about half the size but it was still an impressive structure.[20] Butchers were most visible but market halls also attracted a host of other trades, including non-food shops. The Blackburn market hall that opened in 1848, for example, was occupied by confectioners, booksellers, furniture dealers, metalware dealers and clothing trades, while provision shops were mostly outside. It seems therefore that by mid-century some market halls were 'closer to a general shopping centre than a provisions market'.[21]

There were other common sources of supply for ordinary consumers besides shops and markets. Street traders were highly visible in the metropolis, the daily lives of costermongers around mid-century immortalized by the bohemian journalist and social explorer Henry Mayhew. They sold mainly fruit and vegetables, fresh fish and street food and beverages – whelks, oysters, pig's trotters, meat puddings, sausages, fried fish, tea, coffee, milk and so on. However, they also sold a great variety of manufactured goods and clothing. Although street traders could be found in most towns and cities they were not nearly as important in Manchester as they were in London, and they were also declining in numbers and subject to attack from moral reformers who regarded them as unregulated and therefore necessarily suspect.[22] Like street traders, itinerant traders or pedlars can be seen as residual rather than dominant or emergent forms of consumption. Caution is needed here, however, as precise numbers are difficult to ascertain and some scholars believe that their numbers actually expanded after 1830.[23] We can say that they still represented a vital source of supply to many consumers, particularly as they provided much-needed credit. The so-called Scotch drapers or tally tradesmen had a reputation for sharp practice and sometimes drew much opprobrium, not least because they often resorted to courts of requests to recover debts from the husbands of women who, it was supposed, had been hoodwinked into spending beyond their means.[24] Both pedlars and street traders dealt in second-hand clothes and so did some specialist retailers, selling mostly to working-class consumers. Articles of dress were frequently recycled in the first half of the nineteenth century, though the increasing popularity and affordability of cheap cotton goods and ready-made clothing eventually undermined the business. One disgruntled vendor complained to Mayhew about young men of the present day who were 'had by 'vertisements, and bills, and them books about fashions which is all over the country and town ... I'll back a coat such as is sometimes sold by a gentleman's servant to wear out two new slops'. By 1850 the largest outlet for goods often made from 'shoddy' or 'devil's dust', Moses and Son, was doing an extensive trade selling ready-made suits which, according to the firm's publicity, 'a Beau Brummel would have been proud to wear, at prices that a mechanic could afford to pay'. Consequently, the trade in second-hand clothes was pushed to the margins and wearing 'cast-offs' came to be stigmatized, confined to the very poor.[25] Conversely, the second-hand trade in furniture continued to be buoyant throughout the first half of the nineteenth century and well beyond, as wealthier consumers increasingly traded their tables, chairs and sideboards for more fashionable goods when opportunity arose.[26] Whether middle-class shoppers believed that furniture conferred moral qualities on its owners, as one modern scholar has argued, may be a moot point, though what is not debatable is the passionate middle-class love affair with material culture.[27] As in so many other ways, Queen Victoria was merely reflecting middle-class sensibilities by collecting photographs of all her possessions in richly bound albums.[28]

Discourses of consumption

The Great Exhibition held in Hyde Park in the summer of 1851 showcased manufactured goods from across the world, though naturally products of British industry predominated. Visitors from all over the country and beyond were attracted to the glittering spectacle of the Crystal Palace and the thousands of things on display inside; a total of six million visits were recorded before doors closed in October. Most contemporaries considered it a complete success, eloquent proof of the ability of free trade capitalism to deliver material progress and international peace.[29] Some modern scholars have contended that although goods on show at the Great Exhibition were not ticketed, the event represented a crucial turning point in the making of consumer culture in Britain, describing the modernist plate-glass and cast-iron structure in which it was housed as nothing less than a huge department store. The Great Exhibition, it has been argued, gave the advertising industry a major fillip, as it bathed commodities in a romantic light and encouraged advertisers to develop more elaborate modes of representation for the commodity form that played on its 'fetishistic' character.[30] Contemporary evidence provides some support for this view. The caricaturist George Cruikshank, for example, imagined goods exploding outwards from the Great Exhibition when it closed, in a remarkable surrealistic illustration (Figure 1). Harriet Martineau, popularizer of political economy and ideas about separate spheres for men and women, was not being complimentary when she called the Great Exhibition the 'Sublime of the Bazaar'; while *Punch* imagined a delighted visitor recommending it to a friend in these terms: 'It is much better far than going a-shopping. The whole place is full of some of the prettiest things in the world – laces – silks – brocades – and such lovely jewels – and the beauty is, you may look at them ever so long, without being expected to buy a single thing!'[31]

The Great Exhibition did help bring the consumer more to the fore, even perhaps at a linguistic level. As was noted in the previous chapter, the term 'consumer' had traditionally been negatively freighted but this gradually changed around mid-century. For the inventor and mathematician Charles Babbage, the problem with the Great Exhibition was that it did not go far enough in this respect, hamstrung as it was by the commitment of its promoters to public improvement and 'rational recreation'. Babbage placed a universal category of the consumer at the centre of his account of the event: 'All men are *consumers*, and as such their common bond of interest is to purchase every thing in the *cheapest* market.' His major complaint was that goods were not openly priced at the Great Exhibition, for this undermined its fundamental role, which was 'to instruct the consumer in the art of judging of the character of the commodity'. The decision to separate display from exchange he asserted, 'puts aside the greatest of all interests, that of the consumer'. In other words, according to Babbage, the interests of what was later to be called the 'discriminating consumer' were subordinated

FIGURE 1 *George Cruikshank, 'The Dispersion of the Works of All Nations from the Great Exhibition of 1851', in Henry Mayhew,* 1851: Or, the Adventures of Mr and Mrs Sandboys and Family *(1851). © The British Library Board (1600/745).*

to a certain extent as being too vulgar, for the moment at least.[32] Significantly, just over a decade later when an International Exhibition was held in South Kensington, objects on display did have price tags. If Babbage was pleased by this change, others were not, one writer complaining that it was nothing less than 'a gigantic advertisement ... The Palace of Puffs'.[33]

Historians are generally wary of overly specific turning points, and for good reason. If the Great Exhibition and other similar events that followed provided an impetus for advertising, their effects should not be overestimated. Indeed, self-styled experts on advertising speculated at the time about why the impact of the Great Exhibition had apparently been so limited, given the expectations that had been raised by it.[34] Nevertheless, important changes in the orchestration of consumer desire – including more elaborated and sophisticated discourses of consumption – did occur during the first three quarters of the nineteenth century, even if developments were more gradual than sometimes thought. Although the origins of modern advertising can be traced back to the late seventeenth century when rhetoric rather than unadorned description began to be used to sell goods, the most important developments were bound up with wider transformations wrought by the industrial revolution. Industrialization and urbanization made ordinary consumers less able to provide for their own needs and widened and deepened the market for consumer goods, making it more imperative for manufacturers to publicize them. A good deal of money early on was spent advertising literary products, as well as condiments and boot polish. Warren's Blacking, Rowland's Macassar Oil, Lea and Perrins' Worcestershire Sauce, Schweppe's Mineral Waters and Colman's Mustard were some early well-known brands that advertised nationally. Ready-made tailors such as Moses and Son also spent heavily, probably £10,000 a year by the mid-1850s. Though some cultural historians have contended that workers were largely excluded from consumer culture until the late nineteenth century, this was not the case.[35] These early branded goods were targeted directly at a very wide market, and workers fully participated in the new world of goods that was opening up, as economic historians have rightly emphasized.[36]

The largest expenditure in this period was on patent or 'quack' medicines such as the cure-all pills produced from the 1820s and 1830s by James Morison and Thomas Holloway. The latter was an early convert to the power of advertising, and the Holloway brand became emblazoned across the world – Holloway once even used the Great Pyramid as a hoarding and may have tried, without success, to persuade Charles Dickens to puff his pills. By 1855 his annual advertising budget exceeded £30,000 and it continued to rise.[37] Advertising was therefore a ubiquitous feature of British society by mid-century, though the range of products that were puffed remained limited. Moreover, and despite resistance to advertising on the part of many manufacturers, an important shift can be discerned in both scale and technique around this time; advertising changed from being connected to a special event – such as the launch of a product – to a routine business activity and outlay.[38] Thus, a writer in the *Quarterly Review* pointed to the emergence of 'that liberal and systematic plan of advertising which marks the complete era in the art'; while the author of an early advertisers' guide declared more straightforwardly that there was no point employing it 'with a niggardly spirit'.[39]

Advertising saturated the urban landscape, bombarding the senses of its inhabitants from all directions. Some early forms, such as advertising vans that crowded the streets, were even potentially dangerous. Ingenious horse drawn constructions, like the giant wheeled hat memorably ridiculed by Thomas Carlyle in *Past and Present* in 1843, threatened to run over pedestrians until they were suppressed by the London Hackney Carriage Act of 1853, by which time their role was being taken over anyway by advertising on omnibuses.[40] Impoverished sandwich-men crowded the pavements, which were often chalked with brand names and notices of sales. Visually the city was dominated by posters, much of it being literally papered over during this period. According to the 'King of the Bill-Stickers' interviewed by Dickens's *Household Words* in 1851, the trade had been boosted by the English State Lottery during the eighteenth century but fierce competition had set in after its abolition in 1826. Violence was common, as different companies scrambled for business and pasted their own bills over those of their rivals, often creating a bewildering, kaleidoscopic effect on every available wall or building.[41] During the next decade or so the trade of bill posting was to become more well-ordered and well-regulated, in line with the sanitization of other 'disreputable' forms of urban labour, such as that of dustman.[42] The impetus for the cleanup came from Leeds, where Edward Sheldon began to rent sites in an effort to control advertising space more effectively. This was facilitated by the emergence of advertising contractors who purchased the right to post bills on properties, as well as by legal changes; in London the Metropolitan Police Act of 1839 made the practice illegal without the owner's consent and the Town Police Act of 1847 tightened control further. Sheldon eventually established the United Kingdom Billposters' Association in 1862, which enforced a code of practice on members that prohibited overlapping and restricted numbers. By the third quarter of the nineteenth century, the earlier confused visual order of the city had been replaced by a much tidier pattern, though the clamour of commerce was louder and more insistent than ever.[43]

Moving from the street to the home, advertisers used handbills and direct marketing to publicize their wares, quickly exploiting the opportunities afforded by the introduction of the penny post in 1840. The growing reading public was also addressed more systematically and with growing sophistication by means of the press. The number of titles expanded from the turn of the century and the space devoted to advertising in their pages gradually increased. Accurate figures are very difficult to ascertain but one rough estimate of the total national expenditure on newspaper advertisements suggests figures of £160,000 for 1800, £252,000 for 1820, and £424,000 for 1840. As such estimates can easily be doubled, it seems likely that at least £1 million was being spent on press advertising annually by the late 1840s. Technological advances that revolutionized the production of newspapers accelerated this trend; *The Times*, which installed a steam press as early as 1814, led the way, carrying 150,000 advertisements or 10 per cent of the national total in 1838. In answer to critics who complained that the paper was cornering the market, the editor retorted: 'Our monopoly is the monopoly of BARCLAY and PERKINS' porter, of TWINING'S tea, of Mr Cobden's agitation, and of FORTNUM and MASON'S hams.' Although provincial newspapers lagged behind, their number also swelled; out of 130 provincial newspapers in 1833, only two had circulations of more than 4,000 but by 1849 there were a total of 289, with twenty-seven selling over 4,000 copies a week.[44] Expansion was encouraged after mid-century by the repeal of the legal restrictions that held back the press. The Advertisement Tax, which dated from 1712 and amounted to 1s. 6d. per insertion, was repealed in 1853, while repeal of the Stamp Act – a hated symbol of state oppression for radicals that hiked the cost of each newspaper by 4d. – followed two years later.[45] However, change was unspectacular as newspaper editors were reluctant to accept the imperative of advertisers and break column rules, insert illustrations and use different type to catch readers' attention.[46] The range of goods advertised also remained quite limited early on, being dominated by estate agents and auctioneers, though by the 1850s many retailers including watchmakers, jewellers, tailors, drapers, milliners, coffee and tea merchants and grocers were making regular use of the metropolitan and provincial press.[47]

Advertising agents sprang up as middlemen between manufacturers, retailers and the press, helping to place advertisements in suitable publications and receiving commission from the owners of newspapers for their services. Their origins can be traced back to the late eighteenth century when some coffee houses acted as agents for newspapers they provided for their customers.[48] A key figure in the development of the modern business was Charles Mitchell, who established an agency in London in 1836 and went on to publish the hugely successful *Newspaper Press Directory*, which comprehensively described the different markets covered by various publications throughout the country. This was not the first publication of its kind but it was the most thorough. Like many later defenders, Mitchell insisted that advertising was an art as well as a trade, and he stressed that in order to be successful agents had to study carefully not only the newspapers themselves but also 'the classes to whom they are addressed, the towns in which they circulate, and the interests they advocate'. Mitchell's *Directory* remained the standard guide until the end of the nineteenth century and played an important role in the creation of more systematic links between advertisers and readers of the expanding press.[49]

These gradual but profound transformations provoked sustained criticism from intellectual elites, a jeremiad underestimated by some social historians.[50] It cut across the ideological spectrum, encompassing the radical William Cobbett, who regularly fulminated against advertising from the early 1800s, the romantic-conservative Thomas Carlyle, who referred to 'the all-deafening blast of puffery', and the Whig-liberal T. B. Macaulay, who condemned advertisers for their 'despicable ingenuity'.[51] Such attacks appeared regularly in middle-class periodicals throughout the nineteenth century, though the tone was often less barbed, the writers assuming a resigned but knowing attitude, as if the trickery so frequently manifested was merely as inevitable facet of modern commercial life. Results may have been regrettable but they were frequently also humorous, one commentator wryly pointing out that Morison believed so wholeheartedly in his own product during his final illness that he 'took more pills as he grew worse, and was in the very act of calling for a fresh box when he expired'.[52] Spokesmen for the emergent 'art' of advertising expressed the view that consumers were gradually becoming cannier, or as one nicely put it, 'The public have begun to feel the "alarming sacrifice" is more often on their own part than on that of the vendor.'[53] However, Victorian advertisers were reluctant to restrain their discourse and temper their claims, for stretching the meaning of words and things was central to their practice. One of the most trenchant attacks on the increasingly pervasive discourse of consumption was made by an ex-Chartist, James Burns, in an excoriating, marvellously titled book, *The Language of the Walls*. Burns was no innocent observer – he had written puffs himself to help support his family when he had been short – and the work exposed in detail 'the infamous tricks of these leeches'. For Burns, heightened competition had encouraged false and inflated claims to be made not only about goods but also about other areas of social life, including politics and religion. In fact, puffing was fast becoming an accepted norm: 'One of the leading characteristics of the age is Quackery', Burns wrote, and its spread had poisoned national morality.[54] Another more polite critic was making a similar point when he described advertising in this way: 'Magical and cabalistic, compelling mere words to alter, confuse, and confound the reality of things, or to endow them with ideal properties, qualities, and perfections beyond the belief of credulity itself.'[55]

Practices and representations

Unlike the previous century, the majority of the population were affected by the spreading consumerism which occurred during the first half of the nineteenth century. Rapid urbanization and population increases swelled the market and workers increasingly depended on cash, losing the means they once had to supplement their diet by growing their own foodstuffs. Urban workers usually fared better than rural, although diet changed as they became more dependent on bakers, brewers and retailers generally; there was a preference for hot, tasty food that required little preparation – bought bread, potatoes and bacon were mainstays, washed down with tea.[56] From the point of view of the poor consumer, some of these changes were negative and working-class radicals made much of this, as we shall see in the following chapter. But there were positives; the sphere of consumption was a source of pleasure as well as anxiety. Most of the sources that provide a glimpse of how working people experienced early Victorian consumerism were written by outside observers, as is so often the case. Despite this, more sympathetic middle-class writers open a fascinating window onto this world. One of the best examples is an article about London street markets on a Saturday night – after workers had been paid – written by a Mrs White, which appeared in a popular periodical in the middle of the so-called hungry forties. White vividly recreated the markets and stalls that proliferated around Spitalfields and Shoreditch, up the Tottenham Court Road and the Edgware Road. Here the senses were bombarded by musicians, cries of vendors, ballad singers, beggars and the overwhelming stench of bodies and poor quality, often rancid fish, poultry and vegetables sold by the better shops and street foods – pickled salmon, slices of fried sole, shrimps, oysters, sausages and so on. The gas-heated atmosphere was fetid and overwhelming but also vibrant and alive. 'Low' drapery and bonnet shops made it difficult for the 'simple housewife' to resist bargains, while stalls selling cheap shoes, belts, braces, toys, prints, ironware, jewellery, and haberdashery crowded the pavements, impeding the flow of the throng.[57]

There is the usual mixture of disgust and desire in White's account that one would expect but also a real attempt to sympathize with the lives of the poor and their small pleasures. She draws attention to the many couples who comprise the majority of the crowd, 'Humble artisans and their wives making their periodical preparations (such as they are) for the home-feast on the morrow.' Occasionally, the men in 'fustian jackets' are seen carrying a small child and White admonishes other social explorers of her class who wag a disapproving finger at such behaviour, reminding them that working men have feelings also: 'It is something for the poor man to claim the privilege of a parent once a week, and show the world he too has children, and a heart to lay them in.' White also celebrates the canny working-class housewife who had 'learnt economy in a hard school' and who purchases half a shoulder of mutton from the butcher's shop that will do for three meals. Thus, shopping is represented as both a necessity requiring particular skills and fraught with dangers for ordinary consumers, but also a source of great sensory delight and familial affection. And nothing is wasted: at the end of White's account a pathetic beggar scuttles away to enjoy leftover bones he has managed to buy for threepence.[58] Similar themes were highlighted just over twenty years later by Thomas Wright, the self-styled 'journeyman engineer', in his better known description of Saturday trading in the metropolis. Wright concluded that Saturday shopping constituted 'one of the most animated and characteristic phases of working-class life in this country, and illustrates perhaps more strikingly than any other phase of their social life, the magnitude, importance, and collective wealth of the working classes'.[59]

Shopping got under the skin of life for the poor as well as for those in more comfortable circumstances, for men as well as women. Such rituals of buying and selling were not confined to large cities either but were to be found wherever wages were regularly spent. If the smells of working-class shopping districts sometimes disgusted bourgeois observers, more uniformly positive reactions were prompted by the increased diffusion of material things among the common people. Elizabeth Gaskell drew attention to how house-proud Mrs Barton was, for example, prior to the economic catastrophe that caused widespread hunger and personal tragedy in Lancashire textile districts. The working-class home is drawn in intricate detail in her novel, including the tin candlestick, the checked curtains and geraniums in the window sill, the cupboard full of crockery and glass, the Pembroke table with a bright green Japanned teatray and crimson teacaddy. This was a real home, cosy with stencilled patterns on the wall, a place for family and friends, before the vagaries of the capitalist economy laid waste to it all.[60] A few years later, a correspondent for the liberal *Morning Chronicle* described the shops he had seen in Merthyr Tydfil, including ironmongers, grocers, druggists, booksellers and drapers who displayed 'a profusion of wares adapted to the wants and the tastes' of local consumers, mainly relatively affluent iron workers and coal miners.[61] The writer observed how local workers greatly enjoyed shopping and approvingly noted how the love of material possessions was widely shared after venturing inside their homes, which were 'stuffed with furniture, even to superfluity; a fine mahogany eight-day clock, a showy mahogany chest of drawers, a set of mahogany chairs with solid seats, a glass-fronted cupboard for the display of china, glass, and silver spoons, forming indispensible requisites for the principal room'. Chartism had once been an important force in the area but had now died out, according to the correspondent, who implied that it had been finally laid to rest by spreading affluence.[62] Middle-class observers often presumed that commodities had the power to pacify and civilize hitherto dangerous elements. This was a key argument used against radical advocates of democracy, as we shall see in the next chapter.

For working-class women, shopping was a form of labour as well as pleasure, involving calculation and foresight. That was no doubt why it was so often approved by those further up the social scale. But the real beneficiary of increasing levels of consumption in the first three quarters of the nineteenth century was the rising middle class. The Victorian middle class especially had a deep love for material things as has already been noted. Local studies of cities and towns such as Edinburgh, Glasgow, Birmingham and Colchester have demonstrated just how bound up with class formation and identity consumption practices were.[63] Middle-class consumers did not simply ape the styles of aristocratic elites – which frequently involved lavish expenditure on luxuries or conspicuous consumption – but developed their own consumption habits as a way of asserting their distinctive status and place in the social hierarchy. This involved thrift, often caused anxiety but was also expansive. The lighter, more airy and less densely furnished style of interior design favoured by the middling orders in the early part of the century gradually gave way to a more cluttered, heavily upholstered look. As one scholar has observed:

> The characteristic mid-Victorian liking for clutter required increasing expenditure on tables, chairs, sideboards, chiffoniers, escritoires, pianos, dumb waiters, (all covered with tasseled velvet cloths and runners), upon Staffordshire figurines, Doulton china, brass candlesticks, coal-scuttles, papier-mâché models, vases, stuffed birds, wax fruit, and framed photographs. Rapid fashion changes in something as fundamental as carpets regularly forced the 'up-to-date' into making new acquisitions as the flat-woven body carpets of the 1840s gave way in the 1850s to fitted pile or tapestry carpets.[64]

The 'home' as both an ideological but also a quintessentially material construct took on a heightened significance. From the 1850s and 1860s the middle class began limiting family size, spending more income on the 'paraphernalia of gentility'; by the end of the century a professional man's family was less than four, compared to six in the average working-class family.[65] Evangelical religion, with its stress on separate spheres for different genders, the sanctity of the domestic realm and women's role in maintaining it, encouraged new practices. Women were seen to play a key role in creating the middle-class home, certainly, but it should not be thought that men were entirely passive either. They were usually responsible for buying goods such as wine, books, pictures, musical instruments and wheeled vehicles but they also accompanied their wives on shopping expeditions. In 1820 a civil engineer in the west midlands, John Raistick, shopped with his wife for furnishings in Birmingham and carpets in Kidderminster, for example.[66]

An increasing propensity to consume was encouraged by the consolidation of Christmas as a consumerist festival by the early- to mid-Victorian middle class. Many scholars have drawn attention to this phenomenon and have pointed out that previously presents had traditionally been exchanged at New Year, by those who could afford them at least. This changed in the first half of the century and the foodstuffs and material goods that came to represent an authentic Christmas also became firmly established. Turkeys were imported in huge numbers from the continent by the early 1840s, for example, sending cards became common, and the Christmas cracker was patented in 1847 by Tom Smith, a London confectioner (the 'crack' was added in 1860). The popularity of the Christmas tree from 1850 soon established a market for ornaments.[67] Not surprisingly, the demand for children's toys expanded enormously, which gave a tremendous boost to German toy manufacturers.[68] The press greatly benefited, naturally; annuals appeared for children, special numbers of magazines and newspapers were issued and, by the 1840s, Christmas was established as the most important book publishing season in the year.[69] Advertisers were in the forefront of all these developments. Typically, intellectuals sometimes wagged a finger at what was seen as increasing profligacy. Charles Dickens's most famous short story 'A Christmas Carol', which was first published in December 1843, was an attempt to remind the better-off of their Christian duty towards the poor; while George Cruickshank's wonderful caricature 'A Swallow at Christmas', which had appeared two years before in the *Comic Almanack*, mocked the gluttonous, insatiable appetite of middle-class consumers who summoned up delicacies from across the globe to fulfil their consuming desires, regardless of the season.

Dickens may have been critical about the lack of charity at Christmas but he also benefited from and indeed helped further the commercialization of the festival; his early 'Christmas Books' were designed to tap into this growing market. Moreover, Dickens regularly enthused about consumerism more generally as offering welcome signs of progress.[70] Conflicting responses like these were shared by many commentators. If there was sometimes nostalgia for the passing of the traditional, small-scale shop with its outdated practices (including honesty, critics often asserted), there was frequently a great deal of pride in what the new shopping thoroughfares and frontages said about the progressive nature of Britain's economy and society. A periodical article in the mid-1840s suggested that 'the tremendous wealth, importance, and enterprise of this mighty metropolis of shopocrats' was eloquent proof of the nations' greatness. The writer also noted the shopping mania that had gripped consumers in the capital, fuelled by the never-ending hunt for a bargain.[71] As plate glass and brass continued to spread over subsequent decades, London's shop windows could accurately be described as 'a museum which puts all others to scorn'.[72] And as in a museum, the city's inhabitants could while away their time just looking at the profusion of goods on sale, could stroll idly through a showcase of desirable objects if they so wished: the identity of what scholars call the urban 'flâneur' was considerably extended. If not on the same scale or to the same degree perhaps, shopping gradually became more of a spectacle in other cities and towns throughout the country. Shop windows became much more attractive as men like Ablett experimented with new ways of arresting the customers' gaze. 'Dressing the shop-window is an art', wrote John Fisher Murray in *Bentley's Miscellany*, 'one of the fine arts, in fact, requiring an eye for the harmony of colour and an accurate knowledge of the effect of light and shade in drapery'. No wonder then that those most adept at baiting such 'lady-traps' were generously rewarded by their employers.[73]

Changes in language registered a passionate desire for things. The term 'shopping' – in the sense of browsing for pleasure without necessarily any intention of purchasing specific goods – can be traced back to the mid-eighteenth century, as we have seen. However, after the Napoleonic Wars the term was used much more commonly as the practice became generalized; what was frequently referred to as 'going a-shopping' became a recognizable leisure pursuit for growing numbers of middle-class consumers. It drew a good deal of ridicule and disapproval from commentators and gender was invariably at the root of their reaction. As we saw in the preceding chapter, consumption and its associations had long been negatively freighted; shopping was regarded as an essentially female activity and shopping for pleasure routinely censured as the occupation of the idle and superficial. Fashion especially was thought to take hold of the weakest minds and the most immoral individuals – actresses and prostitutes were its easiest victims, according to William Hazlitt.[74] As style was democratized during this period, such anxieties increased. Greater numbers of consumers could afford the printed cotton fabrics that replaced heavy woollens and linen, for instance, and the popularity of fashion magazines from *La Belle Assemblée* launched in 1806, through the *World of Fashion*, which from 1850 gave away free patterns each month, to Samuel Beeton's *Englishwoman's Domestic Magazine* that featured elaborate colour fashion plates from 1860, fuelled middle-class fashion consciousness.[75] From the 1840s onwards, as cheap shops spread and the trade in ready-made clothing grew, a chorus of commentators mocked the supposedly female mania for shopping and fashion.

A writer in *Punch* in 1844, for example, described shopping as a sport, the feminine equivalent of fox hunting or game shooting. The commentator differentiated between 'street-shopping' and 'bazaar-shopping', which required different techniques to ensure best results. For the former, which was mainly concerned with 'hosiery, drapery, and jewellery of the richer sort', it was best to 'walk leisurely along, keeping a sharp look-out on the windows', while the advice when 'bazaar-shopping' was to 'beat each stall' separately in order to turn up the new and the unexpected: 'Many patterns, colours, novelties, conveniences, and other articles will thus strike your eye, which you would otherwise have never wanted or dreamt of.' The writer also noted how, when shopping, 'one thing suggests another; as bonnets – ribands for trimming, or flowers; and handkerchiefs – perfumery', and that if anything seemed to be very cheap it should be immediately snapped up as a bargain.[76] A comic song from 1850 conveyed the exasperation of a husband who is unable to quell his wife's consuming desires after she buys a pretty scarf: 'To Swan and Edgar's when we got/Of things she purchased such a lot/A shot of silk, would it had been shot/When we went out a shopping.'[77] Cruikshank provided his own inimitable take, representing the modern female shopper as both gullible and insatiable, rendered almost hysterical by the promise of a bargain and therefore easy prey for the owners of the new emporia; in the print it is the women who are sacrificed on the altar of profit (see Figure 2). Such weakness was regarded as especially dangerous when, under the common-law principle of coverture or the law of necessaries as it was called, husbands could be held responsible in court for debts incurred by greedy

FIGURE 2 *George Cruikshank, 'Alarming Sacrifice',* Comic Almanack *(1851).*
© Private collection.

wives. Little wonder then that moralists like Sarah Stickney Ellis denounced the evils of credit and sang the praises of thrifty housewives.[78] Working-class men eager to achieve a measure of respectability shared these anxieties, which cut across class. Joseph Livesey, for instance, a weaver turned cheese seller from Preston who was on the make, warned of the 'evils of shopping' that could soon destroy the plebeian home, as the 'thorough-going shopping woman' was also prone to the temptations of drink and idleness.[79] Such views were not only sexist but, as we have already suggested, they were also untrue as both middle-class and working-class men actively participated in the developing world of consumption.

Given this level of concern, it was no wonder that female consumers received a constant stream of instruction on how to buy wisely. If female shoppers were seen as hedonistic hunters after elusive bargains, they were also often themselves represented as quarry for unscrupulous tradesmen, who lured them with many cunning tricks. Ablett described these in detail when trying to make amends later in life and they were regularly condemned at the time in the press. A common tactic was to lure the shopper by ticketing articles in the window at bargain prices, then passing off inferior goods for those on display over the counter. 'Selling-off' goods that had supposedly been fire-damaged at what seemed to be a serious loss to the shopkeeper was another widely adopted ploy. According to Mrs White writing in the popular periodical *Ainsworth's Magazine*, cheating was now systemic, particularly in the drapery trade, the result of cut-throat competition and indicative of the diffusion among the middle class of an axiom of free trade that had been championed by the Anti-Corn Law League, which was to 'buy in the cheapest market, or at least what promises to be so'. The radical Chartist newspaper, the *Northern Star*, picked up this exposure of the pitfalls of modern consumption, though it typically turned up the heat, vehemently denouncing the 'tricks of the base bourgeoisie'.[80] It is worth noting, however, that the ruses of unscrupulous traders were not always successful; in his 1862 novel, Anthony Trollope described how they could backfire on the shopkeeper if customers proved feisty and stood up for their rights.[81] Moreover, shoplifting was in fact first identified as a social problem in this period, rather than accompanying the emergence of the full-fledged department store in the late nineteenth century, with which it is usually associated.[82] Some feminist scholars have gone so far as to suggest that shoplifting represented a form of 'resistance' to the patriarchal implications of capitalist consumerism, though the contemporary evidence tends not to support such sweeping claims.[83] What we can say with more certainty, however, is that theft by consumers and deceitful trading methods were often seen as two sides of the same coin. As one writer put it: 'The wonderful bargains of the cheap shops and shoplifting go on together – the one produces the other. Shoplifters are the natural result of "selling off at a ruinous sacrifice"; and it is no wonder that the avowed bargain-hunter is, as a matter of course, suspected of being a shoplifter.'[84]

3

Alternative Paths: The Politics of Consumption

Middle-class consumer politics

In the late eighteenth and early nineteenth centuries, middle-class consumers organized against slavery in the Caribbean. Women were in the forefront of campaigns to abstain from purchasing slave-grown produce, sugar in particular, the demand for which had grown tremendously along with the craze for tea drinking.[1] Propagandists for the abolitionist movement sought to politicize rituals of consumption that helped define polite society. They published pamphlets that revealed how genteel consumer practices in the metropole were indissolubly connected to barbaric forms of production in the colonies. William Allen, a Quaker mill owner, put the case succinctly in 1792: 'The CONSUMER of West India Produce, may be considered as the *Master-Spring* that gives motion and effect to the whole Machine of Cruelties.'[2] Adopted when petitioning government against the slave trade was seen to have failed, the tactic of abstention was commonly regarded as dependent on female support, as women held the domestic purse strings and could also exert moral pressure in the private sphere. Fashion was harnessed to the cause; Josiah Wedgwood cashed in by producing a jasper cameo depicting a kneeling black slave with the motto 'Am I not a man and a brother?' that became all the rage. The abolitionist leader Thomas Clarkson wrote how, 'at length the taste for wearing them became general; and thus fashion, which usually confines itself to worthless things, was seen for once in the honourable office of promoting the cause of justice, humanity, and freedom'. Though most abstainers were middle-class, aristocratic and working-class women also backed the cause. Clarkson estimated that there were about 300,000 abstainers in the early 1790s, but the Abolition Society refused to promote the tactic after 1792 and it fizzled out. However, the campaign reappeared again with renewed vigour in the 1820s, when it was taken up by ladies' associations that spread throughout the country.

Women canvassed other consumers and tried to get them to pledge support and substitute slave-grown West India sugar with 'free'-grown East India product, thereby salving an emerging humanitarian conscience whilst supporting new forms of free trade imperialism. Some even tried to put pressure on small traders; the ladies' association in Worcester, for example, who boycotted those who sold or used West India sugar. All this activity probably did not have much direct effect in hastening abolition of the slave trade but it no doubt educated many people about the ethical ramifications of global trade networks and gave middle-class consumers in particular a sense of their collective power.[3]

However, it was the issue of the Corn Laws which really galvanized middle-class consumers, spurring them to organize politically on a mass scale. Revised in 1815 by a parliament dominated by great landowners, the Corn Laws propped up prices for agricultural goods and protected home producers by banning the import of foreign foodstuffs until the price of wheat reached the high figure of 80s. (£4) per quarter. Political economists denounced the measure as contravening the free trade teachings of Adam Smith and some politicians inveighed against it, opposition gaining momentum over subsequent decades, especially after a new Corn Law was passed with some difficulty in 1828 that introduced a sliding scale of duties. The cause of free trade was one of the crucibles within which middle-class consciousness was forged in the first half of the nineteenth century, and the role of the consumer was vital to it.[4] In one of the most widely read pamphlets on the question, Colonel Perronet Thompson tried to both persuade and threaten opponents, pointing out that although 'the middle classes' were not enamoured by the prospect of revolutionary change and might not have to go without bread themselves, they would inevitably be radicalized by the collapse of their businesses and 'the general stagnation of trade and the impossibility of rising in the world by honourable industry' brought about by protection. But this was not only a middle-class question for Thompson; the reduction in consumption was felt everyday by 'the poorest man in England' when he weighed his 'penny roll'. He drew the conclusion that 'the manufacturing and commercial interest' and the 'manufacturing labourers' were robbed equally by unfair legislation passed by those who enjoyed exclusive political power, and he suggested making common cause to gain gradual extension of the suffrage.[5] As we saw in the previous chapter, the purchasing power of middle-class consumers was growing at this time and Tories, Whigs and radicals all attempted to harness this for political ends. In many localities during the agitation leading up to the passage of the Reform Act of 1832 and after, for example, what was now termed 'exclusive dealing' was adopted, which involved trading with those shopkeepers who sympathized with your beliefs, and boycotting others.[6]

The question of the relationship between changes in economic policy and widening political representation and citizenship rights was to remain important throughout the campaign against protectionism. Consumer power was construed as intimately bound up with political power for some free traders; as the great liberal historian G. M. Trevelyan remarked in his monumental biography of one of the key figures in the struggle against protection, for John Bright the 'connection between a good coat and the right to the franchise seemed an obvious first postulate of civilised society'.[7] In September 1838, the Manchester Anti-Corn Law Association was founded, and out of it developed the Anti-Corn Law League the following spring after a motion in favour of Corn Law repeal had been resoundingly defeated in the Commons. Led by a talented group of manufacturers and agitators, including Bright, Richard Cobden and George Wilson who served as the League's chairman, it became the most successful consumer organization in early Victorian Britain. Although local associations in other parts of the country affiliated to this body, Manchester men dominated the ruling council of the League from the start and the city was home to its headquarters.[8] The League promulgated a simple message and mobilized middle-class consumers by means of an extensive propaganda campaign which involved countless public meetings and many conferences as well as the distribution of thousands of tracts, pamphlets, handbills and periodicals. In an effort to bridge divisions of class, the League angled its appeal to the mass of consumers imagined as 'the people', maintaining that aristocratic landowners – parasitic vestiges of an outdated feudal order – were impoverishing the majority through the imposition of an unjust tax on the staff of life. Employing a discourse shot through with scriptural allusion and authority, ideologues demonized 'monopoly' as antithetical to freedom, a power used by landowners to maintain 'the people' in a condition of abject slavery. They argued that monopoly power also had deleterious effects on public and private realms as both national security and domestic family life were undermined by it. The latter theme is illustrated by Figure 3, a League membership card, which juxtaposed an impoverished working-class family ground down by the iniquitous Corn Laws with a far more prosperous and healthier domestic scene post repeal. If the immediate solution to the problem of scarcity was abolition of the Corn Laws, the eventual goal was far wider than this, being nothing less than the creation of a new economic and political order, one in which government kept out of the market and the middle classes gained full recognition and control across society as a whole.[9] During the economic downturn of the late 1830s, the notion that hunger was caused or exacerbated by the operation of the Corn Laws appealed to some sections of the working class, even if the demand for middle-class hegemony was harder to swallow. Consequently, twenty-three Anti-Corn Law Operative Associations were established in various localities between spring 1839 and summer 1843, though many of these were ephemeral.[10]

For those who believed in free trade most wholeheartedly, however, it was far more than a solution to distress at home. As contemporary commentators frequently pointed out, free trade constituted a religion for many of its adherents. It was a broad church, certainly, but its message was frequently

FIGURE 3 *Anti-Corn Law League membership card, 1839. © People's History Museum, Manchester.*

couched in messianic language and like all religions it held out the promise of a better life in the future, not only for consumers in the metropole but also for those who inhabited less 'civilized' regions. Tory romantic critics like Thomas Carlyle may have ridiculed this creed as representing nothing more than a 'bagman's' or commercial traveller's 'millennium', but it was no less real for those who sincerely believed it.[11] The internationalist mission of free trade was preached by Cobden, who believed that the *douceur* of commerce would harmonize national interests and inaugurate an era of world peace. Stronger economic ties brought about by free trade would not only bind peoples and nations closer together, Cobden prophesied that it would make redundant the desire for empires and the vast military expenditure these entailed, and it would also 'at a far distant period' refashion global politics on the lines of the municipal system of government. In sum, the campaign for free trade was for Cobden no less than the beginning of 'the greatest revolution that ever happened in the world's history.'[12] Other activists shared this vision and helped spread the word about the wider benefits that putting consumers in the driving seat of history would bring. The Irish nationalist leader Daniel O'Connell threw his weight behind the campaign at an Anti-Corn Law dinner at Manchester in 1840, declaring his faith in the power of free trade to improve the condition of Irish peasants and other impoverished peoples throughout the British Empire. O'Connell looked forward to a time when increased trade would eventually enable Ireland to industrialize:

'I want so to increase their demand for your manufactured articles, that that demand may require a greater supply; so much greater as not only that England may increase her manufactures, but that it may augment until Ireland shall also become a manufacturing place.'[13] In similar vein, the popularizer and vulgarizer of political economy, Harriet Martineau, wrote a short novella for the League in 1845 which described how savage head-hunters in the South Pacific were civilized and domesticated by habits of trade introduced by white sailors. *Dawn Island* was a racist work, certainly, but it was also resolutely optimistic, holding out the promise of a better life for all consumers across the globe, united by their shared motivations and material desires.[14]

The Anti-Corn Law League failed to convince workers at home that free trade would solve their problems, either immediately or in some distant utopian future; Chartists, for instance, reviled O'Connell for his free trade principles.[15] The break point in the relationship between the League and the working class came in 1842 – in the short to medium term at least – when a massive strike wave broke out throughout industrial districts in the potteries and northern England, lowland Scotland and South Wales. A trade depression had led manufacturers to reduce wages in many trades, causing dire distress and provoking numerous protests and lockouts. Many blamed the League for stage-managing the conflict, an erroneous charge that was later put about by the Tory *Quarterly Review*.[16] Although they did not direct affairs, the League nevertheless made the most of this opportunity, often employing highly melodramatic and inflammatory language to stoke the flames during what was an undeniably profound social and political crisis. Leaders denounced those protectionist spokesmen who had suggested that workers might not be able to buy wheaten bread any longer but could at least afford coarser fare, Cobden, for example, warning in the Commons that 'if the people continue to descend in the scale of physical comfort, and to eat potatoes, the hope of moral improvement which the friends of humanity indulge, must be altogether disappointed'. For Cobden and many others the consumption habits of the majority were signs of national superiority and advancement, which contrasted starkly with the consumer practices of the 'primitive' Irish, whom the 'Corn Law Rhymer' Ebenezer Elliott described as 'Erin's root-fed hordes'. The League blamed widespread hunger experienced in the present on the Corn Laws, claiming that they had reduced desperate workers to a state of near-barbarism. Rumours circulated that some were killing dogs to eat or even practicing cannibalism in this, the richest, most highly civilized country on the face of the earth.[17]

Speeches and pamphlets were often saturated in bloody imagery at this time. In the spring of 1842, before the strike commenced, the Unitarian minister William Field, for example, delivered a sermon based on Ecclesiasticus: 'The bread of the needy is his life; he, that defraudeth him of it, is a man of blood.' Field went on to observe that in some parts of the country individuals had been seen 'feeding themselves, out of the same trough, with the same food, which the swine were eating!'[18] Similarly, the Presbyterian minister Alexander Harvey gave a lecture to the Glasgow Young Men's Free Trade Association later that year in which he described the Corn Laws as 'a ravenous beast which devours at once the people and their food'. What made the situation unbearable was the existence of acute scarcity in the midst of excess: 'It is not possible to imagine a more terrible visitation than for a people to be subjected to starvation in the sight of plenty,' Harvey declared. He also maintained, as did other prominent supporters of repeal, that the crisis was not caused by over-production but was instead due to a lack of effective demand: 'We deny that there is over-production; the real evil is diminished consumption. The labourer, in dear years, has to give all his earnings for bread, and has nothing to spare for clothes ... we tell the monopolist you have laid an embargo on our commerce and shut up its outlets, and what right have you to complain that our warehouses are crammed and our people naked.'[19] The crisis of 1842 also caused the leaders of the League to use the language of class more openly. The imaginary notion of 'the people' as an undifferentiated mass of consumers began to disintegrate as class conflict intensified across diverse trades and localities. Cobden's remarks in a letter to Robert Peel after the Corn Laws were repealed in 1846 about the League being 'a middle-class set of agitators' are famous but other free traders also spoke the language of class at this earlier juncture.[20] As for workers, they remained largely unimpressed by lurid rumours put about by the League, which many no doubt found frankly insulting, and the general strike heightened class antagonism between them and their employers, who were generally keen supporters of free trade. Not surprisingly, they backed off the League; only three Operative Anti-Corn Law Associations were founded following the industrial unrest of 1842 and, during the remainder of the 'hungry forties', free trade was a lost cause among the working class.[21]

The real significance of the campaign for free trade during this period was that it helped unify the middle classes, providing a *Weltanschauung* or secular religion which enabled them to regard individual and national material progress as ethically sound and not merely the result of base, instinctive drives. Free trade helped moralize capitalism in Britain at a crucial moment, though whether this economic creed was ever accepted by the majority is highly questionable, despite confident assertions to this effect by some recent historians.[22] One of the most interesting aspects of the Anti-Corn Law League was how it politicized the consumption practices of middle-class consumers, whose appetites for goods were rapidly growing. The ideology of free trade that it promoted legitimated expansive consumer desire, making it possible to regard quotidian acts of shopping as steppingstones to a better life for all. Extensive use was made of material culture to communicate the League's message, including commemorative teapots, plates and mugs, as well as cushions, handkerchiefs and waistcoats embroidered with free trade slogans.[23] However, the intertwining of political economy and culture is brought out most clearly by the great fund-raising bazaars organized by the League, first in Manchester in 1842, then in London three years later.

The National Anti-Corn Law League Bazaar was a truly spectacular affair; widely publicized by both the provincial and metropolitan press, it served as a kind of dress rehearsal for the Great Exhibition of 1851. The journalist Douglas Jerrold, himself a zealous free trader, struggled to find sufficient hyperbole with which to describe the event. He imagined the goods speaking to visitors, proclaiming their utopian promise: 'Let us accomplish our mission; let us go forth over the earth, civilizing, aiding, comforting man; and bringing, in return, plenty to the board, and peace to the hearth, of the toil worn men and women who have fashioned us!' The Bazaar for Douglas was pregnant with meaning: 'As a spectacle, it was magnificent in the extreme; but not more grand materially than it was morally. The crowd who saw it, thought as well as gazed. It was not a mere huge shop for selling wares; but a great school for propagating an idea.' The League transformed Covent Garden Theatre into a temporary department store in the spring of 1845, where shoppers could purchase a wide range of fashionable commodities, from fabrics and furniture to the latest domestic appliances such as stoves and washing machines, which were retailed on stalls organized and staffed by the wives and daughters of male members of the League. Many observers besides Jerrold waxed lyrical over the profusion on display, which they read as signs of the potential of free trade to deliver the goods literally. The *Morning Chronicle*, for example, described it as an 'extraordinary museum' and noted that 'as a spectacle, it is unsurpassed in beauty, attractiveness, and interest by any that our metropolis affords. It is a great social and political fact.' In just seventeen days, the National Anti-Corn Law League Bazaar attracted approximately 170,000 people and raised over £25,000 for the League – about £1.5 million in today's money.[24]

When protectionism was finally defeated after the Corn Laws were repealed in 1846, the League disbanded.[25] Cobden and Bright continued to reach out to workers, however, and were especially keen on the freehold land movement which emerged around mid-century – that sought to enfranchise members who contributed to a fund to purchase property and eventually qualify to vote as forty-shilling freeholders – precisely because they saw it as a way of reinforcing an identity between the suffrage and property ownership. Both Cobden and Bright feared democracy in principle but they did believe in a kind of 'pocketbook democracy' and felt that the thrifty consumption practices of some groups of workers had earned them the right to the vote.[26] The most zealous free traders were also only partially satisfied by repeal of the Corn Laws and campaigned to remove duties on other imported goods such as sugar, tea and coffee, which were becoming staples of working-class as well as middle-class diets by this time. They established the Financial Reform Association in 1848 to campaign for government retrenchment and abolition of all customs and excise duties and made determined attempts to mobilize working-class consumers behind their cause. A pamphlet in 1862, for example, denounced indirect taxes levied on 'necessaries and comforts' that came 'crushingly down on the poor consumer.'[27] Although the organization failed to recruit many workers, some were attracted to John Bright's campaign for a 'free breakfast table' that he launched towards the end of the decade. Articles in the *Co-operator* and in the radical *Reynolds's News* appeared backing the reduction of import duties and indirect taxes, though on the whole this demand sparked little popular enthusiasm.[28] Free trade may have been generally regarded by the majority of the organized working class – for those active in the co-operative movement, for instance – as a necessary precondition for the continued expansion of their own voluntary associations. But it seems unlikely that they shared the belief in free trade as a kind of panacea in itself, a belief that remained largely restricted to the ranks of the middle class. An editorial in *The Times* admitted as much in 1859, observing that free trade seemed to constitute 'an article of national faith' so long as 'the more intelligent classes' dominated the political apparatus. However, continued friction between workers and their employers, the editor went on resignedly, demonstrated that 'the sound economical creed which they have fortunately adopted is, for the present, almost exclusively confined to their own country and class'.[29]

Working-class consumer politics

Workers used their consumer power in order to gain some protection against market exploitation from the second half of the eighteenth century onwards. As bread was the staff of life for the majority it was no wonder that securing regular supplies of corn at reasonable prices first occupied their attention. Increasingly, corn mills were being converted into mills for manufacturing and millers often therefore gained greater monopoly control in some localities – they had long been condemned in popular culture for grinding poor consumers, and opportunities for this became more common. Consequently, at least forty-six flour and bread societies, in effect co-operative retailing schemes, were established in various parts of the country between 1759 and 1820, the majority founded from the late eighteenth century onwards.[30] One of the most successful of these was the wonderfully named Hull Anti-Mill Society, which began in 1795. Petitioning the mayor and aldermen to lend financial support for the venture, the 'poor inhabitants' of the city expressed their determination to defend themselves against 'covetous and merciless men' by pooling their meagre cash resources and building their own mill. It took two years to raise enough money to erect a mill but the venture soon proved so successful that local millers indicted the society as a nuisance in 1811 before a jury at York that – believing poverty a greater nuisance – found in favour of the society. By the mid-nineteenth century a new steam mill had been erected at considerable cost and membership continued to expand until it stood at over 4,000 by the late 1860s.[31] Some historians have seen these mills as a continuation of the 'moral economy' that arguably characterized social and economic relationships in the eighteenth century.[32] As we saw in Chapter 1, according to this view economic relations were not separated out or disaggregated from other aspects of social and cultural life as they were to become in the nineteenth century when the 'free market' became hegemonic. Morality and economics were thought of as being bound together and the actions of unscrupulous corn dealers and millers who sought only to inflate their profits were seen as subversive of this idea. Working people and their social superiors arguably had a more reciprocal (though of course highly unequal) relationship with one another during this period, and sometimes combined against the rapacious capitalist order that was emerging. Evidence from the Hull Anti-Mill lends some support to this view. Paternalist motives were present early on, certainly; although most of the £2,200 which the original mill cost came from modest subscriptions, members of the local gentry did donate around £350, as well as two large bowls of punch to celebrate the opening.[33]

More systematic thinking about and practical organizing around consumption was spurred by the development of Owenite socialism after the end of the Napoleonic Wars. Robert Owen and other early socialist writers extended the eighteenth-century critique of luxury in a new context: the inexorable growth of industrial capitalism meant that the gulf between scarcity and excess was exposed with a new intensity. The rising middle class was avidly consuming a proliferating range of goods while labourers and their families frequently went hungry. Many Owenite writers denounced the profligacy of the rich and advocated an ascetic attitude towards consumption, refusing to accept that happiness could be straightforwardly measured in terms of the individual acquisition of material 'comforts'.[34] Arguing for the harmful effects of consumerism across society, Owen himself observed that while the wealthy wasted their augmented wealth on conspicuous consumption, the middle classes spent theirs on 'fine clothes and extravagant dwellings and palaces of business', and the working classes poisoned themselves with alcohol and adulterated food.[35] Owenites maintained that the solution to this state of affairs lay in a fairer distribution of the products of labour – which ought to be exchanged on the basis of the labour-time embodied in goods – and they established a number of labour exchanges to this end before this phase of the movement collapsed in the mid-1830s. They also tried to reverse the current trend, emphasizing that restraint in private habits of consumption should be combined with opulence in relation to social consumption. Such ideas were built into the fabric of the movement's community experiments, notably Queenwood in Hampshire. Thus, when he visited in 1844, the 'social missionary'

G. J. Holyoake reported that Harmony Hall itself was done out in fine style, no expense being spared in its construction or furnishings.[36] Less spectacular but more important in the longer term were Owenite co-operative stores that sold unadulterated basic goods at fair prices to members of local societies. Pioneered by sympathetic middle-class individuals such as Dr William King of Brighton, but also by working-class trade unionists in that town like William Bryan, these early co-operators regarded so-called Union Shops as the building bricks of a New Moral World where private property would be abolished and where people would live in co-operative communities. Despite the fact that Robert Owen disagreed with the usefulness of this strategy, it caught on, with over 250 of these stores established throughout the country between 1826 and 1835.[37]

Working people combined in trade unions and co-operative societies to try to ameliorate the effects of heightened competition, frequently establishing both producers' and consumers' co-operatives in order to employ themselves and mitigate exploitation in the marketplace. The situation was made worse by the fact that hunger was overtly politicized by the Poor Law Amendment Act of 1834, which was introduced by the Whig government but commanded wide support among ruling elites. The New Poor Law dismantled the safety net represented by the Old Poor Law that dated back to Tudor times. Drawn up soon after the Swing riots had convulsed the English countryside in the south, it sought to ratchet up the pressure on poor consumers by abolishing outdoor relief and making life within workhouses – 'bastilles' as they were called by their critics – as unbearable as possible. The main target of the act's chief architects, Edwin Chadwick and William Nassau Senior, who wrote the report on which the Act was based, was the Speenhamland system, which had pegged outdoor relief to the price of bread (although this system was declining anyway). According to Chadwick and Senior, this had 'demoralised' labourers who were keen to assert their rights but not so keen to work for the going rate of pay. In short, the act attempted to incentivize workers by reducing their benefits or the 'social norm of consumption' of those at the bottom of the economic hierarchy.[38] Henceforth – in theory at least, for in practice implementation was often softened – working people would be denied 'comforts' unless they had earned them by the sweat of their brow. On entering the workhouse, paupers had to relinquish any meagre possessions they had and their families were broken up, housed in separate quarters. Moreover, dietaries in the institution consisted of what Chadwick notoriously referred to as 'coarser fare', a term that radicals threw back at him unrelentingly. Many of the new unions even abolished Christmas in the workhouse, withholding from inmates seasonal treats like roast beef and plum pudding.[39] A mass movement soon organized against the act, made up of an alliance of sympathetic humanitarian Tories such as John Walter, editor of *The Times*, nonconformist preachers such as the Reverend Joseph Rayner Stephens and radical working-class activists, including many women. These groups denounced the measure as deliberately cruel and unchristian, a brutal assault on the families of the poor. The act moved the politics of hunger and what became known as the 'gruel question' centre stage; Charles Dickens's novel *Oliver Twist* (1837) is merely the most long lasting instance of a far wider contemporary debate that fed directly into the Chartist movement towards the end of the 1830s.[40]

It was in this context that Chartist activists politicized shopping, arguing that the problem of hunger would not be solved until working people obtained the franchise and gained a handle on political power. They first used the tactic of trading only with shopkeepers who supported their political cause – or 'exclusive dealing' as it was called – that can be traced back at least to the crisis preceding the passage of the Reform Act of 1832 when Tories, Whigs and radicals all employed it, as has already been noted.[41] However, the latter group really made it their own, seeing in exclusive dealing a way of hitting back at middlemen or the rising 'shopocracy', as Bronterre O'Brien dubbed them in the *Poor Man's Guardian*. The Owenite Allen Davenport suggested that the tactic might be used to pressure this group into siding with workers and was even moved to poetry: 'The little shops must fall in spite/Of puffing and appealing/Unless their owners shall unite/And share Exclusive Dealing.' For Davenport, exclusive dealing had a utopian as well as a practical dimension, for if working people could learn to trade only with themselves they might effect 'a moral revolution that shall expel from society all who are able but not willing to create the means of their own subsistence'.[42] A few years later, Chartists eagerly adopted the tactic, which was practiced in many localities in the industrial north. Women were to the fore in the early years of the movement, and housewives who were at the end of their tether in 1839 threatened many shopkeepers; in Carlisle that summer, special constables had to be sworn in to protect them. A short while before this, in May, exclusive dealing had been given official backing by the Chartist Convention, the anti-parliament that sought to challenge the legitimacy of the existing state apparatus. Political shopping was a component part of the Chartist manifesto, which also included the boycott of excisable goods, a run on the banks, the formation of a people's militia and a 'sacred month' or general strike. This strategy, designed to maximize working-class power – the editor of the *Northern Star*, William Hill, thought it the best way of getting rid of 'a middle-class of money-mongers and capitalists' – generated a great deal of debate in Chartist ranks. Nevertheless, although many thought the time was not yet ripe for a general strike and were reluctant to recommend direct confrontation, exclusive dealing was widely supported within the movement. The London radical Henry Hetherington regarded it as an offensive weapon, describing it as nothing less than a 'tremendous field-piece … (a) steam-gun is a child's toy to it'.[43]

It was a small step for Chartists to move on from boycotting hostile shopkeepers to setting up their own joint stock co-operative stores and trading with each other. The earliest Chartist co-operative was probably established in Hull in April 1839 and many quickly sprung up in other manufacturing towns in Scotland, northern England and south Wales. They sold unadulterated basic commodities such as flour, tea, coffee, sugar, butter, cheese and bacon at market prices. Newcastle became a particularly innovative centre; the North East of England Joint Stock Company opened a 'People's Provision Store' there in November 1839 that boasted three departments selling a wide range of groceries, dairy produce and meat. Organizers hoped that this combination of working-class purchasing power would 'reduce the middle classes to live according to Scripture; and eat their bread by the sweat of their brow'.[44] The most important theorist of this strategy was Robert Lowery, who also came from Newcastle and who wrote a widely circulated pamphlet on exclusive dealing in which storekeeping was portrayed as a means to achieve fundamental political and economic change. Harnessing the collective power of working-class consumers would enable them to have more of the good things in life, Lowery believed, rather than supplying other classes: 'All those splendid shops we see in every town have been furnished by us; all those fine houses in which those gentry dwell, with their snug parlours, fine drawing rooms, and costly furniture, have been furnished by the profits on our labour; and if we have done so much for others, may we not do as much for ourselves?' Exclusive dealing would, Lowery prophesied, 'change the face of society: we may become builders, cultivators, merchants, and producers for ourselves, and sit under our own vine and fig tree, none making us afraid'.[45] Another Chartist from the north-east, Thomas Devyr, reckoned political shopkeeping would undermine 'the middle class foundation' of an exploitative economic system and that eventually 'the whole fabric of rottenness would tumble into one undistinguished ruin'.[46]

There was a great deal of diversity and experimentation as one would expect; some co-operatives limited shareholding as a protection against take over by wealthier members, others redistributed profits to members while some used them to support the cause – by relieving Chartist prisoners, for example. Unsurprisingly, many of the co-operative stores that were founded during this enthusiastic period quickly collapsed, riven by internal disputes or financially undermined when officers absconded with funds; there was no legal protection until the passage of the Industrial and Provident Societies Act of 1852. Nevertheless, in the early Chartist phase, many radicals firmly believed that they could turn the joint stock principle against emerging industrial capitalism, using collective ownership of capital to regulate and control the market in the interest of working-class consumers and producers. It is misleading to dismiss their optimism as merely utopian or naive, especially as the joint stock form of organization was malleable and contested around mid-century.[47] Exclusive dealing and co-operatives represented attempts to regulate the market in favour of working-class consumers; the latter were also important forcing beds of democratic practice. Unlike the Anti-Corn

Law League, the Chartists affirmed the concept and language of 'democracy' and sought to utilize the power they had as consumers to hasten what they regarded as an inevitable process of democratization.[48]

The period 1841–2 was crucial in the politics of consumption. As we saw in the last section, the general strike polarized class relations in the summer of 1842 and completely discredited attempts by the Anti-Corn Law League to forge an alliance with the working classes and convince them that free trade was the solution to the manifold problems facing them as poor consumers. Hunger was widespread during the economic depression of the early 1840s and many labourers and their families were reduced to subsisting on a diet of potatoes, though they had been accustomed to much better fare. With poverty criminalized, their demands for enfranchisement rejected by Parliament and their own solutions such as co-operatives failing in an increasingly hostile environment, workers' ire was raised further by hard-hearted observers who told them that at least they could 'rejoice in potatoes'. Little wonder, then, that desperate measures were sometimes resorted to during what was in effect a profound crisis of the state. The Tory home secretary, Sir James Graham – who described the strike as 'the mad insurrection of the working classes' – even advised the young Queen Victoria to cancel her holiday to Scotland, fearing her train might be intercepted by rioters as it passed through northern manufacturing districts.[49] Consumer protests helped fuel the crisis, some of them exhibiting features of the older tradition of 'moral economy'. When paternalistic bonds between plebeians and patricians reached breaking point in times of dearth during the eighteenth century, labourers resorted to highly ritualized and disciplined forms of direct action as a last resort. This period witnessed a resurgence of the 'moral economy', the crowd's anger ignited by particular targets – a vicar who had advised the poor to use dock leaves as a substitute for tea, parsimonious local shopkeepers, John Bright himself. Figure 4 is a woodcut by the popular caricaturist C. J. Grant, which portrayed the Duke of Wellington as a 'modern Nero', playing the fiddle with petitions for relief strewn at his feet, while crowds of angry workers roamed the country torching ricks and looking for food. The most widely publicized clash occurred in Stockport and focused on the local workhouse, which was ransacked by a crowd that distributed hundreds of loaves found in its stores.[50] In the autumn after the strike died down, the state responded harshly, with many local Chartists sentenced to transportation and hard labour by kangaroo courts. The following spring a show trial was held at Lancaster for Chartist leaders but now the carrot was employed rather than the stick. Defendants were allowed to get off charges of seditious conspiracy on a technicality, though the judge, Baron Rolfe, used the opportunity to reinforce the distinction between economic pressure by workers, which was seen as legitimate, and political action that had to be kept separate otherwise protest was deemed treasonable.[51]

This sundering of economic from political spheres of activity was to have profound repercussions for working-class organization and ideology. We see

FIGURE 4 *C. J. Grant, 'The Modern Nero'*, Penny Satirist, *30 October 1841. © The British Library Board (LOU.LON 45).*

this clearly, for instance, in the rules of the Rochdale Society of Equitable Pioneers founded in 1844, which eventually served as a model for a growing movement after mid-century. These included the complete remodelling, 'as soon as practicable', of 'the powers of production, distribution, education and government ... to establish a self-supporting colony of united interests'. But the Rochdale Society's rules also voiced a strong commitment to political neutrality and it was this that represented a more important turning point than their decision to award dividend on purchases to members, as other societies had distributed profits for over a decade.[52] The founders of the Society – twenty-eight or so textile operatives and skilled workers – were deeply involved in social movements such as Owenism, factory reform and trade unionism and it seems likely that all of them supported the People's Charter, so the formal exclusion of politics was mainly a matter of expediency.[53] Nevertheless, although the decision to turn their backs on more confrontational forms of politics and attempt to sidestep the question of state power may have been a realistic assessment of the changed situation, it does indicate an important move away from the more explicitly political forms of shopkeeping that emerged out of exclusive dealing. It was some time, however, before the leadership of the Chartist movement publicly rejected exclusive dealing. O'Connor, for instance, was still recommending its use in the general election of 1847, though it was marginalized if not yet totally rejected at the Chartist Convention the following year. There was some resistance to the abandonment of this weapon in certain localities by female Chartists in particular, but the tide had turned against linking up politics and popular consumerism so closely.[54] A few Chartists criticized this strategic shift at the time, accusing consumer co-operation in particular of helping to depoliticize the working class. Karl Marx's supporter Ernest Jones, for example, who debated the significance of co-operation in Halifax in 1852 with Lloyd Jones, the old Owenite convert to Christian Socialism, threw out a series of sharp questions: 'What carried Catholic Emancipation? Was it a cake of soap? No! it was political power. What carried the Reform Bill? Was it a pat of butter? No! it was political power. What is it that is driving on the middle class tyrants and the aristocracy to a semblance of reform? Is it your co-operation that they fear? – no, it is ours.'[55]

Liberal consumerism and the onset of 'equipoise'

If consumption issues tended to pull classes apart before mid-century, afterwards they tended to pull classes closer together. The emergent category of the consumer was universal in scope, in theory at least, and the interests of consumers could be portrayed by sympathetic members of the political elite as transcending class divisions. Significantly, from 1842 taxation policy increasingly prioritized the interests of poor consumers; the budget introduced by Conservative prime minister Sir Robert Peel that year modified the sliding scale on corn, removed indirect taxes on hundreds of basic goods that pinched working-class consumers especially and shifted the burden on to direct taxation that was reintroduced, initially for a limited term but which was to remain indefinitely. 'We must make this country a cheap country for living', Peel wrote to his friend John Wilson Croker, and 'Peel's Bombshell Budget' as some Chartists called it was designed to take some of the heat out of the politics of hunger and make it easier to portray the state as impartial, concerned with promoting justice and fair play for all consumers.[56] This approach was later continued by William Gladstone when the Liberal leader was Chancellor of the Exchequer and the 'Gladstonian fiscal constitution' that took shape over the next two decades was informed by these priorities.[57] Gladstone embraced the free trade utopia and fully believed in the healing effects of the diffusion of comforts that his fiscal reforms were intended to facilitate. His 1853 budget – nicknamed 'The People's Budget' – extended the income tax to more of the middle classes and further reduced or abolished duties on over a hundred commodities, including soap, tea, butter, cheese, cocoa and eggs, articles that, as Gladstone remarked, 'enter largely if not into the necessaries of life, at any rate into the solace and comfort of the people'. The advertisement duty was also repealed, which helped fuel the remarkable expansion of the press as well as consumer culture more generally from this time. Gladstone's budget of 1860 went even further, raising income tax and cutting more duties, and it was his taxation policy more than anything else that endeared him to large sections of the working class, creating the idea of a moralized capitalism.[58] It also constituted a key component part in a distinctive politics of consumption that undergirded popular liberalism – a specifically liberal consumerism – that, while never doubting the benefits free trade would confer on the mass of consumers, eschewed the dogmatism of Cobden and Bright and tried to assuage the criticisms of democratic radicals by bringing more cheap goods within reach of the masses.

Liberal consumerism therefore aided class conciliation post-mid-century, making possible a fragile social and political 'equipoise'.[59] A number of issues and institutions encouraged its growth. One of the most important issues that drew widespread support concerned the adulteration of food and drink, which was commonplace. Abuses were exposed in the 1820s by a German chemist, Frederick Accum, but nothing was done until the 1850s when the cause was taken up by the *Lancet* and its radical editor, Thomas Wakley, who instigated an investigation by Dr Arthur Hassell, physician and lecturer in medicine at the Royal Free Hospital. Between 1851 and 1854, the 'Analytical Sanitary Commission' documented in gory detail each week in the journal how fraudulent and often dangerous practices had reached epidemic proportions. Tea was frequently adulterated with mineral dyes and old tea leaves, bread and flour with alum, milk was usually diluted with water, beer pepped up with 'grains of paradise', children's sweets coloured with chromate of lead, copper was added to pickles to lend colour, lead was found in snuff and so on. These reports were eventually collected together and published by Hassell in book form that received a great deal of publicity in the popular press.[60] *Chambers's Journal*, for example, compared the activities of those who practiced adulteration to that of Thuggees in India, a criminal gang whose members would befriend travellers before poisoning and robbing them. It declared that 'the adulteration of the necessaries of life by those through whose hands they pass from nature's great laboratory to the consumer's table, is a crime for which it is difficult, in our opinion, to find language strong enough or punishment too signal'.[61]

A Select Committee of the House of Commons was set up following these revelations that confirmed the picture and concluded that the problem had considerably worsened since the early nineteenth century. All consumers suffered but the poorest suffered most, as they had to buy the cheapest goods. There were some attempts at voluntary improvement after this. A number of firms started to take purity seriously, recognizing its commercial potential. Moreover, co-operative societies helped to improve standards, though even they sometimes faced problems educating their working-class members who had come to prefer adulterated foodstuffs. The state eventually intervened in 1860, when the Adulteration of Foods Act was passed, but the measure was almost completely ineffective, as local authorities were not compelled to appoint public analysts. Hassell and others were bitterly disappointed and reformers had to overcome a great deal of resistance, not only from manufacturers and retailers but also from politicians such as John Bright who regarded adulteration as a form of legitimate competition. Marx wrote that the act showed 'the tenderest consideration for every free-trader who determines by the buying and selling of adulterated commodities "to turn an honest penny"', and modern historians have confirmed his opinion.[62] Pressure mounted over the following decade until a new Adulteration of Food, Drink and Drugs Act was passed in 1872, which tightened up the law and led to more than 1,500 convictions during the next three years. As a select committee later reported, one measure of the success of this act was that consumers were now 'cheated rather than poisoned'.[63]

Another consumption issue that helped to build bridges between classes was the plight of those who laboured in the expanding retail sector. The Early Closing Association was founded in 1842 and was led by concerned middle-class individuals such as the journalist Samuel Carter Hall and the Baptist preacher George Dawson. It drew support from high-profile public figures such as Charles Dickens and aimed to curtail the extremely long hours that were often endured by those who worked in warehouses and shops in the metropolis and other towns and cities.[64] The organization's annual report for 1847 referred to 'the worse than negro slavery to which the young men and women so employed are subjected'. Supporters emphasized particularly the deleterious effects of overwork on the health of shop workers and their lack of opportunities for self-improvement. The movement gathered more steam after mid-century, publicized by the popular press and backed by medical men who estimated in 1853 that about 1,000 shop workers died annually as a result of long hours, while 3,000–5,000 more returned to their homes in the provinces to die.[65] By this time, a few large respectable drapers in the capital were closing at seven o'clock, many more at eight, though change was very slow and excessive hours remained the norm throughout the nineteenth century, especially in smaller shops. The association was reinvigorated after the launch of a campaign for Saturday half-holidays at a large public meeting at London's Exeter Hall in 1856, which was chaired by Lord Shaftsbury. Aristocratic women such as the Duchess of Sutherland and the Countess of Shaftsbury quickly rallied to the cause, promising never to shop on Saturdays after two o'clock.[66] The *London Review* noted that excellent progress had been made a decade later, at least in larger establishments, and observed that 'it is hardly possible to convey an adequate idea of the boon thus conferred on the over tasked shop-assistants ... The British navvy works hard, but his lot is enviable in comparison with that of the unfortunate milliner cooped up in a close atmosphere from Monday morning until Saturday night.'[67]

The fact that consumption generated anxieties for some sections of the middle classes no doubt made it easier to perceive shared interests with those worse off. For sure, middle-class consumers as a whole voted with their pocketbooks and eagerly bought into the expanding world of goods, as scholars have reminded us.[68] However, many felt uneasy and took some time to 'make their peace with indulgence'.[69] Mainstream professional economists like J. S. Mill continued to prioritize production and it was not until 1871 that an alternative perspective was suggested by W. S. Jevons in his *Theory of Political Economy*. Jevons argued that value was created by the consumer rather than the producer – goods being desired according to the 'marginal utility' that consumers gained from them – but he was an isolated figure and such views were thought maverick until Alfred Marshall made them more respectable during the fin de siècle by adding a dose of social duty to individual desire.[70] For their part, designers and art critics set themselves the task of reforming middle-class taste and tried to educate consumers to reject the profuse, overly ornamental style that dominated Victorian design. The most radical of these critics, John Ruskin, went on to elaborate a searching analysis of Victorian consumerism in works such as *Unto This Last* (1860) and *Fors Clavigera* (1871–84), which attacked the middle-class cult of things as a sign of wastefulness and ethical bankruptcy, thus endearing himself to working-class radicals for the rest of the century and beyond.[71] But it was far more moderate individuals such as Henry Cole, Richard Redgrave and Owen Jones that had helped organize the Great Exhibition in 1851, who were instrumental in moulding middle-class taste, the latter arguing that consumers had yet to find a language of design appropriate to their own quintessentially commercial age in which religious strictures – against excess and showiness, for example – no longer held their earlier force.[72] After the Great Exhibition closed, taste reformers opened a Museum of Ornamental Art at Marlborough House in London to display what they considered to be examples of good design, for the continued edification of the consuming public. There was also a Chamber of Horrors, where visitors could study examples of bad taste and be in turn amused, if the objects had been bought by others, or humiliated, if they had bought the objects themselves. Some manufacturers and retailers were angered by this preaching – Dickens even penned a damning portrait of Cole in *Hard Times* – and the Chamber of Horrors was eventually shut down, though the question of what exactly constituted good taste did not disappear.[73]

Zealous taste reformers may have alienated as many middle-class consumers as they converted but less dogmatic advice found a ready audience, as furnishing the bourgeois home presented many pitfalls for the unwary. Writing anonymously in the *Cornhill Magazine* in 1864, for instance, the art journalist and nephew of the president of the Royal Academy, Charles Locke Eastlake, warned young middle-class newlyweds furnishing their first home about the unscrupulous wiles of salesmen: 'At the furniture warehouse, they are in the upholsterer's hands; at the china-shop, they are as easily talked over by the obsequious vendor of wine-glasses and dinner-plates. The carpet merchant leads them by the nose.'[74] Eastlake went on to condemn the heightened fashion consciousness and emphasis on showiness that he believed characterized the present age and which generally substituted for sound design and good taste. He repeated this theme towards the end of the decade in his influential work *Hints on Household Taste*, which was intended to instruct readers on how to 'furnish their houses picturesquely, without ignoring modern notions of comfort and convenience'. Carpets were singled out for special censure: 'It may convey the notion of a bed of roses, or a dangerous labyrinth of rococo ornament – but if it is "fashionable" that is all-sufficient. While it is new, it is admired, when old, everybody will agree that it was always "hideous".'[75] Clearly, navigating one's way through this new world of consumption was often not easy, even for those with means to enjoy the material comforts made possible by economic advance, and many consumers sought guidance from works by Eastlake and others. Religious injunctions against excess had to be overcome before the new world of goods could be completely embraced and anxieties over what to consume remained.

If guidebooks like the one by Eastlake helped to ease anxieties of middle-class consumers in the private sphere, working-class co-operatives served as models for what could be hoped for in the public sphere. They were widely praised after mid-century by free traders like Cobden and Bright and liberal intellectuals including J. S. Mill, the latter regarding them as opening up the possibility of a middle way between capitalism and socialism, achievable without violence and bloodshed. Christian Socialists like the barrister Edward Vansittart Neale and the lawyer John Malcolm Ludlow also sang their praises, the latter regarding co-operatively owned workshops in particular as a means of avoiding the proletarian revolution that he had witnessed first-hand in Paris in 1848. Ludlow played a key role in gaining state recognition for co-operatives, helping to draft the Industrial and Provident Societies Act of 1852 that provided protection against fraud, which had led to the collapse of many earlier societies when officials ran off with funds. However, the act also hamstrung co-operative growth in many ways; societies were not allowed to own land or to engage in banking or wholesaling until restrictions were removed by the Industrial and Provident Societies Act of 1862 that Neale had helped get on to the statute books.[76] Co-operators soon took advantage of this and set up the English Co-operative Wholesale Society the year after, and a similar body was established in Scotland in 1868. Leading members of the Rochdale Society such as Abraham Greenwood and J. T. W. Mitchell had been pushing for this for years and the wholesale society soon exceeded their expectations, building supply chains and investing in production and transport that kept the stores stocked with goods, as well as providing invaluable support for local societies facing boycotts from hostile private traders.[77] The co-operative movement became a major institutional prop for liberal consumerism: its leadership supported free trade and colluded in the separation of the political from the economic domain, believing that co-operators only needed to be left alone by the state in order to achieve their ultimate ambitions. In this way, working-class consumption was formally depoliticized in the third quarter of the nineteenth century, a fact that was often underlined by middle-class commentators, including one who visited the Rochdale Society and approvingly observed: 'Their transactions bear no sign of political bias, no religious test, or passport of secret favour.'[78]

Co-operatives were also embraced by the liberal bourgeoisie because of their presumed effects on working-class manners and morals. It was thought that they helped inculcate values like thrift, independence and respectability, teaching workers the rules of the capitalist market and therefore soothing class conflict after the clashes of the 1830s and 1840s, a view that was rehearsed ad nauseam by later academic historians who singled out the establishment of the Rochdale Pioneers Society as marking a watershed.[79] This interpretation was encouraged at the time by the self-appointed early historian of co-operation, George Jacob Holyoake, whose significantly titled history of the Pioneers, *Self-Help by the People*, which appeared in book form in 1858, sought to build bridges with middle-class sympathizers.[80] Co-operatives were also frequently lauded because they were regarded as encouraging a more rational and efficient – and hence more masculine – approach to consumption. This, at a time when middle-class men worried, often unfairly, about the reckless spending habits of their wives and daughters. Addressing the annual meeting of the Social Science Association, an important early liberal think tank, the engineer Jeremiah Head recommended co-operation to the better off because it would result in less waste and cheaper prices. But he also hoped that it would abolish 'false sentimentality' and lead to the adoption of a more systematic, methodical approach to shopping by middle-class women who, Head believed, often failed 'to look at the commercial business of buying from a sufficiently serious point of view. They appear rather to regard streets of shops as their natural promenades – places for air, exercise and amusement. They delight in seeing what that is pretty or attractive is displayed in the windows; and the result not infrequently corresponds with that recorded in the fable of the spider and the fly.'[81] Head considered that the boundless and irrational desires stimulated by the developing fantasy world of consumption could only be contained by the masculinization of consumption practices and that working-class co-operation might keep these desires in check. For many middle-class supporters, the appeal of co-operation lay precisely in the idea that it fostered 'manly' virtues and a rational, calculating mentality. Sections of the lower middle class acted on these ideas, establishing many of their own retail co-operative societies, notably the Civil Service Supply Association founded by post office employees in London in 1865, which sought to keep prices down but pursued no wider social or political ambitions.[82] Initiatives like these again highlight just how fraught consumerism was for many members of the middle class.

Liberal consumerism was severely tested by the so-called Cotton Famine that hit the Lancashire cotton textile industry in the early 1860s. As mills closed rendering thousands of textile workers unemployed, profound tensions were exposed. Even the description proved contentious, critics pointing out that the problems were not caused by a 'famine' in raw cotton resulting from the disruptions of the American Civil War but that they were the inevitable consequence of overproduction by Lancashire mill owners who had run their mills full pelt and glutted the market. In short, the Cotton Famine raised questions about the ability of free market capitalism to deliver the good life to the majority as impoverished workers were reduced to pawning their possessions and begging in the streets. These were not Irish peasants either; they were a respectable, thrifty and hard-working proletariat – the world's first affluent workers in fact – who had enjoyed relatively high wages, which they spent on more and better foodstuffs and clothes and on filling their homes with decent furniture and pictures, sometimes even a piano. The Poor Law could not cope and soon the boundary line between 'deserving' and 'undeserving' that it had been designed to police collapsed, clean-living operatives and their families falling into the gutter and losing all the material possessions they had laboured so hard for.[83] The foundations of liberal consumerism were severely shaken, Gladstone chastising capitalists for their immoral conduct as co-operative stores went to the wall. The crisis provoked a response from the state in the form of the Public Works Act, which provided employment and helped prop up the social norm of consumption of working-class families. Far more important, however, was the charitable response; indeed, the Cotton Famine generated the first large-scale international humanitarian aid campaign in world history, which eventually raised about £2 million probably ten times the amount raised for victims of the Irish Famine around twenty years before. Most of the money came from the concerned middle classes, and many of them visited Lancashire to witness the worst effects of the Cotton Famine first hand. They later wrote about what they saw, producing a kind of 'famine literature' that provided momentum for the charitable campaign. Naturally, the gift did not come without conditions, and working people sometimes bit the hand that fed them. Towards the end of the crisis in the spring of 1863, a series of riots occurred, for example, that tested 'equipoise' to the limit. The most serious disturbances at Stalybridge saw the old radical preacher J. R. Stephens once more denouncing the 'skilly' dished out to workers in relief soup kitchens. The good behaviour of the majority at this crucial juncture did not go unrewarded, Cobden, Bright and Gladstone all arguing that the decorum of 'Rochdale man' – who worked hard to lay up his shares in the co-operative store and whose behaviour provided a model of suitably masculinized consumption practice for his own class as well as for others – proved beyond doubt that he was now worthy of the vote. Consequently, the Second Reform Act of 1867 enfranchised about a million rate-paying urban male householders, which neatly equated to the membership of the growing co-operative movement.[84]

PART TWO

Making a Mass Market: 1870–1920

Preface

The period from the beginning of the economic downturn historians used to call the 'Great Depression' until the immediate aftermath of the First World War constituted a distinct phase in the history of consumer culture in Britain. Many of the characteristics that have come to be associated with a recognizably modern society were forged during these decades. Living standards for the majority continued to rise significantly, despite uneven distribution and periodic reversals. Representative democracy was extended, with the vote being granted to different categories of working-class men as a kind of reward for respectable conduct. Business enterprises grew in size, a trend that deeply affected the consumer goods sector, which experienced a 'retailing revolution'. Big capitalists emerged who sought to better control markets and therefore consumer demand through the creation of cartels and syndicates. At a time when regional identities were very strong, branded goods that were heavily advertised in the cheap daily press and sold in multiple shops helped knit together a national community of consumers. The growth of popular tourism to holiday resorts like Margate and Blackpool and the rise of commercialized sports also provided new ways of spending money. Such changes took place within the context of the 'new imperialism' – the territorial and commercial invention of 'Greater Britain' that deeply penetrated British society. No longer regarded as posing a serious revolutionary threat by ruling elites, workers were frequently condescended to as 'the masses', innately gullible and driven by instinctive drives. Ex-Chartists and a younger generation of radicals sometimes despaired about the new working class, believing that they had been bought off by material possessions and cheap amusements.

The development of consumer culture was inextricably bound up with the profound transformations that occurred during this period. Advertisers may not have conjured up consumerism and conditions had necessarily to be ripe. But they did shape desires and mould consumers in particular ways. Although apologists for advertising typically stress that its practices are almost as old as human society, this is misleading; the modern advertising industry fully emerged only during the fin de siècle. The key factor here was the expansion of advertising agencies that were hired by many large firms to push branded commodities across national markets. The language of goods became further refined by advertisers who increasingly regarded themselves as professionals, often with artistic pretentions. This was one way of heading off criticism as consumer culture continued to be divisive, generating deep anxieties as is shown by the history of the department store, which reached its apotheosis during this phase. Run by autocratic big capitalists like William Whiteley and Gordon Selfridge, they created 'dream worlds' for female shoppers, though male consumers were also catered for. These forms inflamed the fears of those who continued to consider shopping potentially dangerous as it gave women too many opportunities to indulge their appetites and drag their husbands into debt. Department store bosses often played on the idea of female empowerment, presenting themselves as champions of women's rights. The politics of consumption polarized opinion more starkly than it had been for a generation or more as different groups vied with each other to speak for consumers. Embodied by the co-operative movement, democratic consumerism grew tremendously and harnessed working-class consumer power for radical social and economic change. Liberal consumerism had to reinvent itself to defeat the challenge to free trade made by tariff reformers who argued for a distinctively imperial consumerism to meet the threats posed by heightened global competition.

4

Image Worlds: The Rise of Modern Advertising

The age of advertising

It is a commonplace that the Victorian middle class regarded their society as the embodiment of the idea of 'Progress'. They took great delight in reading about the myriad ways in which this idea manifested itself, so it was not surprising that many enterprising authors exploited this appetite for self-congratulation by publishing books that traced how Victorian society had brought almost everything to near-perfection. The earliest history of advertising, which appeared in 1874, followed this pattern. In this work, Henry Sampson narrated the development of the practice from its supposed origins in classical antiquity, through to the refined art of the present day. It was a resolutely progressive story, Sampson emphasizing how, despite its long antecedents, advertising had been completely transformed and improved during the previous half-century. The order and control that now characterized billposting, for example, demonstrated that advertising had itself become a vital constituent part of modern urban civility, parading the material results of economic advance for both the edification and amusement of the widest possible audience.[1] Though Sampson thought advertising was already fully developed, the 'age of advertising' properly emerged over only subsequent decades, which witnessed revolutionary changes in the organization of the industry and the techniques it employed to talk about commodities and tempt buyers.

The writer George Gissing captured this shift in a novel that was published two decades after Sampson's history. *In the Year of Jubilee* (1894) represented a bitter indictment of the shallowness of a burgeoning consumer culture and metropolitan suburban life during the fin de siècle. For Gissing, advertising was a key symbol of modern life, unstoppable yet essentially degenerate.

Luckworth Crewe, the advertising agent protagonist in the novel, believes that before 'advertising sprang up, the world was barbarous' and asks a potential client, 'Do you suppose people kept themselves clean before they were reminded at every corner of the benefits of soap?' Riding on an omnibus, the novel's heroine, Nancy Lord, is distracted by the advertisements that Gissing suggests have corroded her belief in anything loftier: 'Somebody's "Blue"; somebody's "Soap"; somebody's "High-class Jams"; and behold, inserted between the Soap and the Jam – "God so loved the world, that He gave His only-begotten Son, that whoso believeth in Him should not perish, but have everlasting life." Nancy perused the passage without perception of incongruity, without emotion of any kind. Her religion had long since fallen to pieces, and universal defilement of Scriptural phrase by the associations of the market-place had in this respect blunted her sensibilities.'[2] We will return to such attacks later in this chapter but first it is necessary to get a better idea of the growing reach of the advertising industry.

The increasing salience of advertising would not have been possible without the continuing expansion of the market for a wide range of affordable commodities during the last quarter of the nineteenth century. Defenders of laissez faire capitalism, like the Board of Trade's chief statistician Robert Giffen, eagerly pointed to the growth of working-class demand in answer to mounting criticism from those who argued for more state intervention to help the poor. In a widely circulated work of 1884 he argued that absolute scarcity had been abolished and that there had been massive increases in money wages of between 20 and 100 per cent in different trades since the 1830s, while prices had remained relatively stable. Admittedly, those at the bottom of the social ladder or the 'residuum' had not benefited as much as they might have done but overall working-class consumption of basic foodstuffs such as butter, tea, eggs, cheese and sugar had increased enormously. Taken with other changes such as the advance of popular education, statistics demonstrated that what had taken place was nothing less than 'a complete revolution in the condition of the masses'.[3] Giffen's view was admittedly partial; the seasonal or casual nature of employment in some sectors of the economy – agriculture and dock labour, for instance, as well as the prevalence of low-paid domestic work and 'sweated' trades – meant that acute poverty remained a structural feature of working-class life. Even skilled workers could quickly sink if struck down by illness, injury or merely if they were unlucky enough to survive into old age, as the influential poverty studies conducted by Charles Booth, Joseph Rowntree and others graphically demonstrated.[4] Nevertheless, leading trade unionists such as Joseph Arch, president of the National Agricultural Labourers' Union, concurred with Giffen about the plenteous present, reminding readers of the dearth he had experienced in his own youth during the 'hungry forties'. So too did socialists like Annie Besant who, though stressing that meat was still dear and rents expensive for workers, had to admit the force of the argument for material improvement and endeavoured to shift the ground with the observation that multiplying desires brought new problems, or as she put it, 'greater material comfort may co-exist with lesser satisfaction'.[5] And as we saw in Chapter 2, working-class consumers were targeted early on by firms that produced the first nationally advertised goods, including patent or 'quack' medicines, soap and starch, sauces and relishes, jams and pickles, mustard and so on. This trend increased to keep pace with and grow popular demand.

Transformations in processing, packaging and branding helped satisfy this demand. Technological breakthroughs undoubtedly played an important role here. Bottled meat extracts dated back to mid-century, for example, though they did not achieve a wider sale until production was industrialized in the 1860s; the Bovril Company led the field by the late nineteenth century.[6] Product innovation helped secure the success of Cadbury's Cocoa Essence from 1866, as the firm was the first to employ a process which allowed it to extract a finer, more palatable oil from the cocoa bean and market its product as 'purer' or less adulterated than that of its major rivals, Fry's and Rowntree's. Interestingly, the latter initially rejected advertising because of the Quaker principles of its founder but, facing decline, even this firm advertised heavily by the 1890s, employing elaborate stunts such as advertising its Elect Cocoa on a barge during the 1897 Oxford and Cambridge boat race.[7] Cigarette manufacture was revolutionized by the purchase of an American invention, the Bonsack rolling machine, by W. D. & H. O. Wills in 1883, which allowed them to take the lead in packeted cigarettes with the Woodbine brand launched towards the end of that decade.[8] In soap manufacture, W. H. Lever in Britain and Procter and Gamble in the United States pioneered vegetable soaps from the 1880s with Sunlight and Ivory. New technologies were vital for some products, clearly, but marketing was the real key to the success of cheap household goods, as in reality there was little to choose between them once competitors had caught up. We have already seen how patent medicines manufactured by entrepreneurs such as Thomas Holloway or Thomas Beecham paved the way; the latter started selling pills in boxes before mid-century though the business did not really take off until the late 1860s. Both men spent massively on advertising, Holloway laying out £50,000 in 1883, Beecham claiming double that sum in 1895.[9] Branding also became far more vital as the century wore on; John Player registered his first brand name, 'Gold Leaf', in 1877. A picture of a sailor framed by a lifebelt with the slogan 'Player's please' was used from 1882 to market Player's Navy Cut cigarettes, with great success. Both Player and Wills included collectable cards to strengthen brand loyalty. American developments continued to exert an important influence in Britain in relation to soap and also processed breakfast cereals such as those made by the Quaker Oats Company and Kellogg's, as well as canned and bottled convenience foods produced by manufacturers such as Henry Heinz and Joseph Campbell.[10] Although Giffen's 'residuum', which comprised a substantial proportion of the working class – perhaps a third of the population scraped by on about a pound a week at the turn of the century – could not afford the more expensive consumer goods like sewing machines, bicycles and typewriters, which instalment schemes were making more affordable, even they were not shut out of the market for these cheap, everyday products. And it was no coincidence that these goods were ones that made life more bearable for the poor, promising to cure their many ills, pepping up a scanty meal or providing narcotic comfort.

As in the earlier period, various methods of publicity were employed to advertise these commodities, though forms were significantly extended and developed; a qualitative as well as a quantitative change can be discerned during the last quarter of the nineteenth century. The dominant form of outdoor advertising remained posters, their attractiveness increased by the introduction of colour lithographic reproduction from the 1880s. Now arranged in more orderly fashion, they were a ubiquitous feature of city streets, described either as 'the horrors of the walls' by their detractors or 'the people's picture galleries' by their admirers. Initially at least, many fine artists were involved in their design, including Walter Crane and Frederick Walker, whose poster for Wilkie Collins's play *The Woman in White* in 1871 is often taken as marking a turning point in the development of poster art in Britain.[11] Old ways of trumpeting commodities coexisted with the new. Down at heel sandwichmen – 'the unfortunate individuals who let themselves out for hire as walking advertisements', as a sympathetic contemporary observer described them – still traipsed streets chalked with brand names; retailers like Thomas Lipton made them wear Indian costumes to sell his tea. From the 1870s, advertisements were projected onto the sides of buildings in London and in subsequent decades advertisers experimented, with varying degrees of success, with the use of airships and sky signs, causing much public outcry.[12] Other media continued to be widely used by advertisers, including handbills and direct mailing – junk mail is not new – as well as circulars specifically targeted at particular groups of consumers; in 1907 the Reliable Advertising and Addressing Service had a register of 30,000 car owners geographically arranged, for instance, and the company claimed to be able to deliver a quarter of a million circulars in a single day. Promotions, free gifts and prize schemes, celebrity endorsement by famous actresses such as Lillie Langtry and all manner of ingenious stunts were very common, the latter sometimes ascribed to the influence of the American showman P. T. Barnum. Lipton was particularly addicted to them and his monster cheeses, distorting mirrors and various other gimmicks proved highly popular with working-class consumers, lending grocery shopping some of the humour of the music hall stage.[13]

It is impossible to gauge the exact extent of the advertising industry with any real certainty at this time. A commentator on the eve of the First World War suggested that between £80 million and £100 million was being spent annually on advertising, though estimates vary widely. By this time the advertising industry employed at least 80,000 people, probably more, which was comparable to the number who worked in the greengrocery trade. One thing that is clear is that the business of advertising had expanded tremendously since mid-century. The transformation of the popular press, aided by the repeal of the 'taxes on knowledge' as we saw in Chapter 2, as well as technological advances such as the mechanization of typesetting, were vital to this expansion. Probably half of the total expenditure went into press advertising. The circulation of London newspapers increased enormously in the second half of the nineteenth century; the *Daily Telegraph* rose from 27,000 in 1856 to 300,000 in 1880, while *Lloyd's Weekly* claimed one million in 1896. The number of daily papers published outside London also rose, from 52 in 1864 to 129 in 1889.[14] However, change was relatively slow initially, advertisers held back by the conservative practices of papers such as *The Times*, which refused to break the column rule for advertisements or allow block illustrations, although these did appear in the *Illustrated London News*.[15] While the notion of a 'Northcliffe revolution' has been rightly questioned by historians of journalism – the changes that occurred during the fin de siècle had deep roots and were not simply spun out of Alfred Harmsworth's brain – the latter did undoubtedly play a very important role. Harmsworth had attempted to make his fortune out of 'quack' pills before following the lead taken by George Newnes, whose weekly *Tit-Bits*, published from 1881, was selling 900,000 copies a week by the end of the decade. Newnes was more an advertising man than a journalist, and was forever dreaming up competitions and other gimmicks to boost sales. Best known for the scheme that offered insurance against railway accidents to loyal readers, when on holiday at the seaside Newnes even hired donkeys and had cloaks made for them inscribed with the motto, '*We* don't read *Tit-Bits*'.[16] Similar tactics were used by Harmsworth in *Answers*, which first appeared in 1888 and boasted a similar circulation by the late 1890s. Harmsworth went on to launch the *Daily Mail* in 1896 and four years later Arthur Pearson entered the field with the *Daily Express*. The advertising revenue from manufacturers of branded goods was central to the success of all these titles. And although Harmsworth sometimes genuflected against the vulgarity of advertising, he urged his advertising manager on the *Daily Mail*, Wareham Smith, to take a more daring approach to layout early on in order to attract readers. The confinement of advertisements within column rules was ended and illustrations became common. The policy proved a success, the paper reaching the milestone circulation figure of one million copies a day during the Boer War.[17] In short, advertisers began more and more to call the tune, images of the goods they pushed and the discourse they used to talk about commodities increasingly becoming the most important aspect of many popular newspapers.

What did commentators mean precisely when they described this era as 'the age of advertising'? It was a matter of quantity, certainly; though the urban environment was saturated with advertisements earlier in the century as we have seen, the scale had altered. As one middle-class writer wearily observed in 1907:

> Our daily life is permeated with advertising; advertisements in our paper and in our correspondence at breakfast; advertisements in the train, throughout the stations, on omnibuses, hoardings, shop fronts, and on the sky-line; advertisements in the office correspondence, probably on the blotting-pad and the hanging almanac; advertisements on the table, if we dine at an hotel or a restaurant; advertisements blazing from the housetops as we drive home from theatre or concert, where the programme was disguised in advertisements: from the hour we rise to the hour we retire we are assailed by advertisements.[18]

The omnipresence of advertising was undeniable but the changes briefly detailed thus far in this chapter were qualitative as well. Although advertising has frequently been treated by cultural historians as being essentially about images, it was also a highly lucrative business and the advertising industry in the broadest sense – comprising an ensemble of commercial discourses and images but also practices and institutions – was assuming a much more central place in British society in the three decades or so before the First World War. As one recent study has emphasized; 'From the 1880s onwards ... advertising began to be used in new ways, to direct culture, to impose a cultural version of the rationality of the machine on the divergent consumption patterns within the mass market.'[19] Moreover, the reach of advertising was crucially extending into areas where hitherto it had been absent or else regarded as an unwelcome if not positively unwholesome influence. In short, advertising was beginning to colonize other areas of social and cultural life.

Take the relationship between art and advertising. Initially, fearing the debasing effects of commercialism, fine artists tried to keep their distance from advertising, though they were also sometimes content to take the rewards it offered. Walter Crane produced poster designs and later denounced the vulgarity of the hoardings, for instance, and the spats between the Royal Academicians, Sir John Millais and W. P. Frith, and the advertising industry are well known. Thomas Barratt, the advertising manager for Pears soap, bought Millais's painting *A Child's World* in 1888, renamed it *Bubbles* and used it as an advertisement. The picture featured a cherubic little boy looking wistfully at a bubble he had blown. The year after, W. H. Lever did the same with Frith's painting *The New Frock*, which featured a young girl proudly holding up her dress for all to admire, relabelling it 'So Clean'. In both cases what incensed the artists particularly was that their intended meaning had been twisted by advertisers for their own commercial purposes. Millais had wanted to convey a sense of the transience of childhood with his image; the entry for Frith's painting in the Royal Academy catalogue included a phrase from Ecclesiastes, 'Vanitas, vanitatum, omnia vanitas'.[20] The boundary line between art and commerce was shifting during this period; if individuals such as Barratt and Lever pulled in one direction, taste professionals and poster designers pulled in another, during the 1890s at least. Some tried to redefine poster designing as art practice by staging exhibitions and by writing in periodicals such as the *Idler* and the *Magazine of Art*, the editor of the latter attempting to ease Frith's anxieties with the reassuring platitude that 'Art, like Truth, can only dignify and beautify that with which it comes in contact', and that commerce cannot 'degrade' if it is 'conducted with decency'.[21] Advertising had the upper hand in this contest by the turn of the century as posters came to be seen predominantly as a way of selling branded goods rather than an artistic form in their own right. Poster collecting, which had been popular for a while, peaked in the mid-1890s and then declined rapidly. Commercial discourse became increasingly well-orchestrated by means of publications such as *Advertisers' Review*, *Advertising World*, *Billposting and Outdoor Publicity*, *Advertising News* and *Advertiser's Weekly*. The artist–designer that sold an image to a manufacturer or advertiser who subsequently linked a product to it was now anachronistic, as the commodity became the main focus. Thus, the editor of the *Advertisers' Review* gave this no-nonsense advice in 1899: 'Don't have the object of your advertisement hidden away in an obscure corner where it requires to be searched for.' Faced with this commercial onslaught, the art discourse began to wane and designers were subordinated to advertising agencies that hired them as part of well-planned campaigns tailored to the specific requirements of their clients.[22]

Advertising was also beginning to colonize the political realm, albeit in more piecemeal fashion. Indeed, one of the first people to pick up the phrase 'age of advertising' was the Conservative politician Lord Randolph Churchill in a speech in 1884. Interestingly, he used it to condemn the free trade policy of Gladstone's Liberal Party, which he argued was now dominated by commercial interests; 'We live in an age of advertisement', Churchill declared, 'the age of Holloway's pills, of Colman's mustard, of Horniman's pure tea; and the policy of lavish advertisement, has been so successful in commerce that the Liberal Party, with its usual enterprise, has adapted it to politics.' For Churchill, Gladstone was 'the greatest living master of the art of personal political advertisement', who made certain that his every act was broadcast on 'large and glaring placards'.[23] Five years later the editor of the *Pall Mall Gazette* observed that when the history of the present time is written, 'an interesting chapter will have to be devoted to the Age of Advertisement', and he went on to stress how the modern press represented the cutting edge of this development. Pointing to the fact that Sir Algernon Borthwick, owner of the *Morning Post* and friend of Conservative prime minister Lord Salisbury, was about to be treated along with other newspaper men at the 'Barratt banquet' organized by the managing director of Pears soap, the editor considered the change entirely positive: 'Tea and cocoa and soap and all the rest of it have helped to give the masses the best and cheapest Press in the world. The morning cup of cocoa pays as it were for the morning paper ... The Age of Advertisement is essentially democratic.'[24]

Some politicians drew the appropriate lesson from such transformations, emulating and refining modern publicity techniques. In the vanguard here was the Conservative leader Joseph Chamberlain, who cannily marketed himself – the orchid in his lapel serving as a kind of logo – and enlisted the *Daily Mail* in the formidable campaign he waged on behalf of tariff reform, as we shall see in Chapter 6. An insightful writer in a London periodical in 1897 accurately described Chamberlain as 'an advertising statesman' who conducted himself like 'a pushing tradesman', comparable to 'the Universal Provider of Westbourne Grove', William Whiteley.[25] Theorists such as Graham Wallas, the Fabian socialist best remembered for introducing psychology into political analysis, worried deeply about this trend, observing in his major work published in 1908 that in contemporary society 'advertisement and party politics are becoming more and more closely assimilated in method'. He used the memorable example of a fictitious brand – 'Parramatta tea' – to illustrate how advertisers sought to forge unconscious associations with the exotic in consumers' minds, especially by means of images, and argued that such methods were now being used regularly by party politicians who believed that most of their constituents regarded them merely as commodities, or 'a packet with the name of Liberal or Conservative upon it'.[26] The force of Wallas's argument was demonstrated during the 1910 general election, which witnessed the extensive use of political advertising on hoardings and in the press.[27] The increasing permeation of the political sphere with the epistemologies and practices of the commercial domain was demonstrated most clearly at the outbreak of war, when government leaders brought in advertising men such as Hedley Le Bas and Charles Frederick Higham to organize its recruitment campaign. As numbers of recruits began to tail off in the autumn of 1914, a more aggressive poster and press campaign deliberately crafted to invoke fear and guilt was launched. Its early success led the *Daily Mail* to praise Lord Kitchener for appointing Le Bas and appreciating that 'advertising for people to go to a war is just like advertising for people to buy a popular cigarette or a new boot polish'.[28] And as it got nearer to centres of political as well as economic power, advertising gained respectability, its professional status asserted from 1917 by the Association of British Advertising Agents.

Monopoly and market control

Developments in the business of advertising in the late nineteenth century were intimately bound up with changes in the wider economy. In response to the two decades or so of falling prices and uneven economic performance that began in the mid-1870s and which some historians used to call the 'Great Depression', capitalist manufacturers started to look for new ways to guarantee regularity of demand for their products. Various means were adopted, including industrial combination, price-fixing agreements, trade campaigns, cartel quotas and the political control of overseas markets through imperial expansion. Another crucial initiative was extensive and systematic advertising. Ironically, then, modern advertising – which as Chapter 8 will demonstrate was portrayed after the Second World War as a defining feature of a 'free' capitalist society – developed specifically as a way of securing greater organization and control of markets by large producers. As one critic has written, the decades after 1880 'saw the full development of an organised system of commercial information and persuasion, as part of the modern distributive system in conditions of large-scale capitalism'.[29] From the late nineteenth century onwards, the increasing concentration of industry and the growth of combines in various sectors of the economy, including distribution, retailing and the manufacture of consumer goods such as tobacco and soap, was frequently discussed by middle-class intellectuals across the political spectrum and drew opprobrium from working-class leaders of the co-operative movement who sounded warnings about the dangers of monopoly power for the poor consumer.[30] In sum, after the 1880s most markets were no longer characterized by competition between a multitude of individual firms but were instead oligopolistic, the various consumer goods markets, for example, dominated by large companies that sought to corral consumers and shut out upstart adversaries by the use of highly expensive national advertising campaigns for their branded products.[31]

Branding was a key lever of market control. Before the late nineteenth century, products tended to carry the names of firms or individuals and the notion of an abstract name invented specifically for a product was novel. Brands were designed by advertisers to make commodities stick more effectively in consumers' minds, thereby encouraging consumer loyalty and guaranteeing demand. They endowed products with more extensive meanings, forging various associations with their use and linking them to images that worked on both an emotional and ideological level. Their success was underpinned by trademark legislation that protected manufacturers' intellectual property. The first act was passed in 1862 but the law was strengthened considerably by the Trade Marks Registration Act of 1875, which established a national register of trademarks. Other acts followed until a relatively tight legal framework was created, tighter than that in the United States or France; trademarks had to be logos and not merely names, though after the Patents and Trade Marks Act of 1883 words could be registered so long as they were 'fancy words not in common use'. This led to a wave of branding, and eventually 'fancy words' came to mean invented words, such as Bovril, the meat extract, or Mazawattee, a brand of tea.[32] The most innovative manufacturers of consumer goods immediately grasped the usefulness of branding; Lever hired W. P. Thompson, a trademark and patent agent, who suggested 'Sunlight' as far more distinctive and memorable than 'Lever's Pure Honey Soap', which it replaced. Lever aggressively protected his brands through the courts, suing imitators of 'Sunlight' soap twice in 1886, for example, and he later introduced other highly successful brands, including 'Lifebuoy' in 1894 and 'Lux' in 1899. Indeed, branding became almost an obsession for him, Lever's firm making up 9 per cent of total registrations in 1897.[33] The definition of a trademark was further liberalized by another act in 1905, which relaxed the bar on geographical locations but outlawed the use of most surnames. Overall, across the period we witness a shift from brands being merely descriptions of products to abstract inventions. Registrations rose from 454 in 1876 to over 7,000 per annum in the 1920s and names such as 'Bovril' (1886), 'Hovis' (1890), 'Oxo', 'Vimto' and 'Bisto' (1908), became part of the language of everyday life.[34] Advertisers used myriad ways to ensure brand names penetrated the culture, including the popularization of catchphrases, a staple of the music hall comic. The most famous probably was that used by Barratt, which was accused of debasing a common courtesy: 'Good morning! Have you used Pears soap?'[35]

Advertising agencies developed to market brands more effectively. Their origins can be traced back to the late eighteenth century, as we have seen, but they changed significantly in the late Victorian period, from being essentially space brokers or middlemen operating between the press and manufacturers, to being much more specialized and powerful businesses in their own right. By the turn of the century, newspapers employed their own advertising managers, while advertising agencies moved from selling space and offered their expertise to manufacturers instead, designing elaborate campaigns for them and booking space as part of this activity. Some published handbooks, such as Henry Sell's *Philosophy of Advertising* (1885) that emphasized the importance of branding among other things, and Sell's hugely popular *Dictionary of the World's Press*, which appeared annually from 1885.[36] Their numbers steadily grew – one estimate suggesting there were 92 advertising agents and contractors in 1866, 220 in 1886, and 339 by 1906 – and although agencies were initially concentrated in London they soon spread to other cities and indeed expanded to continental Europe, the empire and the United States, tailoring campaigns to specific markets.[37] Many large firms such as Player's, Colman's, Cadbury's, and Pears employed them from the 1880s; according to Wareham Smith writing in 1907 about 90 per cent of total advertising business was by this time done through agents, though it is worth noting that some British manufacturers, unlike most of their American counterparts, preferred to support their own in-house advertising departments, including Lever who micro-managed this side of his operation.[38] The major agencies employed many staff and offered an extensive range of services: 100 people worked for Mather and Crowther in 1894, for instance, and the firm was organized into a separate media department that dealt with newspaper and outdoor advertising, a production department that handled typesetting, engraving and printing, an art department and an editorial department.[39] The London office of T. B. Browne was memorably described by William Stead Jr. as 'the great camera obscura of the advertising world' in 1899, by which time the firm employed over 200 people, not only in London but also in its offices in Manchester, Glasgow and Paris.[40] Indeed, Stead emphasized the global reach of this business, which established a separate department to deal with colonial advertising. Browne's had strong links with publications in Australia, Canada, South Africa, India and the East and West Indies, managed to cut out the middleman and supplied advertisements directly without the help of intermediaries.[41]

Advertisers drew on a number of stock themes to sell goods. Perhaps the most important centred on ideas of domesticity and gender. As so many of the cheap branded products were intended for use in the home for either cleaning or cooking, it was little wonder that women were specially targeted. Lever's genius was apparent here – he helped turn soap from a humble everyday item into a much more desirable commodity. Before his intervention in the mid-1880s, soap makers had tended to cater to local markets and avoided aggressive advertising. The trade in tablet soap was limited and manufactures mostly sold long bars to grocers who cut off pound lumps that were retailed by variety rather than as proprietary articles. Lever sold his soap in bars wrapped in parchment and packed in a colourful carton emblazoned with his brand. Along with many other cleaning products, the purity and hygienic powers of the brand were trumpeted from the outset. Lever was also prepared to listen to consumers; he withdrew 'Sunlight Self-Washer' because although it lathered easily it also sweated drops of pungent oil, then later reintroduced an improved variety after a Lancashire buyer had remarked, 'I mun ha' some more of yon stinking soap.'[42] Most importantly, he spent a great deal of money on advertising, perhaps as much as £2 million over the first two decades.[43] Countless colour posters and newspaper advertisements portrayed the benign effects of Sunlight Soap, showing how it transformed washing days by lessening the labour of working-class women, thus making them simultaneously more efficient and more cheerful. From the beginning, the theme of the idealized housewife was played on continuously. One famous poster featured the question, 'Why does a woman look older sooner than a man?' – purchased by Lever from a Philadelphia soap maker – promising that Sunlight Soap would check the ageing effects of domestic drudgery. Another advertisement observed that 'if home is to be the very dearest spot on earth it can only be such if the mother or wife brightens it with the sunlight of her cheerful smile … When things go right in the kitchen, the laundry and the bath, the good housewife's face is lit up with a loving, smiling calm.'[44] In a final example, a mother is tormented by some weighty questions on her daughter's wedding day: 'Does your daughter know what SUNLIGHT SOAP can do? Have you told her that for a few pence, without boiling or bleaching, she can have all her husband's shirts and collars washed at home with SUNLIGHT SOAP and made to look snow white?'[45] Clearly, advertisers like Lever fully realized the power of psychological suggestion to provoke feelings of guilt and fear in prospective consumers, long before the publication of landmark texts in the field such as Walter Dill Scott's *The Psychology of Advertising* (1908). Though writers like these undoubtedly helped to make this aspect more explicit, Lever already knew very well that consumers' desires were malleable and that the 'whole object of advertising' was to create a 'hypnotic effect ... to build a halo round the article'.[46]

Themes of patriotism and empire were also omnipresent during this period. Associating goods with symbols of British national identity such as the monarchy, John Bull, Britannia and the Union Jack, had been common from the early nineteenth century at least; Rowland's had been granted a Royal Warrant for their macassar oil, for example, in the 1830s.[47] However, during the 'age of advertising' such connections were forged relentlessly by manufacturers and their agents. The jubilee celebrations of 1887 and 1897 turned Queen Victoria into an icon of a developing consumer culture, and all manner of jubilee kitch or souvenirs flooded the market.[48] Trading on empire became hugely popular: indeed the 'age of advertisement' and the 'age of empire' seemed to some observers to represent two sides of the same coin, as in the humorous cartoon reproduced as Figure 5. In this image, the cartoonist imagined what might happen if commercial firms sponsored not only Her Majesty's armed forces but also their tribal adversaries.

Soap manufacturers were to the fore in making connections between empire and commerce and cultural historians have usefully demonstrated how advertisements for Pears Soap and Sunlight Soap typically conflated the use of these products with the progress of Western 'civilization', suggesting that cleansing the 'savage' and the metropolitan working class were component parts of the same imperial project.[49] Soap was important, certainly, though imperialist iconography saturated advertising more generally. A full-page magazine advertisement for Eno's titled 'How Kandahar was won' that appeared in 1889 quoted the soldier turned travel writer, G. W. Vyse, who reckoned that this famous victory during the Afghan War was due to ample supplies of effervescent fruit salts on the British side, which made each of them 'fit to overthrow half a dozen Ayab Kahns'. Other letters featured in the advertisement testified to the way in which the health of colonial officials and soldiers – and thus the success of the British Empire – depended on a regular dose of Eno's, which was nothing more than a mixture of bicarbonate of soda.[50] Not surprisingly, the Boer War provided a rich and highly lucrative subject, the advertising agent S. H. Benson proving typically inventive. Benson organized the Bovril War Cable Scheme at a cost of £10,000, whereby a team of ninety cyclists supplied up to date despatches to 1,000 Bovril stockists who publicized details on bulletin boards outside their shops, much to the

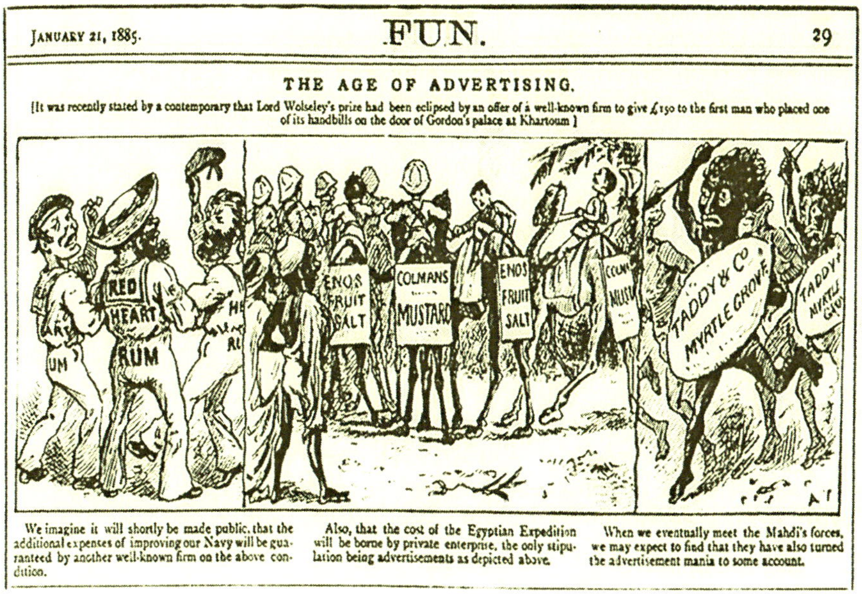

FIGURE 5 *'The Age of Advertising'*, Fun, *21 January 1885. © The British Library Board (P.P.5273.c).*

annoyance of newspaper proprietors. An advertisement for the firm also claimed that the route taken by General Kitchener's campaign against the Boers in South Africa spelt out the word Bovril.[51] Historians continue to contest the popularity of imperialism at this time and the ideological effect of this often racist commercial propaganda is impossible to gauge with absolute certainty.[52] As we have seen, however, despite the longstanding ubiquity of pro-imperialist advertising, patriotism and banging the empire drum had to be supplemented with more insidious appeals when recruitment faltered during the First World War.

Benson's attempt to usurp the power of the press was merely a single skirmish in a protracted confrontation between advertising agencies and the owners of the new mass circulation press such as Alfred Harmsworth and Arthur Pearson around the turn of the century. Newspaper magnates liked to believe that they were masters of modern communication, able to mould public opinion and exert real political influence through their publications. There was some truth in this of course, but advertising men like Benson retorted that the modern press was essentially merely a commodity designed to sell other commodities, a kind of circulating showcase for the latest branded goods and shopping opportunities. The force of their argument could not be gainsaid – the cheap daily press and the high circulation Sunday papers would not have been viable without advertising revenue. Harmsworth and his peers knew this and it hurt them deeply but they could not escape the logic of their subordination. Advertisers had changed the visual appearance of newspapers as space was now bought in blocks rather than columns, one agent commenting in his autobiography that the 'wishes of the advertiser regulate the character of the display made in the advertising columns'.[53] In the battle for trade, newspaper proprietors tried to outdo each other's publication figures, making often-inflated claims that were repeatedly contested by advertising agencies. An important moment occurred in the spring of 1899, when Benson organized an Exhibition of Advertising at Niagara Hall, London. This was a big event, with 150 exhibitors and thousands of visitors but it was shunned by most of the press owners and ignored by the major London papers. At the exhibition's launch, Benson publicly humiliated Newnes – the one press magnate who did attend – by reminding him that advertisers held the whip hand over the modern press.[54] The following year, the Advertisers' Protection Society was established to put pressure on papers to publish accurate circulation figures. According to them, Harmsworth Publications was the worst offender, because their circulation figures were artificially inflated by competitions of various kinds. Although he had started as a quack himself, Harmsworth sometimes affected a disdain for advertising, though he knew that his fortune depended upon it.[55] While admitting the dangers of commercial dominance, a study of the press published just before the First World War tersely summed up the situation: 'Advertising is the newspaper's backbone. The world is only beginning to recognize how vitally necessary it is to business.[56]

While newspaper magnates and advertising agencies battled it out, manufacturers fought among themselves to maintain market share. Firms combined to try to defeat competitors and pushed their brands more extensively by means of costly advertising campaigns. A number of 'wars' were thus precipitated, the first in the tobacco industry. Facing stiff pressure from American manufacturers in the domestic market, W. D. & H. O. Wills, John Player and a number of other British firms merged to form the Imperial Tobacco Company in 1901, which then launched the biggest advertising campaign ever witnessed in Britain, dubbed the 'tobacco war' by the press at the time. Patriotism was frequently invoked, naturally, one of the advertisements advising consumers, 'Don't be fooled by Yankee Bluff/ Support John Bull with every puff!' A truce was eventually called in 1902, when American and British firms agreed to trade in their respective countries but co-operate together to supply to the rest of the world.[57] The war that broke out in the soap trade became a major cause célèbre. Soaring raw material costs and falling returns convinced W. H. Lever that combination was inevitable if profitability was to be maintained and in 1906 he hatched a plan to unite the soap industry under the control of a parent body or trust. A major consideration was reduction of overall advertising costs, which were spiralling upwards. Lever also reduced the weight of a bar of Sunlight Soap from 1 lb to 15 oz at this time, thus making the consumer pay the

FIGURE 6 *'The Greedy Soap Trust'*, Daily Mirror, *22 October 1906. © Trinity Mirror Limited.*

same for less. As we have seen, Lever's business was built on advertising and he fully appreciated the importance of the modern press to its success but he shared Benson's view regarding which partner was the more important in the relationship. No doubt resenting this shift and influenced by President Theodore Roosevelt's activities as a 'trust-buster' on the other side of the Atlantic, Harmsworth used his papers to attack Lever's attempt to construct a soap trust, urging female consumers in particular to boycott his products. In Figure 6, just one in a series of cartoons that appeared in the *Daily Mirror* during the campaign, Lever is represented as an arrogant shopkeeper, trying to pass off the short-weight soap made at 'Port Moonshine' (rather than Port Sunlight, where the soap was made near Liverpool) to an elderly working-class woman. The boycott proved highly effective – suggesting that female consumers were influenced more by cost and were not easily taken in by idealistic images – and sales of Lever's products plummeted by 60 per cent towards the end of the year, with many working-class consumers switching to co-operative-made goods, much to Lever's chagrin. He eventually had to shelve the idea of a trust, though only until the end of the First World War when the company swallowed up competitors such as Pears. Moreover, the litigious Lever pursued Harmsworth through the courts for libel, eventually winning record damages.[58]

Public restraint, private licence

Criticism of advertising did not abate during this period but in fact intensified. Attacks came from across the political spectrum, against sky signs that proliferated in London, which were often huge, lofty constructions erected on the roofs of buildings.[59] Another common cause of complaint were posters, or the 'horrors on our walls' as they were called by the London *Standard*.[60] Sensationalist images – of sexualized female acrobats and violent crimes, for example – that were commonplace despite the passage of the Indecent Advertisements Act in 1889, were condemned as immoral and as exerting a bad influence on young people in particular. In response, the Bill Posters' Association stepped up efforts to regulate its members and established a censorship committee to vet advertisements.[61] But it was advertisers' encroachment on rural rather than urban space that inflamed tempers most. *The Times* tolerated posters on city streets by the early 1890s, excusing them as 'amongst the most striking symbols of the fierce commercial competition of the age', and admitting that 'they cause a good deal of pleasure to a great many persons who live very dull lives'. However, as far as places of natural beauty were concerned, the editor asserted 'we must cry "Hands off" to the advertiser'. The paper also published letters on 'The Advertising Plague' that complained: 'Fields and hillsides are being covered with unwonted crops of hoardings ... Night succeeds day only to be utilized for the electrical announcement that "Messrs. so-and-so's soap is the best."'[62] 'Northumbrian' in the radical weekly, *Reynolds's Newspaper*, also denounced the many 'horrors' which 'meet the eye at every turn' and asked, 'Is all sense of artistic beauty to be sacrificed to this craze, the greedy grasping for speedy wealth?'[63] Not surprisingly, advertisers and their supporters, such as the journalist George Augustus Sala, fought back, the latter accusing the 'hysterical' letters appearing in the press as being merely 'the outcome of a sickly, maundering, puling, querulous dislike and jealousy of trade and commerce'.[64]

Calls for greater legal control grew louder following the formation of the Society for Checking the Abuses of Public Advertising (SCAPA) in 1893. The origins of this body go back to a series of letters from Alfred Waterhouse, a well-known architect, and Richardson Evans, a barrister turned journalist, which appeared in the *National Review* over two years before. With Waterhouse as its first President and Evans as Secretary, SCAPA campaigned for greater powers over advertising for local authorities, taxation on posters and a boycott of products whose advertisements were deemed offensive. It drew limited though diverse support, soon boasting 500 members and a council which included four MPs and four members of the House of Lords. A heterogeneous mix of intellectuals and artists were attracted to the cause, including Sir John Millais, Rudyard Kipling, Walter Crane and William Morris. Interestingly, the latter was initially reluctant to join, writing in the organization's journal, *A Beautiful World*: 'To tell you the plain truth, much as they (advertisements) annoy me personally, I cannot help rejoicing at the spectacle of the middle classes so annoyed and so helpless before the results of the idiotic tyranny which they themselves have created.'[65] Evans elaborated his ideas in detail in his book *The Age of Disfigurement*. In this well-intentioned but confused work, Evans expressed concern for the deadening effects of advertising on the urban working class, predictably arguing in Arnoldian terms that garish hoardings made it more difficult for authentic, elevating 'culture' to reach the 'masses'. Although Evans saw modern advertising as symbolic of the way contemporary society was dominated by 'the race for profit', his intention was not to fundamentally challenge the values of the age. Statutory intervention was urgently required to protect rural beauty spots but Evans's preference overall was for voluntary methods such as limited boycotts of the worst offenders, which would help 'direct consumption into moral lines'.[66]

SCAPA enjoyed early success when regulations restricting sky signs in London were consolidated in 1894 but its membership was mainly restricted to upper-middle-class intellectuals and it never gained wider appeal. Evans's concern for the aesthetic well-being of urban workers was genuine enough; he accused advertisers of making 'war upon the working-man' and robbing them 'even of the treasure that costs nothing, and yet is of priceless worth'.[67] However, he made no attempt to construct a popular movement and his Tory outlook isolated him from radical and socialist organizations that were equally concerned about the aesthetic as well as the physical environmental damage that, they argued, was caused by the spread of consumer capitalism.[68] SCAPA tried unsuccessfully to steer five bills onto the statute book prior to the passage of the 1907 Advertisements Regulation Act, though it had made some headway at the local level before then, helping the Dover corporation, for example, to get the huge sign erected by Quaker Oats on the cliffs to be removed in 1901.[69] The 1907 act received wide support in parliament, only a few disgruntled Conservative and Irish MPs voting against a measure that sought to protect public parks and the beauty of rural landscapes. Pressure was maintained for further control, however, as the act was frequently evaded, for it was not entirely clear what constituted a rural landscape. Roadsides were not included, causing continuing friction. Consequently, local residents occasionally undertook direct action; in the village of Eynsford in Kent, hoardings promoting 'Carter's Little Liver Pills' were torn down in autumn 1909 and other advertisements were washed off by 'several old women … to the accompaniment of the village Brass Band.'[70] Nevertheless, the trend was for greater regulation and by 1925 some thirty-five counties and fifty-nine boroughs had introduced by-laws to restrain public advertisements under the terms of the 1907 act.[71]

Many advertisers themselves supported cleaning up and regulating public advertising and this no doubt helped placate middle-class and elite anxieties about the consequences of mass consumerism. Shorn of the worst excesses, it became more acceptable. The popular middle-brow magazine *Review of Reviews* roundly condemned what it dubbed 'The Advertising Fiend' in the mid-1890s, for example, and although the 1907 act was regarded as a step in the right direction, more regulation was thought urgently necessary, for everywhere one could see 'houses and fields and hedgerows, disfigured and vulgarised by flaring posters or metal plates, shrieking … some cocoa vendor's lie about his cocoa, or some tyre-maker's or whisky-distiller's false and fulsome praise of his tyres and his whisky'.[72] However, criticism in the paper was seriously muted thereafter, as advertisers' bid for professional status gained momentum. The establishment of the Incorporated Society of Advertisement Consultants just before the First World War was an important moment here and the popular press by this time made every effort to puff the emergent profession and underline its utility and 'efficiency'.[73] The relative success of central and local government to regulate public advertising contrasts starkly with the failure to check the inflated and often fraudulent claims advertisers could make about their clients' products. In short, provided that lies were not shrieked at some beauty spot but were confined to city streets or the pages of newspapers, they were deemed acceptable. When it came to their private consumption practices, consumers had largely to depend on their own common sense, often a very poor guide.

The question of advertisers' responsibility for promoting patent or 'quack' medicines focused this issue most clearly. As we have seen, the morality of these goods had been subject of debate for decades but it reignited again in the late nineteenth century, played out in the courts in the Carlill vs. Carbolic Smoke Ball Company case in 1892. The company's advertising had claimed that its product would ward off influenza – the pandemic of 1889–90 had killed about one million people – and promised £100 to anyone who caught the flu after using it. Mrs Carlill, a disgruntled consumer who had fallen ill despite the ball, successfully sued the company to make good its promise, though the case did go to the Court of Appeal and the judgement changed contract law thereafter.[74] Criticism of quack medicines and misleading advertising intensified over the next two decades, stimulated by other legal cases such as the action brought in 1905 by the Bile Beans Manufacturing Company against George Davidson, a chemist who was passing off his own pills as an alternative to the 'real' thing. The company lost the case, the Scottish judge finding that the plaintiff's business was conducted by fraud, as the pills contained no secret health-promoting ingredient. There was clearly some legal protection against quacks and their agents, though the cost of suing the wealthy owners of the companies that manufactured these remedies was prohibitive.[75] From 1907 onwards, however, progressive doctors went on the offensive in the *British Medical Journal*, exposing the generally useless or sometimes positively harmful composition of popular remedies; 'female' pills contained iron or lead, for example, while so called 'nerve tonics' either had a very high alcohol content or contained chlorodyne – a mixture of chloroform, morphine and prussic acid.[76] These revelations were eventually collected and published by the British Medical Association (BMA) in two volumes – *Secret Remedies* (1909) and *More Secret Remedies* (1912) – which made grim reading.

The contemporary debate on patent medicines, the role of advertising and the meaning of consumer culture more generally was at the heart of the novel published by the Fabian socialist H. G. Wells in 1909. *Tono-Bungay*, probably Wells's finest literary achievement, narrated the rise and fall of Edward Ponderevo, who makes a huge fortune selling a quack medicine – the 'secret of vigour' that causes kidney damage – after which the novel is named.[77] Wells meticulously describes how goods are brought to life by modern advertising in this great work. Ponderevo disseminates the Tono-Bungay brand nationwide by means of slogans and poster campaigns tailored to appeal to particularized local markets, and then the product range is diversified to include 'Tono-Bungay Hair Stimulant' and 'Tono-Bungay Lozenges', which contain a touch of strychnine to add 'kick'. As Ewart, an armchair socialist who grasps the meaning of it all most clearly, confides to Ponderevo, 'It's advertisement has done it. Advertisement has revolutionised trade and industry; it is going to revolutionise the world. The old merchant used to tote about commodities; the new one creates values … He takes mustard that is just like anybody else's mustard, and he goes about saying, shouting, singing, chalking on walls, writing inside people's books, putting it everywhere, "Smith's Mustard is the Best." And behold it is the best!'[78] Wells portrays advertising as much more than a mere symptom of decay; it functions in the novel as a structural feature of a pathological social and economic formation and this is the key difference between Wells's approach and that of earlier novelists such as Gissing. Ponderevo's initial success owes much to Lord Boom, a press baron modelled on Alfred Harmsworth who, ironically enough, employed Wells to write articles on the labour question for the *Daily Mail*.[79] Boom's support is vital in order to effectively push fraudulent goods to a mass market but when things finally go awry he quickly turns against Ponderevo, causing the latter to despair: 'I have called it Tono-Bungay, but I had far better have called it Waste … It is all one spectacle of forces running to waste, of people who use and do not replace, the story of a country hectic with a wasting aimless fever of trade and money-making and pleasure-seeking.'[80] Moreover, rampant capitalist consumerism is shown to drag down not only the nation but also exert a devastating global influence; Ponderevo dreams of marketing Tono-Bungay throughout the empire while, in an attempt to save the business, his nephew journeys to West Africa in search of a radioactive substance aptly named 'quap', vitally important for the manufacture of 'Capern's filament' used in electric light bulbs that will soon illuminate the modern homes of imperial consumers. Wells's bleak narrative sounds a prescient warning about the logic of an imperial consumerism that will inevitably lead to both racial killing and ecological catastrophe.[81]

The campaign by the medical profession against quack remedies was covered by a few sympathetic journals such as the *Saturday Review*, which described the BMA's second volume of revelations as 'The Book of Tono Bungay' and underlined the cruelty inflicted by misleading advertisements for products that claimed to cure life threatening illnesses.[82] In response to this mounting pressure, the Liberal government established a select committee to investigate the subject, which sat over three parliamentary sessions from 1912 and interviewed numerous witnesses, including doctors, vendors of patent medicines and newspaper proprietors. In his evidence to the committee, Dr Alfred Cox, secretary of the BMA, condemned the way in which the press and patent medicine manufacturers were in league. The former was to a large extent financially dependent on the latter – it was estimated that upwards of £2 million per annum was spent on advertising these goods in the press – and leading titles like the *Daily Express*, *Daily Chronicle*, and *News of the World* had refused to publicize the BMA's findings. Other witnesses pointed out how adverts for patent medicines were often deliberately mixed up with editorial matter. When the committee eventually published its report in 1914, it came down hard on the manufacturers of quack medicines and their publicists, recommending that the sale of and advertisements for cures for serious conditions such as cancer, tuberculosis, diabetes, kidney disease and so on should be immediately banned. The committee also emphasized the importance of enabling the state to force manufacturers to make public the ingredients that they used in their products and prohibiting them if these were fraudulent or dangerous.[83] Despite the fact that there was widespread support for intervention – the report quickly sold out – no action was taken until twenty-seven years later. The war got in the way but the medical profession was also deeply divided on this subject; many doctors frequently recommended patent medicines to their patients, some received kickbacks from companies that produced them and some were shareholders and directors of those companies.[84] Clearly, ruling elites during this period deemed the health of individual consumers, the majority of whom were working-class people who often could not afford to see a doctor, less important than the aesthetic sensibilities of the wealthy.

5

Shopping as Pleasure: Department Stores

Cathedrals of commerce

William Whiteley caused an outcry when he opened a refreshment room in his London department store in 1872. The *Graphic*, a middle-class illustrated weekly, listed the catalogue of horrors that it believed would follow this innovation, for it was feared that eating and drinking on the premises would allow female consumers to recover their energies on a shopping trip and enable them to resume the hunt for bargains, or 'return once more to the slaughter' as the paper put it. According to the editor, department stores such as Whiteley's were nothing less than 'Halls of Temptation', luring unwary women with 'ten thousand pretty things'. The delights they offered were both material and erotic; following luncheon an afternoon shopping spree had 'all the attraction of a delightful dream, with a slight dash of an orgie'.[1] Undeterred by such criticism, Whiteley continued to expand his business in Bayswater, selling provisions and opening a butchery department in 1875. Local shopkeepers whose profits were being squeezed went on the offensive against 'the gigantic Westbourne Grove monopoly', as Whiteley's emporium was described by a correspondent to the *Bayswater Chronicle*. Butchers were particularly incensed, marching through the streets banging meat cleavers against marrow bones and burning an effigy of the self-styled 'Universal Provider' on Guy Fawkes Day the following year.[2] According to one recent historian, by the early 1880s such conflicts had subsided as local traders learnt to appreciate the progressive effects of Whiteley's success and – like the middle class more generally – had come to terms with the disorienting effects of modern consumerism.[3] Although the neatness of this argument is appealing, we should be careful not to underestimate how consumer culture continued to be contested over the longer term.

Department stores have been well served by historians. However, most early studies were written by non-professional historians or else were commissioned by companies themselves, reflecting the way in which the history of shopping, like consumption more generally, was marginalized by academics.[4] More serious scholarly work began to appear from the early 1980s onwards, an influential study of the Bon Marché in Paris that was opened by Aristide Boucicaut in 1869 demonstrating in particular how proper investigation of these forms needed to combine economic, social and cultural approaches.[5] Large European stores such as the Bon Marché and the Louvre in Paris and Wertheim in Berlin, but also North American stores including Marshall Field's in Chicago, Wanamaker's in Philadelphia and Macy's in New York, are often now regarded as much more than just shopping venues, being seen instead as major symbols of capitalist modernity in their own right, signifying the utopian promise of mass consumerism – a cornucopia of goods for all, eventually if not perhaps immediately.[6] There is some truth in this perspective, though it underplays the importance of evolutionary and incremental growth to the emergence of large stores. If we accept the definition of a department store proposed by an early seminal study of the subject – that is, a large retail store with four or more separate departments under one roof selling different goods, including either women's or children's wear – then such forms can be discerned much earlier in the century, as we saw in Chapter 2. Supposed innovations like fixed and ticketed prices, elaborate displays and showrooms can also be traced right back. Moreover, undue concentration on department stores detracts attention from other, arguably more important, developments that were in train, notably the rise of multiple retailers such as Lipton's and working-class co-operatives, discussed in the following chapter. After all, despite their iconic status, department stores only accounted for less than 2 per cent of total retail sales in Britain in 1900, including 10 per cent of women's and children's wear.[7] Overestimation of the newness of these forms also reinforces the self-promotional efforts of charismatic owners who liked to regard themselves as genuine innovators spearheading a completely new phase in what H. Gordon Selfridge liked to call the 'romance of commerce'.[8]

The subject received a further boost over recent decades by the increasing prominence of feminist scholarship and gender history. Working across a variety of disciplines, scholars interested in the experience of middle-class women in particular have found late nineteenth-century department stores fertile ground. Some have portrayed them as necessarily confining for women, arguing that the commodity culture they helped to generalize was a kind of seduction that merely disempowered female shoppers.[9] These one-sided critiques have been largely superseded by much more nuanced accounts of how consumer culture and department stores in particular opened up new possibilities for middle-class women to transgress and redefine the boundaries of the public and private spheres, presenting to women, in the words of one historian, 'a new definition of gender that carved out a space for individual expression similar to men's'.[10] This chapter discusses these themes, though it is worth noting at the outset how much of the literature on this subject develops leads originally suggested by the great French naturalist writer Émile Zola in his 1883 novel *The Ladies' Paradise* (*Au Bonheur des Dames*). Gender was at the heart of Zola's fascinating work, which still remains the best way into this particular subject. Female consumers gain erotic pleasure from the delights of the store in the novel and the owner, Octave Mouret, is represented as a seducer of women throughout. But he is also dependent on their whims and in the end Mouret prostrates himself before the poor good-hearted shop girl Denise and begs her to marry him, Zola thus suggesting the possibility of humanizing consumer capitalism and harmonizing class and gender antagonism more generally.[11] This was a patriarchal view, certainly, but it was also a far more optimistic view of capitalist development than Zola presented in novels like *Germinal* (1885), which saw industrial workers ground down by industrial labour to the point of despair. Little wonder that *The Ladies' Paradise* was warmly received by middle-class periodicals when an English edition of the complete work first appeared.[12]

Contemporary commentators often described these stores in high-blown language, the Paris correspondent for the *Daily Telegraph*, for example, referring to the Louvre as a 'cathedral of commerce' in 1888.[13] But what precisely did they mean by this term? Size of course was an important aspect; the new stores were colossal affairs that dwarfed traditional shops. Whiteley had started modestly, selling ribbons, lace and fancy goods in Bayswater in 1863 but four years later he was already operating seventeen departments, having branched out into silks, linens, ladies' outfitting, gloves, mantles and jewellery. He then grew his business opportunistically, buying up adjacent premises and offering new lines when he could. Ignoring angry traders, Whiteley expanded into gentlemen's outfitting, household goods, furniture, ironmongery, stationery, hairdressing and banking among other things in the 1870s, eventually occupying a whole row of Westbourne Grove and employing 6,000 staff. His timing was fortuitous as fashionable shopping had gravitated westwards in the capital by the 1860s, with Oxford Street drapers such as Marshall and Snelgrove and Regent Street stores including Swan and Edgar among the chief attractions. Bayswater was close by but still relatively sleepy until the pushing trader began his enterprise, just after an underground station opened at Kensington. The suburbs were mushrooming and thousands of female consumers travelled by tube to the West End. Whiteley successfully fought those members of the local vestry that sought to hold him back and helped to redraw the map of this part of London.[14] The local paper may have allowed his critics a voice but it also readily admitted to the progressive influence of his business: 'The Bayswater boulevard can only be compared with King's Road, Brighton, *the* place for shopping, lounging, and promenading, where everybody meets everybody.'[15]

Such piecemeal growth was typical of the evolution of department stores but enterprising storeowners eventually invested in purpose-built structures boasting huge frontages and acres of plate glass. When Whiteley's store was burnt down by a mysterious fire, the new building on Queen's Road which rose from the ashes in 1887 was a truly impressive construction. Along with his competitors, Whiteley quickly adopted new technologies of display during this decade, including electric lighting, glass cabinets and full wax mannequins instead of headless and armless models.[16] Creating a more luxurious and relaxing ambience that allowed shoppers to wander aimlessly was key to the success of the new emporia. The shopping experience was made more pleasurable, plateglass and lighting being used to heighten the visual appeal of commodities; like cathedrals, atmosphere and light were central to their impact. As many scholars have pointed out, department stores emulated the Crystal Palace in this respect – indeed, Whiteley claimed that he began to imagine 'universal providers' shops' with plate-glass fronts after visiting the Great Exhibition – though as we have already suggested, pinning origins down so precisely is misleading.[17] By the turn of the century, the experience of West End consumers had been undeniably transformed, leading the society hostess Lady Jeune to ask rhetorically, 'What is shopping in these days, but an unsuccessful struggle against overwhelming temptations?'[18]

As with many other aspects of modern consumer history, the American influence here was vital and continuing. As early as the mid-1880s if not before, journalists were complaining about the 'Americanising of many of our institutions', including 'the barriers which formerly divided different kinds of tradesmen'.[19] However, the arrival of H. Gordon Selfridge on the scene took this influence to a new level. Selfridge had been superintendent at Marshall Field's in Chicago before striking out alone and opening his lavish new store on Oxford Street in the spring of 1909. He brought with him driving ambition, a passion for display and publicity and a love for modernity; 'Learn to forget the past', he had told his staff at Field's, 'and deal more and more with the present'. For Selfridge, the shop window was a pre-eminent way of encouraging consumer longing and he had a keen sense of the importance of theatrical techniques for making commodities come to life and drawing consumers of all classes and ages into the store. He placed special emphasis on the need to appeal to children, supporting the introduction of a special 'Children's Day' and a separate department for them and declaring to staff that 'children are the future customers of this store, and impressions made now will be lasting'.[20] When the Oxford Street store opened in a blaze of publicity, it dwarfed its rivals; eighty feet high with eight floors and 100 departments, it had six acres of floor space, nine passenger lifts and twenty-one of the largest plate-glass windows in the world. Quintessentially a place of leisure and relaxation, with a dining club and reading rooms, shoppers could idly wander through the store, just looking at the goods on show without fear of being importuned by the intrusive shop walker who usually stalked large stores, supervising sales staff and ejecting any unwanted visitors; Selfridge was asked to leave a London store himself once after admitting he had no intention of buying anything. Selfridge also fully realized the uses of advertising, spending around £36,000 on the opening. He worked hard to get the popular press on his side, nurturing close relations with men like Alfred Harmsworth and Arthur Pearson and placing large display advertisements in their papers. Consequently, they lent vital support from the outset, the *Daily Express* stating that Selfridge had inaugurated no less than 'a new era in shopping'. Thus, the mass press puffed the stores in return for lucrative contracts and both can therefore be regarded as related parts of a maturing economic and cultural system that depended for its vitality on the constant stimulation of mass consumption. It is worth noting that Selfridge differed here from men like Whiteley who were initially reluctant to spend money on press advertising, preferring alternative forms of publicity. Moreover, other conservative attitudes and practices were still widely shared. Stores such as Waring and Gillow's that specialized in furniture, Marshall and Snelgrove the drapers and Peter Robinson that sold mainly ladies' wear, for instance, were reluctant to become full-blown department stores. Different stores also tended to cater to different constituencies of class and status. Selfridge's democratic and forward looking approach challenged such rigidities of buying and selling.[21]

Although the metropolis certainly witnessed vital developments, other parts of the country did not lag behind. We saw in Chapter 2 how early department stores sprang up in northern cities and provincial stores continued to be dynamic engines of change. In Liverpool, David Lewis opened his first store in 1856, which followed the successful model provided by working-class retail co-operative societies, operating on principles of cash sales, low prices and high turnover. Specializing initially in men's and youth's clothing, Lewis sold women's wear from the mid-1860s then branched out to many other lines, pitching his appeal towards poorer consumers and marketing his concern as 'the Friend of the People'. Importantly, in terms of their democratic appeal, northern stores like Lewis's were ahead of their London counterparts. Lewis also strove to cut out the middleman wherever possible by manufacturing his own goods, which generated friction with various trade associations.[22] He eventually established a provincial empire, opening stores in Manchester in 1877, Sheffield in 1884 and Birmingham the year after. The latter changed the topography of the city and proved hugely popular, the local press noting on the evening of its first day's trade that 'the lighting up of the windows on each storey attracted a great crowd, and Bull Street was for several hours well-nigh impassable. The building and its contents form one of the town's attractions.'[23] Similarly, the rebuilt Fraser's store in Glasgow made the city one of the most sophisticated shopping centres in Britain in the late 1880s. With its broad column spaces, light walls and integrated plate-glass frontages – made possible by iron-frame construction – it was in the vanguard of store design at the time. The interior of the store was carefully designed to entice consumers and encourage them to part with their cash, featuring sweeping staircases, passenger lifts, luxurious carpets, large mirrors, mahogany panelling and electric lighting.[24] Department stores thrived not only in large cities but also helped create the appeal of seaside resorts and other picturesque towns such as Bournemouth, Margate and Chester, where Beale's, Bobby's and Brown's ('the Harrod's of the North') attracted large numbers of consumers.[25]

The owners of many of these stores in the late Victorian and Edwardian period were celebrity consumer capitalists, flamboyant individuals who were often notorious for their sexual exploits and the authoritarian rule they exercised over staff. They were masters of publicity, having more in common with theatrical impresarios than thrifty, guilt-ridden shopkeepers like William Ablett. Selfridge advertised heavily in the press as we have noted and he was not alone; Harrod's, which could trace its beginnings back to the grocery shop started by Charles Harrod in Knightsbridge around 1853, had its own advertising department and manager by the early 1890s and in February 1904 spent £2,500 on newspaper advertising on one day alone. And although Whiteley was loath to spend money on press advertising, he fully understood the value of publicity, even when it was adverse, and puffed his business whenever he could, distributing an almanac to his customers at Christmas, for example.[26] Other owners were skilled showmen, drumming up business in all manner of ingenious ways. David Lewis, for example, even turned antagonism from local traders to his advantage, publicizing the court case that resulted from the congestion in Manchester streets in 1881 caused by stunts intended to attract consumers, including puppet shows and coloured balloons. The trial was held at the High Court in London and although Lewis and his partners lost and were fined £40 and made to enter recognizances for £500 not to repeat the nuisance, Lewis appeared in person and used the opportunity to expose the inflated prices charged by his competitors. Portraying himself as a champion of the working class, Lewis had 100,000 copies of his account of the trial published. He also dreamt up elaborate promotions, chartering Brunel's *Great Eastern* steamship in 1886, for instance, and converting it into a huge floating advertisement, complete with bar, music and dance hall, fairground rides, photographic studio and coffee shop, which drew over half a million visitors.[27] Two decades or so later, Selfridge became renowned for his stunts, negotiating a deal with the *Daily Mail*, for example, which enabled him to display Louis Blériot's plane in his store to 150,000 visitors after the pioneer aviator's successful flight across the English Channel in 1909.[28]

For some commentators, department stores were analogous to cathedrals because they appeared to be temples of a new religion – modern consumerism. As with so many aspects of the subject, Zola touched on this theme in his seminal work. Mouret's store is repeatedly described as a new kind of religious space in *The Ladies' Paradise*, one in which erotic and acquisitive desires are frequently confused; in one scene a crowd of shoppers causes a cloud of fine dust to rise from the floor of the store, which is 'laden with the odour of Woman, the odour of her underlinen and the nape of her neck, of her skirts and her hair, a penetrating, all-pervading odour which seemed to be the incense of this temple dedicated to the worship of her body'. Mouret's competitors share his sense of the religious significance of the department store, one of them even getting a priest to bless his new shop, described by Zola sardonically as 'an astonishing ceremony: all the pomp of the Church was paraded through the silk and glove departments, God circulated among women's knickers and corsets'.[29] Despite their relative insignificance quantitatively, department stores no doubt attracted such interest from intellectuals because although they often seemed to embody the increasing 'alienation' of modern consumers and their enslavement to commodity capitalism, they were also simultaneously symbols of a progressive consumer culture that held out the promise of the good life for all, defined in terms of a never-ending accumulation of things. They not only sold goods, like churches and cathedrals department stores also traded in dreams and can therefore be regarded like early cinemas as 'dream palaces', with which they were associated in both the elite and popular mind at the time. They served to re-enchant the world in new ways and functioned as beacons of hope for the future, helping therefore to 'organise the imagination' of consumers, to borrow the felicitous phrase of the American sociologist, C. Wright Mills.[30]

Gender, desire and labour

Shopping was represented as an inherently female activity during this period, while department stores were commonly portrayed as an essentially female domain. As we have seen, historians have underlined how shopping in these new spaces allowed middle-class women in particular to challenge and transgress existing boundaries between public and private spheres, mixing up different classes and genders.[31] Growing consumerism was fuelled by spreading fashion consciousness, evidence of which abounds; more sophisticated forms of display were employed by the new stores but also new ways of addressing and constructing women as consumers emerged that made it easier for them to forge different identities through goods. We can see this in the popularity of illustrated fashion magazines such as *Myra's Journal of Dress and Fashion* and the *Queen* during the last quarter of the nineteenth century, for example, which according to design historians fostered 'an intensified consumer literacy'. Through editorials which plugged the latest trends as well as advertisements, these magazines enabled more and more women to engage in a fantasy world of consumption outside of the home.[32] Probably 120 or more fashion magazines were established between 1880 and the turn of the century and in their pages women were constructed as urban spectators and ramblers or *flâneuse,* and were encouraged to regard the city's streets and stores primarily as sites of pleasure.[33]

A growing propensity to consume fashion goods is also evidenced by the increasing number of sales that regularly punctuated the annual cycle and which seemed to become more extensive with each passing year. At these times especially, lower middle-class and working-class women were encouraged to shop in these 'cathedrals of commerce'. Smaller department stores that opened in London's suburbs and other urban centres, such as John Barnes in Hampstead, the Bon Marché in Brixton, Binns in Sunderland, Howell's in Cardiff, Bobby's in Margate, Broadbents in Southport and so on, also made extensive use of sales.[34] These events added new momentum to the shopping experience, especially those held at Christmas and the New Year, when according to some critics masses of women were tempted by the generally illusory promise of getting a bargain into making purchases 'of endless things for which they have no use whatever'.[35] For some even less enthusiastic commentators the sales seemed to induce a kind of shopping madness that threatened to overturn respectability. An observer of Whiteley's January sales in 1881 described the contagion of bargain hunting in the following manner: 'Ladies, dauntless in the cause of dress, were charging into the serried ranks of jackets, dragging them off their pegs, and bearing them away in all directions to be tried on at leisure.'[36] Continuing longstanding anxieties, female consumers were still often portrayed as innately gullible, as in the cartoon reproduced as Figure 7, which represented them as geese about to be caught in traps laid by foxy sales assistants.

Sometimes seemingly quite inconsequential events brought middle-class male anxieties into the open. For example, as we saw at the start of this chapter, Whiteley applied for a licence to sell wine and beer in the store's refreshment room in 1872. By this time he was employing over 600 staff and serving more than 4,000 customers a day. The resulting debate exposed concerns about female shoppers in this new space. The Liberal editor of the local paper came out against Whiteley's request, noting that 'sherry and silks, or port and piques, need not of necessity go together when ladies go "shopping."' Bourgeois fears were heightened by the fact that alcohol and prostitution was seen to go hand in hand and that fashionable West End shopping areas were also frequented by many prostitutes. The purported link between female consumers of fashionable goods and commercialized sexuality goes back at least to the eighteenth century – William Hazlitt made this connection as we saw earlier – but it re-emerged in these debates.[37] Whiteley passionately refuted claims about the potential immorality of his customers but magistrates ignored his arguments and refused his application, arguing that they did not want to see the store become 'a place of assignation'.[38] Department store owners cut through such narrow-mindedness and appealed directly to women over the heads of male authority. They claimed woman's cause as their own and went to great lengths to cultivate good relations with female consumers, for obvious reasons. Selfridge's advertising addressed women specifically in the most flattering terms, for instance. The lavish press advertisements for his store foregrounded female consumers, literally

FIGURE 7 *'Selling off Winter Stock'*, Snap-Shots: Humorous Pictures and Amusing Reading, *19 January 1895. © The British Library Board (PENP.NT194).*

putting them on a pedestal and representing them as empowered figures whose every need this modern 'cathedral of commerce' had been designed to serve. Such imagery, which was a common visual feature used in advertising for a wide range of commodities, has been seen by some cultural historians to lend support to a positive reading of consumer culture for women.[39] We ought to be careful here, however, as the gulf between representation and reality was frequently very wide and the effects of department stores were never that straightforward. There were gains certainly but there were also more negative implications.

Anxieties about the impact of department stores were magnified particularly by shoplifting, which increasing press coverage and widely publicized court cases helped fix in the public imagination. Consumer theft long predated the emergence of the modern department store but in the second half of the nineteenth century it became medicalized and pathologized. Shoplifting by otherwise respectable middle-class women was increasingly diagnosed as 'kleptomania' in Britain, France and elsewhere, a medical condition seen as caused by women's mental and physical health problems.[40] A contributor to the *Cornhill Magazine* in 1860, for instance, admitted that kleptomania was not merely an 'imaginary disease' because he knew 'a young lady, of good sense and most respectable station, (who) could never be trusted in a shop alone'. The writer concluded with a troubling question: 'If this disease can happen in the upper classes, why may it not exist in the lower strata of social life?'[41] When working-class consumers had purloined goods in the past it was seen as straightforward theft and punished accordingly; the bill abolishing the death penalty for shoplifting had been rejected six times by the House of Lords before it was passed in 1820 and working-class women continued to receive harsh sentences for the crime afterwards, including transportation and penal servitude, especially if they were habitual offenders.[42] Turning it into a disease may have conveniently let some middle-class women off the hook but it opened the prospect of their proletarian sisters getting away with their misdemeanours scot free. Despite such fears, courts generally treated middle-class shoplifters leniently and a light-hearted note characterized much cultural discourse, as in the ballad *Ladies, Don't Go Thieving*, which was hawked around London streets in 1867:

A beauty of the West End went,
Around a shop she lingers,
And there upon some handkerchiefs
She clapped her pretty fingers.
Into the shop she gently popped;
The world is quite deceiving
When ladies have a notion got
To ramble out a-thieving.

Whiteley once estimated that female shoplifters outnumbered males by three hundred to one. Mostly from the middle and upper class, Victorian fashions made it easier for them to hide goods and they were occasionally caught with remarkable caches; in 1885 one woman was found to have 24 ½ yards of velvet, forty-two silk handkerchiefs, two pairs of gloves and some ribbons concealed in her clothes. Unsurprisingly, Whiteley came down hard on those caught though most department store owners preferred to turn a blind eye.[43]

The ambiguous legal position of women as consumers did nothing to quell male bourgeois fears. Under the law of coverture, a husband was liable for his wife's debts and although the situation gradually changed after the passage of the Married Women's Property Act in 1870, women's responsibility for debt remained unclear well into the twentieth century. Different judgements in the county and higher courts caused more confusion. Judges in the former, established in 1846 to help recover small debts, often sympathized with husbands and found against traders. In 1864 the Court of Common Pleas ruled that a husband could deny liability for his wife's debts if the goods could be deemed not 'necessary' – the so-called law of necessaries – but definitions of what constituted 'necessaries' were vague and fluid.[44] Female consumers clearly had some agency, then, and could sometimes manipulate the law to their advantage. The case of Laura Bell in

1878 caused traders particular consternation. Bell was a former prostitute who ran up debts of £1,000 until a firm of milliners sued her husband, Augustus Thistlewayte, for the money. In her defence, Bell maintained that her current allowance of £500 a year was not sufficient for a lady of fashion, and the jury agreed. The West End firm of Debenham and Freebody pursued a case against Mr Mellon for a debt of £43 incurred by his wife through the lower courts, to the Lords, then on to the Court of Appeal. They all found against the plaintiff, provoking a national debate on the status of women as consumers. An amendment to the Married Women's Property Act that followed in 1882 was welcomed by traders as women were now thought to be liable, but wives still lacked full contractual rights and responsibilities and so store owners continued to complain about the impossibility of recovering debts from married women. Whiteley tried to get around the problem by institutionalizing cash transactions but many other stores continued to offer their customers credit.[45]

The exact nature of kleptomania continued to be debated throughout the late Victorian and Edwardian period. A writer in the *English Illustrated Magazine* in 1910, for instance, noted that many people continued to disbelieve in the existence of such a medical condition, explaining shoplifting instead as a result of 'moral turpitude'. A recent interview with a manager of a fashionable West End store and sentences passed by some magistrates, 'Peter Penn' continued, suggested that such scepticism was widely shared. Criticizing this trend, the writer asserted that the condition was a mental illness which only truly afflicted wealthier women and that these poor unfortunates should therefore be treated differently. It was all a matter of status and reputation:

> Admitted, there should be one law only for both rich and poor, yet publicity, and imprisonment more so, of course, constitute a much severer penalty to the woman of fashion and means than to a woman of the lower orders who, if caught stealing would be summarily dealt with as a thief, and nothing more. The latter is supposed to be urged to the commission of a crime in order to relieve poverty, but the lady kleptomaniac has no excuse. And having no such excuse, and being aware of the more exacting penalty which would follow detection and exposure we may suppose that the impulsion to theft is stronger ... It seems reasonable to conclude that a lady who would commit a theft, however paltry it must be, is, to a certain extent, irresponsible; that, in short, she is mentally deficient.[46]

It would be stretching things too far to suggest that shoplifting in this period can be understood as 'a performative tactic that makes visible the ways in which femininity is always a construction or a masquerade'.[47] Nevertheless, the widely reported acts of middle-class female shoplifters undoubtedly raised disturbing questions about the pitfalls of modern consumer culture and placed the owners of department stores, the authorities and the law in a very tricky position. The idea of legal impartiality was important to maintain, as 'Peter Penn' grudgingly admitted, but how then to ensure that the poor woman or 'professional shoplifter' did not run amok in the 'halls of temptation'?

Not surprisingly, concern about female extravagance was mainly voiced by middle-class men fearful of the impact on their pocketbooks. More sympathetic responses to the effects of department stores were forthcoming from women who worried about the working lives of their sisters that served behind the counters. The earlier emporia had been staffed mainly by male assistants and they continued to be employed in large numbers in some stores until the First World War; in Peter Robinson's, for example, there were 300 male to 100 female assistants. However, the new cathedrals of commerce hired young women in vast numbers and they came to embody the 'new shopping'. Harrod's employed over 1,000 by the late nineteenth century, as did Bainbridge's and Kendal Milne.[48] Many of them worked like dogs. The so-called living-in system was the norm in London, with shop girls sharing a room with four or five others. Wages were low and they had to cope with the demands of standing for very long periods and breathing stale air, as well as the frequent impertinence of customers. Calls for improvement can be traced back to the middle-class Early Closing Association founded in 1842, which was discussed in Chapter 3. Pressure increased during the 1870s with the establishment of the Shop Hours Labour League in 1883. Its president, Thomas Sutherst, summarized the effects of prolonged shop work in a book titled *Death and Disease Behind the Counter* that was published in 1884: 'The whole system – mind and body – begins to wither and decay, evolving different forms of infirmity and disease, until the poor victim of this vicious system either drops into a premature grave or passes the remainder of life in bodily suffering.' Conditions in large stores were usually better than those found in smaller shops. The working day at Debenham and Freebody, for example, was 7 am to 6 pm in winter and 7 am to 7 pm in summer, with the store closing at 2 pm on Saturdays. Conditions were improved slightly by the Shop Hours Regulation Act of 1886 that established a working week of between seventy-five and ninety hours a week.[49]

Change, however, was very slow, especially outside the West End. Nearly a decade after the Shop Act was passed, Lady Jeune eloquently pleaded the case for these exploited workers:

> How often has one seen a thin, pallid, anaemic girl, behind the counter, hurrying here and there, full of resource, of quickness, of anxiety to please, working from morning to night, without knowing that she is not fit to be doing such work than she is to draw a cart. How well one knows that air, light, and rest would put colour into her cheeks and light into her eyes, but that she cannot allow herself the time and money for such a luxury.[50]

Lady Jeune argued for an urgent improvement in conditions, including the provision of seating for shop girls, but she rejected the need for legislative intervention, trusting in voluntary action by employers and pressure from other sympathetic shoppers. More radical critics, such as the socialist and trade unionist Isabella Ford, also had little faith in the efficacy of state action as a remedy for shop workers' problems, emphasizing instead the necessity for greater organization and self-activity on their own part.[51] Public debate on this issue intensified following labour activist Margaret Bondfield's reports of shop life in the *Daily Chronicle* in 1898, which were gained through undercover investigation. Like the figure of the prostitute or the needlewoman in earlier decades, during the fin de siècle the shop girl became a highly charged and complex symbol, talked about in newspapers and periodicals, sung about and represented on the stage of the music halls and popular theatres. In this discourse, the effects of shop work were invariably construed in both moral as well as physical terms; ground down by arduous labour, shop girls were seen, unfairly of course, to turn frequently to drink and 'dissipation'. The link between consumption and sexuality is once again discernible here, fuelled by the sensationalist journalism of writers such as W. T. Stead who was keen to find another scandal after his lurid exposure of sexual trafficking in the *Pall Mall Gazette*.[52] Represented as prone to the constant temptations of finery, shop girls might be able to rise in the world by making a good match occasionally (like Denise in *The Ladies' Paradise*), but they were more often considered likely to end up in the gutter.[53]

While department stores were typically portrayed by contemporary commentators as quintessentially places of female consumption, they also catered for the needs of male consumers. Men may have been 'hidden' by the new stores to an extent but one did not have to look very hard to find them. The notion of a 'Great Masculine Renunciation' – whereby men supposedly turned their backs on style and colour from the late eighteenth century in favour of the uniform dark suit – has been convincingly overturned by modern scholarship that has demonstrated how many male consumers were as prone to the temptations of fashion as any style-conscious woman in the late Victorian and Edwardian period.[54] As the author of a well-known guidebook published for the drapery trade explained in 1912, male consumers often preferred ready-made suits to made to measure ones as they were now often very good quality and well-cut. Moreover, there was another reason, which was that the customer 'has an opportunity of judging its finish, the lining and other trifling matters which go towards making up a satisfactory garment'. The modern male shopper was therefore regarded as increasingly fashion conscious and highly discerning, fussy even. Discussing catalogues, Burgess went on to underline how the contemporary male was 'just as much interested as the lady buyer' in the latest thing.[55]

Naturally, store owners fully recognized the potential of this market themselves. David Lewis started off selling men's and youth's clothes at first, before branching out into women's clothing later on. Whiteley's expanded into gentlemen's outfitting in 1868 and his 'appeal to the male proved as successful as his appeal to the female customer', according to the company's historian. Selfridge's described itself as 'The Man's Best Buying Centre' from the outset.[56] There was backlash against this from journalists like G. A. Sala, who impugned the masculinity of young gentlemen that 'have not the slightest objection to going out shopping with their Mamas, their sisters, or their *prétendues*'. Consequently, department stores went to some lengths to placate masculine unease, a number even providing separate entrances off the main thoroughfares for their male clientele.[57] Occasionally, middle- and upper-class men's love for fine clothes also provoked open class conflict. During riots by the unemployed in London's West End in 1886, for example, an angry crowd almost completely wrecked Marshall and Snelgrove's and numerous other fashionable shops were looted. Enacting symbolic revenge on wealthy consumers and with a nice touch of black humour, rioters stripped the coats from dummies in a ready-made tailor's shop in Oxford Street and replaced them with 'their own ragged garments'.[58]

Although shop girls attracted disproportionate attention, many others were employed behind the scenes in department stores. Most of the clothing sold by David Lewis, for example, was manufactured in its own extensive workshops that supplied the demand for both bespoke and ready-made goods, making it a factory as well as a shop. About 300 tailors and 200–300 shoemakers worked in the Manchester store that opened in 1877. Many more were engaged in the lucrative mail-order business, which did a huge trade in fashionable textiles such as velveteen in the 1880s.[59] Other stores were big employers of labour. By the early twentieth century, around 600 members of staff were engaged on the retail side at Debenham and Freebody, while at least 3,000 were employed in its workrooms.[60] Although some storeowners tried to create a paternalist culture within their enterprises, labour relations were often strained. Whiteley provided decent living-in accommodation, reasonable food in the staff canteen and encouraged recreational activities but he also ruled employees with a rod of iron. They were liable to instant dismissal and a multitude of rules governed their behaviour, offenders' names complete with cutting comments were posted in the dining room and fines were levied, all money going into Whiteley's own pocket. Not surprisingly, the place seethed with discontent, one informant telling a reporter from the *Pall Mall Gazette*, 'So far as I know, whether male or female, those who are employed by Whiteley regard their master with feelings of intense dislike … His whole system is one of slave-driving from top to bottom.' Though shop girls were relatively powerless against such tyrannical rule, tailoring workers had greater room for manoeuvre. They went on strike in 1895, garnering support from Lady Dilke and other opponents of sweating, parading Whiteley's effigy on horseback through the streets on Guy Fawkes Day, evoking memories of his conflict with the butchers nearly twenty years before.[61] Pressure such as this, and also increased competition from rival shops and co-operatives, led to department stores seeking better protection and access to capital through limited liability; Harrod's had gone public as early as 1889, followed by D. H. Evans in 1894, Binns of Sunderland in 1897, Whiteley's in 1899, Dickens and Jones in 1900, Fraser's of Glasgow in 1909 and so on.[62] Autocratic store bosses often remained in place despite the change, Whiteley remaining until 1907 when he was shot dead in his store by a man named Rayner, most likely an illegitimate son that Whiteley had refused to recognize. Petitions calling for the reprieve of the death sentence that was passed on his murderer were remarkably popular and eventually proved successful; a vicar even asked his congregation to sign and workers at the Carriage and Wagon Depot of the Midland Railway sent their own petition.[63]

Private acts, public narratives

An important reason why department stores figured so saliently in the cultural imagination of both contemporaries and later historians was that they linked private acts of consumption with public narratives. In other words, they pushed shopping onto the public stage, sometimes politicizing it directly. Whenever they could, the owners of these cathedrals of commerce identified their stores with the nation and the progress of the British Empire. Cultivating royal patronage was an obvious tactic, with Whiteley counting Queen Victoria and the Princess of Wales among his customers early on. He took the lead in decorating Westbourne Grove for Victoria's Golden Jubilee in the summer of 1887, borrowing the royal family's insignia for the store's clock tower for the occasion. The whole shop front was festooned with red, white and blue drapery, while the colonies and dependencies were also represented. The *Pall Mall Gazette* noted admiringly that the 'tremendous building is nearly buried beneath the flags, bunting, trophies, loyal prayers, patriotic inscriptions, and pleasant assurances to the colonies'.[64] Other department stores were similarly decked, including Marshall and Snelgrove's. Whiteley later received a royal warrant as 'General Furnisher to Her Majesty' after he decorated Buckingham Palace. In 1896 he even appropriated Nelson's Column on Trafalgar Day, decorating the monument from top to bottom with laurel wreaths and flying Nelson's famous signal ('England expects that every man will do his duty') from the roof of his store. During the diamond jubilee the year after, Whiteley flooded London with royal souvenirs and even petitioned the queen to include the store on her tour through the city on 28 June. Victoria rejected such crass commercial identification, though she toured the district a week earlier to see the whole of Bayswater decorated in grand style.[65] Perhaps peeved by the snub, Whiteley let himself be outdone by his competitors' stores that were illuminated by gas jets and electric lights for the jubilee, filling the night sky with signs of patriotic devotion.[66]

Consumerism was inextricably bound up with national pride, connected to imperialist ideology more perhaps by the myriad commodities on sale than by occasional pageantry. One of the most lucrative areas of trade for department stores before the First World War was mail order and much of this went to consumers in the empire, especially the many soldiers and civilians for whom it provided employment. By the 1890s, perhaps a third of Harrod's trade was with the empire. The Army and Navy Co-operative Society – a middle-class co-operative that aimed to save money for its members but had no wider goals, unlike working-class co-operatives – originated primarily as a mail-order business, circulating annual price lists to officers and their families, which became a kind of shopping bible throughout the British Empire.[67] The company's profusely illustrated catalogue for 1907 ran to over 1,200 pages. Within it could be found almost every commodity imaginable, from an artificial leg to a fishing rod, a dinner gong to a croquet set. A separate section on 'Barrack Furniture and Camp Equipment' was housed on the second floor of the London store on Victoria Street. All kinds of furniture, bedding, camping and outdoor cooking equipment was for sale, carefully designed for ease of transport and use in foreign climes; different sorts of travelling chests, collapsible beds and bedsteads, chairs and tables as well as a variety of mosquito nets could be purchased for private as well as official expeditions. To protect themselves from wild animals or angry 'natives', customers had to move to the smaller premises on Howick Place, just behind the main store and connected by a bridge, where one could choose from a wide range of rifles and revolvers, as well as ammunition including the store's own cartridge – the 'Victoria'. Such goods took up over forty pages in the catalogue. Shipping costs were surprisingly low; a 50 lb package could be sent to India, for instance, for as little as 15s.[68] In a very real sense 'Britishness', embodied in the goods that simultaneously met colonial travellers' immediate needs and reminded them of home, was eminently portable.[69] Where the British went, their things went with them.

As the arms race quickened and the prospect of war drew closer, department stores in the metropolis beat the patriotic drum ever more loudly. Both Harrod's and Selfridge's strongly supported the Territorial Force established by the Secretary of State for War, Richard Haldane, in 1907. They encouraged male staff to enlist and participate in competitive sports activities organized by the territorials two years later – Selfridge's even had its own separate company within the London regiment. Harrod's brought its diamond jubilee forward to try to steal some of the limelight from Selfridge when he opened his new store in 1909, and celebrations commenced with a meeting to puff the territorials. Haldane had agreed to address this meeting but withdrew at the last minute, after such a close public identification was vetoed by the Liberal Prime Minister, Herbert Asquith.[70] Socialists worried deeply about these strengthening links between shopping and war, condemning them as evidence of the increasing militarization of British society. Noting the spectacular boom experienced by big stores in London, for example, a correspondent for *Justice*, the weekly newspaper published by Britain's first Marxist party, the Social Democratic Federation, condemned Haldane's planned appearance at Selfridge's for cementing militarism and consumerism, and later articles continued this line of criticism.[71]

The stores also fuelled popular patriotism with the inauguration of the 'All-British Shopping Week' in the spring of 1911, following a series of articles on the 'All-British Woman' in the *Daily Express*. Promoted by the Union Jack Industries League, numerous stores lent enthusiastic backing including Harvey Nichols, Harrod's and Selfridge's and stores in other English cities followed their lead, though none in Scotland. A reporter from the *Express* visited Selfridge's just before the start of the event, reassuring male readers that their needs had also been catered for. Shop windows in the West End and the City were crammed with thousands of posters of 'Britannia and the Lion' during this 'Imperial Pageant' and the paper assured readers; 'In these miles of streets everything that man or woman can need will be exhibited – and everything will have been produced within the Empire.' Unsurprisingly, the monarchy strongly supported this campaign, Queen Mary declaring before the coronation of George V in June 1911 that only British-made materials would be used in her gowns.[72] When war finally broke out, department stores made great efforts to bolster patriotic spirits. 'Rule Britannia!' played daily in the Palm Court at Selfridge's, a shooting range was opened on the roof, campaign maps displayed in the windows and German-made articles exhibited so that customers could boycott them, while the Army and Navy sent parcels to the front.[73]

The Crystal Palace at Sydenham functioned both as a proto shopping mall and an amusement park in Edwardian England, a place where consumers could while away their time as well as buy fashionable goods. That was why it was chosen for the Festival of Empire arranged as part of the coronation celebrations in 1911. One of the main objects of the festival was to bring the things of empire to life and for nearly six months the Crystal Palace became *the* space of imperial consumerism. The journalist John Holt captured this dimension perfectly in a series of articles in the *Daily Mail*. For Holt, Sydenham Hill represented a fitting venue, as from here one could look down on 'the heart of the Empire' and ponder its meaning, which he thought was to be found in the goods themselves:

> This soap with which we will wash our hands this evening lies beside the water chatties in an Indian bungalow also. These boots, the new and polished brothers of the ones we are wearing, have their counterparts tramping the Western prairies or hurrying through the busy streets of Melbourne. Those cartridges with which we will litter the moors next autumn are bringing down larger game than grouse in equatorial Africa. A dusky potentate and fellow citizen of ours enjoys the same music from the same talking machine that beguiles our suburban evenings. Savage and civilised, the whole Empire share our blankets and our breakfast

> foods, work with our machinery, play with our toys. It is when we realise that our pantry and our wardrobe are duplicated in a thousand corners of the earth that the unity of the Empire and the dependence upon one another of its various parts are brought home to us.[74]

Flows of goods such as these constituted the lifeblood of the imperial system, binding the savage and the civilized together in a larger, quasi-religious endeavour. More prosaically, Holt's puffery was sandwiched between advertisements for some of the commodities on display at the Crystal Palace: Hovis bread, Eley cartridges, Manfield boots, Lyons tea. Advertisements for the latter reassured readers that 'Indian tea is British tea. British capital is invested in the Indian Tea Industry: the gardens are owned or managed by British planters; the tea is manufactured by ingenious machinery of British make; and it is dispatched to the United Kingdom in British ships. Indian Tea, then, is of especial interest to the patriotic Briton.'[75]

As this chapter has emphasized, shopping in department stores allowed women greater access to public space and afforded them many new employment opportunities. Department stores may have been regarded by many contemporary male commentators as emblematic of women's enslavement to consumerism but they also offered the possibility of a kind of liberation, for some at least. The debate on their effects echoes that concerning the meaning of fashion for women – the use of cosmetics in particular – which has often been interpreted as a sign of patriarchal subordination but which has also been read, more sensitively, as allowing some women to manipulate their identities, to masquerade in order to increase their power in unequal contexts.[76] If it is not hard to find evidence to support Zola's view that the big stores seduced female consumers, we should not forget that increasing numbers worked in these cathedrals of commerce as managers, buyers and window dressers as well as shop girls, not to mention the women who pursued interesting and rewarding careers in the many enterprises that expanded alongside the stores, such as fashion journalism, advertising agencies and dress design. Selfridge liked to claim that he not only satisfied women's consuming desires but also emancipated them and although women, it must be insisted, emancipated themselves, there was a grain of truth in this typically self-aggrandizing statement. Selfridge's press advertising put female consumers firmly in the driving seat. Figure 8, one of a series of striking images produced by Fred Pegram to help launch Selfridge's, shows a haughty consumer queen receiving the store as if in homage from a supplicant male architect; this 'great house' is dedicated to female pleasure.

More importantly, Selfridge's business success depended on his female employees, the journalists and copywriters who kept his store before the public in newspapers and periodicals and the female shoppers who could make or break his fortune. Women with means recognized this

FIGURE 8 *Fred Pegram, 'The Dedication of a Great House', 1909. © Victoria & Albert Museum, London.*

interdependence and they bought into it, literally, as approximately 49 per cent of Selfridge's investors were women.[77]

Aware of their reliance on female workers and consumers, Selfridge and other department store owners in London and elsewhere understandably liked to publicize their support for women's emancipation, which they regarded as a modernizing impulse, analogous to their own revolutionary transformation of retailing. They knew that many of the elite women who supported the suffrage campaign were among their best customers and that they shared a deep love of things, especially home furnishings. As the suffragette journal, *Votes for Women*, observed about an exhibition of modern furniture: 'No one is more keen about the home than the Suffragette.' Agnes Garrett, sister of the liberal suffrage leader Millicent Garrett, made a living as an interior designer as well as being an honorary secretary of the National Society for Women's Suffrage, but even the militant Emmeline Pankhurst ran a number of furniture stores for a while before devoting herself fully to the suffrage cause.[78] It is hardly surprising therefore that Selfridge flew the suffragette flag over his store in 1909, or that Fenwick's tearoom was used by suffragettes in Newcastle as their headquarters. Department stores manufactured and sold a range of goods including tea services and articles of female attire in purple, white and green, the movement's symbolic colours. Recreational facilities provided at Selfridge's included an Operatic and Dramatic Society that produced a play early on written by the society's director, titled *The Suffrage Girl*.[79] The stores also advertised widely in the suffrage press. In the run up to the so-called Women's Pilgrimage organized by the National Union of Women's Suffrage Societies (NUWSS) that drew contingents from different parts of the country and culminated in London in the summer of 1913, Swan and Edgar's advertised suitable clothing for the march in the pages of *Common Cause*, the hats trimmed with ribbon in the organization's colours.[80]

The year before, things had not been quite so harmonious. In March 1912 women belonging to the Women's Social and Political Union (WSPU), a militant middle-class dominated body, had smashed nearly 400 shop windows in the West End, causing approximately £5,000 worth of damage. Attacks were indiscriminate and included a host of small shops though big drapers like Swan and Edgar's, Marshall and Snelgrove's, D. H. Evan's and Liberty's were also targeted. The *Daily Mirror* reported that the 'hammer-women have done more than break windows – they have killed a fashion', because shoppers were afraid to be seen carrying large portmanteau bags following the campaign. Department store owners were confused by the way in which many of their own customers had seemingly turned against them, especially after they had lent support to their cause. Mr Lasenby Liberty wrote to the *Standard* wanting Mrs Pankhurst 'to state the mental process by which they deem the breaking of the very shrines at which they worship will advance their cause'. Suffragettes were now forcing storekeepers to come out publicly in favour of votes for women, or suffer the consequences. In a letter to retailers, the WSPU reassured them that 'the Suffragettes bear no grudge against you personally ... the women are good friends to you', but went on to remind them that real power lay in the hands of the woman with the pocketbook: 'Without them and their support what would become of that flourishing business of yours?'[81] In short, these women were no longer content with patronage and calculated support from retailers, they wanted some measure of real control. This desire also explains why suffragettes established their own shops and meeting places both in London and elsewhere at this time, initiatives that represent other rather more constructive attempts to use their collective strength as consumers for their own ends, albeit with limited success.[82] Violent tactics not only served to alarm department store owners but it also divided the middle-class 'suffragettes' in the WSPU from more working-class 'suffragists' in the NUWSS who rejected window smashing along with militancy in general. And the latter organization continued to enjoy support from traders such as Swan and Edgar's as we have seen, though this did not stop the firm from successfully suing officials of the WSPU for the damage that had been inflicted on it in 1912.[83] Clearly, militant feminism and consumerism were uneasy bedfellows before the First World War. Moreover, attempts to build cross-class alliances based on consumption within the women's suffrage movement foundered, not least because the consumer power of many working-class women was already being organized independently within the co-operative movement.[84] The barriers to understanding here are exemplified by a work written by the suffragette Teresa Billington Greig titled *The Consumer in Revolt*, which developed a trenchant argument for women's liberation based around consumption but which ignored entirely the largest organization of working-class women that Britain had ever seen – the Women's Co-operative Guild.[85] It is that organization to which we will now turn our attention.

6

Co-op Commonwealth: Consumer Organizing

Cultures of co-operation, cultures of shopkeeping

Mrs Layton, a typically overworked mother who had to manage on her husband's meagre wage of just over a pound a week, joined her local co-operative society in London in the mid-1880s. She had fully grasped the intimate connection between consumption and class inequality long before married life. Layton wrote in her autobiography about how as a young girl she had been moved by the sight of impoverished matchbox makers who were kept waiting outside the manufacturer's big house for their pay, the smell of roast meat coming from his kitchen tormenting them all the while. 'Several women passed remarks regarding the smell', she recalled, 'and wished they could be invited to dine off that joint'. At the age of ten Layton helped out in a kind of pawn shop in the neighbourhood that exchanged articles of clothing for food, which reinforced her early consumer consciousness. As she later remembered: 'I have seen a pair of children's boots left in pawn for a loaf of bread and a small quantity of butter.' She was encouraged by the owner of the shop to cheat the poor in these pathetic exchanges, until an aunt caught her and reminded her that she had perhaps deprived a poor child of a slice of bread, a thought that made Layton feel 'so thoroughly ashamed … and so sorry' that she 'was days getting over it'.[1] Originally motivated by the 'divi', Layton was so enthusiastic about co-operation that she 'walked two miles to the Store' for even small purchases. But material advantages quickly became intertwined with social and educational attractions. The store was a doorway to an expansive culture and Layton was soon participating in teas, socials and educational classes, and joined a branch of the Women's Co-operative Guild (WCG), the separate women's organization linked to the movement that had been founded in 1883.[2] As she read co-operative literature and spoke at branch meetings, she developed a gender as well as a class consciousness; here was a movement which empowered the ordinary 'woman with the basket', unlike Mother's Meetings at which middle-class ladies gave out patronizing advice to their social inferiors, where Layton had previously 'boiled over many times'. Growing in confidence year by year, she eventually became president of a branch of the guild and later vice president of the WCG, speaking at many local and national conferences and even taking part in deputations to parliament on maternity care during the First World War, where she staunchly defended the cause of unmarried mothers. As Layton concluded: 'From a shy, nervous woman, the Guild made me a fighter.'[3] Although some socialist women made attempts to emulate co-operative methods and develop their own alternative politics of consumption towards the end of the century, their efforts were inconsequential compared to those of the WCG.[4]

Consumers' co-operation made tremendous strides in the last third of the nineteenth century because it got under the skin of life and it increased the individual and collective power of both female and male workers. However, until relatively recently, historians regarded this success as evidence of the 'incorporation' of workers into a capitalist system that was now accepted by them as constituting an inevitable framework for action, and have portrayed co-operative societies as a means by which the 'labour aristocracy' among the working class learnt the rules of the game and internalized supposedly bourgeois values such as respectability and thrift.[5] Some ex-Chartists encouraged this view, most famously Thomas Cooper in his autobiography published in 1872, where he compared unfavourably the abjectly poor but politically conscious Lancashire workers of the 1830s and 1840s with the 'well-dressed working men' of the present day, who were interested only in betting and talking about their shares in coops and building societies.[6] It was hardly surprising then that the loudest proponents of the gospel of improvement, including Samuel Smiles, sang the praises of consumers' co-operation. In *Thrift* (1875), for example, Smiles congratulated the Rochdale Pioneers for having spread this salutary model, which has 'given the people an interest in money matters and enabled them to lay out their earnings to the best advantage'.[7] However we read its meaning, this enterprise was made possible by the increase in working-class demand from around mid-century, as noted in Chapter 4. After the temporary setbacks caused by the Cotton Famine, working-class living standards continued to rise until 1873 when a financial crisis and slump in wholesale commodity prices by about 40 per cent began a period of over two decades that were later misleadingly labelled the 'Great Depression'. Although punctuated by severe slumps in 1879, 1886 and 1890, most workers were in fact better off by the mid-1890s but from then until the outbreak of the First World War the standard of living for the working class was squeezed as prices rose. The general picture was accurately delineated at the time by the pioneering statistician A. L. Bowley, whose research into changes in the cost of living for the working class revealed a story 'of Victorian real wage amelioration and Edwardian immiserization'.[8]

Ideologists like G. J. Holyoake valorized co-operation and the consumer. He rescued mutual trade from the enormous condescension of Marxists and Christian Socialists, memorably criticizing J. M. Ludlow for regarding 'the consumer as a guzzler – a person all throat and gastric juice'.[9] And this consumer-driven movement grew at a tremendous rate so that by the early 1870s many local co-operative societies in the industrial north, north-east and east midlands especially had put down solid roots. Individual membership rose from 350,000 in 1873 to 628,000 a decade later, by which time there were well over 1,000 retail societies in existence. The total number of societies peaked in 1905, when there were 1,452 with 2,153,000 members. By 1914, total membership stood at over 3 million. Confirming Bowley's picture, the highest percentage increases in membership occurred before the turn of the century, with a slowdown in the early 1900s but growth thereafter. Some areas remained inimical to co-operative trade. Ports and holiday resorts such as Liverpool and Blackpool witnessed only sporadic advance because of the prevalence of casual labour and irregular earnings. With the exception of cities such as Gloucester and Plymouth, southern England was largely untouched by co-operation, including London until the 1920s.[10] Despite these limitations, the movement assumed a more visible national presence in the late nineteenth century. The foundation of the Co-operative Union as the central, federal body that provided legal advice, published literature and propaganda and promoted education aided this. It organized the annual congress held every spring from 1869, events which were attended by thousands of delegates from all over Britain and abroad by the turn of the century. Middle-class intellectuals and politicians who supported co-operation were honoured as presidents of early congresses – figures like Thomas Hughes, Thomas Brassey, Thorold Rogers and Alfred Marshall – but they were replaced from the early 1890s by working-class activists such as the indefatigable chairman of the English Co-operative Wholesale Society, J. T. W. Mitchell, thereby demonstrating the increasingly self-confident working-class character of the movement. National identity was further encouraged by the production of the *Co-operative News* from 1871 and the *Scottish Co-operator* from 1894.[11] Co-operatives had undoubtedly become a defining feature of working-class community life by the late nineteenth century. Stores had their own distinctive atmosphere and the movement's mutualistic ethos was communicated at a quotidian level by means of the goods they sold and the ritualistic distribution of 'dividend' that punctuated working-class life.

The goods stocked by the stores were increasingly manufactured by the movement itself, produced in factories owned by the English and Scottish Co-operative Wholesale Society (CWS, formed respectively in 1863 and 1868). Packaging of everyday foodstuffs that these organizations specialized in manufacturing such as flour, tea, pickles, jam and biscuits, carried the ubiquitous 'Wheatsheaf' logo (which the CWS staunchly defended against competitive rivals who wanted to use it), while boots and shoes made in CWS-owned factories were branded 'Progressive'. One key to the success of the wholesales was undoubtedly the much-vaunted purity of the goods they made. At a time when adulteration was rife, the 'Wheatsheaf' was a valuable guarantee of quality, so it was little wonder that capitalists wanted to borrow the logo as some of them were waking up to the commercial advantages of selling honest goods. Not all members of local co-operative societies were totally loyal buyers of CWS products, however, and stores invariably also sold commodities produced by private firms that were sometimes preferred by members, which generated frequent complaint.[12] It was not all honey and harmony in the co-operative movement and the tension between often fiercely independent local societies and the CWS did not abate; in 1890 societies in England and Wales only obtained 37 per cent of their produce by value from the CWS. Indeed, while the movement evolved organically as a federation, the separation of power between societies and the wholesales made it often appear dysfunctional.[13] Despite this 'seepage' of trade, the growth of the CWS was quite spectacular, making it one of the largest businesses of its kind in the world by the early twentieth century with a truly international reach. The English CWS established its own bank in 1872, which enabled the wholesale to help societies by granting loans and overdrafts. Numerous factories were opened to meet the expansion of working-class demand, competing directly with big capitalists such as W. H. Lever and Thomas Lipton for the soap and tea trade, for instance. Directors of the CWS, elected from the local societies, pursued a policy of backward vertical integration to meet this challenge, securing palm oil supplies from Sierra Leone and the Gold Coast and establishing tea plantations in Ceylon before 1914. Annual net sales grew inexorably, decade by decade, from £507,217 in 1870, to £3,339,681 in 1880, £7,429,073 in 1890, £16,043,889 in 1900, £26,567,833 in 1910, and a staggering £105,439,628 in 1920. Many of the movement's leaders drew from this advance the lesson that complete transformation of the existing social and economic order was not only feasible – it was already happening.[14]

A distinct culture grew up around co-operative stores and education was central to that culture. Like the earlier Owenite socialists, co-operative activists nationally and locally believed that continued advance depended on the growth of a committed, well-informed membership. Most societies consequently put aside a percentage of their annual surplus for the provision of libraries, lectures and classes in co-operative history and theory. Co-operators realized that outside agencies, whether state schools or capitalist newspapers, most often instilled a competitive ethos, and that they had to depend on their own efforts. As the American trust-busting journalist Henry Demarest Lloyd remarked: 'At a very early period in the movement, co-operation set before itself the task of becoming mentally independent as being quite as important as that of becoming independent in its groceries.'

For J. T. W. Mitchell, education of the right kind was necessary for successful association, enabling individuals to 'extinguish superstition and jealousy' that so often caused their ventures to founder and create a 'bond of united interest which no power on earth could break asunder'. Co-operative education also had a more ambitious purpose, according to Mitchell, eventually making it possible for working people to 'free themselves from the toil and misery which oppressed them' and bring about 'a heaven upon earth'.[15] Societies had their own education committees that organized provision and the one in Rochdale, on which Mitchell served, was very active; in the mid-1870s the society's library contained 12,000 volumes and its central newsroom supplied members with twenty-seven daily and fifty-five weekly periodicals. From the turn of the century, classes spread and, by 1914, nearly 17,000 children were being taught a heroic version of the movement's history using a textbook titled *Our Story*.[16] Many more thousands of people of all ages became deeply attached to the store through participating in the extensive social life that developed around it. For the CWS journalist Percy Redfern, the vitality of the movement culture depended not only on formal instruction but also on making the store 'the hub of pleasure as well as profit'. Local societies therefore organized a wide repertoire of social events that punctuated the calendar at regular intervals – celebrations to mark the opening of a new building or commemorate an important milestone in the society's history, tea parties and musical soirées, sports and games events and day trips to the country or seaside. Some societies established clubs for co-operative ramblers, photographers, naturalists and cyclists. Most effort was devoted to music, with many societies organizing large choirs which regularly competed against each other or combined for large events such as the annual National Co-operative Festival at the Crystal Palace. The scale of activity in this area was remarkable – 10,000 voices made up the co-operative choir that performed at this festival in 1897.[17]

A particular sense of the past was vital to this movement culture. It was communicated through classes as we have seen, but towards the end of the century scores of local societies also began to publish their jubilee histories to mark fifty years of successful trading. Usually written by one of the officers of the society, these texts were distributed free to members as part of a wider celebration, which demonstrated a considerable outlay for larger societies such as the Bolton Co-op that had 36,000 members in 1909, its jubilee year. For sure, the amateur historians who wrote these texts tended to portray the society as a powerful engine of material improvement but the tone was invariably and proudly class-conscious, with an emphasis on co-operation's wider ambitions both in the immediate area as well as more broadly. Indeed, one of the most striking characteristics of the movement in its golden age was this dynamic (if not always harmonious) relationship between local rootedness and national and international reach. As we have seen, the CWS was a global business and the culture of the movement was also internationalist in outlook. Delegates from other national movements both in Europe and beyond attended annual congresses in large numbers before the First World War. Co-operators began to realize that as capitalism was mutating and entering a different phase characterized increasingly by large companies and monopolies, so must they trade and associate on an international scale if the vision of a 'Co-operative Commonwealth' was ever to become reality.[18]

Evidence suggests that more and more activists in the movement came to share this wider ambition from towards the turn of the century, though Mitchell was a utopian long before then. In 1878 he had declared his faith in revolution through consumption: 'It was quite possible, if they joined together, to produce everything that they ate, everything that they wore, and everything that they used, and also to gradually get hold of the land'. Mitchell went on to deny that bringing everything under working-class ownership and control was 'a utopian idea', arguing that it was nothing more than an eminently 'practical idea of trade'.[19] In his presidential address to the annual congress in 1892 – held, fittingly, in Rochdale, Mitchell's home town – he took the opportunity to elaborate his 'ideology of consumption' in more detail, explaining how, by combining their consumer power and concentrating 'all their trade into one channel', the common people would be able to regain 'the profits of all trade, all industry, all distribution, all commerce, all importation, all banking and money dealing'. Mitchell believed, perhaps rather naively, that this could be done peacefully, without state legislation or the confiscation of property and not just in Britain but also globally.[20]

Despite this far-reaching ambition, co-operative culture only embraced a proportion of working-class consumers. Some were effectively excluded because of their poverty and hand to mouth existence that made it more difficult to maintain the regularity of habit on which co-operative success depended. Although co-operation was not confined to any putative 'labour aristocracy', membership of a society was undoubtedly a sign of respectability and was often beyond the reach of the lower echelons of the working class. More importantly, perhaps, most workers who shopped at the co-op did not belong to the committed minority but were rather more flexible in their consumption habits, and could be tempted by bargains on offer elsewhere. And bargains were often to be had; the late nineteenth century witnessed greater competition in retailing and the growth of multiple shop firms that could make use of economies of scale in buying to undercut rivals. Though the idea of a 'retailing revolution' detracts from the slow, evolutionary change that had characterized this sector over the longer term, the number of firms operating 25 or more branches grew most rapidly in this period, from just 10 in 1875 with 725 branches, to 94 in 1900 with 9,256 branches, to 180 in 1920 with 20,602 branches.[21] The largest of these firms eventually became household names with chains of shops all over the country selling foodstuffs but also clothing and other household goods: Sainsbury's (from 1869), Lipton's (from 1871), Boots (from 1883), Home and Colonial Stores (from 1883), Marks & Spencer (from 1884), and Maypole Dairy Company (from 1887).

Owners of multiple firms emulated co-operative societies in some respects, utilizing the principles of low prices, cash transactions and high turnover of stock. From the first store in Glasgow in 1871, Lipton spread out across Scotland before moving south of the border in the 1880s. By the end of that decade, annual turnover was £1.5 million and there were over thirty shops and nearly 1,000 employees. Like the CWS, whenever he could Lipton tried to secure supplies direct from source, whether it was ham from Ireland or tea from Ceylon, thus cutting out the middleman and reducing expenses.[22] But unlike co-operatives, Lipton also frequently made extensive use of advertising to puff his goods and, as we noted in Chapter 4, his success depended as much on his talent for showmanship as it did on the efficiency of his business. Lipton had visited the United States before opening his first shop and American methods had made a deep impression. Lipton advertised heavily in the expanding press, naturally, but taking his cue from the American showman and businessman P. T. Barnum, he became particularly famous for his promotional stunts. He paraded giant cheeses through the streets, offering a monster cheese weighing five tons for the Queen's jubilee celebrations in 1887 (Victoria declined the offer). Another stunt involved a troop of thin men marching to his stores carrying signs saying 'Going to Lipton's', while fat men left the stores with signs saying 'We've just been to Lipton's'. Any trick to catch the consumer's eye and keep the Lipton brand before the public was tried. And like a good showman, Lipton also rubbed shoulders with music-hall celebrities such as Harry Lauder, as well as royalty, donating all the tea (and £25,000 cash) to the Princess of Wales fund for the poor in 1897. A knighthood followed soon after.[23]

Most shopkeepers were unlike the celebrity grocer Thomas Lipton. In 1900, multiple retailers only controlled 3–4.5 per cent of total retail trade, rising to 6–7.5 per cent in 1910 and 7–10 per cent in 1920. Comparative figures for co-operative societies are 6–7 per cent in 1900, 7–8 per cent in 1910 and 7.5–9 per cent in 1920. The rest of the retail trade, the vast majority, was made up of shopkeepers of all kinds and descriptions – grocers, bakers, ironmongers, butchers, pawnbrokers, drapers, fishmongers, greengrocers, tobacconists, wine merchants, chemists, stationers and booksellers – and combined figures for these other retailers was 86.5–90 per cent in 1900, 81.5–85.5 per cent in 1910 and 77–82.5 per cent in 1920.[24] There were relatively small shifts in the sector, certainly, but the persistence of small shopkeepers and their continued importance cannot be denied, despite the fact that many commentators thought that their days were numbered and they would inevitably be squeezed out by large 'combines' and the co-op. Their continued popularity is explained by a number of factors. Private stores were convenient, part of the ecology of working-class neighbourhood. Crucially, they were also deeply embedded in the social texture of everyday life, their success inextricably bound up with that of the community they served. In short, small shopkeepers did not compose a distinct stratum completely separate from the wider working class but were bound to that class in an ambiguous, liminal relationship. They frequently functioned as 'bankers of the poor', offering credit or 'tick' that enabled consumers to make ends meet until payday.[25]

As working-class mothers most often controlled the family purse strings, cultivating and handling this relationship was a particularly important skill for them to develop. The pawnbroker of course was the most obvious source of credit available to working people, but other forms of credit developed in the late nineteenth century, including the check trading system that emerged out of credit rotation societies. The most famous of these was the Provident Clothing and Supply Co. Ltd, founded by Joshua Waddilove in Bradford in 1880.[26] Shopkeepers in general, however, also made it possible for poor consumers to better eke out a living on a pound a week or so. This nexus was often strained to breaking point if the community was in crisis – during a strike, for instance – when traders had to be careful not to alienate their customers but also avoid going under. Even respectable workers who tried to be loyal to the co-op often used these shops when times were hard because of an economic downturn, industrial unrest, accident or illness. Despite regular denunciations of the 'evils' of credit trading from the movement's leaders, many co-operative societies even offered some forms of credit before 1914 and this became much more common in the interwar years.[27] Nevertheless, the attitude of the co-op was generally hostile towards practices that for a great many families were a necessary part of daily living. Shopkeepers developed their own identities and support networks, establishing trade associations from the late nineteenth century which enabled them to fix the prices of many commodities – including bread, sugar, cheese, soap, ham as well as many other common goods – much to the chagrin of co-operators. They also attacked the co-op directly, first in Scotland in the 1890s and then nationally from the early twentieth century by means of a Traders' Defence Association that tried, unsuccessfully, to boycott local societies. Unlike their continental counterparts, British shopkeepers generally remained attached to the main political parties but they were not therefore politically inert, playing important roles within both Liberal and Conservative parties, increasingly in the latter by the end of this period as economic and social pressures on them – both real and imagined – grew more intense.[28]

Challenges to liberal consumerism

During the late nineteenth century, most co-operative leaders continued to believe that the separation of politics from economics was sacrosanct and that it had facilitated the success of their movement, despite the fact that two other rising ideologies which also spoke to the interests of ordinary consumers – protectionism and socialism – threatened to bridge that divide. It is to the competing appeals to the consumer made by these ideologies that we must now turn. The onset of economic depression in 1873 and the spread of protectionist policies across Europe in the decade that followed forced a rethinking of attitudes towards free trade. Calls for 'retaliation' and 'reciprocity' – that is, the end of what critics called 'one-sided' free trade between Britain and countries that practised protectionism – were commonly heard in the press and various chambers of commerce declared against free trade. Protectionist clubs and organizations sprang up in places such as Sheffield, Birmingham and Wolverhampton, including the National and Patriotic League for the Protection of British Interests, which was aimed squarely at workers. At a meeting in Hyde Park in 1878, its secretary R. H. Armit declared that their object was to end 'the Bright-Gladstone Free Trade bastard policy'.[29] The growing popular appeal of protectionism may account for splits within the ranks of the co-operative movement at this time; Conservative co-operative societies were operated successfully in Bacup, Darwen, Oldham and even in Rochdale during the 1870s, though they did not spread.[30] Eventually in 1881, a National Fair Trade League (NFTL) was established. Led by William Farrer Ecroyd, the owner of a worsted manufacturing firm in Burnley and Conservative MP for Preston, the League's manifesto argued for a preferential system of tariffs that would maximize the potential of the empire to supply Britain's demand for food, raw materials and luxury goods, whilst enabling colonies to purchase British manufactures at a reduced rate. Ecroyd stressed that what he wanted was 'real free trade' rather than 'one-sided trade', a 'Free-trade Empire' that would 'promote the prosperity of all classes'. Public response during its early years was disappointing, most likely because the economy picked up. Over the course of the decade, however, manufacturers and consumers increasingly recognized the advantages of protection for British products in home markets and entry to foreign markets by means of retaliation and the League spread throughout the country. By the mid-1880s, the number of provincial branches stood at 500, while more than 100,000 pamphlets were being distributed weekly.[31]

The NFTL attempted to speak on behalf of working people in their role as consumers. Producers were important for fair traders and the movement did indeed gain a good deal of support from workers in industries such as silk weaving and sugar refining that were hit hard by foreign competition. But the NFTL also sought to wrest ordinary consumers away from free trade ideology, which according to the Lancashire manufacturer Robert Boyd had hoodwinked working-class consumers into believing that they were getting a better deal when in reality they were only making other classes richer. Thus, free trade according to Boyd was 'nothing but class legislation, apparently in favour of the consumer, but which will in reality bring about the annihilation of both producer and consumer'.[32] Fair traders such as Ecroyd similarly argued that fiscal policy should favour working-class consumers, who would then be able to afford to pay small increases on certain foodstuffs. He advocated a duty of 10 per cent on French manufactures and lambasted English capitalists who invested overseas and took advantage of cheap, unprotected labour while domestic producers and consumers were increasingly impoverished.[33] These were common themes in fair trade propaganda but they were also echoed in the radical press, including *Reynolds's Newspaper* that regularly advocated taxation of foreign luxuries. 'Gracchus', for example, though against taxing the common people's food, strongly supported taxing luxury imports and even advised workers to back the League if they made this distinction clear. 'Northumbrian' went further, advising workers 'to turn the free trade fetish over' and tax 'Lady De Fitzurse's silk jacket and French boots and the champagne which her noble spouse drinks'.[34]

The impact of this agitation on the Conservative Party was significant. After their defeat in the 1880 general election, many leading Tories became more openly sympathetic towards protectionist schemes, including Lord Randolph Churchill and Lord Salisbury. When the party briefly returned to power in 1885, many of Salisbury's leading men were favourable to protection, including Lord Dunraven, undersecretary for the colonies. Aided by the extension of the franchise – the Third Reform Act enfranchised about 2.5 million men – the cause gained ground: 'Fair trade, you have no idea what a hold it has upon the artisans,' observed Joseph Chamberlain after the 1885 general election.[35] Gladstone's Irish Home Rule Bill, which split the Liberal Party the year after, transformed the situation; Liberal Unionist MPs who were strong free traders lent their support to Salisbury in order to maintain the union with Ireland on condition that the issue of fair trade was sidelined. Despite being hamstrung in this manner, protectionists calculated that they could count on support from sixty-four members in the new parliament, enough to disturb the Cobden Club. Checked at Westminster, the NFTL shifted its focus, maintaining pressure through Conservative associations and the Primrose League, but the campaign lacked leadership. A relatively unknown, recently elected Sheffield MP, Howard Vincent, put himself forward as spokesman for fair trade at the party's Oxford Conference in November 1887. Vincent's motion to back this policy received overwhelming support, with only about a dozen delegates out of a thousand voting against it. Salisbury worked hard to silence controversy; as the NFTL's weekly journal, *Fair Trade*, reported, ordinary party members were 'sat upon both by local and national chiefs'.[36] Although it could be argued that in the short term fair trade achieved little, it illustrated much, not least substantial popular disillusionment with the ideology of free trade.[37] As one working-class Conservative noted, the cause of protection made steady progress among 'the masses' after the Oxford vote, with radical working men's clubs welcoming lectures on the subject because they realized that 'our present so-called Free Trade system is not Free Trade at all, but that it is a system that is mainly in the interests of the capitalist, foreign investors, pensioners, people with settled incomes, and most likely the majority of the rich'.[38]

Protectionists were not the only ones trying to wrest ordinary consumers away from Liberal free trade in the late nineteenth century. Socialists made their own appeal, though their attitudes varied. Some rejected it wholesale but the issue often provoked responses that were more complex because many of them shared the ambivalence of the wider working class. Free trade ideology exerted a tenacious hold over popular consciousness at the end of the nineteenth century for two main reasons. First, it was integral to a progressive view of history that was widely accepted among labour leaders, furnishing a belief that things were better than they had been in the past as well as the hope that improvement would continue into the future.[39] The Leeds socialist Tom Maguire saw the coming struggle as fundamentally about alternative versions of the past, which pointed to alternative paths of development. Writing in the *Christian Socialist* in 1884, Maguire argued that it had been 'the Bright and Cobden cry of "Free Trade and Corn Law Repeal"' which, combined with 'capitalist combination', had 'annihilated Chartism'. Socialist advance depended therefore on the recovery of lost traditions: 'Ernest Jones and Bronterre O'Brien are forgotten, ridiculed out of history. John Bright and Richard Cobden are household words.'[40] The second major obstacle that radical critics of free trade faced was that the policy had demonstrably worked from the point of view of the organized working class. Trade unions, friendly societies and consumer co-operatives had come to accept that their security and future success was bound up with the continued separation of the political state from civil society. They had internalized the division between political and economic domains as the best framework for action and were extremely wary of state intervention that challenged this separation – hence the suspicion or even hostility towards social reform legislation voiced by some working-class leaders and their frequent repudiation of tariff reform.[41] Socialists thus faced a very difficult task and found it far from easy to replace the hope furnished by free trade ideology with their own brand of utopianism.

Many tried, however. Henry Champion, a leading figure in the Social Democratic Federation (SDF), preferred to side with fair traders rather than 'the Free Trader of the foolish Manchester kind', and even wrote in the protectionist's national newspaper urging them to back demands for the rights of labour. Though Champion often traded on xenophobic fears of foreign immigration among the working class, he also tried to convince trade unionists that their own organizations were no more than forms of protection and that free trade and capitalist exploitation went hand in hand.[42] Others linked consumer exploitation to the growth of capitalist monopolies, whose covert machinations served to expose the mythological nature of the 'free' market. James Blackwell, for instance, condemned the way in which workers were robbed as consumers by the 'rings' that raised prices of basic foodstuffs. 'Every commodity now is apparently susceptible of being made the subject of a "corner"', Harry Quelch, editor of the SDF's national weekly paper *Justice* wrote, 'and the great salt syndicate is being followed by syndicates in coal, in paper, in firebrick, and other commodities'. Quelch attempted to dispel what he described as 'the bourgeois economic heresies of the Manchester school', most especially the 'Liberal Free Trade humbug' or 'the "Free Trade" Fraud', which he considered to be the major ideological obstacle blocking socialist politics before the First World War.[43] Liberal free traders had also routinely denounced monopolies as inimical to the consumers' interest, certainly, but Liberal politicians had done nothing to check their growth in practice. The SDF's condemnation of free trade as little more than 'false consciousness' was the clearest position taken by any socialist organization but others on the left were also highly critical, demonstrating the limitations of the idea of a shared liberal 'Free Trade culture' at this time.[44] Shortly before the foundation of the Independent Labour Party (ILP) in 1893, Keir Hardie argued that socialists had to throw over free trade which may have 'cheapened the necessaries of life; but it has not improved the relative position of the worker'. Hardie did not underestimate the ideological hold of free trade nor its pernicious effects, once declaiming at a public meeting: 'The hanging wind of Free Trade radicalism had swept over the nation and destroyed all that is most beautiful in our nature.'[45]

Socialists thus strongly contested Liberal claims concerning the material advantages of free trade and the 'cheap loaf' and were frequently 'sickened at the sight of a few fat plutocrats lolling back in velvet-lined carriages, and a great army of workers pining in the slums'.[46] However, they found it difficult to develop a more positive attitude towards the world of goods, or at least towards mass-produced commodities and modern consumer culture. Some kinds of consumption were heartily approved on the left. Following John Ruskin's advice that one should not give any object houseroom that did not beautify its surroundings, William Morris and the Arts and Crafts Movement made healthy profits furnishing the homes of the wealthy. Liberty's department store helped feed this elite consumerism in the metropolis from the late nineteenth century.[47] Educating the taste of well-heeled consumers was one thing, reforming the consumption practices of 'unenlightened' workers was another matter entirely. In fact, though Annie Besant noted how the spread of popular education allied to increases in purchasing power had 'developed tastes which crave for gratification', there was little serious thinking about how to address the actual predilections of workers as consumers.[48] Instead, there was an overriding emphasis on the importance of restraint in terms of private consumption allied with increased social expenditure, as well as almost unanimous condemnation of existing practices. As John Burns famously put it: 'The curse of the working classes is the fewness of their wants, the poverty of their desires, the over-loading of a few sensuous tastes, the absence of a varied set of elevated and healthy desires.'[49] Often underpinned by nonconformist belief, this fundamentally ascetic approach to consumption represented a serious obstacle to understanding. Robert Blatchford was another who recommended the cultivation of the mind in preference to the satisfaction of the body. In his best-selling pamphlet *Merrie England* (1893) he contrasted the worker imagined by the 'Manchester School' who was interested only in the satisfaction of animal needs – 'With them it is a question of bread and cheese and be thankful' – with his own ideal which he summarized as 'frugality of body and opulence of mind'. Although not quite so hard line as Burns (who was a teetotaller), Blatchford also emphasized the psychological satisfaction that knowledge, social intercourse and music conferred, particularly music, which was 'more delightful and more precious than all the vanities wealth can buy, or all the carnal luxuries that folly can desire'. Popular consumerism for Blatchford was a kind of cheap trick played on working people that obscured inequalities. He admitted that free trade capitalism had made it possible for workers to buy more things but questioned the real value of many modern comforts, turning his nose up at 'cheap and vulgar' carpets or 'fifth-rate music' played on 'cheap pianos' that working people often preferred to 'the songs of the gushing streams and joyous birds', ignoring the fact that goods such as carpets and pianos made possible the social intercourse and catered to the emotional needs that he prized so highly. One wonders how many workers who read *Merrie England* thought Blatchford rather a snob.[50]

Protectionist and socialist arguments gained traction in the last decades of the nineteenth century as it became clearer that many members of the working class were shut out from the free trade utopia. Average real wages may have risen considerably during this period but improvement was unevenly distributed and gains were very precarious. The researches of social investigators exposed what a narrow path a great many working-class families negotiated between scarcity and survival. Charles Booth's monumental study of the London poor began to appear in 1889, and demands for state intervention became more urgent thereafter. Booth's work demonstrated that the experience of poverty was a structural feature of the working-class life cycle, regardless of workers' behaviour as individuals. No matter how hard they worked as producers or how thriftily they laid out their income as consumers, poverty was an inescapable feature of working-class life. It meant that if they were lucky or rather unlucky enough to survive into old age, prospects for the vast majority were very bleak indeed as they were imprisoned within what Booth's fellow investigator Seebohm Rowntree was later to describe as the 'poverty cycle'. They clung on heroically with help from Poor Law and family, though Booth observed how 'a growing neglect of parents by their children is reported' in the more anonymous context of big cities. It was not only the London poor whose lives were deformed in this way either, as research by Rowntree and others made abundantly clear.[51] These revelations helped fuel public debate about the limits of voluntary solutions to the problem of poverty and a fault line opened up between 'individualists', who continued to advocate a laissez faire approach and 'collectivists', who urged state action as the only effective option.[52] And although working-class organizations had been traditionally hostile to state intervention, even bodies such as the friendly and co-operative societies were converted to social reform from the turn of the century, as it became more and more apparent that many workers were simply too poor to benefit from voluntary associations.[53]

If Booth's research furnished ample empirical proof that wealth had failed to trickle down sufficiently under free trade and that the lives of many consumers was in desperate need of improvement, the work of the radical economist J. A. Hobson provided a more theoretical explanation of the problem of unemployment that caused so much deprivation. Hobson agreed with the optimists that the 'standard of consumption' had been raised for all classes in recent decades but disputed claims that even the lot of 'the residuum' had improved significantly.[54] Moreover, Hobson also stressed that any increase had been far less rapid than the growth in productive power and rejected the widely held belief in Say's law, which stated that supply created its own demand, arguing for a radical approach to tackle a fundamental imbalance that affected the whole economy, not just a few trades subject to seasonal fluctuations. What was required, Hobson maintained, was 'a commensurate revolution in the consuming habits of the people' to match the massive growth in productive power unleashed by industrial capitalism. It was patently obvious, he thought, that at the moment many who desired to consume simply lacked the necessary means, while the well-off could not spend all their income, which was diverted into unproductive investment, much of it overseas, thus exacerbating domestic unemployment. For Hobson, the key issue was therefore the disequilibrium between production and consumption that was only worsened by private interest working through the market. Rejecting simplistic, piecemeal remedies for unemployment such as bimetallism, land reform and labour colonies, Hobson proposed a general 'raising of the standard of consumption' that would require a political commitment to what he called 'progressive consumption' to solve the problem of working-class underconsumption.[55] This entailed boosting working-class purchasing power by means of a redistribution of income through death duties and increases in income tax, enabling poor consumers to buy more goods and in turn stimulate employment. Such ideas served to destabilize further liberal consumerism but they also helped to save free trade finance and restore the hegemony of the Liberal Party, as we shall see in the next section.

Consumers in revolt

Liberal consumerism was under sustained pressure from the late nineteenth century as people increasingly questioned the ability of free trade to deliver the goods. The crisis of liberal consumerism involved a fundamental assault on the Gladstonian fiscal constitution. By the turn of the century, divisions had opened up within the business community, with important elements in the City and industry moving away from free trade and lending support for reciprocity and retaliation targeted against the 'dumping' of specific foreign goods, as in the Brussels sugar convention of 1902. Eventually, both zealous Cobdenites and moderate free traders came to the conclusion that the fiscal state was at 'the end of its tether' and recommended a shift from direct to indirect taxation to right matters.[56] On the other hand, protectionist demands became intertwined with arguments in favour of closer links with the colonies, thus forging stronger bonds between imperialism and consumerism, which free trade ideology had obscured with a benign, progressive internationalism.[57] The idea of an imperial zollverein was taken up by the charismatic Joseph Chamberlain, who stressed the material benefits for working-class consumers that would result from preferential trade agreements, making this a central ambition after he became secretary of state for the colonies in 1895.[58] His critics at the Cobden Club did not tire of underlining the weaknesses of his economic arguments but this was to miss the point.[59] For Chamberlain, empire was never simply a material calculation; the idea of a 'Greater Britain' also signified an alternative utopia, a world-historical mission to replace the vision of civilized, peaceful advance through free trade imagined by the Anti-Corn Law League half a century before.[60]

Chamberlain was a new kind of politician. He not only grasped the significance of the new imperialism and helped bring it into being but also understood the present as 'an age of advertising'; scholars have taught us much about the interconnections between modern advertising and the new imperialism in recent years as we have previously noted and Chamberlain's career evidences these linkages. He saw in imperial consumerism an exotic, romantic fantasy world that would appeal to the imaginations as well as the pocketbooks of working-class consumers. His political influence depended on his abilities as 'an advertising statesman', as an insightful article in the *Speaker* observed. According to the writer, what distinguished Chamberlain from his contemporaries was that he had fully embraced commercial forms of publicity and conducted himself like 'a pushing tradesman' or 'the Universal Provider of Westbourne Grove', William Whiteley. Moreover, Chamberlain's involvement in the scandalous Jameson Raid suggested that he could be as disingenuous as 'the patentees of rival soaps and pills'.[61] The briefest backward glance at Bright or Gladstone is sufficient to underscore the shift that had taken place here; though committed to Britain's industrial and commercial hegemony, for them politics was necessarily above business, involved the creation of 'character' and was therefore a quintessentially moral practice.[62] Moreover, neither was afraid to go against the grain – over Crimea or Ireland, for example – while Chamberlain happily trimmed his views to suit the marketplace of 'public opinion' in an era of 'mass' democracy.[63]

The landscape of politics was transformed utterly by Chamberlain's crusade for tariff reform and imperial preference that began in 1903. Henceforth, he dominated the national political stage, spellbinding audiences throughout the country with his oratory. Like earlier fair traders, Chamberlain addressed his message directly at the working class, in their roles as both producers and consumers. Tariff reform was central to the strategy of 'radical Conservatism', an attempt by the most dynamic elements in the party to come to terms with democracy before the First World War. The issue of employment was important to the campaign but Chamberlain frequently insisted that the abandonment of free trade was also vital in order to protect or raise workers' 'standard of living', that 'the working man in every case is both a consumer and a producer', and that as 'a consumer you will not lose, your cost of living will be as cheap as ever, but as a producer you will gain'.[64] Pointing to the rediscovery of working-class poverty over the previous decade or so, Chamberlain sarcastically mocked 'Cobden Club figures' which purported to show 'that we are progressing in a wonderful way'. Instead, the failure of free trade was palpable, visible in both city and country so that perhaps thirteen million people 'are underfed and on the verge of hunger'. He deconstructed narratives of progress underpinning free trade ideology – attacking the Anti-Corn Law League as a 'middle-class movement that was hated by the Chartists' – and spoke to working-class trade unionists over the heads of their leaders who publicly repudiated tariff reform. Chamberlain argued that many vital problems facing workers, including the dumping of sweated and prison-made goods, as well as the impoverishment of poor consumers, would only be solved by breaching the separation of political and economic domains, which he maintained was already happening, demonstrated by recent legislation that eroded the 'bad doctrine of laisser faire which was the bottom of the policy of Free Traders in times before we appreciated our position as a great Imperial race'.[65]

Chamberlain gave what was probably his best and certainly his most famous speech during the early phase of the campaign in Birmingham, when he deployed his considerable skills as a showman as well as a public orator to great effect. Referring to the 'flaming posters' that had been plastered by Liberals on the streets of the city over the preceding weeks, in which a 'mammoth' free trade loaf was juxtaposed with a much smaller loaf shrunken by the impact of tariff reform, Chamberlain related how he had asked a friend to make two loaves with different quantities of corn that could be purchased for the same amount of money before and after the proposed tax. Chamberlain nearly brought the house down when, with a dramatic flourish, he produced the loaves and playfully remarked:

> Now, gentlemen, I do not know whether your eyes are better than mine, but I admit when I first saw those loaves I said, which is the big one and which is the little one? I know there is a difference, because I know that the small one is the one in which less flour has been used in order to

correspond with the amount of the tax. But I did not realise the important question, which was the big one and which was the little one. (Laughter).

However, Chamberlain also had a serious moral message and he went on in this speech and others to propose an alternative to the narrow self-interest that, he argued, characterized liberal consumerism. It was a vision of the British people as imperial consumers in which the 'great mission' of the working class loomed large, a mission to build an empire 'greater, more united, more fruitful for good, than any Empire in human history (great cheering)'.[66] Many powerful supporters found such rhetoric highly seductive, including the newspaper magnate Alfred Harmsworth who believed that tariff reform represented no less than 'a social and commercial revolution'. The *Daily Mail* strongly backed Chamberlain and even organized an opinion poll or 'a general election in advance' – with cash prizes ranging from £10 to £1,000 for the most assiduous collectors of voting papers – in order to test 'public opinion on the great fiscal question of the hour'.[67]

Faced with this challenge, Liberals coordinated a remarkable counter-attack that represented one of the most imaginative political campaigns in modern British history.[68] Throughout the country a host of organizations, including not only Liberal and Conservative free traders and the Cobden Club but also working-class associations, notably the co-operative movement and the WCG, mobilized against protection. Spearheaded by the Free Trade Union and its auxiliary bodies, the battle was fought by means of colourful posters, pamphlets, open-air lectures, public meetings and free trade shops. As in the 1840s, the people's bread again became an issue of fierce political contention, though free traders also maintained that tariff reform would drive up the price of all basic foodstuffs. The Liberal Party postcard reproduced as Figure 9 shows the hand of tariff reform literally reaching into the home to rob from the housewives' cupboard.

There was even a riot in sleepy High Wycombe when supporters of free trade demolished a 'dump shop' which tariff reformers had opened to display cheap foreign goods that were undercutting the products of British labour. As noted above, a recent historian has suggested that this campaign successfully mobilized a 'Free Trade culture' that had deep roots in civil society, penetrating across classes.[69] Although this view has a good deal to recommend it, there are problems with it. For one thing, voters backed the Liberal cause for various reasons; though the defence of free trade and the 'cheap loaf' was certainly important, it was inextricably bound up with promises of state intervention to remedy the problems facing poorer consumers. Tariff reform therefore increased pressure for social legislation within the Liberal Party, which had to find new ways to shore up popular support for free trade. Moreover, there is little evidence that ordinary consumers were moved either way – working-class autobiographies that discuss this period are overwhelmingly silent on the issue. Expediency was

FIGURE 9 *Liberal postcard, 1905. © Frank Trentmann.*

often the chief consideration. Discussing the attitudes of trade unionists, for example, the dockers' leader John Burns confided to the German economic historian Carl Fuchs: 'They are for Free Trade so long as this seems to further their interests; they will adopt protection or Fair Trade, without dogmatic or theoretic scruples, should they at any time see any advantage in it.'[70]

Defeat in the 1906 general election ended almost two decades of Conservative rule; the party lost 246 seats, polling just 43.4 per cent of the popular vote. Despite this setback, the cause of tariff reform continued to gain momentum. Disseminated through various party organizations, protectionist ideas resonated widely and indeed, it is the vibrancy of the 'Tariff Reform culture' produced during this period that strikes the historian as much as any putative 'Free Trade culture'. The Tariff Reform League boasted 600 branches by 1910, the largest of which had 1,000 members.[71] Its chairman, the press baron Arthur Pearson, brought the sensationalist techniques of the 'new journalism' to the struggle. He sponsored a 'Fiscal Parrot Show' in the *Daily Express* that offered prizes to birds which repeated the phrase 'Your food will cost you more', a slogan which, tariff reformers claimed, had been drummed into free traders 'parrot fashion'. Other stunts included a national tour by an actress and a chorus of artisans who recited tariff reform monologues from a lorry decorated with a huge photograph of 'Our Joe'.[72] A labour wing was also formed – the Trade Union Tariff Reform Association – which had 27 branches in Lancashire alone by the end of 1910 and a total membership of 10,000.[73] Recent revisionist work on the Conservative Party has shown how the issue of tariff reform remained central to the party up to and beyond the First World War. Impressive celebrations were staged to mark 'Chamberlain Day' and it is estimated that membership of the Tariff Reform League had reached 250,000 by 1914.[74] Music hall songs more often extolled the benefits of imperial trade than of free trade, as in 'The John Bull Store', performed at the Alhambra in 1903 with Chamberlain's portrait as a backdrop on stage. Themes of national decline, xenophobia and patriotic rebirth were combined in its verses:

When our Nelson kept the British flag a-flying,
When we hammered Boney on the shore,
There were traders coming hat in hand a-buying
At the counter of the John Bull Store.
When we'd beaten all our foes, then, as everybody knows,
They were begging for the things we made,
For the German, Yank, and Russ, tho' they liked to sneer at us,
Weren't a patch upon John Bull at Trade.

But an altered tale our present day is telling,
For the Empire's glory seems to fade;
We're buying where we used to go a-selling,
And the foreigner has grabbed our trade.

> Just when things are looking black and the orders getting slack
> Comes a champion leaping to the fore,
> With an eye-glass in his eye that the quicker he could spy
> What is wanting in the John Bull Store.[75]

Mass-market goods were frequently emblazoned with symbols of empire as we have seen and connections between imperialism and consumerism were easily forged. Tariff reformers also reached out specifically to female consumers, especially housewives, as we can see from Figure 10, which was produced as a leaflet and a postcard and shows a housewife, disillusioned by hollow promises, forcefully ejecting a Liberal canvasser from her kitchen.

Bodies such as the Women's Unionist and Tariff Reform Association organized drama and study groups in support of the cause and claimed 300,000 members in the late Edwardian period, though its main strength admittedly lay in the south and the west midlands, rather than in the industrial north. Popular conservatism was clearly a dynamic force and much of its dynamism was owing to an ongoing engagement with the consumer.[76]

The Liberal Party saved free trade after its election victory by introducing measures of social reform. As noted earlier in this chapter, historians have stressed how organized workers traditionally preferred collective self-help to

FIGURE 10 *Conservative Party leaflet, 1910. © Conservative Party.*

solve the problem of poverty and distrusted state intervention, but by 1904 the Ancient Order of Foresters, the second largest friendly society in the country, had come out in favour of old age pensions, as had the co-operative movement that acknowledged the inadequacy of voluntary methods three years before. Although the ILP supported local rather than central state intervention throughout the 1890s, during the 1906 campaign 81 per cent of the Labour Representation Committee election addresses mentioned pensions. Liberal addresses prioritized free trade, certainly, but at least two-thirds of them also discussed pensions.[77] Pressured from all sides and realizing the precariousness of their longer-term position, Liberals pledged themselves to universal, non-contributory old age pensions a month after being elected and this cut the ground from under tariff reformers. Although the pension was niggardly – 5s. a week for those over seventy who had not been to prison or were known inebriates – financing the scheme necessitated a complete remodelling of the fiscal regime, which provoked a profound constitutional crisis when the House of Lords refused to ratify Lloyd George's 'People's Budget' of 1909 that proposed substantial increases in direct and indirect taxation to fund the measure.[78] As Richard Haldane, secretary of state for war, confided to the prime minister, Herbert Asquith, the budget represented 'a bulwark against the nationalization of wealth'.[79] There was heated debate in the country, with Winston Churchill urging the necessity of a 'National Minimum' to bridge the yawning gulf between poverty and wealth and heal the 'savage strife between class and class'. Ironically for someone whose liking for fine champagne and good cigars was already notorious, Churchill denounced the decadence of a society characterized by 'the swift increase of vulgar, joyless luxury' in almost Veblenesque fashion, arguing that it was this that threatened national and imperial stability rather than any 'Yellow peril' or 'Black peril'.[80] The budget was eventually forced through after two general elections in 1910 and although the Liberals won both times, portraying the contest as a historic struggle against parasitic wealthy food taxers and their sinister allies in the Lords, their majority was seriously reduced and they were now more dependent than ever on support from Labour and Irish MPs. The party had lost a total of 127 seats by the end of the year and their share of the votes had been reduced to a mere 43.9 per cent, not much more than Conservatives had polled in their crushing defeat nearly five years earlier.[81]

Both Liberal free traders and Tory protectionists failed to mobilize fully ordinary consumers before the First World War. Economic stagnation and rising unemployment fuelled the great wave of labour unrest that swept Britain in the years immediately preceding the outbreak of war, making the battle between free trade and tariff reform appear increasingly marginal. While politicians attempted to corral working-class consumers for protection or free trade with increasing vigour in Edwardian England, this does not mean that their appeals had much more than a superficial impact. To reiterate, what little evidence there is concerning popular attitudes suggests a lack of interest; John Burns's observation about the instrumental attitude of trade unionists on this issue seems highly plausible. In *The Ragged-Trousered Philanthropists* (1914), for example, which was based on the experience of the 1906 general election, workers are pulled back and forth between tariff reform and free trade, their support for either cause often shallow and short-lived. Robert Noonan had many perceptive things to say about the political contest in Hastings where he lived and worked. Compared to Tory posters, he observed, 'Liberal posters were not quite so offensive. They were more cunning, more specious, more hypocritical and consequently more calculated to mislead and deceive the more intelligent of the voters.'[82] The contemporary social investigator Stephen Reynolds may have been less disillusioned and less angry than Noonan but he also emphasized the wide gulf between political parties and working-class consciousness. As Mr Perring remarks in Reynolds's insightful study written in the wake of the 1910 general election: '"Last 'lection was supposed to be between Tariff Reform an' Free Trade. But come to it, they was all chattering 'bout the Navy and Lord Charles Beresford. That's all thee cou'st hear on 'lection day. They tries for to miz-maze 'ee up a-purpose, so's you shall vote according to their opinion 'stead of your own. An' they thinks the likes o' us don't know we'm being fooled. But us do."'[83]

The war finally put paid to free trade's aspirations to be an authentically popular creed. It broke down much of the aversion towards state intervention as major areas of economic life became subject to control, thus collapsing together politics and economics that liberal consumerism had sought to keep separate. Most important, wartime conditions encouraged a more radical politicization of consumption. The membership of the co-operative movement grew tremendously between 1914 and 1919, rising from just over 3 million to well over 4 million, as the material and ideological logic of co-operative methods of trade seemed an increasingly preferable alternative to the anarchy of the capitalist 'free' market. The movement became particularly aggrieved by what it perceived to be unfair treatment by government at local and national level. Co-operators were largely excluded from the food committees that controlled distribution of supplies on the ground and which were often packed with hostile private traders and Conservatives. Matters came to a head with the imposition of Excess Profits Duty in 1916. Designed to quieten public concerns over 'profiteering', the measure made no distinction between private capitalist firms and the co-op and although a loophole was soon found that enabled avoidance of the tax, the episode demonstrated to many co-operators that the state could no longer claim to be impartial and that the movement had to protect its interests itself.[84]

The mass of consumers were also becoming more incensed as war dragged on. The reluctance of the government to introduce rationing fuelled discontent among a public struggling to cope with rising prices and serious food shortages made worse by a relentless U-boat campaign.[85]

Consumers mostly queued patiently for dwindling supplies, though in West Cumberland they resorted to direct action and rioted, recalling earlier traditions of 'moral economy'.[86] Consumer discontent may not have been as serious as it was in Berlin or even Paris but it was sufficient for the government to be very concerned – the co-operative movement was kept under surveillance at this time as a potential 'Revolutionary Organisation'.[87] Government responded to this crisis in a number of ways. At the Ministry of Food, established early in 1917 to ensure the civilian population was properly fed, Lord Rhondda replaced the ineffective Lord Devonport as food controller. Rationing was introduced and a new body – a Consumers' Council – was set up to facilitate communication with organized labour and included representatives of working-class associations, including co-operators. Although the Consumers' Council had little more than symbolic effect and failed to check 'profiteering' that many claimed thrived even after war ended, the strategy of appeasement worked in the short term and discontent subsided. The effects of this phase on the organized consumer were long lasting, however, with the co-operative movement officially entering the political field in 1917 with the formation of a Co-operative Party.[88] In the volatile situation at the end of the war, it was not clear that the politics of production would trump the politics of consumption as far as labour was concerned. In a conference held in London in October 1917, for example, Arthur Henderson, general secretary of the Labour Party, emphasized how urgent it was to 'combine the whole of democracy' and may have even contemplated joining forces with co-operators in a 'People's Party'. Such unifying ambitions were to be quickly dashed as economic slump and industrial 'rationalization' served to further divide ordinary producers from consumers.[89]

PART THREE

A Consumers' Democracy: 1920–2000

Preface

Consumer culture in Britain fully matured during the short twentieth century, from the aftermath of the First World War to the end of the millennium. Citizenship rights were extended to all adult males and most importantly, women were enfranchised in 1918 and 1928. This meant that governments had to attend to the wishes of consumers more than ever before. Although the interwar years were marked by serious and prolonged economic depression, a 'new consumerism' was enjoyed by middle-class families who bought their own homes on cheap mortgages, furnishing them on hire purchase from multiple stores such as Drage's. Despite the fact that many working-class families suffered badly during the depression, those fortunate enough to live in areas of the country that had more buoyant local economies also enjoyed the pleasures of consumption and purchased an expanding range of cheap luxuries. Department stores experienced their heyday, democratizing the 'dream worlds' they offered to consumers. Popular cinema extended its reach, developing in symbiotic relationship to the new consumerism and selling fantasy to ordinary consumers. The Conservative Party responded much more imaginatively to these transformations than the Labour Party, which squandered the possible advantages conferred by its historical links with organized working-class consumers. The co-operative movement became more concerned about the exploitation of ordinary shoppers by increasingly powerful monopolies that, it was argued, were reinventing the sharp practices characteristic of the wartime profiteer.

The ethical approach to consumption taken by the co-operative movement informed government policy during the Second World War. 'Fair Shares for All' and rationing seemed to embody a 'moral economy' approach that disciplined individual consumers, necessary in order to help defeat the threat of fascism. Once again, opportunities were missed and the fall of the Labour Government in 1951 put organized consumers on the defensive. Having gained power by attacking the policy of austerity, the Conservative Party took full advantage of the 'golden age of capitalism' when it finally arrived in the second half of the 1950s. They portrayed themselves as the party of popular affluence, liberating individual consumers from the dead hand of bureaucracy and prioritizing 'choice'. As in the nineteenth century, commentators across the ideological spectrum inveighed against the enervating effects of material goods on the working class in particular; while liberal intellectuals like J. K. Galbraith pointed to widespread 'public squalor' in a society geared to 'private affluence'. The political orchestration of consumer 'choice', aided by advertisers and businessmen, took place within the wider context of the Cold War, with conservatives in the West maintaining that political freedom and freedom of choice were two sides of the same coin. Think tanks like the Institute of Economic Affairs were instrumental in pushing neo-liberal views to a wider audience. Such ideas profoundly shaped a generation, including Margaret Thatcher before and after she took office in 1979. The closing decades of the twentieth century witnessed the neo-liberal apotheosis of consumer culture. As deindustrialization undermined the older solidarities of class, new constituencies of consumers emerged that appeared less homogeneous and more discriminating. The individual consumer became a central reference point for a whole way of life, with a key role for government ensuring greater freedom of choice for consumers. Simultaneously, democratic alternatives to capitalist consumerism withered, as the organized consumer was pushed to the margins. New Labour was a response to this changed landscape. Its architects accepted the neo-liberal agenda and developed it further, explicitly marketing the party as a brand and extending the mantra of choice across the public services.

7

Ideal Home: The Growth of the New Consumerism

Images and realities

Images sometimes seem to capture perfectly the meaning of a particular historical period. Orwell recorded many memorable ones in his famous portrait of northern England on the dole, *The Road to Wigan Pier* (1937), none more striking perhaps than that of the prematurely aged working-class woman he observed from the window of a train, who caught his eye for a moment while she was unblocking a drainpipe in the backyard of a slum.[1] It is a hopeless, desolate scene that vividly conveys the waste of human capacities caused by mass unemployment. But for many other people, life between the wars was very different, especially if they lived in the West Midlands or the south-east that had more buoyant local economies.[2] Indeed, we get glimpses of these alternative experiences in Orwell's text. Fashionable, ready-to-wear clothes and the cinema were within reach of the majority and fantasizing cost nothing: 'In your new clothes you can stand on the street corner, indulging in a private daydream of yourself as Clark Gable or Greta Garbo, which compensates you for a great deal.' Like many left-wing critics before and since, Orwell regarded these cheap luxuries as a kind of safety valve that had made radical political change less likely:

> Trade since the war has had to adjust itself to meet the demands of underpaid, underfed people, with the result that a luxury is nowadays almost always cheaper than a necessity. One pair of plain solid shoes costs as much as two ultra-smart pairs. For the price of one square meal you can get two pounds of sweets ... Twenty million people are underfed but literally everyone in England has access to a radio. What we have lost in food we have gained in electricity. Whole sections of the working class who have been plundered of all they really need

> are being compensated, in part, by cheap luxuries which mitigate the surface of life ... It is quite possible that fish-and-chips, art-silk stockings, tinned salmon, cut-price chocolate (five two-ounce bars for sixpence), the movies, the radio, strong tea and the Football Pools have between them averted revolution.[3]

Politicians and manufacturers had not conspired to bring this about. According to Orwell, it had just happened through the operation of market forces – 'The quite natural interaction between the manufacturer's need for a market and the need of half-starved people for cheap palliatives.'

Another socialist observer, J. B. Priestley, who had perhaps a deeper understanding of working-class culture than Orwell did, emphasized the democratizing influence of popular consumerism at this time. Its effects were most apparent in what Priestley referred to as 'Modern England', which was pushing aside both the 'Old England' of cathedral cities and the 'Nineteenth Century England' of grimy mill towns. He listed some of its chief characteristics:

> This is the England of arterial and by-pass roads, of filling stations and factories that look like exhibition buildings, of giant cinemas and dance-halls and cafes, bungalows with tiny garages, cocktail bars, Woolworths, motor-coaches, wireless, hiking, factory girls looking like actresses, greyhound racing and dirt tracks, swimming pools, and everything given away for cigarette coupons.[4]

Emanating from America, the symbolic centre of the new England was Blackpool and it was spreading fast: 'Modern England is rapidly Blackpooling itself'. As we have seen, one did not need to look across the Atlantic for the origins of all this as consumerism had deep indigenous roots. Interestingly, Priestley had conflicting feelings about these changes. On the one hand, he considered the essentially democratic nature of the new society admirable, as it was open to everyone who had cash or credit. After a social revolution, there would be more of it, he thought. However, sinister forces were also discernible, encouraging passive consumption by the majority rather than active engagement. 'Too much of this life is being stamped on from outside, probably by astute financial gentlemen, backed by the Press and their publicity services', Priestley noted, and he went on to warn more ominously still that the eventual effect of increasingly monotonous work allied to the supply of cheap luxuries might be to 'create a set of people entirely without ambition or any real desire to think and act for themselves, the perfect subjects for an iron autocracy'.[5] We will return to the politics of consumption later in this chapter but first it is necessary to briefly sketch the economic and social changes that were occurring between the wars, transformations that have been described by some historians as constituting a distinct phase, a 'new consumerism'.[6]

The two key features of the interwar economy were increasing consumption and the expansion of the home market, with both middle- and working-class consumers benefiting. This trend began in the 1920s and despite being knocked temporarily off track after depression hit in 1929, it had resumed by 1934. National income per head rose by about a third across the interwar period as a whole, reflecting increasing productivity and a relatively static population and although not all of this went to wages and salaries, a good deal of it did. As world commodity prices fell in the thirties, so too did the cost of living as wage rates either stagnated or fell only by a small amount. The unemployed and those on short time struggled to make ends meet, certainly, but absolute poverty was abolished and real incomes of most working-class people increased overall. Numbers of workers employed in service industries multiplied with hotels, restaurants and the entertainment industry all witnessing marked growth. Distributive trades saw the greatest increases, with numbers employed rising from 1,661,000 in 1920–2 to 2,436,000 in 1937–8. Demand for shop workers, clerical staff, transport employees and managers of all kinds grew. Employment opportunities also opened up in new light industries, many of which produced for the consumer market.[7] As Orwell observed, the depression in fact stimulated the desire for cheap luxuries such as rayon stockings and chocolate bars but the period also saw the steady growth of demand for goods at the other end of the scale like motor cars. As the electricity supply industry expanded, so too did sales of commodities such as electric cookers, vacuum cleaners, refrigerators and wireless sets, the latter proving the most immediately popular as radio brought cheap entertainment directly into people's homes. A growing army of travelling salesmen helped impel the consumer boom, linking manufacturers and wholesalers with retailers.[8] Notwithstanding these positive signs, we should remember that in his 1936 study of family budgets in York, the social investigator Seebohm Rowntree found that over 30 per cent of workers 'are not getting enough to eat to keep them in health, and that this is due not to lack of knowledge but to lack of means'.[9]

However, even the poorest in York could enjoy looking around the new chain stores such as Woolworths, Littlewoods (founded in 1923) and British Home Stores (founded in 1928). By 1939 these chains had a combined total of about 1,200 stores and commanded nearly 20 per cent of total sales by multiple retail organizations.[10] F. W. Woolworth began trading in Britain when its first store opened in Liverpool in 1909, having been established in the United States in the 1870s, and the firm expanded rapidly to become the most important foreign multinational in British retailing, owning 375 branches in 1929 and 759 a decade later.[11] The modernist aesthetics of its store frontages transformed many high streets and the opening of new branches was reported enthusiastically by the local press. Woolworths and its competitors caught the eye of contemporaries because they seemed to embody the democratic spirit of the new consumerism. Despite the greater inclusivity of some department stores in the late nineteenth and early twentieth centuries, most still employed floorwalkers whose main job was to eject 'tabbies' – demanding female customers that rarely bought goods. Chain stores that specialized in cheap, mass-produced non-basic goods including tinned food, confectionery, biscuits, crockery, glassware, toiletries and clothing, expanded the range of commodities available to consumers and, crucially, they allowed everyone to browse freely, without any pressure to purchase. Rowntree himself underlined the fact that they provided a form of 'entertainment' and that 'thousands of people enter the stores just for the fun of having a look round.'[12] Multiple retailers of foodstuffs with roots in the nineteenth century, including Sainsbury's, Home and Colonial and Lipton's, as well as footwear outlets such as Stead and Simpson, newspaper and book sellers like W. H. Smith, furniture stores with multiple outlets and Boots the chemists, also expanded their operations considerably during this period. Trading on a reputation for purity, for example, Sainsbury's built up gradually from its London base, owning 129 shops in 1920 and 255 shops by 1939.[13]

Marks & Spencer was another great success story, launching the 'St Michael' brand in 1928 and bringing fashionable ready-to-wear clothing to greater numbers than ever; its turnover rose spectacularly from £2,493,000 in 1929 to £23,448,000 in 1939, by which time it had opened or extended 258 stores.[14] Figure 11 is a local newspaper advertisement for a new 'super store' which opened in north London that typically featured modernist design at a time when most co-operative retail stores in northern England were already looking like relics from the Victorian era. It was also pitched to a mass market – all goods were priced at under 5s. (at least for the opening period), and weekly clubs brought them within reach of less well-off customers in the longer term. Declaring a handsome profit at the annual general meeting of shareholders in 1936, Simon Marks, the chairman and managing director of Marks & Spencer, credited success to the company's recognition of the importance of 'consumer's choice'. His conclusion was resolutely upbeat: 'Goods and services once regarded as luxuries have become conventional comforts and are now almost deemed necessities. A fundamental change in people's habits has been brought about.'[15]

The interwar years were the golden age of the department store, despite the focus of much historical writing on the earlier period. For it was between the wars that department stores made most determined efforts to democratize their 'dream worlds' of consumption. Harrod's recognized the new direction in 1925, opening inexpensive departments for gowns and coats. Other stores outside London such as Binns in Sunderland and Howell's in Cardiff expanded their range of goods, catering especially to the desire for simpler, more functional styles that transformed fashions for clothing across age and gender lines, as well as fashions for household furnishings, where the heavy Victorian look was replaced by lighter designs.[16] Pressed increasingly hard by the multiples and the co-operative movement – discussed in more detail later in this chapter – and affected badly by economic downturn, they fought

FIGURE 11 *Advertisement for the opening of a Marks & Spencer store, November 1936. © Marks & Spencer Archive, Leeds.*

back by successfully widening their appeal. Many, though not all, advertised extensively in the national and local press and also used other means; recent research has suggested that this was money well spent. Pushing out into the growing suburbs and outer suburbs, their numbers consequently grew from 175–225 stores in 1914 to 475–525 stores in 1938.[17] More sophisticated display strategies were used to attract consumers and more imaginative ways deployed to create an engaging shopping experience and a stronger brand image for the store. Fraser's, which nearly went bust in 1932, introduced 'quick serve' counters and expanded its bargain basement, for example. Some stores used stunts that tapped into popular culture; under its flamboyant store chief Jimmy Driscoll, Kennard's of Croydon brought the town to a halt with elephants loaned from the circus to promote its 'jumbo' birthday sale. Driscoll also arranged regular visits from celebrities, had a Wurlitzer organ installed in the store's restaurant, laid on donkey rides and even staged a Wild West 'Shoot Out'. Similarly, Bentall's of Kingston attempted to turn the store into a theatrical venue and exhibition centre, displaying Sir Malcolm Campbell's record-breaking car *Bluebird*, providing cabaret and orchestral performances and even showcasing Anita Kittner, a young Swedish performer who regularly dived sixty-three feet into a small pool, much to the crowd's delight![18] David Lewis's, now under the control of Frederick Marquis (Lord Woolton from 1939), opened ambitious new stores in Glasgow (1929), Leeds (1932), Hanley (1934) and Leicester (1936), and replaced the old, formal display of goods that characterized its stores with elaborate tableaux that created a context for commodities; tweeds were shown within a representation of a crofter's cottage on the Island of Harris, for instance. Building on a long tradition, Lewis's also made extensive use of exhibitions and attractions such as flower displays, brass band concerts and a miniature scale model of Blackpool, which proved immensely popular. As the store's historian has observed, 'A trip to the city began to be associated not only with the cinema or the football match, but with a trip to Lewis's.'[19]

Department stores innovated in more prosaic but no less vital ways between the wars. Amalgamation was a key response to the challenges they faced. Debenham's took over Marshall and Snelgrove in 1919, then Harvey Nichols, while Harrod's had bought up Dickens and Jones in 1914, then Kendal Milne of Manchester in 1919 and Swan and Edgar a year later. Selfridge bought a chain of London and regional stores, including the Bon Marché in Brixton and Whiteley's in 1927, eventually overstretching himself and selling out to the John Lewis Partnership in 1940. Debenham's emerged in the 1930s as Britain's largest group of stores. Despite these developments, many independent family firms such as Fenwick's survived, adapting themselves to local conditions.[20] But others sought greater access to capital that would allow them to expand by becoming public limited companies, as did Lewis's in 1924. Under Marquis's leadership, advantages of scale and modern techniques of 'scientific management' were introduced similar to innovations in industry associated with the influence of the American management theorist, Frederick Winslow Taylor. The emphasis was on rationalization and efficiency. Following the example of chain stores, Lewis's was the first department store to use central buying, opening a London office with forty buyers in 1923 that replaced local buying by managers of individual departments. Control of what became known as 'Lewis's Group' from 1929 was in the hands of a board of management rather than an individual autocrat, which instigated modern methods of retail inventory, clear expenses, departmental accounting, stock control and a more rational classification of goods. Department stores also made greater efforts to bind workers more closely to the enterprise by strengthening paternalist provision through better canteens, extensive recreational facilities, medical services, pension schemes and so on. 'Lewis's Group' took a lead here too but the name that became most closely associated with this trend was John Spedan Lewis, who introduced a profit-sharing scheme into the London stores he inherited from his father in 1928. Alarmed by the militancy of shop workers during the war, he hoped to damp down class conflict in retailing by such means, spreading the system through the John Lewis Partnership that was established in 1929 and diversified in 1937 by buying up the Waitrose chain of grocery stores. Notwithstanding inflated claims about the beneficial effects of profit-sharing, the firm in fact was no less hierarchical than its rivals and it seems unlikely that its employees were any more contented than other department store workers.[21]

The 'new consumerism' manifested itself most insistently at the level of everyday life through advertising, which achieved a new respectability during the First World War, as we saw in Chapter 4. Advertisers like Hedley Le Bas and Charles Higham were employed by politicians to boost civilian morale, gaining knighthoods in the process and causing left critics such as the philosopher Bertrand Russell to complain that this newly established relationship demonstrated how people might be allowed to vote in democratic countries but were in reality 'hypnotised into the opinion which is officially considered desirable', by means of government propaganda in the press and the cinema.[22] The war dignified advertising, making it easier for the industry to adopt the mantle of professionalism in its immediate aftermath and slough off the stigma of quackery, or at least attempt to. Big industrialists helped polish the industry's image, including W. H. Lever who picked up the idea of the necessity for truthful advertising from a magazine article in 1921. He later puffed the increasing influence of advertising by comparing its effects to the growing desire for global co-operation and world peace. 'Leagues of Nations may totter and sway', Lever declared in a speech at New York in 1923, 'but the eternal principles, which are the fundamentals of honest business, will continue to advance humanity to brotherhood and abolish the artificial barriers between the several nations. Advertising only means keeping up with the times and the big advance in modern business.'[23]

Around this time, Higham lobbied the American-based Associated Advertising Clubs of the World to hold their annual meeting in London and in July 1924 London staged an Advertising Convention at Wembley, the slogan for which was 'Truth in Advertising'. Attracting approximately 5,000 delegates, many of them from overseas including 2,000 from America alone, the meeting was opened by its patron the Prince of Wales (the future ill-starred Edward VIII) who praised advertising for leading to greater efficiency in distribution and therefore lower prices and greater employment, representing no less than a solution to the world's economic and social problems. Unsurprisingly, many other speakers at the event were sanguine about the industry's future prospects, which led on to the establishment of the Advertising Association in 1926.[24] Higham himself naturally had the highest ambitions for advertising, recommending its more systematic use by fascist organizations such as the Freedom League, which he believed were 'bent on preserving the British Constitution and combating the tyrannical aims of Bolshevism'.[25] Critical outsiders pointed up the oxymoronic nature of the convention's key theme – advertisers of patent medicines often claimed that their remedies cured cancer and tuberculosis at this time – including writers like the young radical novelist Ethel Mannin, who had worked for Higham as a copywriter during the war. *Sounding Brass* (1926), probably Mannin's finest achievement, narrated the rise and fall of Jim Rickard, head of Premier Publicity, who steals and cheats his way to the top and spouts the new gospel of advertising proclaimed at the convention with the evangelical zeal of a missionary. At a dinner party held to celebrate the event, Rickard declares that the purpose of the convention was to 'conserve for ourselves, and for posterity, ideals of conduct and standards of advertising practice born of the belief that truthful advertising builds both character and good business', sentiments supported by a manufacturer of 'the Only Satisfactory Cheap Car on the Market' who exclaims ecstatically, 'To seek the truth and to live it'. The overwhelming majority of guests lap this up enthusiastically, apart from one cynical advertising man who deflates the gathering by reminding them that Christ had attempted to do exactly that and had been crucified in return.[26]

Somewhere between £85 million and £200 million was spent on advertising annually between the wars, but there was qualitative as well as quantitative change with the practice of advertising becoming more sophisticated. This has sometimes been seen as a consequence of the influence of works such as Walter Dill Scott's *The Psychology of Advertising* (1908), and a more explicitly psychological approach is discernible in contemporary advertisements.[27] Higham himself wrote in his treatise on the subject published in 1925 that psychology put advertising on a 'scientific' footing and he asserted: 'Research work has proved that we reach the unconscious through the power of imagination; that we prevent it functioning when we merely reason and use our will.' Psychology constituted an important weapon for Higham, invaluable in breaking down the rational resistance of consumers and encouraging them to spend. But he did not credit it unlimited power and neither did the advertising industry as a whole: in the end, the ethical appeal of 'truth' (whatever that word might mean) was more telling, as delegates to the Wembley Convention agreed. Greater organization and better technique proved more vital weapons than psychology and helped boost claims of professional status; the Incorporated Society of Advertising Consultants introduced a syllabus and examinations for its members in 1925.[28] Agencies became increasingly adept at market research, designing campaigns for particular products and building 'brand architecture'. The American company J. Walter Thompson was in the forefront here. A London branch opened in 1899 but it had closed during the war. After it reopened in 1919, JWT quickly became one of the top five agencies in the country, handling the 'Lux' account for Unilever, for instance, and conducting extensive research on consumer attitudes in the late 1920s, interviewing 3,200 housewives – an unprecedented number – in twenty towns and cities across England to ensure the relaunched brand's success as 'a magical kind of product' rather than simply a laundry soap.[29] Advertisers clearly did not treat consumers as passive dopes but listened carefully to them and tried to adapt their messages accordingly. They also worked on the visual appeal of advertisements, often using artistic images to lend distinction to goods and services, like the London, Midland and Scottish Railway Company that commissioned a group of Royal Academicians to design its posters in 1924. The attractive posters they produced helped to allay the remaining criticism of middle-class pressure groups such as the Society for Checking the Abuses of Public Advertising, which continued to decry what the *Observer* in 1923 called the 'painted cant' of the hoardings. In similar fashion, in the early 1930s Shell successfully managed to differentiate both its oil and its petrol from those of its competitors – despite the fact that there was nothing to choose between them – and soothe the anxieties of the middle-class owners of motor cars who purchased its products, by means of a poster campaign that seemed to demonstrate that the company cared for art and nature.[30]

Domesticity and identity

Most of the women recruited into paid labour during the First World War returned to 'home and duty' when hostilities ceased. They were encouraged to do so by politicians and the media, which emphasized women's domestic mission as homemakers and the importance of the home for the stability of both nation and empire. Some historians have seen this as women being coerced back into the domestic sphere by patriarchal forces but the story is more complex than this.[31] Nevertheless, the domestic realm assumed a new importance during the interwar period. There were social as well as ideological aspects to this revalorization of the home. For one thing, the average size of working-class families fell from approximately six surviving children around the turn of the century to just over two by the 1930s, a change that affected first skilled then unskilled workers.[32] Those fortunate to be employed, therefore, had more disposable income to spend on their homes. Popular newspapers addressed women as consumers and homemakers, as did a proliferating number of women's magazines such as *Good Housekeeping* from 1922 and *Woman's Own* from 1932.[33] There was also a boom in house building and the manufacture of things to go in them, and more people aspired to own homes than ever before. Literary historians have stressed the importance of discursive shifts, arguing that there was a redefinition of ideas of English national identity between the wars and that changing notions of home and gender were central to this redefinition. In short, a trend has been discerned away from predominantly masculine public languages of the nation that characterized the period of high imperialism before the First World War, towards a more introspective, private and domestic discourse.[34] Female consumers bridged ideological and social spheres but they were not simply corralled passively into domesticity. Historians of the mass press, for instance, have shown that although women's domestic duty was often discussed in popular newspapers, other identities were also available to them; the press was polyvocal and the messages it articulated were often not straightforward.[35] This section considers such complexities in more depth.

A most striking example of the new domesticity was the '*Daily Mail* Ideal Home Exhibition', which had begun in 1908. Staged at the Olympia Stadium in Hammersmith, it was the brainchild of Wareham Smith, the paper's advertising manager. Up to 200,000 people visited the first exhibition with attendance climbing steadily over subsequent years. The editorial Alfred Harmsworth wrote announcing the exhibition's opening emphasized its key themes, particularly the futuristic nature or modernity of the event and its usefulness for British manufacturers. Harmsworth hoped it would 'demonstrate that good taste is combined with moderation of price in twentieth-century British furniture'. A range of new commodities promised to both ease the labour of homemaking and increase efficiency, even improving the health of the next generation by making 'the House Beautiful' a much more hygienic space; eugenic concerns were addressed by a special 'Babyland' feature.[36] The continued success of the exhibition between the wars was aided by the growth of house building and home ownership. In 1920 private builders only built 100 houses, compared to 600 built by local authorities but over the next decade the former raced ahead, constructing 140,300 homes in 1930 whereas local authorities only built 61,800. By 1939, the figures stood at 230,600 and 100,900 respectively. Owner occupation rose from around 10 per cent in 1914 to about 32 per cent on the eve of the Second World War. Although the lower middle-class were most affected, the prospect of owning one's own home became more realistic for lower-income groups too as the cost of house building fell; the same house that cost £1,000 to build in 1920 cost £350 to build in 1932. Mortgages also became more affordable and widely advertised. Consequently, the demand for home furnishings and appliances to fill the spreading suburban utopia was greatly stimulated.[37]

The Ideal Home Exhibition guided consumers through this changing world, promoting labour-saving gadgets that would allow middle-class women especially to become more efficient housewives rather than managers of servants. Some 200 exhibitors displayed their wares in 1935 and at least 500,000 visitors attended the event that year. The Goblin vacuum cleaner was a major attraction, the qualities of which were sung by twenty-four 'Goblin Girls' who belted out a catchy jingle.[38] Though one might read all this as subordinating women, it is worth remembering that a nice home had more positive aspects. This point was only too obvious to those who lived in slums, like the young woman interviewed by Mass-Observation (who could have been the one Orwell witnessed unblocking a drainpipe), and who dreamt about owning a modern home with a nice kitchen and garden that might tempt her husband from the pub and encourage him to treat her decently.[39] Naturally, cynicism as well as hope characterized popular attitudes, as in the song 'My Little Bottom Drawer', performed by Gracie Fields in the 1934 film *Sing as We Go*, which poked fun at the romantic image of the perfect home with all mod cons: 'We'll have a bathroom / Oh! What a bathroom / With a wonderful bath / Where we can keep the coal / Horse-shoe for luck – pail for the muck / And a President Hoover's cleaner for the floor / If the plans go all to pot / I can sell the bloomin' lot / All packed up in me little bottom drawer.'

Though the domestic realm was undoubtedly a key site of consumption, young consumers in particular spent their money on other things such as clothes, cosmetics, cheap luxuries and entertainment – principally dance halls and cinema. The consumer power of young people was increasing and although we need to be careful not to overestimate the pace of change – 'teenagers' did not properly emerge until the 1950s – new opportunities for paid employment and leisure were opening up, especially for young female workers.[40] The decline of domestic service and the rise of the leisure and holiday industries and light manufacturing meant that there were more young women with money in their pockets and they spent eagerly on cinema going, which became the major form of commercial entertainment interwar, with millions attending each week. Authority figures worried that films would encourage criminal behaviour, though such fears were ungrounded, based on little more than class and cultural prejudice. Commentators on the left criticized popular cinema for distracting people from the realities of economic depression and class struggle, including the novelist Graham Greene who suggested that Gracie Fields's films helped safeguard capitalist profits, though their popularity owed much to the fact that Fields frequently played a feisty, class-conscious millworker.[41] Sexism often marked responses; bemoaning the £1.5 million a week that women spent on cosmetics during the 1930s, the journalist John Hilton wrote that a young woman would not go to the cinema unless she had 'the latest perm' and had 'done her face with the proper night lotion and day lotion, and has had her eyebrows put in a more fetching place, and has got her lips done into a ruddy blob and her fingernails varnished the colour of stale blood, so that you expect the flies to settle on them'.[42]

Like the popular press, however, cinema provided alternative forms of identity for young women and alternative images of femininity and lifestyle that often proved a welcome distraction from the difficulties of everyday life. Cinemagoers clearly wanted 'escapism' – a loaded term that entered the language in the 1930s – and preferred musical romance and historical melodrama to crime and war films, let alone documentaries or social realism, much to the disgust of many intellectuals. They did not want 'real' life, as one of them remarked to a social investigator at the time: 'We don't go to the pictures to learn.'[43] We need to understand these practices and not simply condemn them as so many contemporaries did. Eighteen-year-old Constance Badrock put it succinctly in 1937: 'The critic may say I am easily pleased, but to think that for a few coppers, one can enter that world of make believe and leave behind all the worries and cares, well I say: "Long live the Films!"'[44] Rather than regarding popular cinema negatively as offering merely 'escapism', it makes more sense to approach cinema, as well as related forms of consumption and pleasure like department stores, more positively, as sites of fantasy that provide space – albeit a commercialized space and one regulated by the state in terms of censorship – for the free play of consumers' imaginations. Indeed, oral testimony suggests how linked department stores and the cinema were in the popular mind and how important the desire for fantasy was. When Lewis's opened its new department store in Leeds in September 1932 it had five floors, four escalators and a host of uniformed 'Ask Me' girls to direct shoppers to one of its 157 departments; 120,000 people visited on opening day.[45] One of these was the young Muriel Jordan, who vividly remembered the event over sixty years later: 'But oh! It wa' fantastic. I mean really, it wa' fantastic ... it was so modern. It was like the cinema, you know ... An' when they opened it, in the ladies' bathroom, toilets an' things, for the first week they had powder-bowls of face powder wi' puffs – wi' swan's down puffs.'[46] Jordan grew up in a working-class family that was committed to a co-operative movement informed by a utilitarian consumption ethic, so her testimony suggests just how widely shared the desire for fantasy and glamour was at the time. Mediated by magazines such as *Picturegoer* and *Film Weekly* that were replete with articles on movie stars and advertisements for the cosmetics, toiletries and other products they supposedly used, cinema and department stores fed off one another. As a shop girl from Leeds wrote in a letter to *Film Weekly* in 1933; 'People consider me smartly dressed, but this is undoubtedly because I copy the clothes I have seen in films. Powders, soap and odds and ends are those used by my favourite film stars.'[47]

It would be mistaken to think that women were the only ones affected by the 'new consumerism'. Men of all kinds were also actively engaged in the world of goods, though naturally young male consumers adopted new fashions most eagerly. Multiple retailers such as Joseph Hepworth and Montague Burton ('The Tailor of Taste') dominated the manufacture and distribution of men's clothes, the latter eventually leading the field, owning nearly 600 shops in 1939. Its factory in Leeds was alleged to be the largest in the world, employing 10,000 workers by the late 1930s. Burton's played safe in terms of fashion, concentrating on producing reasonably priced made-to-measure suits ordered from its shops and believing 'style monotony' to be the best route to a large market.[48] Although the strategy proved highly successful, with the typical male look remaining generally conservative in this period, new lines were becoming more popular, including sports jackets, flannels and pullovers, now often supplied in brighter colours.[49] Moreover, lifestyle magazines like *Men Only*, which appeared from 1935, championed the tasteful but still sometimes adventurous middle-class male consumer and attempted to quell anxieties about the supposed effeminising effects of fashion consciousness. Despite this emphasis, however, the magazine also spoke to other constituencies, even courting the pink pound, for instance.[50] Towards the other end of the social scale, the dole was sometimes thought to undermine the masculinity of working-class men, depriving them of their breadwinner status and power as consumers as well as producers. This possibility seemed even more likely after a household means test was introduced in 1931, sparking rumours in working-class communities that under its terms the unemployed would be forced to sell what remaining possessions they had.[51] While full participation in the expanding masculine realm of consumption required a decent income, clearly it is important to recognize that even those on the most slender means were not entirely excluded. The protagonist in Walter Brierley's 'proletarian' novel *Means Test Man*, for example, is a long-term unemployed Derbyshire miner who feels that he is no longer a 'full-blown citizen' because he is unable to buy new furniture for the home or clothes for his child. Nevertheless, encouraged by his wife and in an effort to 'keep respectable' – vital in order to get a job – he replaces his threadbare suit at one point in the novel with a 37s. made-to-measure from Burton's.[52]

If increasing levels of consumption were often interpreted positively by politicians and intellectuals as welcome signs of material progress, some doubts still remained. More specifically, there was disquiet concerning a purported lack of taste in the design of goods in general use and apparent in many homes, particularly those of the working class. In the forefront here was the Council for Art and Industry (CAI), established by the government Board of Trade in 1934 under the chairmanship of Frank Pick who, as boss of London Underground, had commissioned modernist advertising posters for the Tube in an effort to educate the public.[53] Pick was an odd mixture, an admirer of Ruskin and Morris but no political revolutionary and he believed that he could use the CAI to help spread the gospel of good taste throughout society. The first report produced by the organization, *Education for the Consumer*, published in 1935, argued that suitably discriminating choice on the part of shoppers would drive improvement in design and that 'what is required in the consumer is, first, conscious realization of the possibility of beauty in things of everyday use, and second, quicker understanding and appreciation of it when it is placed before him'.[54] The report went on to recommend the systematic teaching of art and design in elementary and secondary schools, and Pick worked hard to get these ideas put into practice in London and elsewhere, with limited success. Recalling mid-nineteenth century taste reformers, a later report produced by the council bemoaned the 'accumulation of patterns' in working-class homes, which, it concluded, were 'often conflicting and tiresome. There seems to be general reluctance to look at anything bare and plain.'[55] The report went on to make suggestions on how to furnish a three-bedroom working-class home for less than £50 in suitably modern and efficient style.

While a heightened domesticity no doubt stimulated consumption, manufacturers, advertisers and retailers appealed to other identities of both male and female consumers. Moreover, although a revalorized home dovetailed with a more inward-looking, private discourse of Englishness, we should not underestimate the continuing appeal of the British Empire as a means of selling goods. Its dominant symbols – the Union Jack, Britannia and the monarchy – continued to be used to lend commodities a patriotic appeal. And although the meaning of the British Empire was changing into something much softer and less aggressive than it had been in its heyday before the First World War, its civilizing effects continued to be taken for granted. This was exemplified by the Empire Marketing Board (EMB), which attempted between 1926 and 1933 to harness the consumer for the empire. Established by Stanley Baldwin's government after it had reneged on its promise to introduce protection, the EMB represented a short-term compromise with supporters of tariff reform before the Ottawa Agreement of 1932 finally buried free trade. There was widespread party political support for the EMB and its Publicity Committee included two directors of the Co-operative Wholesale Society, the managing director of Harrod's, the head of a major advertising agency, and Frank Pick, again a dominant force. An extensive campaign was organized, comprising a nationwide series of public lectures, the distribution of millions of pamphlets, Empire Shopping Weeks in various cities, and advertising using the press, posters, the BBC and film. Private companies employed its designs on postcards, jigsaw puzzles, Christmas cards and an Empire Card Game. The discourse of the EMB recast the British Empire as an interdependent system of co-operation, a 'family' in a moral as well as an economic sense in that the empire was now seen as necessary for international peace. Though price remained more important for working-class consumers than the imperial origin of goods, the effects of the EMB should not be underestimated.[56] Shopping and empire continued to be linked after the body was disbanded, by Selfridge for instance, who decorated his Oxford Street store lavishly on the theme of 'The Empire's Homage to the Throne' for the coronation of George VI in 1937. Eighteen imposing panels representing key moments and individual heroes of British and imperial mythology covered the front of the store, while sculptures at the corners of the building portrayed the dominions and India. Interestingly, the centrepiece of the display erected above the main entrance was a monumental winged figure surmounting a crown with the motto 'Let Peace Prevail'.[57] Selfridge hoped that the £50,000 he spent on these decorations would boost the store's failing fortunes but he was to be disappointed; crowds came to witness the spectacle, which unsurprisingly divided opinion, though most preferred just to look rather than spend.[58]

The politics of consumption

Orwell may have been on to something when he flippantly observed that artificial silk or rayon stockings were anti-revolutionary. The Conservative Party understood this perhaps. It issued a one-off magazine in 1928 aimed at newly enfranchised 'flapper' voters called *Women of Today and Tomorrow*, which contained an article comparing the ample supplies of artificial silk stockings under a Conservative government in Britain with the scarcity experienced in Communist Russia, where only a single factory produced these goods.[59] We have already seen how the party also pushed empire shopping but this was only a component part of a broader strategy that sought to address the interests of the mass of consumers, women in particular. And it proved largely successful, the Conservatives wresting the consumer from the Liberals between the wars while simultaneously managing to contain the challenge of Labour in this sphere, despite Labour's advantage of close relations with the co-operative movement. The latter fully recognized the importance of rayon stockings that replaced heavy 'cashmere' stockings for women after the First World War and which were manufactured by the CWS factory at Leicester. Significantly, though the factory was expanded in the mid-1930s until it employed over 1,500 people, it struggled to meet demand from local retail societies, which may have reinforced Conservative claims about the efficacy of free market capitalism.[60]

Determined efforts were necessary to get the consumer onside: the prospects of success had not seemed very promising for the Conservatives in the early 1920s. Demands for a specifically imperial consumerism had stalled, while the panacea of free trade still carried a good deal of influence in the popular mind. Moreover, calls for greater government regulation to aid the consumer had gained considerable ground during the war and in its immediate aftermath. The critique of 'profiteering' that had become more prominent in the latter stages of the conflict helped politicize consumption as we saw in the preceding chapter, causing the co-operative movement to enter the political sphere formally. Ordinary consumers were widely regarded as being at the mercy of the capitalist 'profiteer', who remained a potent and widely despised figure in the popular imagination throughout the 1920s. Conservatives worked hard to slough off negative associations between private business and consumer exploitation, though this was no easy task. Pressure to intervene in markets for particular commodities and keep prices down increased in the run-up to the 1924 general election, with both Conservatives and Labour attempting to woo consumers, particularly women. While the Labour Chancellor of the Exchequer Philip Snowden pointed to the fact that he had introduced 'a housewife's budget' when in power that had cut food duties by £30 million, the Conservative leader Stanley Baldwin promised a thorough investigation of and firm action to address the problems facing the mass of consumers.[61] Baldwin was as good as his word, establishing a Royal Commission on Food Prices in 1925 that exposed how consumers were getting a raw deal, followed by a Food Council to check abuses soon after. Unfortunately, however, this body had no statutory powers and therefore functioned mainly as a way of deflecting criticism rather than a means of attacking the root causes of exploitation.[62]

Consumers' anger was fuelled by the idea that powerful 'vested interests', organized as 'combines' or monopolies, fleeced shoppers on a daily basis. Since the late nineteenth century, co-operators had been very concerned about the impact large-scale industrial and commercial organizations might have on their movement, arguing that the emergence of 'trusts' and other forms of capitalist co-operation made a mockery of the notion of a self-regulating, competitive market. Their criticisms seemed to be confirmed by the new wave of amalgamations that occurred after the First World War, which profoundly affected the distributive and retailing trades. Mergers transformed the ownership of department stores, for example. Selfridge, who believed that giant stores were 'the spear head in the progress of civilisation', bought up many, including Whiteley's in 1927, eventually overstretching himself, as we have noted. As boss of the Drapery Trust, the high-living fraudster Clarence Hatry took over scores of provincial department stores as well as Debenhams, before going bust in 1929.[63] Greed prompted much of this expansion no doubt but 'rationalization' in this sphere was also regarded vital in order to make better use of economies of scale and meet the challenges posed by multiples and co-operatives. The arrogance of monopoly power was revealed all too plainly before the Royal Commission on Food Prices, when Lord Vesty and Sir Edmund Vesty, owners of the international meat importation business that was able to influence prices and profits, treated their questioners with complete disdain and were repaid with servility.[64] Perhaps the clearest indication of the dominant economic tendency was the merger between Van den Berghs, Jurgens and Lever Brothers, which led to the creation of Unilever Limited in England and Unilever NV in Holland. When this merger came into force in 1930 the company controlled thousands of high street shops, trading under well-known names such as

Home and Colonial Stores, Liptons and Mac Fisheries.[65] Co-operators were vociferous in their criticism of such developments, feeling that they were under illegitimate as well as legitimate forms of commercial pressure as they were denied supplies of goods by certain capitalist manufacturers organized as the Proprietary Articles Trade Association and other bodies, which regarded the movement as their outright enemy.[66] Little wonder then that the critique of 'profiteering' and the anti-monopoly theme assumed greater importance in co-operative discourse during the 1920s as it became more apparent which way the tide was running. The illustration from the cover of a pamphlet published by the movement in 1930 and reproduced as Figure 12 captured these fears; here the bloated owner of a capitalist 'combine' – 'the modern highwayman' – robs a defenceless working-class housewife, thereby taking food from the mouths of her children.

Although the co-operative movement was in a beleaguered position in many respects, it also had good grounds for optimism between the wars. Despite the depression, its economic strength improved significantly. The decline of Britain's old staple industries led to stagnation of membership and turnover in some of its old heartlands in the north-west and north-east, certainly, but striking progress was made in the areas that experienced economic growth, particularly London and the south-east, and historians

FIGURE 12 *Fred Hayward,* The Co-operative Boycott and Its Political Implications *(1930). © National Co-operative Archive, Manchester.*

have yet to properly investigate how working-class consciousness was shaped by co-operative activity in this period. The membership of 6.5 million in the early 1930s included over a fifth of the population between the ages of sixteen and sixty-four. There were almost 1,200 local societies, which owned around 12,000 shops, 300 warehouses and factories, a bank, an insurance society and from 1929 a national Sunday paper, *Reynolds's News*. The movement was the biggest distributor of tea in the country, milled a third of total flour imports and baked one in five loaves. The wholesale and productive societies had an annual trade of over £100 million in 1935; despite the difficult circumstances, in the decade ending 1935 the CWS opened nearly forty new departments, factories and workshops. About 300,000 people were co-operative employees, making the movement second only to government as an employer of labour. Organized consumers owned a total of £160 million of capital in retail societies.[67] Such facts furnished eloquent proof of the efficacy of planning and the democratic control of business, as the movement remained comparatively free from boom and slump during the depression. However, there were serious underlying weaknesses. Co-operatives were outstripped by the multiples and department stores in the sale of dry goods and fashionable commodities such as radios and vacuum cleaners that were in the vanguard of the 'new consumerism' – foodstuffs continued to be the mainstay of their retail business throughout the interwar years. The movement controlled almost a quarter of the national trade by 1939 and was particularly important in the supply of milk and bread.[68] Little wonder then that its leaders were most concerned about the way ordinary consumers were being squeezed by 'combines', which, they argued, maintained inflated retail prices of everyday goods despite significant falls in wholesale prices, a practice thoroughly exposed in 1925 by the Royal Commission on Food Prices.

In this hostile context, the movement's leaders became convinced that state regulation was required to help check the dangers posed by monopolies and trade associations. The Co-operative Party consequently introduced a Trust and Combines Bill in 1925, though that soon failed. Emboldened by the election of nine Co-operative MPs and the formation of a second Labour government in 1929, however, the Joint Parliamentary Committee of the Co-operative Union quickly drafted a Consumers' Council Bill that proposed the establishment of a body with far-reaching powers to replace the discredited Food Council in order to properly investigate the practices of trade associations and private companies. This new Consumers' Council would be able to summon witnesses, examine accounts and set prices for a wide range of basic commodities including food, clothes and fuel. The mass press and trade associations denounced what it regarded as a direct attack on the sanctity of the free market, perceived as essential for capitalist growth, and so did Conservative politicians, who fought hard to block the bill's progress through parliament. Nevertheless, despite strong opposition, the bill had its second reading in May 1930, provoking heated debate in the Commons. While Labour MPs tried to play down its socialistic nature, Conservative opponents led by Sir Philip Cunliffe-Lister described the 'orgy of despotic price-fixing' that he believed the bill would unloose and asserted, 'This is not Socialism by the back door; it is Socialism through the front door.' Price-fixing was portrayed as characteristic of centralized and authoritarian revolutionary regimes, destined like French Jacobinism and Russian Bolshevism to lead to economic inefficiency and rapid decline. Interestingly, some Liberal MPs were amongst the bill's supporters, including Harry Nathan, MP for Bethnal Green who later went over to Labour and who proved an uncompromising critic of Tory cant about the free market: 'You have the great vertical and horizontal trusts, and price rings, which are open to the public gaze, and the concealed trusts which can be found out only by such investigations as are contemplated by the Bill.' The fact that the Labour government was in a parliamentary minority did not help expedite matters and its position steadily weakened before it collapsed in late August 1931. With its fall went the chance of regulating markets democratically to protect working-class consumers.[69]

The enemies of co-operation took the opportunity afforded by the election of a National Government in 1931 to redouble their attempts to hamstring the movement. The press barons Lord Beaverbrook and Lord Rothermere led a campaign for the taxation of the dividend, the latter blaming the 'Curse of the Co-ops' for undermining the competitive ethic. Although the mass press supported the monopolistic economic tendencies of the period as evidence of greater efficiency and was indeed itself part of this general trend, like fascist movements on the continent which Rothermere especially much admired, it directed its campaign at the small private trader squeezed by department stores and multiples on the one side and by the co-op on the other.[70] Many Conservative members of the new government were sympathetic to the charge that the co-op enjoyed an unfair advantage as it was largely exempt from income tax, and set up the Raeburn Committee to investigate the situation. The committee was not impartial – one of its members was on the board of directors of Peter Robinson, the department store – so the fact that it eventually backed removing some exemptions was hardly surprising. However, neither the committee nor the government were prepared to go the whole way and instead compromised by taxing co-operative reserves, that is, the surplus that was not distributed as dividend.[71] Taxing the total dividend would have ruined the movement and leading Conservatives including Stanley Baldwin and Neville Chamberlain did not want that; they regarded the co-op as a bulwark against revolution rather than its ally because it encouraged the growth of working-class property ownership. Beaverbrook was furious at what looked to him like a climb down and tried to continue the fight but was soon defeated by an energized movement that campaigned hard to safeguard its interests. For co-operators, 'the great tax ramp' as they called it was a matter of life and death, for the very principle of mutuality was at stake; it was not an insignificant affair as some earlier studies have suggested.[72] One means of protest was the collection of a national petition, which was eventually signed by 3,428,000 people, making it the largest petition to Parliament since the Chartist period. Ultimately, the attack on the co-op in the early 1930s backfired on Beaverbrook and his supporters, as it politicized consumption explicitly and served as a marvellous advertisement for the movement. Total membership increased at a healthy rate in the second half of the 1930s until it stood at over 8.6 million on the eve of the Second World War.[73]

Although there was a great deal of joint activity at the local level in the interwar period, organized consumers did not receive much help from the leadership of the Labour Party, which identified more closely with working-class producers and did not share co-operators' anxieties about the rise of monopolies.[74] The Co-operative Party managed to negotiate an agreement with Labour in 1927 but the interests of workers as consumers was nevertheless marginalized, with damaging repercussions for the labour movement as a whole, both at the time and in subsequent decades, as we shall see in the next chapter. This did not mean that Labour leaders ignored the problems faced by consumers entirely but they tended to pursue their own solutions to them. The issue of consumer credit provides illustration of the approach taken. The 'new consumerism' was facilitated by the increasing availability of affordable credit; furniture multiples like Drage's were in the vanguard here with its '50-pay-way' system but most department stores also offered hire purchase.[75] Although there was still a stigma attached to it, gradually hire purchase became more widely accepted, even among working-class consumers who had traditionally been very suspicious; many local co-operative societies offered extended credit from 1923 onwards, for instance, in the form of so-called mutuality clubs.[76] Abuses were common in a business that had an annual turnover of probably £100 million by the late 1930s. Retailers charged very high margins for credit – often 100 per cent or more – and heavy-handed tactics were frequently used to recover debts from customers, Drage's being seen as one of the worst offenders in this respect. Under existing law, goods bought on instalment were only hired by the consumer and could be reclaimed by the retailer (the notorious tactic of 'snatching back') if payments were not timely, regardless of how much of the purchase price had already been paid. High-pressure salesmanship not infrequently pushed working-class households into debt, drawing sharp criticism from magistrates and County Court judges who had to deal with the victims.[77] Ellen Wilkinson, Labour MP for Jarrow, introduced a private member's bill in 1937 to deal with the worst abuses such as 'snatch back' and intimidation that received a wide measure of cross-party support and led to the Hire Purchase Act the following year. Wilkinson's taking up of this cause and her preference to work independently rather than through the co-operative movement – which after all had championed working-class consumers for generations – was an important pointer to the future; the emphasis was on the statutory protection of vulnerable consumers rather than their active empowerment.[78] The act represented a progressive step in many ways, admittedly, but it also indicated reluctance on the part of even left-wing Labour members like Wilkinson not only to work with organized consumers but also to think beyond the capitalist market to the 'Co-operative Commonwealth'.

The consumer was brought centre stage more than ever before in interwar Britain. Not only was there growing popular consumerism but also political parties increasingly vied with each other to address the consumer interests of new constituencies after the widening of the franchise in 1918 and 1928. The Conservative Party was most successful here, presenting itself as the housewife's ally at the same time as it encouraged industrial and commercial combination that made consumer exploitation more likely. Significantly, the party also forged closer relationships with the advertising industry, hiring Bensons to run its general election campaigns in 1929 and 1935.[79] Recognizing that free trade had lost popular support, the National Government under Conservative control abandoned the policy finally in 1932, formally aligning itself with a specifically imperial consumerism. Even the co-operative movement, which had traditionally supported free trade, cared little about it by this time and raised hardly any protest about the change.[80]

Professional economists continued to contest the role and significance of the consumer, with a key opposition opening up during the depression. For John Maynard Keynes, writing in 1936 in his landmark work *The General Theory of Employment, Interest and Money*, the lack of popular demand or the 'insufficiency of the propensity to consume' was the root cause of the 'evils of unemployment'. He proposed that the poor spent more of any extra income they received on immediate consumption rather than savings or investment – that is, their 'marginal propensity to consume' was greater. Government policy, Keynes argued, should therefore be aimed at stimulating popular demand, as consumer spending would boost overall economic activity by means of the operation of the 'multiplier'. Keynes praised Mandeville as well as J. A. Hobson as members of that 'brave army of heretics' in the past who had warned about the dangers of underconsumption, which had caused so much hardship between the wars.[81] A very different perspective was proposed by William Hutt in a book that appeared the same year but which remained relatively unknown until the counter-revolution against Keynesianism in the last quarter of the twentieth century. Hutt borrowed or coined the term 'consumer sovereignty' in this work and argued that individual 'consumer choice', operating though the 'free' market and unhindered as far as possible by government interference, was the mainspring of economic growth.[82] These alternative views may have directly confronted each other sooner, had not another war intervened that rendered the notion of 'consumer sovereignty' irrelevant if not decidedly unpatriotic.

8

Mass Consumerism: From Austerity to Affluence

Fair Shares for All?

The idea that the individual consumer was king would have been regarded as ludicrous in Britain during the war against fascism. That did not mean, however, that consumers were ignored by government; far from it. Supplying their wants and maintaining their support by means of a policy of 'Fair Shares for All' was considered a key part of the war effort from the outset. Surveys undertaken by the social research organization Mass-Observation revealed that food shortages caused by the reduction in imports due to enemy action against merchant shipping was high on the list of popular grievances, which the wartime coalition government was naturally keen to address. The price mechanism was therefore put on hold and private consumption severely constrained by controls and restrictions that were imposed on production and demand in order to meet the needs of a wartime economy. Consumer spending consequently plummeted compared to pre-war levels, falling by about 15 per cent for foodstuffs in 1942, more than 30 per cent for clothing and perhaps as much as 75 per cent for household goods. This represented the largest reduction in personal consumption in modern British history.[1]

Although ration books were issued to the population when war was declared in September 1939, rationing was not introduced immediately, though plans had been instigated long before to avoid the problems encountered in the First World War, when food shortages had caused riots and Britain had been nearly starved into surrender. A Food (Defence Plans) Department had been formed as a section of the Board of Trade in 1936 and it was realized that defeat in war was inevitable unless the consumer was guaranteed his or her share, but there was no comprehensive policy until the second Ministry of Food was set up at the beginning of the war, which acted as sole purchaser of imported and home produced food. Rationing faced stiff opposition initially, from the right-wing press and the First Lord of the Admiralty, Winston Churchill, who along with other Conservatives rejected a comprehensive scheme when the issue was discussed by cabinet in October, arguing that such far-reaching state intervention might damage morale. It soon became apparent that the public were strongly in favour, as inaction generated discontent. Commodity divisions were duly established by the Ministry of Food, each controlled by a director, while regional divisions and 1,500 local food control committees implemented rationing and its enforcement on the ground. The cost of foodstuffs spiralled and although the Ministry of Food used subsidies to keep prices down, they rose by 30 per cent during the first few years of the war and would have been much higher without this intervention.[2] Straight rationing was introduced from January 1940 for bacon, butter and sugar, then rolled out piecemeal, underlining the reluctance in some quarters to abandon laissez faire; meat was rationed from March 1940, tea from July and other goods including margarine, cheese, eggs, preserves, soap and chocolate followed. Consumers had to register with retailers who were allowed buying permits based on numbers of customers. The major advantage of this arrangement was that it guaranteed entitlement to basic foods but it was also inflexible. Until December 1941 imperishable goods such as tinned and dried foods were not rationed, which meant that the better off got more. Consequently, a points rationing system based on coupons was introduced; non-rationed foods were given a points rating and all adult consumers allotted sixteen non-specific points every four weeks, which they could use in any shop they liked. This scheme maintained a degree of fairness but also introduced a certain amount of choice that allowed consumers to indulge their taste for luxuries sometimes. Clothing and footwear were also rationed from June 1941 (opposed again by Churchill), and from 1942 manufacturers had to conform to Utility standards that severely limited the amount of fabric and styles that could be offered and, consequently, fashion was strangulated. The general approach was summed up in the official slogan of 'Make Do and Mend'.[3]

An important turning point occurred in April 1940, when Lord Woolton took over from the ineffectual W. S. Morrison as Minister of Food. One of Neville Chamberlain's last acts before Churchill became prime minister, the appointment of this talented retailer indicated a more serious approach by government to the food issue. Woolton fully understood the necessity of sophisticated publicity if the consuming public were to be brought on side, and promoted a policy of 'Fair Shares for All' by means of regular radio broadcasts targeted specifically at housewives, who, he repeatedly emphasized, were making a major contribution to the war effort on the 'Kitchen Front'. The Ministry of Food also used short propaganda films that were shown in cinemas as well as 'Food Facts' that were placed as weekly newspaper advertisements, one of these declaring in November 1941 that 'the British Housewife is helping to make a second front – the Kitchen Front – against Hitler'. Large sums were devoted to this extensive campaign, about

£500,000 on press advertising alone by June 1941.[4] As a highly successful retailer, Woolton had firm faith in private enterprise best serving consumers. As one modern scholar has pointed out, his 'own philosophy tended more towards the virtues of self-help and the nightwatchman state'.[5] Nevertheless, Woolton recognized that extensive though not complete state control of food during the war was vital in order to shore up morale, much more so than the prime minister, who continued to underestimate the importance of such mundanities – a blind spot that may have proved disastrous, especially in the early years of the war when the military situation looked bleak and wartime radicalism was at its peak domestically.[6]

Woolton has been treated kindly by historians.[7] The largely uncritical tone was established early on in accounts of the ministry's work that began to appear even before the war was over. Thomas Jones, for example, who was chief divisional food officer for Wales and the Midlands, emphasized Woolton's common touch, recalling how he had joked with housewives and workers on his many trips around the country, undertaken to publicize the ministry's work.[8] However, there were many inherent flaws in the system of rationing as Woolton sought to simultaneously placate private enterprise and big business and secure popular support for his policy, a difficult if not impossible task. Manual workers employed in heavy industry, for instance, complained that 'fair shares' did not take proper account of how their particular needs were greater than those of other groups. Another major grievance was that wealthier consumers could still eat off ration in restaurants which were not subject to control. In March 1942 Home Intelligence reports for the Ministry of Information drew attention to the fact that some sections of the public thought that dining in restaurants contributed to a feeling that 'inequality of sacrifice' persisted. Woolton attempted to stem such criticism by capping restaurant charges at five shillings but this was simply evaded by charging for extras such as cabaret and music. More important, Woolton tried to win over working-class consumers by such measures as the provision of free milk for poor mothers and their children and the introduction of British Restaurants, where cheap, basic meals could be purchased off-ration in canteen-like surroundings. This experiment in social feeding was very successful and in 1942 there were 2,119 British Restaurants serving 619,000 meals a day, run mainly by local authorities.[9] Notwithstanding the undeniable problems, Mass-Observation reported in March 1942 that the government food policy was working and that there was a large measure of public approval for Woolton. Although there were frequent grumblings about the monotony of the diet, Home Intelligence reports confirmed this view, pointing out from 1942 that food rationing was regarded as the 'finest achievement of the war' and 'one of the chief causes of the excellent morale of the country'. An important measure of the policy's success is that working-class consumption of foodstuffs in many cases rose during the war and nutritional standards improved.[10]

Nevertheless, and despite these successes, organized consumers were highly critical of both government policy and Woolton at the time and their views have been largely ignored in the recent historiography. The co-operative movement met about a quarter of the people's needs during the war and its officials played an important role in the organization of food rationing at both a local and national level. CWS factories were turned over to wartime production – everything from army uniforms to aircraft fuselages – and as a major importer it worked closely with government to ensure supplies of basic foodstuffs such as cereals, butter, margarine, bacon and canned fish.[11] In short, the co-op really came into its own during the war. The movement regarded the policy of 'Fair Shares for All' as closely aligned with its own project, which sought to substitute mutual for private ownership and control. But co-operators were also acutely disappointed that rationing was not implemented sooner and continued to complain about how Woolton often preferred to fudge in order to please his capitalist friends. Perhaps the most concentrated attack came from the Co-op-Labour MP George Darling in a book entitled *The Politics of Food* that was widely discussed in co-operative circles after it was published in 1941, particularly by branches of the Women's Co-operative Guild, whose members played a vital role in making rationing a success despite the guild's long-standing commitment to pacifism.[12] Darling criticized government for its failure to introduce a comprehensive rationing scheme immediately, reckoning that this was because it was 'primarily concerned with the problem of welding vested interests into the fabric of the State'. The Ministry of Food, he argued, fixed prices to suit the food trades, which meant that millions of poor people still went hungry. Producers therefore dominated consumers, who were continually fleeced. Though Darling admitted that Woolton had made a difference and that food control was better organized in this war than it had been in the last, his determination 'to preserve competitive trading practices' had 'prevented the public from enjoying the full benefits of State enterprise'.[13]

The unprecedented level of state intervention meant that capitalist consumerism went on the defensive during the Second World War. Advertising was severely curtailed due to paper shortages, manufacturers had to reduce drastically the number of lines they produced and all brand names were eliminated for the duration of hostilities. They were replaced by standardized products such as 'Orange Squash S.W.153', where the code letters and numbers were sole indication of the manufacturer's identity.[14] However, it was not simply the practical exigencies of war that curtailed consumerism; there was also a general sense that it was wasteful and therefore unpatriotic when the country was in such mortal danger. One of the clearest signs of this new sensibility was the passage of the Pharmacy and Medicines Act in 1941, which made illegal the most cruelly misleading claims that were still frequently made by advertisers of patent or 'quack' medicines, which many doctors continued to prescribe to their patients.

Although the measure was not radical enough according to left-wing MPs such as Aneurin Bevan, who believed that it did not sufficiently attack big business or 'vested interests', the act did represent an important step towards regulation of the advertising industry. Interestingly, it also attracted cross-party support, the noted physiologist and independent Conservative member for Cambridge University, A. V. Hill, remarking during the second reading of the bill in the House of Commons that 'we have been too respectful and tolerant for too long of the exploitation of the sick and suffering. It is time we realised that laisser faire in this matter means cruel scandals, that laisser faire is not freedom but simply everyone for himself and the devil take the hindmost.'[15] In this context, the views of the most trenchant critics of advertising, such as those of the educationalist Denys Thompson, did not seem that extreme, though they would have appeared preposterous just a few years before. Thompson's ironically titled intervention, *Voice of Civilisation*, which appeared in 1943, was influenced by the work of the exiled Hungarian sociologist Karl Mannheim who prophesied that 'the renunciation of absolute freedom of choice – if it should become necessary – will not weigh too heavily on the consumer, mainly because the greater part of the population has never had this freedom of choice and has been forced by poverty to buy standardized goods'.[16] The levelling effects of the war and the state-sanctioned moralization of consumption pointed towards the possibility of a new kind of society for Thompson, one in which branding and advertising would be dispensed with absolutely. He therefore applauded the 'healthy clearing' that had occurred during the war and considered that 'it is not easy to see why any advertising should return, except the genuinely informative and desirable kind'.[17]

Denys Thompson no doubt overestimated the solidarity and anti-commercialism fostered by war. Recent revisionist historians have emphasized the persistence of divisions, inequalities and individualist forms of behaviour that undercut complacent myths about the 'people's war' and a unified 'Kitchen Front'.[18] One aspect that has received much attention is the black market, which some historians argue constituted the dark side of 'fair shares', its extensiveness proving the hollowness of claims about how we were all in it together. There is some truth in this view, certainly; although it is impossible to quantify accurately its exact extent, a widespread black market existed for many goods in short supply, even if it was far less extensive and well organized than those which emerged in America and Germany.[19] However, revisionists have tended to read the evidence rather simplistically and have often failed to differentiate sufficiently between popular attitudes during the war years and in its immediate aftermath, when there was spreading disillusionment with rationing and continuing austerity. The black market became better organized after American bases increased the availability of scarce goods and it was frequently admitted and condemned. A survey of attitudes undertaken by Mass-Observation in May 1943, for example, revealed that most people supported stiffer penalties for blackmarketeers, who were routinely described as 'traitors' or 'Fifth Columnists', and also discerned a common '*underlying* feeling ... that Black Market offences are highly anti-social and unpatriotic'.[20] People tended to distinguish between profiteers who made huge sums from big rackets and deserved to be punished harshly and those who turned a blind eye to 'grey market' activity occasionally, buying luxury goods 'under the counter' and gifting or swapping coupons and rations with friends and relatives, practices that they thought ought to be tolerated. The most recent and thorough account of this subject has usefully suggested that these seemingly paradoxical positions did not mean that rationing was a failure but rather that it was adapted to everyday needs and indeed points to the persistence of a popular 'moral economy' in wartime Britain.[21] Whether one accepts this argument in its entirety, the conclusion drawn in an earlier classic account of the home front remains convincing: 'Rationing was a popular policy, though very far from fair.'[22]

The Labour Party's landslide victory in 1945 was an endorsement of the policy of 'fair shares' and the continuation of economic controls. The majority of the population fully realized and accepted that the economic situation, especially the need to repay American loans and expand government spending on social reconstruction, meant that there would have to be continued belt-tightening and austerity for individual consumers. People braced themselves for the worst and it looked as if it had arrived when bread was rationed in the summer of 1946, which it had not been even during the war and which achieved very little besides further alienating consumers.[23] Discontent was articulated by the British Housewives' League that campaigned to end rationing and controls. A largely middle-class body, the League was supported by many Conservatives though it spoke to grievances that were felt much more widely.[24] The increasing visibility of the 'spiv' on both city streets and cinema screens also testified to the importance of black-market trading that was becoming increasingly tolerated by the mass of consumers.[25] Christian Dior's 'New Look' style with its long, voluminous skirt and wasp waist emphasizing a more traditional, feminine form, which first appeared on the Paris catwalk early in 1947, seemed to symbolize growing dissatisfaction with the constraints on consumer desire, particularly as they were experienced by female consumers such as historian Carolyn Steedman's working-class mother who yearned for a 'New Look' coat. Interestingly, antagonism towards the style was shared among an older generation of women and it crossed political divisions; staunch members of the WCG like Mabel Ridealgh, MP for Ilford North, denounced the 'New Look' as far too sexy as well as wasteful and leaders of the British Housewives' League also came out against it, though opposition did not check the popularity of the fashion among younger women.[26] Although the consumerist forces that threatened to derail Labour's project were becoming difficult to ignore, sympathetic though not uncritical observers could still find grounds for optimism. J. B. Priestley informed readers of the *New York*

Times, for instance, that despite the undeniable drabness and continuing scarcity that was borne most heavily by housewives, things were not as bad as they had been before the war when malnutrition was rife. 'Nobody guzzles, and nobody starves. Both waste and want have vanished', Priestley wrote, and he concluded: 'We live in something that is beginning to resemble a civilized society, and not a dogfight around a carcass.'[27]

While Labour held back domestic consumption in order to pay for an ambitious programme of social provision and pay off Lend-Lease, its political opponents aligned themselves publicly with a resurgent consumer capitalism. Conflicts occurred on many fronts. Department stores had fared relatively well during the war and their owners campaigned vigorously for the repeal of Excess Profits Tax and purchase tax and the ending of the Utility scheme and controlled prices. In Scotland, the struggle was led by Hugh Fraser, president of the Scottish Retail Drapers' Association and one of the most powerful department store bosses in the country.[28] The first of the so-called Bonfire of Controls in 1948 saw the abolition of clothes rationing and a year later restrictions were lifted on furniture and prices fell, moves that the president of the Board of Trade, Harold Wilson, tried to spin to political advantage.[29] Not surprisingly, the future of advertising was hotly debated. As late as 1949, expenditure on press advertising remained only a third of what it had been in 1938 and government action helped keep it down. When Labour took office, the Chancellor of the Exchequer, Hugh Dalton, proposed a 50 per cent reduction in the proportion of a company's advertising budget which could be written off against tax. The *Daily Express* compared the proposal to the taxes on knowledge in the early nineteenth century and roundly condemned the plan: 'Goods that are returning to the shops after years of absence must be brought back to the public notice ... Advertising has an immense part to play in maintaining a healthy and hopeful home market.' Dalton's successor Sir Stafford Cripps ditched this idea in late 1947, though only after the Federation of British Industries agreed to encourage its members to reduce advertising voluntarily. Goaded in the House of Commons by the Conservative MP Oliver Stanley for this apparent retreat, Cripps retorted that he believed in hitting advertising as much as Dalton and threatened to revisit the matter in the future. Stanley addressed the Regent Advertising Club in London soon after, emphasizing in his speech the 'importance of advertising if we were ever to return to a free choice of goods' and crediting 'free consumer's choice' for the existence of most of the comforts enjoyed by present-day consumers. Whether Stanley was consciously borrowing from Friedrich Hayek and William Hutt is impossible to tell but it is significant that this idea, which had been subordinated during the war, was coming more to the fore at this time. Advertisers duly rewarded their friends; earlier that year the Publicity Club of London presented Lord Woolton with what it modestly described as the 'Nobel Prize of Advertising' for his contribution to the industry during wartime.[30] Though the Conservative Party was keen to side with consumer capitalists and was more assiduous in its attempts to win over discontented consumers, it seems unlikely that this fully explains their success in the October 1951 general election, when they narrowly regained political power, as the swing away from Labour was far less than might have been expected, including the female swing to the Tories.[31] And although many Conservatives were eager to unloose the full force of 'free consumer choice' after 1951, post-war austerity had not fully run its course.

The battle of the consumer

The 1950s was a crucial decade in the making of consumer culture in modern Britain. Retailing continued to be characterized by a mixture of old and new forms. Department stores thrived, with 700 listed in the first Census of Distribution taken in 1950. The tendency towards concentration which had begun in the 1920s continued, with Debenhams maintaining its position as the biggest group and operating 110 stores nationwide. Their owners quickly took advantage of the relaxation of economic controls. By 1952 Lewis's Christmas display was almost back to its pre-war standard and when rationing finally ended in 1954 the outlook seemed very positive indeed.[32] Multiple retailers were quick to take advantage of the opportunities that were opening up, as consumers began to have more disposable incomes and expansive desires. Takeovers and mergers marked the menswear sector also, though Montague Burton continued to set the pace on the high street, selling wholesale-bespoke suits and offering 'an egalitarian vision of a sartorial democracy' to a diverse range of male consumers. Market leaders were increasingly challenged, however, by smaller stores that began to offer a less regimented and timeless style. Colour was coming in, sometimes even a 'feminine angle', according to the trade journal *Men's Wear*.[33] The gradual easing of rules governing consumer credit from the middle of the decade also made goods much more accessible; total hire purchase debt more than doubled between 1956 and 1959, rising from £361 million to £742 million. The expansion of mail-order retailing firms such as Littlewoods and Kays played an important role here, as they embedded credit within working-class communities by means of agents that were familiar to customers. Mail order made it possible for goods to be bought on 'easy terms', and browsing through the companies' elaborately illustrated catalogues became a common leisure activity enjoyed by many. Check traders such as the Provident also continued to be important for working-class consumers despite the high rates of interest charged, and they were to remain so until the mid-1970s.[34]

Innovations such as self-service stores and supermarkets represented the vanguard of change. Rather than be served personally by an assistant at a counter, shoppers now had to help themselves to goods from display shelves and carry them to the checkout in baskets. There was resistance to the new practices – some consumers preferring to hang on to their own baskets – but government encouraged change and supported fact-finding missions to America, as well as a visit by an official 'Productivity Team' organized as part of the Marshall Aid agreement in 1947. The co-operative movement was an enthusiastic pioneer of self-service but other multiple retailers like Sainsbury's and Tesco were also keen. The main drivers of change, however, were not retailers or consumers (who had to be persuaded of the benefits) but rather producers of frozen foods and American manufacturers of shop equipment who represented self-service as a more modern, rational and hygienic form of shopping.[35] Though traditional methods persisted, the spread of self-service was quite dramatic; there were only 10 self-service grocery stores in 1947 but three years later there were 500. By 1960, there were 6,350 self-service stores in Britain, including 531 supermarkets, and a decade later the figures had risen to 28,000 and 3,400 respectively. Market share rose from 15 per cent of food shopping in 1959 to 64 per cent in 1969. British stores were similar to those that had proliferated in the United States before the war though they were generally smaller. Contemporary commentators linked the rise of shoplifting to the spread of self-service, as numbers of people charged by police with shop theft in England and Wales almost doubled between 1949 and 1959, from nearly 10,948 to 17,745, increasing to 34,150 by 1968. Official statistics failed to distinguish between different types of shops but the increasing incidence, aided by press coverage, became conflated in the public mind with self-service. Modern shopping often tested consumers' self-control to the limit, it was thought; as a member of the Design Council remarked, good packaging attracted women like 'waving a torch in front of her eyes'. As in the nineteenth century, some magistrates sympathized with those caught shoplifting, believing that the temptations on offer were often simply too irresistible.[36]

Such changes did not occur in a political vacuum: the title of the pamphlet Labour MP Elaine Burton published in 1955 – *The Battle of the Consumer* – was highly apposite. As we have already seen, advertising went on the offensive when war ended, its apologists including right-wing journalists, intellectuals and politicians emphasizing how the industry constituted a defining feature of a 'free' society. Claiming objectivity, F. P. Bishop, for instance, argued that advertising was already cleaning up its own act, with a voluntary code going further than government legislation. Significantly, Bishop and others found support in Friedrich Hayek's influential indictment of socialist 'totalitarianism', *The Road to Serfdom* (1944).[37] Thus, the development of consumerism in post-war Britain was profoundly shaped by the politics of the early Cold War, as it was in the United States and mainland Europe. Indeed, in a crucial sense consumer culture was the real victor in the Cold War.[38] Its influence was felt in many ways. One fairly unusual but nevertheless emblematic example occurred in 1948 when employees of the John Lewis Partnership were forced to sign an anti-communist pledge.[39] Critics of advertising at home were frequently portrayed as supporting drab communist regimes that necessarily limited consumer desires and for a while the killjoys seemed to be winning post-war; outdoor advertising was brought under full control by the Town and Country Planning Act of 1948, for example, and SCAPA was finally wound up a few years later. Advertising expenditure had been greater as a percentage of the national income in 1938 than it was in the mid-1950s.[40] The fight back properly began the summer before the Conservatives were elected in 1951, when the International Advertising Convention was held in London under the strap line 'The Task of Advertising in a Free World'. Three thousand delegates from thirty-seven countries packed into Westminster's Central Hall where the conference president, Lord Halifax, summed up the key theme: 'Advertising in all its forms can be a very powerful force in maintaining freedom. It is closely linked with freedom of speech, freedom of the Press, freedom of choice, and I believe that if any one of these goes, freedom itself will soon depart.' Building on the success of the conference, the Advertising Association decided to launch a public relations campaign in order to improve the industry's image. One tactic adopted was a panel of speakers that toured the country praising the virtues of advertising at public meetings; from the mid-1950s the Association's speakers addressed over 800 such meetings at schools, branches of the WCG and the Workers' Educational Association, and Rotary Clubs.[41]

The co-operative movement was a major player in the battle of the consumer, in the protracted struggle that occurred in the 1950s across the culture and polity over which groups most accurately represented the consumer and could therefore speak on their behalf. It had worked closely with the state in the Second World War and had done much to maintain morale on the home front, as has been already noted. Even its most determined opponents did not dare call it a curse now, at least not in public, and it continued to prosper in the decade or so after war ended. Membership increased from more than 9.7 million in 1946 to 12.5 million in 1958. Annual trade of more than a thousand retail societies grew from over £402 million to nearly £998 million in the same period. By the early 1950s at least one-third of the entire adult population was connected with the co-op in one way or another and it remained a defining feature of working-class life.[42] The organization continued to be plagued by the old weaknesses, however, especially over-reliance on the sale of groceries and coal and a failure to compete successfully with department stores and multiples in the sale of dry goods such as clothes, home furnishings and new consumer durables like washing machines, vacuum cleaners and televisions. It was frequently regarded as being behind the times and selling outdated styles. Sympathetic intellectuals like the historian G. D. H. Cole criticized the movement for lacking imagination and recommended that it venture into new fields including cinema and theatres, and recruit managers from university graduates. Cole thought the movement was too insular, defensively working-class, and he was not alone.[43]

However, co-operators were not entirely backward looking, introducing self-service early on, as we have noted. Some societies were more progressive than others and there were signs that the movement was becoming more style conscious and trying harder to keep up with rapidly changing consumer tastes; the CWS, for example, worked to this end with the Council of Industrial Design, which had been established by the Board of Trade towards the end of the war.[44] There were ideological as well as material difficulties to overcome though and the movement had trouble defining and maintaining its distinctive vision of social and economic change. In debates with allies in the Labour Party, co-operative leaders insisted that their form of common ownership and control was preferable to nationalization but their perspective was marginalized. The movement did not receive much help from the Attlee government – in fact, it had many grievances. Labour flirted with plans to engage in state trading, local co-operative societies were often excluded from many of the new housing estates, and the movement was threatened by plans to nationalize insurance. Well before the Conservatives regained power it had become obvious that co-operators were going to have to face the challenges posed by resurgent consumer capitalism alone. The struggle quickly became overt as trade associations and monopolies threatened the co-op more acutely. Heated contests occurred in particular markets; first in 1952 the co-operative brand Spel fought it out against Unilever's Persil for the synthetic detergent market, then two years later competitive margarines such as Blue Band were pitched against Red Seal. Although they put up a good show for a while, co-op advertising campaigns were poorly funded compared to those of its competitive rivals and they eventually lost out.[45]

The temperature of public debate on consumer culture in general and advertising in particular was raised in the run-up to the introduction of commercial television in 1954. The co-operative movement was opposed to this development, fearing that advertisers would exploit the new media to strengthen their grip on consumers. Sharing with co-operators an ascetic attitude towards consumption, many Labour MPs came out against it, including Aneurin Bevan who famously remarked at the Advertising Association's conference in 1953 that advertising was 'one of the most evil consequences of modern society, which is itself intrinsically evil'. Bevan also proudly revealed in the same speech that he did not own a television himself and had never even seen a television programme![46] The gulf between well-intentioned but puritanical leaders like Bevan and most working-class consumers who understandably desired more material goods was widening in this period, a fact that Conservatives readily exploited.[47] At the same event, Reginald Maudling, economic secretary to the treasury and a leading mover of accelerating the Bonfire of Controls after 1951, backed the individual consumer over the 'gentleman in Whitehall' and asserted that 'the consumer should be enabled to express a preference and choice'. Maudling pledged support for the industry as an intrinsic part of a revitalized capitalism:

'Advertising is an essential part of the machinery of competition which, I and the Government believe, is the best protection of the consumer and the best assurance of industrial efficiency.'[48]

Such oppositions recurred when the contest moved into the formal political arena. In the House of Commons, Herbert Morrison stressed that television advertising would increase the cost of goods for the consumer and the power of 'the rich monopolies'. George Darling voiced similar fears, emphasizing how J. Walter Thompson (JWT) had been hired by private soap firms to defeat the co-op. From an increasingly embattled position, Darling and others maintained that the impact of commercial television on the co-operative alternative had to be understood within a wider context of continuing economic and political conflict. In cabinet, the cause of commercial television was championed by the party chairman, Lord Woolton, while in the Commons young Tory backbenchers like John Rodgers, Charles Orr-Ewing and John Profumo – all of whom had links of one kind or another with the worlds of advertising and telecommunications – used this opportunity to trumpet their support for the 'freedom' of consumers and place themselves squarely on the side of young, aspiring and fashion-conscious couples who wanted more and more modern things.[49] For them, advertising was a vital constituent of a new consumerism that was rapidly developing. Labour puritans, they argued, wanted to choke demand and go back to the grim days of ration books and food queues.[50] Nevertheless, the outcome of this crucial debate on the morality of consumer culture was a close run thing as political parties were divided; many Conservatives were opposed to commercial television and so too were the Archbishop of Canterbury and university vice chancellors, who fretted about the adverse effects it would have on cultural standards and taste. The Television Act of 1954 represented a compromise and ensured that unlike in the United States, commercial television in Britain would depend on commercial subsidy rather than sponsorship in order to prevent advertisers' undue influence.[51]

The advertising industry unsurprisingly received a major boost from the introduction of commercial television, expenditure on advertising increasing from £134 million or 1.6 per cent of national income in 1953, to £323 million or 2.2 per cent in 1959. However, many advertising agencies did not welcome the new media as most of their business was with the press and newspapers were themselves divided, the *Daily Express* condemning it while the *Daily Mirror* lent support. It was Conservative Central Office, not advertising agencies, that described the 1954 act as 'a moment of triumph in the history of the free mind'.[52] Television advertising also intensified cultural anxieties concerning 'Americanization', as it was feared that the crass, hectoring modes and blatant product placement that were seen to characterize television in the United States would be imported wholesale. More worrying still were the 'psychological' approaches pioneered by people like Ernest Dichter, a leading figure in what was called 'motivational research' that specialized in revealing the unconscious sexual drives that supposedly caused consumers to purchase anything from an automobile to a pack of cigarettes. Again, there was a Cold War twist. Vance Packard's *The Hidden Persuaders* (1957), which was fiercely critical of Dichter's work, heightened concerns of left intellectuals who thought that 'subliminal advertising' would render consumers even more powerless than they already were and was akin to 'brainwashing' adopted by totalitarian regimes.[53] Dichter's influence on this side of the Atlantic though was limited – he did not open a London office until 1959 – and even American-owned agencies like JWT had to adapt their practices to suit British audiences, which often meant using indigenous idioms and employing soft-sell techniques rather than more aggressive methods.[54] Adopting a pragmatic approach to motivation research, British agencies were more than adept at sifting the useful, lucrative wheat from the Freudian chaff.[55] They developed extensive campaigns for their clients that drew on an eclectic range of traditions and styles, including documentary film making and the soap opera. Critics of advertising were proved correct as big manufacturers with large budgets dominated the market. Unilever products such as soapless detergents, improved margarines and frozen foods, for example, were pushed most systematically, the company remaining ITV's largest advertiser for three decades. According to a recent study, agencies like JWT attempted to 'assemble' and 'mobilize' housewives using more sophisticated advertising to build brand loyalty. Consequently, commercial television was saturated with commercials for packaged goods such as the Pin-Up home perm, Brillo soap pads, Persil washing powder and Oxo cubes – the latter featuring a 'slice of life' series of advertisements that stared Katie and her 'perfect' patriarchal suburban family. Jingles and oxymoronic slogans – 'Persil Washes Whiter', 'Oxo Gives a Meal Man Appeal' – colonized private life, though whether the products penetrated the consciousness of consumers in any really meaningful sense remains open to doubt.[56]

Having it so good?

In the summer of 1957 Conservative Prime Minister Harold Macmillan famously remarked; 'Most of our people have never had it so good. Go around the country, go to the industrial towns, go to the farms, and you will see a state of prosperity such as we have never had in my lifetime – nor indeed ever in the history of this country.'[57] The second half of the 1950s undoubtedly witnessed an important turning point in the development of consumer culture in Britain. Between 1952 and 1964 consumer expenditure rose by 45 per cent, with the percentage devoted to food, drink and tobacco shrinking, while the amount spent on consumer durables such as television sets, vacuum cleaners, washing machines, electric heaters and cookers more than doubled. Car ownership was perhaps the most obvious symbol of a developing 'affluent society'; in 1952 there were about 2.5 million cars on the road, rising to 5 million by 1959, and ownership was no longer confined to the middle classes either. Increases in wages as well as easier credit made mass consumerism possible; average weekly earnings increased from £7 10s. (£7.50) a week in 1950, to £11 in 1955, to over £18 in 1964, far outstripping the annual rise in prices.[58]

These changes provoked widespread reaction, intellectuals and politicians across the political spectrum frequently pointing to a new acquisitiveness among the working class in particular. In May 1962 Conservative MP Victor Montagu (Lord Hinchingbrooke), for instance, described to the House of Commons how, when visiting council houses in his South Dorset constituency during the previous general election, he had been struck by the many signs of affluence visible in some of them:

> Not day after day but on at least two occasions I found the council house completely transformed. The centre wall had been taken out, the lower storey had a beam across, there was a kitchen at one side, a screen with flowers and a living room on the other side – something that one would expect to see at the Council of Industrial Design as a recent example of modern art. The tea things were brought out on a silver tray – a silver teapot, silver milk jug and a silver sugar bowl – and tea was served. In the corner of the room was a baby grand piano as well as a television set, a wireless and various other things of that kind. When I said, 'Thank you very much for tea; I must go to the next place now,' they said, 'We are very sorry that you cannot stop for cocktails.'[59]

The sarcasm was wasted on Montagu, naturally, but the comicality of the incident caught the attention of the cartoonist for the popular Sunday paper the *News of the World*. Reproduced as Figure 13, George Chrystal imagined the interior of a council flat stuffed with expensive, high-status consumer goods bought on hire purchase by a spendthrift working-class mother and daughter, much to the disgruntlement of the father of the family – the sexist gendering of consumer practices stubbornly persisting.

Another important sign of change was the emergence of the 'teenager'. An American import, usage of the term quickly spread in Britain during the 1950s. By the time Macmillan made his speech it was omnipresent, popular journalists frequently discussing the problems facing this age group and advertisers targeting them as a lucrative market for commodities such as portable radios and gramophones, records, magazines and, of course, new styles of dress. The period also witnessed the birth of youth subcultures, the first being 'teddy boys' with their drainpipe trousers, long 'drape' jackets that harked back to the Edwardian period (hence the nickname), and crepe-soled shoes. The reputed violence of the 'teds' (and later the 'skinheads') generated a media panic and also drew condescending criticism from liberal intellectuals such as Richard Hoggart who, in his influential study *The Uses of Literacy* (1957), regarded them as symptomatic of the corrosion of an

FIGURE 13 *George Chrystal,* News of the World, *27 May 1962. © News Syndication Limited.*

older, more 'authentic' working-class culture by an Americanized commercial culture that was supposedly 'unbending the springs of action'. Hoggart's open disdain for the working-class youth whom he had left behind him as a scholarship boy strikes the modern reader as particularly distasteful. Young men in particular, sporting 'drape-suits, picture ties, and an American slouch', were described aimlessly wasting their time in the new milk bars, pouring their money into jukeboxes. Hoggart concluded: 'The hedonistic but passive barbarian who rides in a fifty-horsepower bus for three pence, to see a five-million-dollar film for one-and-eight pence, is not simply a social oddity; he is a portent.'[60] While most young people did not participate in subcultures they did avidly consume, as studies produced by Mark Abrams – an ex-employee of an advertising agency turned market researcher – made abundantly clear. According to Abrams, teenagers spent more than £1 billion in 1962, fuelling 'a growing fight by salesmen to secure a slice of the young people's pocket money', as a reporter in the *Daily Mail* cheerfully observed.[61]

Political parties had to respond to spreading affluence. An editorial in *The Times* three years before Macmillan's Bradford speech registered the important shift that had taken place in Conservative thought since the late 1940s. It did this by contrasting two policy documents; *Industrial Charter* published by Conservative Central Office in 1947, and *Change Is Our Ally* that had recently been issued by the One Nation Group within the party. The first of these had criticized 'unnecessary controls' but had also accepted the need for substantial planning. According to the editor, victory in the 1951 general election had strengthened the 'new *laissez faire*' with its stress on competition and freedom from controls, and which clearly marked the latter document. Its authors, Enoch Powell and Angus Maude, condemned the preceding three decades as a period that had witnessed the incremental growth of planning, and argued that this trend had to be reversed in order to liberate the consumer. Their credo was simple; 'Efficient coordination depends not on centralized planning but on the exercise of consumer choice based on economic costs competitively determined.'[62] Conservative Party think tanks such as the One Nation Group (founded in 1950), the Bow Group (founded in 1951) and the formally independent Institute of Economic Affairs (IEA, founded in 1955) sought to popularize such views both within the party and more broadly, contrasting 'free consumer choice' that distinguished Western democracies from the lack of consumer choice that characterized communist regimes in the authoritarian East.[63] Sensing that their view of the role of the consumer was winning out the apostles of advertising and their supporters in the political and commercial fields became increasingly self-confident. As the chairman of Unilever, Lord Heyworth, declared at the company's annual general meeting in 1958: 'Advertising is essential to a free economy. A free economy presupposes freedom of choice for the consumer, just as at the other extreme a totalitarian economy restricts freedom of choice by restricting what can be chosen.'[64] Playing on a well-worn theme, Ralph Harris and Arthur Seldon of the IEA asserted that advertising facilitated capitalist progress and would therefore eventually help to civilize consumers in China and India as it had helped civilize consumers in the West. They went on to conflate the modern citizen with the discriminating consumer, categories and identities which were, according to them, complementary sides of the same freedom-loving subject, and they concluded that advertising understood as 'advocacy in the commercial and political spheres' was inevitable 'in a society with developed means of mass communications and with consumers and citizens who must be persuaded rather than browbeaten or coerced into accepting a product or a political party'.[65]

It would be an error to think that all Labour leaders set their faces against consumer culture. If figures such as Attlee, Cripps, Morrison and Bevan – whose conception of socialism differed in many other respects – agreed that it was a bad thing, others did not. The ascetic 'Labour socialism' which marked a leadership formed in the interwar years was largely rejected by a younger generation of 'modernizers' and 'revisionists' that included Hugh Gaitskell, leader of the party from 1955.[66] This latter group eagerly picked up on the increasing diffusion of goods among the working class especially, slow and uneven though this was in actuality, celebrating this as sign of a wider transformation – that the 'age of austerity' was over at last and that an 'age of affluence' was now dawning. In his important book *The Future of Socialism* (1956), Anthony Crosland distanced himself from Owenite utopianism and the co-operative ideal, wholeheartedly embracing the capitalist market and the idea of 'consumer sovereignty' as the best way of securing material well-being for the majority. He welcomed the purported 'embourgeoisement' of the working class, whereby rising levels of consumption was mechanistically thought to be turning workers into middle-class individuals.[67] This crude notion was supported at the time by the influential work of Mark Abrams, who had cultured strong links with the Labour Party and produced private polls for them.[68] Crosland also contested the view that such qualitative as well as quantitative changes had dubious moral or political results, seeing in youth groups like teddy boys, for example, the awakening of a desire for 'sartorial elegance' as well as evidence of the healthy expansion of an 'individual's range of choice and cultural possibilities' among the working classes. 'My working-class constituents', he later remarked, 'want washing machines and refrigerators to relieve domestic drudgery; they want cars, and the freedom they give on weekends and holidays ... They want these things not ... because their minds have been brain-washed and their tastes contrived by advertising, but because the things are desirable in themselves.' Crosland hoped that the democratizing influence of mass consumerism would help integrate citizens into a 'common consumer culture', as had already happened, he naively believed, in America.[69] Fittingly, antagonists in the battle of the consumer often came to literally embody their respective positions, Crosland's flamboyant clothing and 'Hampstead set' lifestyle with its jazz and parties contrasting sharply with Morrison's proletarian background and preference for ill-fitting co-op suits.[70]

An important strand on the centre-right of the Labour Party, which included politicians such as Peter Shore, Francis Noel-Baker and Elaine Barton as well as Crosland, was trying to move closer towards the consumer and consumer issues during this period, arguing that the party needed to diversify away from its traditional bases of support in male-dominated trade unions. However, unlike free market zealots such as Harris and Seldon, they did not believe that 'consumer sovereignty' provided the master key to progress, nor that 'caveat emptor' should be the rule in politics as well as economics.[71] Crosland and other revisionists thought that much advertising was misleading, for instance, and that modern consumerism was full of snares and traps for unwary consumers. The notion that consumers were frequently gullible, ill-equipped to deal with sophisticated techniques of salesmanship and consequently often fleeced, was evidenced in many ways. Newspapers such as the *Daily Herald* and the *News of the World* began to offer consumer advice to readers grappling with the problems of 'affluence' and proliferating 'choice'.[72] Leftish intellectuals such as Richard Hoggart also weighed into the debate, Hoggart condemning advertising for the way it debased language and therefore values, arguments that he put before the Pilkington Committee that was established in 1960 to investigate advertising on commercial television and which led to a tightening of control.[73] Keynesian economists also sounded warnings about how advertising was being used not only to manipulate consumers but also as a means of shutting competitors out of markets in order to maintain oligopolistic power. Nicholas Kaldor had produced some important early studies here but the critique achieved wide publicity after the publication of J. K. Galbraith's popular work *The Affluent Society* in 1958.[74] Noel-Baker later drew attention to the suspicion towards the advertising industry that had grown up following all this bad press, which had also been intensified by the 'advertising wars' among soap manufacturers themselves that made it obvious that the game worked very much to the advantage 'of the big outfit, with an established position and an established share of the market'.[75]

The question remained: How best to educate and protect vulnerable consumers? Labour began advocating consumer protection and a 'Consumer's Charter' from the early 1950s, and Elaine Burton called for the setting up of a consumers' advisory service in her pamphlet. Such demands were strengthened by the recommendations of the Molony Committee in 1962 that led to the creation of the Consumer Council that operated between 1963 and 1970 and which sought, albeit on a shoestring budget, to protect the individual consumer.[76] However, voluntary action preceded these efforts, in the form of the Consumers' Association (CA) which had been set up in 1957 along similar lines as the US Consumers Union and the Swedish Institute for Consumer Research. Founded by an associate of Crosland, Michael Young, who had also been arguing for a consumer advice service since the beginning of the decade, the group appealed particularly to members of the professional middle class, a narrowness repeatedly emphasized by its critics.[77] Nevertheless, the early growth of the CA was impressive; it already claimed a quarter of a million members by spring 1961, rising to over half a million by the beginning of the 1970s. The association sought to educate consumers and help them negotiate their way through the bewildering world of modern consumer goods, mainly by means of its monthly publication, *Which?* magazine, that published results of comparative product tests conducted on 'scientific' lines. The consumer that this organization addressed and constructed was quintessentially individual, rational, efficient and male.[78] The CA also supported legislation to protect consumers and Young even suggested the need for a new Consumers' Party.[79] Although there has been some debate on this subject, it seems unlikely that this body can be construed as a social movement in the full sense. Thousands of middle-class consumers may have subscribed to *Which?*, though it seems unlikely that many of these members had much idea about the wider aims of the organization.[80] It makes more sense, perhaps, to regard the CA as a pressure group that attempted to represent and amalgamate the interests of individual, rational consumers. The result was a politics of consumption of sorts but one which had as its main goal the maximization of individual consumer satisfaction within the existing capitalist framework.

By the late 1950s and early 1960s both the major political parties agreed on the need for greater consumer protection. Most important, they also prioritized an individual model of the consumer and consequently the collective consumer lost out. The co-operative movement, already weakened internally by economic and social factors, was pushed more and more to the sidelines by its erstwhile allies. This was demonstrated most clearly by the movement's establishment in 1955 of the Co-operative Independent Commission (CIC) to investigate its strengths and weaknesses. Gaitskell chaired the CIC and Anthony Crosland served as its secretary, while other members included J. B. Jefferys, author of a major history of retailing and secretary of the International Association of Department Stores, and even the big grocer Alan Sainsbury. The final report which appeared in 1958 recommended sweeping amalgamation of retail societies and various other forms of rationalization designed to maximize economic 'efficiency', including the appointment of university graduates on high salaries to run societies. Any utopian aspirations were brusquely dispensed with, particularly the claim that the co-operative movement sought to eliminate profit. The commission's findings were hotly debated in co-operative circles, then duly ignored.[81] As the co-operative educationalist Fred Abbotts, who was among the CIC's many critics, later recalled: 'You can't inquire into the co-operative trade unless you have some relation to the members. Well, they didn't ... what you got was a very good report on how to run a capitalist business.'[82] The cartoonist David Low ridiculed the movement's failure to adequately respond to its problems. Figure 14 shows a co-op store squeezed between private chains and multiples, the old-fashioned long-whiskered manager advising his young assistant to beware of suspicious characters like Gaitskell, who stands looking on while customers flee away.

Thereafter, the co-op retreated into itself, becoming ever more defensive and inward looking. Membership figures still looked quite healthy on paper but very few members were active in local societies. An incisive study of the problem of member 'apathy' recommended following the example set by the great societies in London and Birmingham – where elections to management and educational committees were fought on explicitly political lines – in order to galvanize members into action.[83] But such advice was ignored and the isolation of the leadership from ordinary co-operative shoppers continued. The abandonment of the dividend in the late 1960s and its replacement with trading stamps that had been introduced by the co-op's competitors symbolized the movement's ineluctable degeneration. The move provoked heated controversy in the Royal Arsenal Co-operative Society in 1970, provoking one senior official to snap, 'We cannot allow a decision of this magnitude to be left in the hands of its members.'[84]

Labour and the Tories not only embraced the protection of consumers rather than their real empowerment, they also both internalized, to a greater or lesser degree, some of the central ways in which individuals were addressed, made sense of and classified within the commercial field,

FIGURE 14 *David Low,* Guardian, *10 June 1960. © Associated Newspapers Limited.*

namely advertising and market research.[85] This intermeshing of politics with commerce goes back a long way as we have seen, to the Edwardian period at least, but it was not until the dawn of the 'age of affluence' that these spheres became thoroughly integrated. Dismayed by this development, the editor of the *New Statesman* offered a pessimistic analysis on the eve of the 1959 general election. Kingsley Martin criticized Gaitskell for treating the election 'as a contest in publicity techniques', likening the event to no more than an 'auction' on employment rates, pension schemes and 'plans for owning more cars, houses and washing machines'. Pointing out that promises of private gratification depended on continued economic growth, Martin went on to argue that it was vital to educate the electorate about the urgent need for expanded social provision provided by the state: 'Someone has to tell the electorate the truth, to treat the voter as a citizen and not as a consumer. We shall soon face the problem of survival unless we remake our industry and our schools at a pace that at present seems unthinkable.' He concluded by suggesting that this was the urgent task now facing socialists that represented – and here Martin drew on the concept recently coined by J. B. Priestley – 'the real alternative to the ad-man's appeal to the ad-mass'.[86]

The Conservative Party spent nearly half a million pounds on what soon became known as the 'TV election', employing a public relations firm to package its image. The Labour MP Richard Crossman questioned the views of the psephologist David Butler, who argued soon after Labour's unexpected defeat at the polls that the party should substitute public relations techniques for political education, which could only happen, Crossman maintained, if it had, 'completely surrendered to Mr Crosland's philosophy of Revisionism'.[87] Labour's capitulation to a commercialized political discourse was hardly complete; powerful interest groups including constituency party members, the trade unions and the co-operative movement continued to speak in a different idiom but the shift at the centre was important. Mark Abrams's relationship with the party is one indication of this. Wanting to make greater use of opinion polls and market research, Gaitskell had recruited Abrams but faced staunch resistance. Under Harold Wilson, however, the National Executive Committee brought Abrams in from the cold, appointing him to an official research post in 1962.[88]

Standing up for individual consumers and extending 'choice' was becoming the common-sense view across the political spectrum. This was demonstrated, for example, by the abolition of Resale Price Mechanism (RPM) in 1964. RPM allowed manufacturers to enforce minimum prices for their goods on retailers and its abolition caused deep rifts in the Conservative Party, contributing to their narrow defeat in the general election that year. The co-operative movement had led the struggle against RPM during the previous decade, which had resulted in the Restrictive Trade Practices Act of 1956. Reflecting Tory support for big business, however, the act only outlawed collective cartels and price-fixing by individual firms remained intact.[89] From the early 1960s, the cause was led by the owner of Tesco supermarkets and ardent Tory supporter, Jack Cohen, who conducted a highly publicized price-cutting campaign, representing himself as champion of the ordinary housewife. Mimicking the dividend offered by the co-op, Cohen began giving away trading stamps with goods, thus effectively undermining fixed prices, and he challenged big manufacturers such as Cadbury's to fight him through the courts. Small shopkeepers opposed change, naturally, but Edward Heath, president of the Board of Trade, strongly supported abolition and forced it through against stiff opposition in cabinet. Labour as well as Tory modernizers also thought it prudent to position themselves as allies of the consumer; after RPM was abolished, Labour leader Harold Wilson congratulated Cohen personally for his efforts.[90] Continuing economic and social changes encouraged this public stance. New developments such as the modernist Bull Ring Shopping Centre in Birmingham, opened by the Duke of Edinburgh as the bill abolishing RPM was making its fraught way through Parliament, could be read as symbolizing how social democratic faith in the 'white heat of technology' was destined to improve the lives of ordinary citizens as consumers as well as producers. Costing

£8 million and covering a four-acre site in the city centre, the Bull Ring boasted over a hundred shops, two markets, three department stores and two supermarkets, all under cover and centrally heated. Easily accessible by car, bus and train, the accent was on shopping as pleasurable leisure activity, with restaurants, pubs, cafes, a crèche and rest areas all provided. As Shirley Lowe, 'shopping correspondent' for the *Daily Mirror*, noted at the time, 'Only a mother who has battled through crowds and traffic and indifference to buy the evening meal and a new dress and a blazer for her child can really see the advantages.'[91]

Nevertheless, critics of this brave new world of consumerism remained, sniping at the margins. Liberal moralists like Hoggart continued to complain about what they saw as the pernicious effects of advertising but this often sounded little more than snobbery; surveys suggested that most working-class people approved of advertising and often found it rather entertaining.[92] More profound if even less influential were the searching analyses developed by some of the ex-communists and independent socialists that grouped together as the New Left. In a penetrating essay, for instance, Raymond Williams argued for a structural understanding of the role of advertising. For Williams, advertising was not merely a kind of unnecessary excrescence that needed only to be properly regulated and its worst abuses reformed, but rather a fundamental, constitutive aspect of the dominant capitalist economy and culture. Moreover, it was becoming all pervasive, colonizing the political as well as the economic fields, a 'magic system' or 'the official art of modern capitalist society' which functioned as a kind of ideological ether for a thoroughly acquisitive society that placed the satisfaction of individual fantasy before social provision. Distinguishing the term 'user', implying a reciprocal, active relationship between buyer and seller, from 'consumer', implying unequal exchange between buyer and seller in an abstract market, Williams argued that advertising served as a 'functional obscuring' of the choice represented by these different terms and identities.[93] If advertising's role was one key target for New Left thinkers, the discourse of 'affluence' was another. The contribution of the social historian E. P. Thompson is illuminating here. Thompson exposed 'affluence' as a trope that served to bolster what was later described as capitalism's golden age. He pointed out that so-called affluent workers had been observed before, as long ago as the third quarter of the nineteenth century. Drawing on this earlier historical experience, Thompson cast doubt on those contemporary commentators like Crosland who believed the diffusion of material goods was leading to a classless society, arguing that what was happening instead was a recomposition and reimagining of class identities.[94] Thompson's argument was to be partially vindicated a few years later by sociological studies that revealed just how tenacious a sense of class continued to be among industrial workers, despite the undeniable changes in lifestyle that had indeed occurred owing to the spread of consumer culture.[95]

9

Consumer Culture: The Hegemony of Choice

Consumers at the end of the 'golden age'

During the last three decades of the twentieth century in Britain, the consumer became truly hegemonic. Before this period, the term 'consumer' had been used largely as a synonym for shopper and there was a great deal of suspicion towards consumers across the ideological spectrum as we have seen. Consumers were still frequently portrayed by commentators and politicians as innately gullible, prone by definition to temptation and passing fancy, and usually feminine – hardly an appropriate bedrock for a whole social, economic and political order. But this changed as gradually people came to be regarded primarily as consumers, whether in the role of patients, tenants, students, voters or parents. Moreover, the consumer was increasingly configured as no longer quintessentially female and weak willed but as rational and male, just as they had been by the Consumers' Association from the outset.[1] Indeed, by the end of the twentieth century, some intellectuals were arguing that it was high time that consumption and the consumer be acknowledged as 'the vanguard of history'.[2]

This profound shift occurred during the fag end of a period described by economic historians as capitalism's 'golden age', when greater numbers of people in Europe and North America enjoyed more disposable income than ever before and the quantity and diversity of consumer goods on sale proliferated at an unprecedented rate. In Britain, the sustained economic growth and high levels of employment after the Second World War that underpinned mass consumerism and stimulated investment came to an abrupt end in 1973 when the Organization of Petroleum Exporting Countries (OPEC) hiked the price of oil, which acted as a trigger, exposing underlying economic weaknesses and leading to a rejection of growth-oriented policies.[3] Consumers were already suffering the effects of inflation in the early 1970s – the rate climbed steadily from 6.4 per cent to 9.2 per cent between 1970 and 1973 – but the economy increasingly appeared out of control after the oil crisis hit, with inflation rising to 16 per cent in 1974, peaking at 24.2 per cent the year after. This trend worked to the advantage of right-wing opinion formers, who, drawing on the work of libertarian thinkers such as Friedrich Hayek and Chicago school 'monetarist' economists like Milton Friedman, painted an apocalyptic picture of the effects of rising prices on both the cost of living for individual households and national stability. Inflation became a key component in the discourse of British 'decline', blown up by influential organs of the press including *The Times* and *The Economist*. However, such anxiety was not shared by the public as a whole it seems while unemployment, though relatively high, (it had risen to 6 per cent by 1976), remained at what was perceived to be an acceptable level.[4]

Continuing a line of criticism that ran back to the 1950s, Conservative politicians blamed soaring inflation on over-powerful unions, whose greed, they maintained, caused a wage–price spiral which undermined the nation. Such arguments were reinforced by the confrontation between the National Union of Mineworkers and the Conservative government led by Edward Heath, who tried to face down striking miners by calling a general election on the theme of 'Who Governs Britain?' in February 1974. The Labour Party attempted to win over consumers during the election campaign; its manifesto promised food subsidies and intervention to curb rent increases, and Harold Wilson claimed that 'the housewife has been in the firing line ever since Mr Heath was elected'. As the *Daily Mail* noted, Wilson took the opportunity to move the debate away from 'the awkward question of the miners' strike and on to the kitchen front'.[5] Significantly, miners garnered much public sympathy and the Conservative Party narrowly lost at the polls, an experience that particularly shook those on the right of the party such as Margaret Thatcher, who took over as leader the following year.[6] When in power, the Labour Party lurched from one crisis to another until the Chancellor of the Exchequer, Denis Healey, made it clear that reducing inflation was to be given priority over maintaining employment in his spring budget of 1975. For the rest of the decade the party tried to restrain wages by means of a 'social contract' with the unions and by imposing a pay freeze on public sector workers, a policy fraught with difficulties. Public sector employees, many of whom were women and non-white workers, were among the most disadvantaged and poorly paid in the country and their patience finally snapped during the so-called winter of discontent of 1978–79, as we shall see in the following section.

Notwithstanding the rhetoric of 'declinism', what was really happening to the British economy during this period was a momentous restructuring away from manufacturing towards services. Deindustrialization transformed patterns of life and labour which in many instances had been established in the nineteenth century and, though this process affected all mature capitalist economies, its impact was more disruptive in Britain.[7] Manufacturing shrank and with it inevitably the number of manual workers, while employment in the retail, finance and the public sector grew enormously. The manual working class did not disappear altogether of course but it was marginalized and deskilled, earning a living from 'Macjobs' that required no craft apprenticeships and conferred no industrial power; its institutions, including unions but also consumer co-operatives, inexorably weakened. Workers were increasingly now cast primarily as consumers rather than producers.[8] Both major political parties had to respond to these challenges. For its part, however, the Labour Party was hamstrung by its historical and institutional ties to workers organized as producers, with the masculine bias that this often entailed.[9] The Conservatives on the other hand were much better placed to take advantages of the changing landscape of consumption. As earlier chapters have discussed, their embrace of the consumer interest went back decades and they could draw on concepts of 'consumer sovereignty' and 'freedom of choice' that had come more to the fore after the Second World War.

The majority of consumers responded enthusiastically to the new opportunities for consumption that opened up in the late twentieth century. The percentage of household income spent on food declined and more went on buying 'arousal' goods, consumer durables such as colour televisions, video recorders and microwave ovens, a wider range of cars and holidays to more exotic foreign destinations – Benidorm replaced Blackpool. Choice and quality remained important considerations for consumers and the period also witnessed the development of 'lifestyle' shopping, whereby individuals were encouraged to see their sense of self more closely bound up with their general consumption practices.[10] The tendency when possible for consumers was to 'trade-up', particularly in the 1980s when aspirational private consumption was lauded by government, portrayed almost as a public duty. High streets were transformed as multiple retailers such as Tesco and Sainsbury's continued to expand, building large out-of-town supermarkets and superstores, following the movement of populations out of urban centres and making shopping more dependent on car ownership. Significantly, even at this early stage of development, in some areas action groups protested against the loss of neighbourhood shops, and occasional attempts were made to establish food-buying co-operatives. However, planners stuck to the belief that bigger was best and that the new shops and shopping centres better suited the modern working wife who now had often to perform a 'dual role'. Unsurprisingly, these changes affected female shoppers variously; some studies suggested that although supermarkets tended to be liked by them, they frequently disliked shopping and resented the growing pressure on their time, especially when in paid employment or bringing up young children.[11]

Discount retailers including Asda and Kwik-Save also emerged, pressuring established firms to reduce prices still more. The total number of shops fell as small shopkeepers continued to be pressed by this heightened competition: in

1971 multiples controlled 37 per cent of market share, independents 55 per cent and the co-op 8 per cent; in 1980 the figures stood at 47 per cent, 46 per cent and 7 per cent respectively; and by 1990 they were 57 per cent, 39 per cent and 4 per cent.[12] Department stores also contracted – numbers fell from 818 to 580 between 1971 and 1989 – though some like Lewis's Group managed to survive by opening new in-store outlets like 'Miss Selfridge', which was initially launched in 1966.[13] Retailer brands became more important as retailers adopted a strategy that Marks & Spencer had been pursuing for decades with its 'St Michael' brand name, while conversely manufacturers' brands declined. By the late 1980s, the big retailer had become the brand. Multiples also assumed more control over suppliers and developed increasingly sophisticated ways of tracking consumers' shopping habits and targeting campaigns at them more precisely.[14]

Tighter control by multiples over manufacturers was not confined to supermarket chains; large retailers in the clothing industry also strengthened their grip over suppliers. As demand became more fragmented and discerning, they forged new relationships with manufacturers, enabling retailers to react more responsively to relatively small changes in consumer taste. Working with manufacturers in the United Kingdom as well as – at the upper end of the market – in Italy and Germany, retail chains secured shorter runs and lead times to maximize flexibility.[15] The Burton Group, for instance, diversified its portfolio, launching Top Shop aimed at young women in 1970, and the segmentation of retail operations continued apace thereafter. Burton's annual report for 1987 noted that British shoppers desired to 'express individuality and a sense of style' and that a greater range and diversity of goods was required to meet this need. The report also highlighted the new emphasis on 'lifestyle'. Rather than forcing people into crude categories, 'more creative and flexible ways of grouping customers' had to be found: 'We look at their attitudes to living, how they want to live and express themselves. What their aspirations are ... What sort of shopping experience are they seeking.' The group eventually comprised numerous outlets targeted at particular market segments, including Burton Retail, Top Man, Principles for Men, Principles for Women, Dorothy Perkins, Top Shop, Evans, Harvey Nichols and Debenhams. In keeping with the emphasis on the total shopping experience, shop formats were completely redesigned; the interior of Top Man, for example, changed from the atmosphere of a disco to a more restrained look pitched at a slightly older consumer.[16]

Not everybody could participate in this more differentiated and expansive world of consumption. Poverty shut out many as one monumental study published at the end of the 1970s demonstrated, and the situation was only to worsen in the following decade as neo-liberalism became ascendant.[17] Moreover, as has already been noted, as the composition of the working class changed, so its institutions were eroded; the history of the co-operative movement during this period is a tale of almost unremitting woe, ending very nearly in total collapse. The organization changed in fact from being a social as well as economic *movement* to a business with ethical pretensions, a very different thing. The challenges the co-op faced were complex, not only the structural remaking of the working class but also an unimaginative and cautious leadership. Business historians have also pointed to the often fraught relationship which existed between individual retail societies and the central buying and productive body the CWS, describing it as a 'dysfunctional federation'.[18] The local roots of the organization and the loyalty of members to individual societies tended to undermine attempts to create a coordinated strategy that could effectively compete with capitalist competitors. Central control was eventually imposed and the total number of societies reduced from nearly 1,000 in the late 1950s to less than 60 by the mid-1990s, dominated by a few huge organizations. By now total membership stood at about 8 million (from a peak of over 12 million in the early 1960s), though the vast majority of these were inactive; the 4 million holders of Marks & Spencer cards at this time may have been more loyal. Manufacturing by the CWS also radically contracted, from 220 factories in 1960 to less than 30 in 1990, which were sold off completely four years later.[19] Most important, the organization failed to keep in touch with ordinary consumers and attend carefully enough to their views and changing tastes. Oral history evidence bears out this point vividly. Born in 1914, Mrs Patrick joined the Leeds Industrial Co-operative Society when she got married, just as her mother had done before her. She found the dividend invaluable during the 1930s when her husband suffered prolonged bouts of unemployment. But none of her three daughters, who were born in the late 1930s and early 1950s, showed the slightest interest in the movement, preferring stores such as Top Shop and Debenhams instead. Patrick reflected that the reason for this was that her daughters regarded the clothes and home furnishings stocked by the co-op as dowdy, unfashionable, and she memorably remarked: 'Our girls woul'n't o' shopped at Cwop if you'd o' clemmed 'em.'[20]

Prospects for organized consumers, however, were not entirely gloomy. Some like the 'social entrepreneur' and founder of the Consumers' Association, Michael Young, had the highest expectations for them, believing consumers might produce new forms of active citizenship to replace what he believed to be increasingly outdated and more exclusive solidarities constructed around production. Thus, the Consumers' Association tried hard to reach out to consumers, establishing 200 advice centres throughout the United Kingdom by the end of the 1970s. The approach taken by government to organized consumerism fluctuated. The Conservatives abolished the Consumer Council in 1970 but soon changed tack and set up the Office of Fair Trading in 1973 and appointed a Minister for Consumer Affairs. When the Labour Party regained power, they made deliberate efforts to address consumers directly, appointing a secretary of state for prices and consumer protection in 1974 and then establishing a National Consumer Council (NCC) the year after. The ideas of Michael Young proved influential here and he served as the NCC's first chairman. Under Young's leadership, the

NCC endeavoured to promote a distinctly social vision of consumerism, which attempted to empower poor and vulnerable consumers disadvantaged in the marketplace by such means as bulk buying clubs, housing co-ops and state-supported advice centres, rather than merely providing help for individual consumers to assess the merits of different commodities. Michael Shanks succeeded Young as chairman of the NCC in 1977 and although he also desired consumers to have as great a role in society as employers or trade unions, Shanks's version of a 'stakeholder' society as an alternative to both communism and monetarism tended to depoliticize issues. Like other 'third way' strategies that emerged in the late twentieth century, criticism was focused on particular public 'vices' and elicited particular single-issue campaigns, rather than providing a wider theoretical critique of government and the market. The NCC helped spread the language of the consumer through the public sector, including into the provision of health, education and housing, where it was hoped that addressing users of these services as consumers would help empower them, making the receipt of benefits, for instance, less demeaning and more compatible with citizenship.[21]

Despite the efforts of the CA and the NCC, the voice of consumers often continued to go unheard and this generated discontent, particularly among tenants of council housing. They began to organize among themselves, launching a series of rent strikes against local councils during the late 1960s and early 1970s. The right-wing press eagerly reported how tenants in Taunton, Sheffield, London and Liverpool took action against increases in rent and the failure of councils to carry out repairs; while in Birmingham a few threatened a rent strike when a number of 'coloured' families moved into council property.[22] Consumer action was particularly apparent in Manchester, where tenants' groups organized themselves to make their hitherto marginalized views known to the city council. Such activity transgressed orthodox political boundaries and was especially troublesome for Labour councillors who dominated the council and who were used to telling ordinary people what was good for them. Tenants' groups helped discredit the top-down tradition of city planners that had resulted in high-rise flats and overspill estates in places like Wythenshawe, which had often fallen into disrepair and had proven unconducive to community life. Groups such as Manchester and Salford Housing Action, established in 1973, informed tenants about their rights and mobilized them against the council, gradually achieving a greater role over the planning process and forcing large-scale demolition to be put on hold in favour of reconditioning existing housing stock.[23]

Consumer grievances were also addressed by new social movements of the 1970s including the Women's Liberation Movement that criticized the sexism which was rife in advertising. 'Decoding' advertisements, feminists argued, was an important aspect of the struggle for sexual equality, for women's subordination was literally inscribed on the city streets, in newspapers and on television. Thus *Spare Rib*, the most important feminist periodical of the time, exposed the male chauvinism of the Advertising Standards Authority and supported the tactics of Affirm that organized direct action, spray painting or tearing down sexist posters.[24] The specific experience of young, predominantly working-class consumers was brought into the spotlight by the punk movement. A major strand in the subculture of punk was its rejection of haute couture and high-street fashion as well as mass consumerism more generally. Punk was characterized by a 'do it yourself' approach to cultural creativity, which comprised deliberately amateurish musical production, a bricolage dress style – bin liners, bondage gear and safety pins – and fanzines as alternatives to the commercialized music press, such as Manchester's *City Fun* and *Sniffin' Glue* edited by Mark Perry, a teenage bank clerk from Deptford in London. One punk wrote about how he improvised the dress style by 'wearing Dad's old pyjamas, and some of the old shirts he wears for decorating. Got into slashing and mutilating anything I can get my hands on. Jumble sales open up new world of clothes; dye old string vests orange, get an old suit and some collarless shirts, which I stencil.'[25] The excesses of capitalist consumerism were regularly denounced in the pages of fanzines and in the lyrics of punk rock itself. However, punk culture was not a 'pure' rejection of consumer culture but was also imbricated within it from the outset, eventually becoming thoroughly commodified and incorporated as a cultural form; punk gear soon became a mini-industry and the subsequent careers of Malcolm McLaren, the entrepreneurial manager of the Sex Pistols, and the fashion designer Vivienne Westwood exemplify this perfectly – one can now buy mass-market versions of the latter's costly creations at House of Fraser department store. Derek Jarman's suitably irreverent avant-garde film *Jubilee* (1978) captured such tensions perfectly at the time.[26] In short, punk was a heterogeneous movement that both left and right tried to appropriate without much success and is best seen, as one historian has recently suggested, as 'a kind of politicised anti-politics', which appealed to young people who felt alienated from mainstream politics and culture.[27] Whatever its contradictions, punk certainly caused heated debate, set out with the intention to deliberately shock, and succeeded. Hence it was interpreted by campaigners against so-called permissiveness, like Mary Whitehouse, as evidence that Britain was degenerating both morally as well as economically.[28]

Thatcherism and the consumer

In 1988 the comedian Harry Enfield introduced the character 'Loadsamoney' on the Channel 4 television show *Friday Night Live*. Created for Enfield by fellow comedian Paul Whitehouse, 'Loadsamoney' was a loud-mouthed, sexist and ignorant but highly paid self-employed plasterer from London who strutted around stage flaunting a wad of notes in the faces of his audience. Whitehouse originally got the idea for the character from observing football supporters in the capital taunting visiting northern fans by waving money at them, chanting to the tune of 'You'll Never Walk Alone'; 'Sign on, sign on, with a pen in your hand – and you'll never work again.' 'Loadsamoney' was hugely popular immediately, with some audiences at least. Enfield told a reporter on the *Daily Mirror* that at a recent show at the Hackney Empire male fans had gone wild for him, though he also recalled that not all audiences were equally enthusiastic – in Salford, he fell completely flat.[29] The term itself quickly entered the language, used by Labour leader Neil Kinnock, for instance, who blamed 'Tory greed' for creating a 'loadsamoney' economy that would eventually cause 'loadsatrouble'. In a wonderful cartoon by Charles Griffin reproduced as Figure 15, Margaret Thatcher was transformed into the Enfield character, siding with 'Yuppies' ('young urban professionals' – a term introduced in the early 1980s) against working-class people who could no longer afford properties in a redeveloped docklands. Embarrassed by the character's success, Enfield and Whitehouse – both on the left – soon killed him off, though he remains a fitting symbol for the decade.[30]

The 1980s is frequently remembered as a period when the consumer was crowned king, and rightly so, though this hegemony did not fall from

FIGURE 15 *Charles Griffin,* Daily Mirror, *12 May 1988. © Trinity Mirror Limited.*

the skies as we have seen. Consumers had played a vital role within the Keynesian economics that underpinned the post-war political settlement but they tended to be understood abstractly and in the aggregate. Policymakers needed to correctly interpret their 'marginal propensity to consume' in order to enable more effective demand management, certainly, but from a Keynesian perspective actual consumers were rather shadowy, elusive figures; Keynes himself was in tune with earlier moralists when he looked forward to a time when satisfaction of everyone's basic or 'absolute' needs would be met, which would only be possible, he believed, if 'relative' needs – the satisfaction of which 'lifts us above, makes us feel superior to, our fellows' – were subordinated to the common good.[31] Thatcherism alternatively rejected such ethical considerations, endowing consumers with unlimited creative power and configuring them as individuals whose desires and aspirations had been suppressed by a bureaucratic, inefficient and paternalistic social democratic order. Tighter control of the money supply and cuts to public expenditure, which drove up unemployment after the Tories regained office in May 1979 to well over 3 million, was one side of Thatcherite economic policy, a more relaxed approach to private consumption another. This was evidenced in various ways: the deregulation of the City of London and the growth of offshore tax havens for the rich; the expansion of personal credit, including mortgages, bank loans and credit cards with department stores and other retailers for those who were lucky enough to be employed.[32]

Margaret Thatcher herself, it should be noted, did not often use the term consumer and avoided celebrations of hedonistic consumerism – predictable given her Methodist background – but she did employ the rhetoric of 'choice', which of course implied the consumer. Discussing Labour's programme in 1975, for example, she attacked plans to end the provision of private beds in NHS hospitals and free places at independent schools as blatant restrictions of 'choice', comparable to the policy of communist regimes in Eastern Europe. Here and elsewhere, Thatcher repeatedly stressed how freedom of choice was the mainspring of economic prosperity that Labour was constantly restricting: 'I believe people deserve more freedom of choice in every field. Freedom to choose where they work; freedom to choose better schools for their children; freedom to own property and their homes.'[33] Speaking before the Institute of Practitioners in Advertising earlier that year she had remarked on the beliefs shared by advertisers and politicians in the West:

> Information is the lifeblood of the democratic way of life … without information there can be no competition. Without competition there is no choice. And without choice there can ultimately be no freedom. What happens when choice is suppressed? Monopoly flourishes – and just how it flourishes can be seen by glancing at Eastern Europe … And so I think it's fair to say that advertising, which is selling what you want to sell in a society that allows you to sell it, provides a service which is in fact a

> guarantee of one of our principal freedoms. The freedom of choice ... With manufacturers vying with one another to make a better product cheaper still, the consumer must be the gainer.[34]

Freedom of choice underpinned both democratic and economic vitality for Thatcher and maximizing consumer choice was one of her core beliefs, a necessity, she thought, if Britain's 'decline' was to be successfully reversed.[35] The reform of public housing, education, health and welfare that began after the Conservative Party won the general election in 1979 aimed therefore to provide more choice and make public services more responsive to the needs of individual users. The ambition of this broadly neo-liberal agenda was to forge a new relationship between the citizen and the state that prioritized the interests of atomized individuals. Choice was increasingly regarded as the right to opt for private provision while organized consumers were unsurprisingly snubbed, the social perspective of the CA withered and advice centres closed down.[36]

Such neo-liberal arguments had been articulated by the IEA from the late 1950s, as we saw in the previous chapter. This think-tank worked hard to promote the ideology of choice throughout the first half of the 1970s but without much luck, as even Conservatives most sympathetic to encouraging 'free enterprise' and defeating socialism remained lukewarm. Arthur Seldon, for example, repeatedly tried to persuade the secretary of state for social services, Keith Joseph, to break up the NHS and introduce greater choice into the health service but Joseph remained stubbornly cautious, fearful of the effects of such a policy at the polls. However, following Conservative defeat in the general election in 1974, Joseph founded the Centre for Policy Studies (CPS) specifically to convert IEA ideas into political action and revolutionize opinion in the party and the country. Thatcher became a keen supporter of both the IEA and the CPS, though it is important to remember that she acted pragmatically and was not as ideologically driven as she is often portrayed.[37] The IEA maintained pressure to dismantle the welfare state, which it argued had been made redundant by working-class 'embourgeoisment' and which merely restricted individual choice. It published surveys on education and healthcare provision conducted between 1963 and 1978 that supposedly demonstrated a long-term trend away from public provision towards greater choice and argued for a voucher scheme to enable individual consumers to shop around.[38] Though political realities continued to block IEA ideas, it promulgated them by means of a constant stream of publications that were discussed enthusiastically in the right-wing press.[39]

Before a neo-liberal transformation could be effected, the old order had to be overturned. Opportunity came with the industrial disputes that began in the winter of 1978, when car workers, lorry drivers and public sector employees engaged in protracted strike action. Labour's 'social contract' with the unions collapsed amid media representations of angry picket lines and uncollected garbage pilling up in the streets, culminating in the story of gravediggers in Liverpool who refused to bury the dead. The phrase 'Winter of Discontent' was popularized by tabloid journalists to capture the mood of the country and the strikes were rapidly mythologized by the right wing press, constructed as a momentous crisis that was turned to great advantage by the Conservative opposition.[40] Thatcher skilfully positioned the party as acting in the national interest at a moment of acute danger and spoke to ordinary people over the heads of union leaders, which the Labour government, she maintained, could no longer control. The ensuing general election was fought on the necessity of curbing union power and substituting the rule of law for 'mob' rule.[41] Citizens were portrayed as consumers deprived by vested interests, by striking transport workers blockading ports or care workers willing to see patients suffer because of their own selfishness. Moving the vote of no confidence that brought down the Callaghan administration in March 1979, Thatcher accused the government of having 'concentrated far too much power in the hands of the centralised State and left too little with the individual citizen'. She attacked high taxes used to fund generous social provision that left many working people with only enough money to buy essential goods. The result, Thatcher argued, was 'a sort of pocket-money society policy' that removed responsibility from individuals instead of empowering them, which 'cannot be attained except by exercising choice and not taking it away'.[42] Thatcherism's success depended on the construction of an alternative hegemony, a common-sense view of the world that chimed with the views of the majority, and there were many aspects to this hegemony. Although we should resist the temptation of seeing consumption as the master key to understanding what was admittedly a complex and unstable political formation, Conservative engagement with voters as consumers was nevertheless crucial to the party's success.[43]

This is most apparent when we consider how committed Thatcher governments were to extending what was referred to as a 'property-owning democracy', to be achieved through employee share-ownership schemes, the sale of shares in nationalized industries and the sale of council housing. The phrase itself can be traced back to the Unionist MP Noel Skelton in 1923 and was initially used in relation to profit-sharing ventures. It was picked up by Anthony Eden after the Second World War, who wanted Conservatives to encourage private homeownership, and the policy of council house sale featured in party manifestoes in 1970 and 1974. One of the strongest advocates of the idea of a 'property-owning democracy' was David Howell, who argued in a number of publications from the mid-1970s that many contemporary problems were due to the fact that people had 'not enough private property' and therefore 'not enough private choice'. Maximizing the latter would produce real democracy, he asserted, not the 'democracy of *Animal Farm*' peddled by the Left. Thatcher was wary of share-ownership schemes to begin with and rejected many of Edward Heath's policies but she took up the sale of council houses enthusiastically, accepting the widely believed view that more home owners was likely to result in more

Conservative supporters. The policy also made it possible for Conservatives to align themselves more easily with the grievances voiced by tenants' associations and also tapped into a widespread dissatisfaction among tenants concerning their treatment and the constraints often imposed on them by local councils. A generous Right to Buy scheme was consequently introduced almost immediately after the Conservatives took power; council house tenants of three years or more received 33 per cent discount of the value of their homes, rising to a maximum of 50 per cent and these rates were increased to 44 per cent after two years up to a maximum of 70 per cent discount in 1986. Enshrined in the Housing Act of 1980, eventually more than 2.5 million houses were transferred into private hands, radically enlarging the 'possibility of choice' according to John Moore, financial secretary to the Treasury.[44]

The Tory press loved the right to buy from the start, the *Daily Express* declaring on its front page that, 'THE sale of the century is ON' when the policy was announced by Michael Heseltine in the House of Commons, and later underlining how homeownership was bound up with the rapid diffusion of high-status consumer goods like cars, colour TVs, washing machines, freezers, fridges, telephones and hi-fi equipment, which pointed to the fact that 'we've never had it so good!'[45] 'Every home a vote winner!' the paper gleefully exclaimed following the Conservative Party Conference in Brighton in 1982, noting how the policy represented a 'decisive step' towards 'the massive extension of the property owning democracy'. More than 11 million new mortgages were taken out that year, many of them by council tenants buying their own homes. The *Daily Express* also published stories of some of these new home owners, picturing couples with wine glasses in hand, recounting how they had benefited materially by the policy but also emphasizing how it enabled them to take more pride in their homes, decorating them according to individual taste now that bureaucratic control by the local council had been removed. Mrs Sowerbutts from Skipton in Yorkshire, for instance, who purchased her council property for half its market value, could not wait to paint the outside of the house because the council colours were 'horrible'.[46] These special features celebrated choice and soothed anxieties of prospective buyers, juxtaposing success stories with advertisements for financial products. As one historian has observed, Right to Buy was 'a masterly manoeuvre', turning what had once been regarded as a social entitlement into a market commodity.[47]

Widening share ownership went hand in hand with denationalization. Like Right to Buy, the idea went back many years, to the Wider Share Ownership Council (WSOC) established in 1958 to promote the idea of a property-owning democracy and to strengthen public belief in the value of free enterprise. The WSOC sought to give individual employee shareowners a lever on economic power and shift the balance away from increasingly dominant financial institutions like clearing banks, pension funds and unit trust companies. Hopes were raised within the WSOC by Thatcher's election but they were soon dashed as the concentration of economic power maintained momentum. Despite privatizations of nationalized industries, the total percentage of shares owned by individuals continued their long-term fall, from 55 per cent of the total value of UK shares in 1963, to 37.5 per cent in 1975, and 21.3 per cent in 1989. There were more shareholders, admittedly, but they owned less as ownership was concentrated in the hands of big institutions, especially pension funds.[48] This did not mean that the policy of selling off shares to the public had failed; far from it. When British Gas and British Telecom were privatized, 96 per cent of eligible employees bought shares – about 250,000 individuals in total. Government ensured that about two million more became shareholders by means of massive press and television advertising campaigns aimed at ordinary men and women, including one memorable advertisement that asked people to 'tell Sid' about the sale of British Gas in 1986.[49] However, shares were often quickly offloaded and the WSOC soon ran into conflict with Thatcherite priorities as it opposed key aspects of policy, including the deregulation of the stock market, which allowed banks and building societies acting as intermediaries to move into the space between individual investors and the ownership of capital. In short, the WSOP argued that passive consumption was being encouraged in the field of shareholding and that the inexorable concentration of financial power continued to go unchecked. Notwithstanding Tory rhetoric, as a recent historian of the WSOC has persuasively argued: 'Thatcherism entailed the rise of an economic form of consumption, governed not by consumer demands, but rather by the designs of an institutional elite.'[50]

Although the rhetoric frequently conflicted with the reality, championing ordinary consumers provided a unifying cause for Conservatives, allowing them to even challenge the rationale of the hitherto sacrosanct National Health Service. Consequently, the notion of the 'patient-consumer' moved from the margins to the centre of debate. Thatcherism totally recast the health service between publication of the consultation paper *Patients First* by the Department of Health and Social Security in 1979, and the introduction of an internal market in 1990, shifting it away from a duty of the state to provide universal care towards individual choice and making it revolve around the patient configured as a consumer. As in housing, the momentum for change came from various sources. Neo-liberal faith in the market was an important driver but so too were patients' groups themselves such as the Patients Association (founded in 1962), the NCC and the CA, which published guides about common conditions and healthcare products, Community Health Councils (founded in 1974) and the College of Health (another of Michael Young's innovations, founded in 1983), which all attempted to speak for consumers of healthcare. These bodies demanded greater information and rights for patients and promoted more choice, for sure, but they also approached the 'patient–consumer' as a collectivity. The 'patient–consumer' was not created by the Conservative government then, but resulted from an interaction between such groups, the state, and the medical profession. But once again, regardless of these plural origins, Conservatives preferred to cast the 'patient–consumer' as an individualized figure and put managers in charge, rather than organized consumers. The internal market was an attempt to widen choice but as general practitioners were budget holders, power now lay in their hands rather than in the hands of patients.[51]

In this political context, it was hardly surprising that advertising and marketing, the cutting edge of the commercial domain, prospered during the 1980s. Indeed, advertising seemed to encapsulate the spirit of the times. As Britain's ability to manufacture things contracted, so its capacity to fabricate seductive images expanded. Between the mid-1970s and mid-1980s the advertising industry demonstrated 66 per cent real growth, with expansion of almost 10 per cent alone in the financial year 1985–86. City brokers had traditionally been wary of the industry and few agencies were floated on the stock exchange but this changed during the decade as advertising agencies came to be positively embraced by City investors. Agencies grew in size and broadened their activities. Some American businesses were taken over by their British competitors and a group of dynamic British agencies – including Saatchi & Saatchi, which had designed the 'Labour Isn't Working' campaign that helped the Conservative Party win the 1979 general election – checked that country's dominance of the industry. Saatchi & Saatchi overtook J. Walter Thompson as the top ranking agency in the United Kingdom the following January, a position which the company retained until collapsing because of debt in 1989.[52] While Saatchi & Saatchi had a global vision of their agency as a 'one stop shop', other agencies such as Bartle Bogle Hegarty (founded in 1982) took a different approach, emphasizing the importance of meeting the needs of local markets and developing 'creative' advertising that connected with consumers' aspirations. The agency maintained that advertisements ought to be constructed around the commodity's 'emotional selling point', making people want to buy it rather than selling it to them. This differed from the influential idea that had dominated advertising textbooks since the 1960s, namely that the best advertising highlighted the 'unique selling proposition' or USP of a commodity, its distinctive features, and underlined the function of written copy. 'Creative' advocates alternatively stressed the centrality of aural and visual aspects to lend emotional appeal. Different agencies pursued different strategies and we should be wary of making too much of this development; after all advertising for Pears Soap and other goods depended on emotional appeal in the late nineteenth century. One aspect of advertising that was distinctive in the 1980s, however, was the way it targeted more systematically both homosexual and heterosexual male consumers with images of the 'new man'.[53]

Selling New Labour

While the Conservative Party capitalized on consumer desires and discontents, channelling them to undermine the post-war settlement and proclaim the virtues of individual choice, the left found the changed circumstances much harder to deal with. In his provocatively titled Marx Memorial Lecture for 1978, 'The Forward March of Labour Halted?', the historian Eric Hobsbawm correctly foresaw the dangers from the radical right but ignored the significance of mass consumption entirely, blaming instead the labour movement's current impasse on disillusionment with the Labour Party during the Wilson years and *economist* militancy – narrow wage demands pursued by trade unions – which frequently pitched groups of workers against each other.[54] However, in his 'Observations on the Debate' published three years later, Hobsbawm pointed to the importance of changes in working-class consciousness since the war, drawing attention particularly to the influence of commercial television: 'Thus the values of consumer–society individualism and the search for private and personal satisfactions above all else, have been daily taken into every living-room for a generation by the media', he wrote. According to Hobsbawm, more important than 'the distortions and bias of news and propaganda' was 'the constant atmosphere of apparently unpolitical advertising and entertainment breathed in by all of us'.[55] Though consumerism was now factored into the analysis, it featured, predictably, as merely a site of 'false consciousness', leading workers down the wrong track.

Hobsbawm's approach was not untypical – most left-wing intellectuals continued to either dismiss or marginalize consumer issues at this time, as they had done for years. In a comprehensive analysis of the strengths and weaknesses of the concept of 'authoritarian populism' (developed in particular by the sociologist Stuart Hall) as an explanation of recent Conservative electoral success, for instance, Bob Jessop and others usefully underlined the complex, contradictory elements that comprised 'Thatcherism'. But they treated right-wing appeals to the consumer merely in passing, and then only as a source of possible future Conservative weakness: 'Insofar as rapid inflation has been the basis for the creation of an *inchoate populist category of "consumers"* (my italics), whose interests in the moderation of inflation have been mobilized to justify public spending cuts, then the reduction of inflation may undermine the argument for further cuts'.[56] Consumerist discourse was not the master key to Conservative success, as has already been noted, and the party had to deal with other issues and constituencies – the unions, of course, but also the City and manufacturers' groups that were not unequivocal supporters of government policy. Nevertheless, the consumer and particularly the rhetoric of 'freedom of choice' was vital to Thatcherism and the failure of critics to appreciate this aspect may have been understandable but it made it harder for them to grasp a vital reason for Thatcherism's appeal. However, from around the mid-1980s onwards the role of the consumer and the question of individual choice could no longer be treated quite so glibly and others on the left who were much more interested in the politics of style and consumption began to explore such issues in more depth. Various currents fed into this developing concern.

Debates in the Communist Party monthly, *Marxism Today*, played an important role in making the left more aware of consumption issues. In its pages, academics such as Stuart Hall and Frank Mort, and 'ideas entrepreneurs' like Charles Leadbeater, stressed how important it was for the left to appreciate fully the politics of consumption as part of what became known as the 'New Times' agenda. These writers sought to slough off Labour's ascetic past and invent a form of socialism that prioritized pleasure rather than drab uniformity.[57] Leadbeater, for example, who went on to be an adviser to Tony Blair, asserted that Labour desperately needed to wrest consumers away from the Tories, who had been most adept at appealing to their interests by means of privatization; television advertisements for British Gas had addressed 'The Sid in Us All'.[58] Elsewhere, Leadbeater asserted that Labour was 'out of touch with the culture of consumerism', which he reckoned had deeply penetrated the affluent working class that identified with Thatcherism, purchasing their own homes and buying shares. Alienated at work, he went on, people found satisfaction and freedom in their homes and in shopping centres.[59] The major lesson for the left was that it should embrace 'choice', a theme elaborated in another article in *Marxism Today*, where Leadbeater argued for the need for a 'progressive individualism' that redrew the relationship between individuals and the state, empowering them as consumers of healthcare and education – a strategy which would require no less than 'a managerial and retailing revolution' across the public sector. Although Leadbeater admitted that a collective sense of the consumer interest was still necessary – people ought to be given more say in how monopolies operated, for instance – the accent of his analysis nevertheless was on individual choice.[60] Other commentators developed more cultural perspectives, including Mort who stressed the splintering of markets and the emergence of 'lifestyle' shopping, among other things. According to Mort, such changes had profound repercussions for Labour that could no longer depend on the old certainties and rigidities of class, which, like consumer markets, were also fracturing along fault lines of gender, age, ethnicity and sexuality. Supporters of Tony Benn and 'the fundamentalist Left' preferred to ignore the new realities and rejected the necessity for 'policies that pull on the common sense of choice'.[61]

Other voices on the centre left were raised in favour of a more sympathetic approach to consumption. The Fabian Society published a pamphlet by Martin Smith, for example, which made the case for redefining socialism from the consumer's perspective. As parliamentary officer for the NCC, Smith had a keen awareness of how the politics of consumption had been ignored by Labour owing to its 'productivist' bias, a blind spot still all too apparent as Labour's Alternative Economic Strategy demonstrated, as it hardly mentioned consumer issues. Smith argued for a less dogmatic approach to markets and for more consumer engagement with public services but he also fully recognized how hollow the much-vaunted notion of 'consumer sovereignty' was in practice, owing to inequalities and the effects of specious advertising.[62] A more prominent figure in the debate was the New Zealand-born member of Labour's shadow cabinet in the 1980s, Bryan Gould. Like Leadbeater, Gould was educated at Balliol College, Oxford, and he played an important role in moving the party towards the ideological middle ground during this decade, unsuccessfully standing for the leadership in 1992. Gould took up the mantra of consumer choice enthusiastically, arguing that the socialist objective should be to guarantee 'the best available standards and the widest area of choice to each member of society'. He conceded that present inequalities restricted freedom of choice for the majority but rejected 'talk of class war', suggesting that socialists ought not to focus on the negatives but instead foreground how their project involved 'the enlargement of choice and the liberation of the individual'.[63] Gould further developed this theme in a later statement of belief, placing particular emphasis on the importance of greater consumer engagement – through surveys and performance measurement data, for example – in order to enlarge individual choice and drive up professional standards across the public services.[64]

Ideas such as these were on the margins of Labour's political culture at this time, though they were to become central later on as we shall see. Many on the left remained unconvinced by the argument that socialism needed to appeal more to material self-interest, believing that it ought to keep faith with the moral tradition that ran back through R. H. Tawney to the early socialists. Such views were only strengthened when *Marxism Today* launched its own credit card and began selling a range of 'socialist chic' products. More particularly, critics then and since, rejected the 'New Times' proposition that a more consumer and identity oriented politics was an inevitable corollary of changes in the economic sphere, namely the spread of 'post-Fordism' or 'flexible specialization' in developed capitalist countries – that is, the manufacture of high quality, customized goods for modern, 'discriminating' consumers. The Italian clothing firm Benetton was often held up as the model here, neatly lampooned by one recent scholar: 'Not only could rich consumers enter the New Jerusalem, but their activity in the shopping malls of England's green and pleasant land would prove instrumental in its construction. A Benetton Britain would be a socialist Britain.'[65]

Equally if not more important than ideology were practical efforts to make the party more consumer friendly. The same techniques used to gather information about markets for consumer goods had been employed by Labour to assess voter opinion since Harold Wilson's time but the 1980s witnessed a step change here. The use of media and publicity was also professionalized, though again the roots of this went back a long way.[66] Peter Mandelson, who became head of Campaigns and Communications in 1985, played a key role. Mandelson recruited advertisers like Philip Gould to join the Shadow Communications Agency (SCA), which produced a report attacking the party's 'cloth cap' image and arguing for an urgent rebranding. The SCA made it possible for advertisers to get closer to the Labour leadership and help shape policy; Boase, Massimi, Pollitt (BMP) was taken on as the unofficial party advertising agency. The centralization of power within the party, supported by Labour leader Neil Kinnock as necessary, supposedly in order to defeat far left groups such as the Militant Tendency, greatly assisted the rebranding process as it enabled the leadership to smother the voices of activists and better control the selection of candidates and the party's image more generally. Kinnock was encouraged to make major policy changes after the party's defeat in the 1987 general election, believing that the packaging was now sound but that the product was still suspect. Consequently, the Policy Review was launched in which market research played a major role, coordinated by Mandelson and the SCA. It was thought vital to find out precisely what the electorate thought – aspirational voters especially – and mould the party around their views. Campaigns Co-ordinator Bryan Gould expressed the ambition succinctly: 'What we ought to be doing', he advised, 'is looking at where policies ought to come from, what the demand is, what interests we ought to be serving. In that way we can make sure that the policy includes its popular appeal from the market.'[67]

Repackaging Labour drew fierce criticism, naturally, with the Marxist political scientist Colin Leys dismissing it all as 'market-research socialism' in *New Left Review*.[68] But it also had its more humorous moments. As part of the image making strategy, which also included nurturing relationships with celebrities and pop stars, Labour replaced its existing insignia, the red flag, with the red rose, to coincide with the annual conference in 1986. The design had been produced by the brand consultancy firm Wolff Olins, although Kinnock later claimed that he was personally responsible.[69] The right-wing press ridiculed the move from the outset and published letters from readers who were enraged by what they saw as a blatant attempt to claim a patriotic symbol – the emblem of St George – by Labour. Thatcher herself voiced this objection, stating that she did not intend to see this national symbol 'hijacked by any political party'.[70] One of the most insightful interventions came from the playwright and journalist Keith Waterhouse, who suggested that the effort would most likely backfire, owing to its origins: 'It is a very middle-class rose, a media consultancy rose, a marketing concept rose. Deepest red it may be like the people's flag, but it is not a people's rose. It reminds me, I am sorry to say, of an advertisement for an underarm deodorant.'[71] Ludicrous or not – and despite the persistence of dissenting voices – the adoption of the red rose was a sign that the Labour leadership now believed in the primacy of style over substance and that the electorate had to be addressed as consumers first and foremost, beliefs that underpinned the more systematic consumer focus that occurred after 1987.[72]

The marketization of the Labour Party in the second half of the 1980s did not solve its many problems. After the party suffered its fourth consecutive defeat in the 1992 general election, Kinnock resigned as leader and was replaced by John Smith, who died prematurely two years later. Tony Blair subsequently took over the leadership and began to mould the party in the image of what became known as 'New Labour'. Significantly, at this time the latter consisted of only a small, relatively isolated band of 'modernizers' – little more than a clique – a situation that changed after Blair became leader. It quickly became apparent that branding was at the core of the New Labour 'project'. We can see this, for example, in relation to the struggle over Clause IV of the Labour Party constitution. Adopted in 1918, the original clause famously contained a vague commitment to socialist transformation, summarizing the party's ultimate objective in the following terms: 'To secure for the workers by hand or by brain the full fruits of their industry and the most equitable distribution thereof that may be possible upon the basis of the common ownership of the means of production, distribution and exchange, and the best obtainable system of popular administration and control of each industry or service.' It was a woolly description that was open to interpretation, as critics have often pointed out.[73] However, the passage served as a kind of symbolic talisman for generations of Labour activists; printed on membership cards it no doubt helped keep alive the dream of a New Jerusalem. Blair and his fellow 'modernizers' believed that the successful relaunch of the Labour brand – necessary to regain floating voters and achieve political power they argued – required a complete and highly public break with the past, especially the 'cloth cap' image of so-called Old Labour. The new clause that subsequently replaced Clause IV following its rejection at a special conference in spring 1995 spoke about the need for a 'dynamic economy', 'the enterprise of the market', 'the rigour of competition', 'a thriving private sector' and 'high-quality public services'. The desire to renounce the party's past helps explain the energy devoted to abolishing Clause IV immediately following Blair's election as leader; out of all proportion, seemingly, from a political point of view, victory on this issue was imperative from a marketing perspective. Veteran party moderates including Roy Hattersley grasped this at the time and despaired, Hattersley remarking that Labour was now 'less of a moral crusade and more of a marketing exercise'.[74] Although Blair typically dressed up the issue in high-blown terms publicly, he also privately understood what was really at stake, later confiding to the consultancy firm Promise that 'Clause IV was a brand moment that he created'.[75]

Emboldened by this success, Blair's supporters further developed the branding and packaging of the party. Extensive use was made of data from opinion polls and focus groups, coordinated by Philip Gould, and BMP was hired to help in the general election in 1997. Great attention was devoted to Blair's youthful and approachable image, tailored to appeal especially to 'Worcester woman', while the electorate was simultaneously reassured that there would be no going back to 'Old Labour' – no renationalization, increased taxes or repeal of anti-trade union legislation. A suitably banal campaign jingle ('Things Can Only Get Better') provided the soundtrack for the subsequent landslide victory.[76] In his first term in office Blair avoided the language of the consumer, preferring instead to talk about the values of 'community', a warm if nebulous concept capable of expansive meaning. Eager to strengthen the party's intellectual credibility, Blair also appropriated the idea of the 'Third Way' from sociologist Anthony Giddens, which proposed a middle path between state socialist planning and the New Right's faith in the market. For Blair, this represented an alternative to the 1945 settlement, now entirely discredited, he believed, as demand management and public ownership had signally failed. Labour therefore needed to learn from Thatcherism, look beyond class and address the heightened desire for 'individual empowerment and opportunity', though Blair studiously avoided the rhetoric of 'choice'.[77]

It is tempting to regard New Labour's espousal of a 'Third Way' as merely another expedient exercise in branding. This would explain its relatively short shelf life after all – Blair dropped the idea during his second term. It was certainly useful organizationally, helping Blair's followers carve out an identity and exert their dominance over the party.[78] Beyond the airy rhetoric, the dominant orientation was articulated clearly by Mandelson in a speech to the Institute of Directors at the Albert Hall in London a year after Labour's electoral success, in which he conflated the political and economic domains absolutely. According to him, the problem with Old Labour was that it had completely lost touch with its 'customer base' and he accounted for New Labour's triumph by its ability to understand its 'customer base, who they are, where they're coming from and what they want'. Having listened to their customers, Mandelson explained, New Labour brought its product to market, utilizing 'all the different components that make up a successful brand – product positioning, packaging, advertising and communications'. In this fundamental sense, Mandelson concluded, 'Politics is no different' to business.[79] Insightful observers, such as the political cartoonist Martin Rowson, exposed the new orientation to ridicule, as in Figure 16, which lampooned the commercialization of Labour evident at the party's conference in 1998. Here we see a wall plastered with bills by the party's financial backers ('Tony's Fixed Grin Sponsored by Araldite'), while round the corner the deputy prime minister, John Prescott – who was instrumental in convincing the trade unions of the necessity for 'modernization' – takes a beating from the police. By this time, strong support for consumer priorities was coming from the Department of Trade and Industry. The White Paper *Modern Markets: Confident Consumers* supported the argument that 'demanding consumers' helped to drive business improvement and emphasized that the present government intended to 'put consumers at

FIGURE 16 *Martin Rowson*, Guardian, *28 September 1998. © Martin Rowson.*

the heart of policy-making', unlike governments in the past.[80] Perhaps not unsurprisingly the paper was weak on concrete proposals to support this commitment and accepted as axiomatic the efficiency of the market in meeting the needs of individual consumers.

One potential ally ignored by New Labour despite its consumer-facing reorientation was the co-operative movement, probably because it was regarded as unwanted baggage from Labour's 'cloth cap' past. *Modern Markets: Confident Consumers*, for instance, promised to work closer with organizations like the NCC and the CA, but said nothing about the co-op, which as we have noted was experiencing its own deep-seated problems. The movement's seemingly unstoppable decline reached crisis point in 1997, when a City financier named Andrew Regan attempted a takeover of the CWS. The structural problems the movement faced had been masked somewhat by the strength of its lucrative banking business but they were revealed in a blaze of publicity by Regan's bid. Regan had bought up CWS food production facilities in 1994, making people redundant soon afterwards, and he now targeted the CWS as a whole, hoping co-operative members would sell their shares to his company, Lanica Trust Limited. However, Regan misunderstood the structure of ownership within the movement – the CWS was mostly owned by societies, not individuals, of course – and he obtained insider information by bribing two CWS officials, who eventually were imprisoned for their part in the affair after the bid was ruled illegal following a lawsuit brought by the CWS. The crisis strengthened the tendency towards coordination or centralization within the movement and led to Blair taking a greater interest in it; he appointed the Co-operative Commission in 2000 to consider how it might be reformed.[81] The prospects were not bright and those leaders of the co-operative movement who looked to New Labour for support at this juncture were to be sorely disappointed.

Epilogue: Satisfaction Guaranteed?

In this book, I have endeavoured to show how economic, social and political factors combined in the making of consumer culture in modern Britain over the past two hundred years. Neither the identity of the consumer nor consumer culture fell from the skies – it was created by the actions of countless manufacturers, retailers, advertisers, media entrepreneurs, politicians and purchasers. The pace of change increased after New Labour was re-elected in 2001. New Labour prioritized the consumer more vigorously than had Margaret Thatcher or John Major as the party sought to reform public services along consumerist lines, a policy which generated bitter controversy.[1] Tony Blair made his intentions clear in a manifesto-like pamphlet on this subject published shortly after his victory at the polls. Although New Labour generally attempted to graft 'choice' onto older communitarian traditions as we have seen, the idea of 'community' was notably absent from *The Courage of Our Convictions*, which emphasized instead the importance of tailoring public services to the requirements of individual consumers unhappy with a 'one size fits all' welfare state.[2] Improvements in standards had been made since 1997, Blair argued, but the key problem with public services was that 'they have not been reformed to deliver in a modern, consumer-focused fashion'.[3] Although Blair reassured readers that 'a right wing philosophy of market choice' was not the solution, the rhetoric of 'choice' dominated the pamphlet, which conflated the citizen with the consumer absolutely. 'Modern public services need to affirm our status as citizens,' he declared, 'while meeting our demands as consumers'. An extensive bureaucratic regime of national standards, inspections and league tables flowed from this analysis, necessary to ensure that dissatisfied consumers could opt for other providers such as academy schools and drive up the quality of public services in the process, or so the argument ran. Blair ended his pamphlet with a warning: if New Labour reforms failed, then the neo-liberal agenda would reassert itself.[4] For some, of course, the irony of this was that New Labour's strategy *was* the neo-liberal agenda, albeit with some distinctive features of its own.[5]

This was not only a one-man crusade but was part of what bound together New Labour in their second and third terms in office. The leadership of the party regarded 'consumer culture' as constituting an inevitable framework for action, which had to be accommodated rather than transformed. Thus in a speech in 2004, Alan Milburn, secretary of state for health, bemoaned how the left had traditionally 'turned its back on choice as the preserve of the right', and he went on to conclude: 'In a consumer society where the consumer is king, vacating this political terrain is not a feasible strategy for progressive politics.'[6] This belief drew on various sources, including 'public choice' theory derived from economics that reckoned that the self-interested individual exerting 'consumer sovereignty' was the mainspring of social as well as material progress.[7] Some New Labour apparatchiks like David Miliband latched on to the ideas of the American economist Albert Hirschman, who had studied consumers of rail transport in Nigeria and advised economists to attend more carefully to the ways in which people could use their 'voice' to alter the behaviour of firms, rather than assuming it was better for them simply to 'exit' particular markets when they were dissatisfied. Miliband thought it sensible to apply these insights to state education when he served as Schools Standards Minister in 2006. Giving parents greater choice over which schools they could send their children to was not sufficient to solve the problems that beset the system, Miliband argued – pupils also had to be given more 'voice', needed to be individually 'empowered' by means of 'personalised learning' and greater curriculum choice.[8]

As with the Conservative Party under Thatcher and Major, New Labour rhetoric unsurprisingly tended to outrun reality when it came to empowering consumers. There was no evidence that parents or pupils wanted 'personalised learning' anyway. As sociologists of education have argued, the strategy was vague, to say the least, and when linked to performance-led school cultures it could be seen more as an authoritarian tool used by top-down management rather than a way of enabling democratic participation from below.[9] Moreover, the private finance initiatives and public–private partnerships used to fund new projects, which were intended to transfer risk from the public to the private sector, represented a poor deal for consumers as private contractors were protected to insure their participation. The further extension of the internal market within the NHS served to enhance the role of fund holders and managers even more, rather than empower patients. Critics like Roy Hattersley and others pointed out at the time how the ideology of 'choice' favoured those who were already privileged and would most likely produce negative social outcomes for the rest, but such warnings went unheeded.[10] New Labour's disregard for the interests of actual rather than imagined consumers was also demonstrated by its disregard for both the National Consumer Council, which merged with Energywatch and

Postwatch to form Consumer Focus in 2008, and the co-operative movement that it kept at arm's length. Rather than defending consumers, New Labour became more interested in rebranding its image after it was tarnished in the public imagination by the Iraq War of 2003. Consequently, in the run-up to the general election of 2005, the party hired commercial consultancy firm Promise Corporation to work on 'brand building'. Promise later outlined the strategy it had adopted at the Market Research Society conference in 2006, explaining how focus groups had shown that voters were disillusioned, feeling let down particularly by Blair's duplicity over weapons of mass destruction. Female voters had been more deeply affected it seemed; they had been attracted to the youthful, idealistic Blair and were now repulsed by the older, cynical liar. What was required, according to Promise, was an election campaign that integrated the 'two Tonys' and they approached the problem 'as they would any other brand', suggesting that Blair adopt a penitent persona to smooth things over. Blair duly played the part before the election, allowing himself to be humiliated by members of the public in various interviews.[11]

While people were being encouraged more and more by politicians to see themselves as consumers and urged to shop around for the best schools, hospitals and care homes, the experience of shopping as traditionally understood continued to undergo constant innovation and change during the first decade or so of the twenty-first century. Some of the changes in what analysts refer to as the 'landscape' of retailing were predictable, following trends in the earlier history that have been traced in this book, but some of them were rather more unexpected. The high street continued its slow decline, urban centres becoming increasingly dominated by charity shops, a dwindling number of department stores struggling to cling on as museum pieces from a bygone era.[12] Chain stores that were an iconic feature of British high streets disappeared: Woolworths closed over 800 shops in 2009, making 27,000 staff redundant; British Home Stores finally collapsed in 2016 with the loss of 163 stores and 11,000 jobs. The review written for the coalition government in 2011 by Mary Portas – a registered trademark herself and 'the UK's foremost authority on retail and brand communication', according to Portas's own website – noted a drop in town-centre sales from 49.4 per cent to 42.5 per cent between 2000 and 2011, while well over 15,000 stores had closed and one in six shops stood vacant.[13] Portas's report did not reverse the decline of course, though it did spawn a television series. The slide was partly explained by the rise of e-commerce or online shopping, as consumers switched to buying a host of goods from the comfort of their own homes. An American company, Amazon, led the way here, selling books at first when the company launched in 1995 but rapidly diversifying. Other major retailers eventually followed suit, including clothing retailers like Marks & Spencer and Next and the major supermarket chains.[14] The mass of consumers were squeezed hard following the financial crisis of 2008, some of the poorest resorting to 'aggravated shopping' in London and elsewhere as we saw at the start of this book. The recession gave a huge boost to discount retailers such as the German firms Aldi and Lidl that increased their combined market share to about 10 per cent by 2015, taking trade from competitors like Tesco that had dominated the sector for decades. Another novel feature of the contemporary 'age of austerity' has been the appearance of local food banks organized by charities such as the Trussell Trust, which in 2015–16 provided more than 1.1 million three-day emergency food supplies to people in desperate need.[15]

The growth of food banks demonstrates that civil society continues to generate a vibrant politics of consumption, beyond the confines of orthodox political activity. Drawing on the valuable work of many scholars, this book has shown how the relationship between citizenship and consumer action has been configured in many ways for many different purposes over the past two centuries, including by abolitionists who boycotted slave-produced goods, free traders in the Anti-Corn Law League who dreamt of a cornucopian future, Chartists who used exclusive dealing and their own stores to strengthen claims for democracy, fair traders who argued for protection and imperial preference, and co-operators who thought workers could use their consumer power to build a 'Co-operative Commonwealth'. The spread of material goods and the 'mass market' did not erode these alternative perspectives – in fact, they were predicated on greater purchasing power. After the Second World War, however, commentators have often assumed that what was termed 'affluence' was necessarily corrosive of political participation and active citizenship. Indeed, 'apathy' was regarded as an inevitable result of 'affluence'. The declining popular interest in political and economic affairs has been explained as a consequence of the way in which the global free trade regime, established by Western capitalist states under US tutelage at Bretton Woods in 1944 and by the General Agreement on Tariffs and Trade in 1947, was felt by most people to have been designed by experts and bureaucrats, remote from their lives and beyond democratic control.[16]

There may be some truth in this view – mass movements of consumers have withered as we have seen – but it also underestimates how consumers continue to think and engage politically. Other scholars have usefully suggested an alternative assessment, pointing to the rise of non-governmental organizations such as the Consumers' Association, of course, but also bodies such as Oxfam, Save the Children, the Fairtrade Foundation and even Mary Whitehouse's National Viewers' and Listeners' Association. They argue that instead of lamenting the depoliticization of the majority, scholars should investigate new forms of politics that have emerged in those affluent capitalist societies where the consumer is increasingly central. Politics has not simply evaporated, then, but has become 'ordinary' and a 'new political history' will therefore need to look for it in novel places.[17] Although such an approach is to be preferred to the bleak determinism of some influential theoretical writing on modern consumerism, there are problems with it. For one thing, it tends to skate over the question of how effective these organizations have been in actually challenging the power of the state; they may give consumers a voice of sorts but how often have their views really altered the direction of state policy, which has become, if anything, even more centralized and less responsive to pressure from below in recent decades. Second, these analyses also underplay the fact that working-class people are seriously under-represented in the voluntary organizations that are pointed to as evidence for continuing political participation.

Nevertheless, consumers continue to be active, finding other ways to connect private vices to public benefits. Perhaps the most notable evidence of their potential in recent decades is provided by the rise of the fairtrade movement, a key component of a much wider phenomenon that is now called ethical consumerism. Although this term encompasses myriad organizations with many different aims, the Fairtrade Foundation has become the standard-bearer for many socially aware consumers. In 2014 sales of fairtrade products in the United Kingdom was estimated at £1.68 billion, making the United Kingdom the largest market for fairtrade goods in Europe. This was less than the previous year, however, when sales had topped £1.74 billion, and this was the first decline in the organization's history.[18] Following the example of a Dutch Christian development aid association which created the Max Havelaar fairtrade label in 1988, the Fairtrade Foundation was established in 1992 by a number of voluntary organizations and pressure groups: the Catholic Fund for Overseas Development, Christian Aid, Oxfam, Traidcraft Exchange, New Consumer, the World Development Movement and the Women's Institute. Its main role was to licence the fairtrade mark to goods from the less developed world, certifying the goods to give small producers a decent margin, enabling them, it was hoped, to pull families out of poverty. Coffee was the first commodity to be certified, followed by tea, chocolate, bananas and so on.[19] The foundation's laudable though vague objects were 'to challenge the conventional model of trade', 'offer a progressive alternative for a sustainable future' and 'empower consumers to take responsibility for the role they play when they buy products from the third world'.[20] Thus, the onus was placed on the conscience of shoppers in affluent countries, who could transform global capitalism through their consumer choices. As Harriet Lamb, the foundation's ebullient CEO put it in 2006: 'You don't have to wait for government to move ... the really fantastic thing about Fairtrade is that you can go shopping!'[21] The foundation grew rapidly, embedding itself in local communities by means of events such as Fairtrade Fortnight which highlighted certified products, and through the creation of Fairtrade Towns – the first in Garstang, Lancashire in 2001 growing to over 500 during the next decade – and there are now thousands of Fairtrade Schools. Lamb attracted major criticism when she spearheaded the strategy of 'mainstreaming', whereby major brands and supermarkets were encouraged to lend their support. Most controversy was caused when Nestlé launched fairtrade-certified coffee in 2005, as the multinational had ruthlessly marketed baby milk in the developed world for years and was the target of a long-running boycott by other consumer pressure groups.[22]

Although the Fairtrade Foundation has tended to downplay criticism, the impact of the organization is far from unproblematic. Numerous studies into whether it has successfully introduced justice and sustainability into international trade have proven inconclusive. Some small producers have benefited, certainly, while for others the effects have been marginal or even negative, as labouring families are often locked more tightly into exploitative relationships.[23] The meaning of fair trade to consumers in affluent countries is similarly complex. Some commentators have interpreted fair trade and ethical consumption more generally as a fashionable mark of distinction flaunted by the more affluent. As environmental campaigner George Monbiot has put it: 'The middle classes rebrand their lives, congratulate themselves on going green, and carry on buying and flying as much as before.' This class reading may be too simplistic, perhaps, but for many consumers price is still the major determining factor. Moreover, recent studies have shown that many consumers have little or no understanding of what fair trade actually stands for, even when they have bought the products.[24] Cynicism is only increased by what has been termed the 'celebritization' of fair trade – the way in which media, film and rock stars have added a veneer of glamour to the practice, which is reflected in the organization's publicity.[25] The involvement of multinational corporations has also served to exacerbate doubts. It has been argued that some large companies have taken up the cause of fair trade mainly for reasons of self-interest, as another way of building brand loyalty; Nestlé, for example, made little effort to create demand for its certified products following the company's conversion.[26] Even the co-op – which led the way here from the late 1990s – can be seen to have adopted fair trade more as a top down 'strategic vision', which traded on the movement's ethical roots and that, it was hoped, would pull it out of terminal decline, than as a response to real pressure from below. It was easier for 'social entrepreneurs' in the business to rebrand the co-op along ethical lines than it was to rebuild a movement in a more meaningful sense and although this led to a short-term 'renaissance', this was only a temporary reprieve.[27] Most important, claims by the Fairtrade Foundation that it is 'empowering' consumers are at best naive. The heightened profile of its brand has enabled the organization to leverage financial support from bodies such as the Department of International Development, which between 1999 and 2008 donated £1.9 million towards the foundation's campaigning work. Scholars have argued that this success demonstrates the organization's ability to channel or 'shepherd' consumers for its own ends, working 'behind the backs' of consumers and purporting to speak on their behalf in order to lobby local and national government. Rather than demonstrating the power of consumer choice, then, fair trade instead highlights its limitations, as the consumer is enmeshed in a complex network of political, economic and institutional power relations.[28]

The Fairtrade Foundation has been keen to assert its commitment to promoting sustainability, though other bodies within the ethical consumer movement have questioned its green credentials. Groups such as the Rainforest Alliance, founded in 1986 to highlight the destruction of tropical rainforests, also certify a wide range of goods and attract corporate support.[29] Clearly, consumers remain divided on how best to tackle issues of climate change and environmental damage, which constitute a crisis that even the most sanguine supporters of free market capitalism now find it difficult to deny, given the weight of scientific evidence. From the end of the twentieth century, many radicals argued that the free trade global system established by Western capitalist governments in the immediate aftermath of the Second World War had served to reinforce the structural impoverishment of poor producers in the underdeveloped world and they called for fundamental reform to put matters right. This critique of the workings of the global economy intermeshed with heightened awareness of capitalism's deleterious effects on the natural world in what became known as the 'anti-globalization' movement. Whether they realized it or not, 'ecosocialists' and others were building on a long tradition of left criticism here, stretching back at least to William Morris, Robert Blatchford and Peter Kropotkin in the late nineteenth century, who regarded environmental pollution as a necessary consequence of the rise of capitalist competition and industrial development.[30] Well-publicized protests against the World Trade Organization took place at Seattle in late 1999, which pushed the issue of the need for thorough fair trade reform for the poor and the environment into the spotlight. Writers such as Naomi Klein in the United States and George Monbiot in Britain took up the assault on corporate capitalism soon after.[31]

The stark disjuncture between government rhetoric and action has been obvious to any intelligent observer ever since. States have attempted to set limits on carbon emissions by means of the Kyoto Protocol of 1997 and 2005 and the Paris Agreement of 2015, but consensus has been difficult to achieve even for vague, theoretical goals.[32] Meanwhile, here in Britain, successive governments have backed plans that will only increase carbon emissions and environmental damage, such as the High Speed 2 rail link and fracking. Capitalist 'progress' and the material inducements it holds out for consumers are shibboleths that no mainstream political party is prepared to question, despite some minor breakthroughs for the Green Party and for pressure groups like the Ethical Consumer Research Association (founded in 1987), which publishes a bimonthly magazine, *Ethical Consumer*. Unlike the Fairtrade Foundation, the latter is very critical of multinational corporations, condemning their adoption of ethical concerns as little more than tokenism.[33]

As individuals, we remain tied to consumer culture by myriad invisible threads and our consumption practices continue to provide a source of great satisfaction but also generate continuing anxieties. Indeed, some recent critics have underlined how material plenitude has signally failed to make us happy in the West and have called for the reinvention of non-materialistic forms of hedonistic pleasure, including deeper appreciation of the natural world, as a more humane, sustainable alternative to the cornucopia of goods.[34] And although changing shopping habits can certainly help raise awareness of the desperately serious problems that confront individuals both nationally and globally, the history of consumer culture suggests that it will not be sufficient to solve them. One might usefully recall Marx's disciple Ernest Jones's exasperation voiced over one hundred and fifty years ago quoted in Chapter 3: 'What carried the Reform Bill? Was it a pat of butter? No! it was political power.' From a very different ideological perspective and nearer to our own time, the editor of *The Economist* expressed similar doubts about the contemporary fair trade movement, observing that 'no amount of Fairtrade coffee will eliminate poverty, and all the organic asparagus in the world will not save the planet'. John Micklethwait went on to point out that 'transforming the planet requires duller disciplines, like politics'. 'Proper free trade' rather than fair trade was the real solution, Micklethwait argued, and he also recommended a global carbon tax and the abolition of agricultural tariffs and subsidies – especially Europe's common agricultural policy – which, he reckoned, propped up rich farmers at the expense of poor producers in the south.[35]

Harnessing consumption can be a powerful motor of social and economic change as we have seen in this book but to be most effective consumers need to actively create associations in order to transform individual practices into a collective project. It seems likely that consumers will continue to do this in the future as they have done in the past. As politics is fundamentally a struggle over the concepts we use to pattern and make sense of the world, criticism of the notion of the 'citizen-consumer' will be vital to secure meaningful change. A relatively new invention, the term tells us a good deal about consumer culture in contemporary Britain. Broadsheet journalists started to refer to the 'citizen as consumer' more frequently from the late 1980s.[36] The term 'citizen–consumer', however, was not coined until the mid to late 1990s. Unsurprisingly, New Labour adopted it enthusiastically, a Green Paper on welfare reform referring to the 'sceptical citizen-consumer' in 1998.[37] The conflation of the citizen with the consumer goes back much further of course, at least to the late 1950s as we saw in Chapter 8, when Kinsley Martin complained that someone ought 'to treat the voter as a citizen and not as a consumer'. Nevertheless, the conflation has been more absolute since the turn of the century, the usage more frequent. It is not an equal partnership as some have pointed out. Ruth Lister, for example, who has observed that 'the suspicion is that it is the consumer rather than the citizen who represents the ideal New Labour [welfare] subject'.[38] Arguably, then, it is the consumer that dominates the citizen in modern Britain, rather than the other way round as one would hope for surely in a healthy democracy.

And behind the notion of the 'citizen–consumer' lies the pernicious fiction of 'consumer sovereignty' – 'a phrase that reeks of dishonesty' as the young Dennis Potter once put it – which continues to mask our lack of real power as citizens despite the undeniable pleasures of consumption.[39] To put matters right will take more than recycling household waste and buying fair trade products. It will require nothing less than a revolution in our relationship to the world of goods and our rights as citizens.

NOTES

Chapter 1

1 *Guardian*, 22 August 2011: 10, 12; 23 August 2011: 13. The author of the report for Tullett Prebon, Tim Morgan, went on to publish a gloomy forecast, *Life after Growth: How the Global Economy Really Works – and Why 200 Years of Growth Are Over* (London: Harriman House, 2013).

2 Zygmunt Bauman, 'The London Riots – on Consumerism Coming Home to Roost', *Social Europe Journal*, 9 August 2011. Available online: http://www.social-europe.eu/2011/08/the-london-riots-on-consumerism-coming-home-to-roost (accessed 3 May 2016).

3 James Treadwell, Daniel Briggs, Simon Winlow and Steve Hall, 'Shopocalypse Now. Consumer Culture and the English Riots of 2011', *British Journal of Criminology* 53, no. 1 (2013): 1–17.

4 Tim Newburn, Kerris Cooper, Rachel Deacon and Rebekah Diski, 'Shopping for Free? Looting, Consumerism and the 2011 Riots', *British Journal of Criminology* 55, no. 5 (2015): 987–1004.

5 *Thought for Today*, [radio programme] BBC Radio 4, 22 April 2009.

6 'Consumer confidence' has been quantified in Britain since the 1990s by the market research firm GfK ('Gesellschaft für Konsumforschun', a German firm established in 1934). Similar measures date back in the US to the 1960s.

7 Rachel Bowlby, *Carried Away: The Invention of Modern Shopping* (London: Faber, 2000): 6–7.

8 Avner Offer, 'British Manual Workers: From Producers to Consumers, c. 1950–2000', *Contemporary British History* 22, no. 4 (2008): 557.

9 These are vast fields but see, *inter alia*, Martin Daunton, *House and Home in the Victorian City: Working-Class Housing 1850–1914* (London: Edward Arnold, 1983); John Burnett, *A Social History of Housing, 1815–1985* (London: Methuen, 1986); Adrian Harvey, *The Beginnings of a Commercial Sporting Culture in Britain, 1793–1850* (Aldershot: Ashgate, 2004); Jeffrey Hill, *Sport, Leisure and Culture in Twentieth Century Britain* (Basingstoke: Palgrave, 2002); Hartmut Berghoff, Barbara Korte, Ralf Schneider and Christopher Harvie (eds), *The Making of Modern Tourism: The Cultural History of the British Experience, 1600–2000* (Basingstoke: Palgrave, 2002); Peter Borsay, *A History of Leisure: The British Experience Since 1500* (Basingstoke: Palgrave Macmillan, 2006).

10 Raymond Williams, *Keywords: A Vocabulary of Culture and Society* (London: Fontana, 1983): 78–9.

11 *Daily Express*, 24 January 1955: 2; Matthew Hilton, *Consumerism in Twentieth-Century Britain: The Search for a Historical Movement* (Cambridge: Cambridge University Press, 2003): 4–5.
12 J. K. Galbraith, *The Affluent Society* (London: Hamish Hamilton, 1958); Vance Packard, *The Hidden Persuaders* (New York: David McKay, 1957); *The Waste Makers* (New York: David McKay, 1960). See also Chapter 8.
13 Intellectuals on the right and the left had denigrated 'consumer culture' as the culture of the 'masses' for some years. For the right, see the work by the Anglo-Catholic conservative poet T. S. Eliot, *Notes towards the Definition of Culture* (London: Faber and Faber, 1948); and for the left, the work of the 'Frankfurt School' Marxists Theodore Adorno and Max Horkheimer, *Dialectic of Enlightenment*, trans. John Cumming (London: Verso, 1997). Note also the discussion in Don Slater, *Consumer Culture and Modernity* (Oxford: Polity Press, 1997): 71–4.
14 *The Times*, 20 July 1964: 5.
15 For a useful exploration of this complexity see Tim Lang and Yiannis Gabriel, *The Unmanageable Consumer* (London: Sage, 1995).
16 Frank Mort, *Cultures of Consumption: Masculinities and Social Space in Late Twentieth-Century Britain* (London: Routledge, 1996): 7; Frank Trentmann, 'Beyond Consumerism: New Historical Perspectives on Consumption', *Journal of Contemporary History* 39, no. 3 (2004): 373–401. In *The World of Consumption* (London: Routledge, 1993), Ben Fine and Ellen Leopold criticized previous analyses of 'consumption' for being too vague as they often lumped together economic and political change, space, identity and so on, and argued instead for a 'systems of provisions' approach that traced the histories of particular commodities through circuits of production, distribution, exchange and consumption. Ben Fine restates the theory in *The World of Consumption: The Material and Cultural Revisited* (London: Routledge, 2002). The present book adopts a messier approach.
17 As Mary Douglas and Baron Isherwood remark in *The World of Goods: Towards an Anthropology of Consumption* (London: Allen Lane, 1979): 3, 'We would like to know how they live, the style and life of those moralists.'
18 John Benson, *The Rise of Consumer Society in Britain, 1880–1980* (London: Longman, 1994): 29. See also W. H. Fraser, *The Coming of the Mass Market, 1850–1914* (London: Macmillan, 1981).
19 Karl Marx, 'The Fetishism of Commodities and the Secret Thereof', *Capital: A Critique of Political Economy. Volume I: The Process of Capitalist Production* (Harmondsworth: Penguin Books, 1976): 163–77; Slater, *Consumer Culture and Modernity*, 111–15.
20 Thorstein Veblen, *The Theory of the Leisure Class: An Economic Study in the Evolution of Institutions* (New York: Macmillan, 1899); David Reisman, *The Social Economics of Thorstein Veblen* (Cheltenham: Edward Elgar, 2012).
21 See Pierre Bourdieu, *Distinction: A Social Critique of the Judgement of Taste* (London: Routledge & Kegan Paul, 1984); Tony Bennett et al., *Culture, Class, Distinction* (Abingdon: Routledge, 2009).
22 Jean Baudrillard, *The Consumer Society: Myths and Structures* (Thousand Oaks, CA: Sage, 1998): 28–9, 76–7, 81–2, 84–6.
23 Some theorists of consumer society have been more positive, especially Walter Benjamin and Michel de Certeau, but they have exerted less influence, on

historians at least. For introductions to their work see Beatrice Hanssen (ed.), *Walter Benjamin and the Arcades Project* (London: Continuum, 2006); Ben Highmore, *Michel de Certeau: Analysing Culture* (London: Continuum, 2006).

24 Joan Thirsk, *Economic Policy and Projects: The Development of a Consumer Society in Early Modern England* (Oxford: Clarendon Press, 1978); Margaret Spufford, *The Great Reclothing of Rural England: Petty Chapmen and Their Wares in the Seventeenth Century* (London: Hambledon Press, 1984); Carole Shammas, *The Pre-industrial Consumer in England and America* (Oxford: Oxford University Press, 1990).

25 Frank Trentmann, *Empire of Things: How We Became a World of Consumers, from the Fifteenth Century to the Twenty-First* (London: Penguin Press, 2016).

26 Neil McKendrick, John Brewer and J. H. Plumb, *The Birth of a Consumer Society: The Commercialization of Eighteenth-Century England* (London: Europa Publications, 1982): 9–15.

27 Ibid., 43–9, 53, 88–91. See also D. E. C. Eversley, 'The Home Market and Economic Growth in England, 1750–1780', in E. L. Jones and G. E. Mingay (eds), *Land, Labour and Population in the Industrial Revolution* (London: Edward Arnold, 1967).

28 McKendrick, Brewer and Plumb, *The Birth of a Consumer Society*, 100–5, 108–12, 118–26.

29 Colin Campbell, *The Romantic Ethic and the Spirit of Modern Consumerism* (Oxford: Basil Blackwood, 1987); Slater, *Consumer Culture and Modernity*, 94–7.

30 See Peter Borsay, *The English Urban Renaissance: Culture and Society in the Provincial Town, 1660–1770* (Oxford: Clarendon Press, 1989).

31 Lorna Weatherill, *Consumer Behaviour and Material Culture in Britain, 1660–1760*, 2nd edn (London: Routledge, 1996): 193–5.

32 Amanda Vickery, *The Gentleman's Daughter: Women's Lives in Georgian England* (New Haven, CT: Yale University Press, 1998): 161, 167–83.

33 Amanda Vickery, '"Neat and Not Too Showey": Words and Wallpaper in Regency England', in John Styles and Amanda Vickery (eds), *Gender, Taste and Material Culture in Britain and North America, 1700–1830* (New Haven, CT: Yale University Press, 2006).

34 Vickery, *The Gentleman's Daughter*, 142, 144–5, 184, 187–9; *Behind Closed Doors: At Home in Georgian England* (New Haven, CT: Yale University Press, 2009).

35 Sidney Mintz, *Sweetness and Power: The Place of Sugar in Modern History* (New York: Penguin Books, 1986); Brian Cowen, *The Social Life of Coffee: The Emergence of the British Coffeehouse* (New Haven, CT: Yale University Press, 2005); Maxine Berg, *Luxury and Pleasure in Eighteenth-Century Britain* (Oxford: Oxford University Press, 2005); Maxine Berg and Elizabeth Eger (eds), *Luxury in the Eighteenth Century: Debates, Desires and Delectable Goods* (Basingstoke: Palgrave, 2003); Erika Rappaport, *A Global Thirst: Selling Tea in the Age of Empire* (Princeton: Princeton University Press, 2017).

36 Beverly Lemire, *Fashion's Favourite: The Cotton Trade and the Consumer in Britain, 1660–1800* (Oxford: Oxford University Press, 1992); Giorgio Riello, *A Foot in the Past: Consumers, Producers and Footwear in the Long Eighteenth Century* (Oxford: Oxford University Press, 2006); John Styles,

The Dress of the People: Everyday Fashion in Eighteenth-Century England (New Haven, CT: Yale University Press, 2007).

37 An earlier, less scholarly study was Dorothy Davis, *A History of Shopping* (London: Routledge & Kegan Paul, 1966).

38 Beverly Lemire, 'Consumerism in Preindustrial and Early Industrial England: The Trade in Secondhand Clothes', *Journal of British Studies* 27, no. 1 (1988): 1–24; Hoh-Cheung Mui and Lorna H. Mui, *Shops and Shopkeeping in Eighteenth-Century England* (London: Routledge, 1989); Jon Stobart, *Sugar and Spice: Grocers and Groceries in Provincial England, 1650–1830* (Oxford: Oxford University Press, 2013); Ian Mitchell, *Tradition and Innovation in English Retailing, 1700 to 1850: Narratives of Consumption* (Farnham: Ashgate, 2014); Nancy Cox, *The Complete Tradesman: A Study of Retailing, 1550–1820* (Aldershot: Ashgate, 2000); *Retailing and the Language of Goods, 1550–1820* (Farnham: Ashgate, 2015).

39 Helen Berry, 'Polite Consumption: Shopping in Eighteenth Century England', *Transactions of the Royal Historical Society* 12 (2002): 375–94; Claire Walsh, 'The Newness of the Department Store: A View from the Eighteenth Century', in Geoffrey Crossick and Serge Jaumain (eds), *Cathedrals of Consumption: The European Department Store 1850–1939* (Aldershot: Ashgate, 1999).

40 Zachary Zeal, *A Seasonable Alarm to the City of London* (London: W. Nicoll, 1764): 13.

41 For an overview, see Paul Langford, *A Polite and Commercial People: England 1727–1783* (Oxford: Oxford University Press, 1989).

42 Jan de Vries, *The Industrious Revolution: Consumer Behaviour and the Household Economy, 1650 to the Present* (Cambridge: Cambridge University Press, 2008).

43 E. P. Thompson, 'The Moral Economy of the English Crowd in the Eighteenth Century', *Past and Present* 50 (1971): 76–136. See also his essay, 'The Moral Economy Reviewed', in *Customs in Common* (London: Merlin Press, 1991). Many historians have taken up the idea of 'moral economy', including John Bohstedt, *Riots and Community Politics in England and Wales, 1790–1810* (Cambridge, MA: Harvard University Press, 1983); K. D. M. Snell, *Annals of the Labouring Poor: Social Change and Agrarian England, 1660–1900* (Cambridge: Cambridge University Press, 1985); Adrian Randall, *Before the Luddites: Custom, Community and Machinery in the English Woollen Industry, 1776–1809* (Cambridge: Cambridge University Press, 1991).

44 See Margot Finn, 'Working-Class Women and the Contest for Consumer Control in Victorian County Courts', *Past and Present* 161 (1998): 119–20, 128–9; Martin Daunton, 'The Material Politics of Natural Monopoly: Consuming Gas in Victorian Britain', in Martin Daunton and Matthew Hilton (eds), *The Politics of Consumption: Material Culture and Citizenship in Europe and America* (Oxford: Berg, 2001): 69–70, 72–4; Frank Trentmann, *Free Trade Nation: Commerce, Consumption, and Civil Society in Modern Britain* (Oxford: Oxford University Press, 2008): 63–5, 429; Trentmann, *Empire of Things*, 578; de Vries, *The Industrious Revolution*, 113–16; John Bohstedt, *The Politics of Provisions: Food Riots, Moral Economy, and Market Transition in England, c. 1550–1850* (Burlington, VT: Ashgate, 2010).

45 Thompson, 'The Moral Economy of the English Crowd', 90. Two other accounts of the transition to capitalist modernity haunt Thompson's text: R. H. Tawney, *Religion and the Rise of Capitalism* (London: John Murray, 1926), and Karl Polanyi, *The Great Transformation: The Political and Economic Origins of Our Time* (New York: Farrar & Rinehart, 1944).

46 Thus McKendrick uses Mandeville uncritically to support his argument in McKendrick, Brewer and Plumb, *The Birth of a Consumer Society*, 16–18, 51–3.

47 Bernard Mandeville, *The Fable of the Bees: Or, Private Vices, Publick Benefits* (Harmondsworth: Penguin Books, 1970). For an insightful analysis see Lucio Colletti's essay in *From Rousseau to Lenin: Studies in Ideology and Society*, trans. John Merrington and Judith White (London: NLB, 1976).

48 John Maynard Keynes, *The General Theory of Employment, Interest and Money* (London: Macmillan, 1936), Chapter 23.

49 From a vast literature see Joel Mokyr, 'Is There Still Life in the Pessimist Case? Consumption During the Industrial Revolution, 1790–1850', *Journal of Economic History* 48, no. 1 (1988): 69–92; Gregory Clark, Michael Huberman and Peter H. Lindert, 'A British Food Puzzle, 1770–1850', *Economic History Review* 48, no. 2 (1995): 215–37; Sara Horrell, 'Home Demand and British Industrialization', *Journal of Economic History* 56, no. 3 (1996): 561–604; Charles H. Feinstein, 'Pessimism Perpetuated: Real Wages and the Standard of Living in Britain During and After the Industrial Revolution', *Journal of Economic History* 58, no. 3 (1998): 625–58; Jane Humphries, 'The Lure of Aggregates and the Pitfalls of the Patriarchal Perspective: A Critique of the High Wage Economy Interpretation of the British Industrial Revolution', *Economic History Review* 66, no. 3 (2013): 693–714; Robert C. Allen, 'The High Wage Economy and the Industrial Revolution: A Restatement', *Economic History Review* 68, no. 1 (2015): 1–22.

50 Emma Griffin, *Liberty's Dawn: A People's History of the Industrial Revolution* (New Haven, CT: Yale University Press, 2013).

51 See my monograph, *Co-operative Culture and the Politics of Consumption in England, 1870–1930* (Manchester: Manchester University Press, 1996): 22–3; Frank Trentmann, 'Knowing Consumers – Histories, Identities, Practices: An Introduction', in Frank Trentmann (ed.), *The Making of the Consumer: Knowledge, Power and Identity in the Modern World* (Oxford: Berg, 2006): 6.

52 Mary Douglas, 'Why Do People Want Goods?' in Shaun Hargreaves Heap and Angus Ross (eds), *Understanding the Enterprise Culture: Themes in the Work of Mary Douglas* (Edinburgh: Edinburgh University Press, 1992): 25, 30.

53 See, for example, T. H. Breen, *The Marketplace of Revolution: How Consumer Politics Shaped American Independence* (Oxford: Oxford University Press, 2005); Dana Frank, *Purchasing Power: Consumer Organizing, Gender, and the Seattle Labor Movement, 1919–1929* (Cambridge: Cambridge University Press, 1994); Lizabeth Cohen, *Making a New Deal: Industrial Workers in Chicago, 1919–1939* (Cambridge: Cambridge University Press, 1990); *A Consumer's Republic: The Politics of Mass Consumption in Postwar America* (New York: Knopf, 2003); Meg Jacobs, *Pocketbook Politics: Economic*

Citizenship in Twentieth-Century America (Princeton: Princeton University Press, 2005); Dana Frank, *Buy American: The Untold Story of American Nationalism* (Boston, MA: Beacon Press, 2000).

54 Daniel Boorstin, 'Advertising and American Civilization', in Yale Brozen (ed.), *Advertising and Society* (New York: New York University Press, 1974): 13.

55 See my monograph, *Wanting and Having: Popular Politics and Liberal Consumerism in England, 1830–70* (Manchester: Manchester University Press, 2015): xi, 139.

56 Gary Cross, *An All-Consuming Century: Why Commercialism Won in Modern America* (New York: Columbia University Press, 2000); Lawrence Glickman, *Buying Power: A History of Consumer Activism in America* (Chicago: University of Chicago Press, 2009); Marie-Emanuelle Chessel, *Histoire de la Consummation* (Paris: La Découverte, 2012); Rebecca J. Pulju, *Women and Mass Consumer Society in Postwar France* (Cambridge: Cambridge University Press, 2011); Heinz-Gerhard Haupt and Claudius Torp (eds), *Die Konsumgesellschaft in Deutschland, 1890–1990* (Frankfurt: Campus Verlag, 2009); Mark Landsman, *Dictatorship and Demand: The Politics of Consumerism in East Germany* (Cambridge, MA: Harvard University Press, 2005).

57 See Sheldon Garon, 'Japan's Post-war "Consumer Revolution", or Striking a "Balance" between Consumption and Saving', in John Brewer and Frank Trentmann (eds), *Consuming Cultures, Global Perspectives: Historical Trajectories, Transnational Exchanges* (Oxford: Berg, 2006); Sheldon Garon and Patricia L. Maclachlan (eds), *The Ambivalent Consumer: Questioning Consumption in East Asia and the West* (Ithaca: Cornell University Press, 2006); Sheldon Garon, *Beyond Our Means: Why America Spends While the World Saves* (Princeton: Princeton University Press, 2012); Jeremy Prestholdt, *Domesticating the World: African Consumerism and the Genealogies of Globalization* (Berkeley: University of California Press, 2008). There are some useful comparative perspectives in Frank Trentmann (ed.), *The Oxford Handbook of the History of Consumption* (Oxford: Oxford University Press, 2012).

58 This is the tendency of Trentmann's encyclopaedic though somewhat confused recent book in which he asserts; 'To attribute the rise in consumption to post-war growth or to neo-liberalism is both historically wrong and politically wrong-headed. The yearning for more goods and services was not the child of standardized mass production. Demand for fashionable cotton, comfortable bedding or an exotic cup of tea or cocoa, for example, were rising before the Industrial Revolution gathered steam in the late eighteenth century. Compared to the booming West in the 1950s and 1960s, early modern Europe and late Ming China were low-growth societies, but this does not mean their material appetites were stagnant.' *Empire of Things*, 678. No one would seriously claim that the 'yearning for more goods and services' was 'the child of standardized mass production' of course but it is difficult not to regard mass consumption as closely intertwined with the development of modern capitalism. Trentmann admits as much himself elsewhere in the book; see his remarks at 53, 71 and 77.

59 Note Victoria de Grazia's important essay, 'Changing Consumption Regimes in Europe, 1930–1970', in Susan Strasser, Charles McGovern and Matthias Judt

(eds), *Getting and Spending. European and American Consumer Societies in the Twentieth Centuries* (Cambridge: Cambridge University Press, 1998).

60 Peter N. Stearns, 'Stages of Consumerism: Recent Work on the Issues of Periodization', *Journal of Modern History* 69, no. 1 (1997): 116.

Chapter 2

1 *Johnstone's London Commercial Guide & Street Directory* (London: Barnard and Farley, 1817), cited in McKendrick's essay, 'The Commercialization of Fashion', in Neil McKendrick, John Brewer and J. H. Plumb, *The Birth of a Consumer Society: The Commercialization of Eighteenth-century England* (London: Europa Publications, 1982): 78.

2 William H. Ablett, *Reminiscences of an Old Draper* (London: S. Low, Marston, Searle & Rivington, 1876): 4–8, 47, 58–9, 68, 79; William Hazlitt, 'On Fashion' (1818), in Jon Cook (ed.), *William Hazlitt: Selected Writings* (Oxford: Oxford University Press, 1991): 148–54.

3 Ablett, *Reminiscences of an Old Draper*, 229, 235–6.

4 Ibid., 30–41, 43.

5 *Spectator*, 24 June 1876: 21.

6 Margaret MacKeith, *The History and Conservation of Shopping Arcades* (London: Mansell, 1986): 1–2.

7 Ian Mitchell, *Tradition and Innovation in English Retailing, 1700 to 1850: Narratives of Consumption* (Farnham: Ashgate, 2014): 140–4; Gary R. Dyer, 'The "Vanity Fair" of Nineteenth Century England: Commerce, Women, and the East in the Ladies' Bazaar', *Nineteenth-Century Literature* 46, no. 2 (1991): 196–222; *Manchester Times*, 12 March 1831.

8 Mitchell, *Tradition and Innovation in English Retailing*, 145.

9 Ablett, *Reminiscences*, 161–5.

10 Michael Moss and Alison Turton, *A Legend of Retailing: House of Fraser* (London: Weidenfeld and Nicolson, 1989): 19–22; Mitchell, *Tradition and Innovation in English Retailing*, 145–7; Bill Lancaster, *The Department Store: A Social History* (London: Leicester University Press, 1995): 7–10, 13.

11 MacKeith, *The History and Conservation of Shopping Arcades*, 8–9; Tammy C. Whitlock, *Crime, Gender and Consumer Culture in Nineteenth Century England* (Aldershot: Ashgate, 2005): 25.

12 Charles Dickens, *Sketches by Boz* (London: Penguin Books, 1995): 214–16.

13 Anthony Trollope, *The Struggles of Brown, Jones and Robinson: By One of the Firm* (London: Penguin Books, 1993): 37; Ablett, *Reminiscences*, 89–90, 208, 222.

14 The older orthodoxy can be found in J. B. Jefferys, *Retail Trading in Britain, 1850–1950: A Study of Trends in Retailing with Special Reference to the Development of Co-operative, Multiple Shop and Department Store Methods of Trading* (Cambridge: Cambridge University Press, 1954); Dorothy Davis, *A History of Shopping* (London: Routledge & Kegan Paul, 1966).

15 Janet Blackman, 'The Development of the Retail Grocery Trade in the Nineteenth Century', *Business History* 9, no. 2 (1967): 110–16; David

Alexander, *Retailing in England during the Industrial Revolution* (London: Athlone Press, 1970).

16 Roger Scola, *Feeding the Victorian City: The Food Supply of Manchester, 1770–1870* (Manchester: Manchester University Press, 1992): 182–92, 205, 211, 221–3, 235–41.

17 Elizabeth Gaskell, *Mary Barton: A Tale of Manchester Life* (London: Penguin Books, 1970): 50–1.

18 M. T. Wild and G. Shaw, 'Population Distribution and Retail Provision: The Case of the Halifax-Calder Valley Area of West Yorkshire during the Second Half of the Nineteenth Century', *Journal of Historical Geography* 1, no. 2 (1975): 202–3; Gareth Shaw, 'Changes in Consumer Demand and Food Supply in Nineteenth-Century British Cities', *Journal of Historical Geography* 11, no. 3 (1985): 291–3.

19 Janet Blackman, 'The Food Supply of an Industrial Town: A Study of Sheffield's Public Markets, 1780–1900', *Business History* 5, no. 2 (1963): 86–8, 95; Roger Scola, 'Food Markets and Shops in Manchester 1770–1870', *Journal of Historical Geography* 1, no. 2 (1975): 164.

20 Mitchell, *Tradition and Innovation in English Retailing*, 155.

21 Alexander, *Retailing in England during the Industrial Revolution*, 57–8.

22 W. H. Fraser, *The Coming of the Mass Market, 1850–1914* (London: Macmillan, 1981): 94–100; Scola, *Feeding the Victorian City*, 250–2; Peter T. A. Jones, 'Redressing Reform Narratives: Victorian London's Street Markets and the Informal Supply Lines of Urban Modernity', *London Journal* 41, no. 1 (2016): 60–81.

23 Gareth Shaw and M. T. Wild, 'Retail Patterns in the Victorian City', *Transactions of the Institute of British Geographers* 4, no. 2 (1979): 280–1.

24 Margot Finn, *The Character of Credit. Personal Debt in English Culture, 1740–1914* (Cambridge: Cambridge University Press, 2003): 258–9; David Brown, '"Persons of Infamous Character" or "An Honest, Industrious and Useful Description of People"? The Textile Pedlars of Alstonfield and the Role of Peddling in Industrialization', *Textile History* 31, no. 1 (2000): 1–26.

25 Fraser, *The Coming of the Mass Market*, 61; Beverly Lemire, 'Consumerism in Preindustrial and Early Industrial England: The Trade in Secondhand Clothes', *Journal of British Studies* 27, no. 1 (1988): 22–3; Alison Toplis, *The Clothing Trade in Provincial England, 1800–1850* (London: Pickering & Chatto, 2011); Vivienne Richmond, *Clothing the Poor in Nineteenth-Century England* (Cambridge: Cambridge University Press, 2013): 40–1.

26 On the second-hand furniture trade, see Pat Kirkham, *The London Furniture Trade, 1700–1870* (London: Furniture History Society, 1988); Clive Edwards and Margaret Ponsonby, 'Desirable Commodity or Practical Necessity? The Sale and Consumption of Second-Hand Furniture, 1750–1900', in David Hussey and Margaret Ponsonby (eds), *Buying for the Home: Shopping for the Domestic from the Seventeenth Century to the Present* (Aldershot: Ashgate, 2008); Akiko Shimbo, *Furniture-Makers and Consumers in England, 1754–1851: Design as Interaction* (London: Routledge, 2015).

27 Deborah Cohen, *Household Gods: The British and Their Possessions* (New Haven, CT: Yale University Press, 2006): 2–3, 6–7, 18–31, passim.

28 Lytton Strachey, *Queen Victoria* (London: Chatto & Windus, 1921): 293.

29 Jeffrey Auerbach, *The Great Exhibition of 1851: A Nation on Display* (New Haven, CT: Yale University Press, 1999); John R. Davis, *The Great Exhibition* (Stroud: Sutton, 1999). The Crystal Palace was moved to Sydenham in South London, where it reopened in 1854. For the working class 'takeover' of the venue in the second half of the nineteenth century see my essay, 'An Appropriated Space: The Great Exhibition, the Crystal Palace and the Working Class', in Louise Purbrick (ed.), *The Great Exhibition of 1851. New Interdisciplinary Essays* (Manchester: Manchester University Press, 2001): 114–45.
30 Thomas Richards, *The Commodity Culture of Victorian England: Advertising and Spectacle, 1851–1914* (London: Verso, 1991): 68–9.
31 Harriet Martineau, 'The Crystal Palace', *Westminster Review* 62, no. 122 (1854): 548; *Punch, or the London Charivari* 20 (1851): 212.
32 Charles Babbage, *The Exposition of 1851; or, Views of the Industry, the Science, and the Government of England* (London: John Murray, 1851): 45, 81, 129.
33 'The Palace of Puffs', *Saturday Review* 13, no. 340 (1862): 485.
34 William Smith, *Advertise. How? When? Where?* (London: Routledge, Warne, and Routledge, 1863): 13.
35 Richards, *The Commodity Culture of Victorian England*, 7–9; Lori Anne Loeb, *Consuming Angels: Advertising and Victorian Women* (Oxford: Oxford University Press, 1994): 7–8.
36 Roy Church, 'Advertising Consumer Goods in Nineteenth Century Britain: Reinterpretations', *Economic History Review* 53, no. 4 (2000): 630–8.
37 E. S. Turner, *The Shocking History of Advertising!* (London: Michael Joseph, 1952): 65–7; T. R. Nevett, *Advertising in Britain: A History* (London: Heinemann on behalf of the History of Advertising Trust, 1982): 29–30.
38 Church, 'Advertising Consumer Goods', 628–9.
39 *Quarterly Review* 97, no. 193 (1855): 211; Smith, *Advertise*, 160. See also Trollope, *The Struggles of Brown*, 4, 8.
40 Nevett, *Advertising in Britain*, 57–9.
41 'Bill-Sticking', *Household Words* 2, no. 52 (1851): 601–6.
42 Brian Maidment, *Dusty Bob: A Cultural History of Dustmen, 1780–1870* (Manchester: Manchester University Press, 2007).
43 Cyril Sheldon, *A History of Poster Advertising* (London: Chapman and Hall, 1937): 3–10; Turner, *The Shocking History of Advertising!*, 76–81, 105, 126–7.
44 Nevett, *Advertising in Britain*, 28–9, 40–1, 46–7; *The Times*, 11 January 1850: 4.
45 See Martin Hewitt, *The Dawn of the Cheap Press in Victorian Britain: The End of the 'Taxes on Knowledge', 1849–1869* (London: Bloomsbury Academic, 2013).
46 Turner, *The Shocking History of Advertising!*, 85.
47 Nevett, *Advertising in Britain*, 37; Church, 'Advertising Consumer Goods', 628.
48 Nevett, *Advertising in Britain*, 61–4.

49 Diana and Geoffrey Hindley, *Advertising in Victorian England, 1837–1901* (London: Wayland, 1972), 16–26.
50 Deborah Cohen, 'Buying and Becoming: New Work on the Victorian Middle Classes', *Historical Journal* 46, no. 4 (2003): 1003–4.
51 Turner, *The Shocking History of Advertising!*, 51, 55; Nevett, *Advertising in Britain*, 111–12.
52 Abraham Hayward, 'The Advertising System', *Edinburgh Review* 77, no. 155 (1843): 8. See also Mrs White, 'A Chapter on Puffs and Advertisements', *Ainsworth's Magazine* 16 (1849): 42–6.
53 Smith, *Advertise*, 34.
54 James Dawson Burn, *The Language of the Walls: And a Voice From the Shop Windows. Or, the Mirror of Commercial Roguery. By One Who Thinks Aloud* (Manchester: Abel Heywood, 1855): v–vi; *Autobiography of a Beggar Boy* (London: William Tweedie, 1856): 174.
55 'The Grand Force!', *Fraser's Magazine* 79, no. 471 (1869): 380.
56 John Burnett, *Plenty and Want: A Social History of Diet in England from 1815 to the Present Day* (London: Penguin Books, 1968): 54; *Liquid Pleasures: A Social History of Drinks in Modern Britain* (London: Routledge, 1999).
57 Mrs White, 'Saturday Night in London. The Street Markets'. *Ainsworth's Magazine* 10 (1846): 137–8.
58 Ibid., 139–40.
59 Thomas Wright, 'Saturday Trading', in *The Great Unwashed By The Journeyman Engineer* (London: Tinsley Brothers, 1868): 210.
60 Gaskell, *Mary Barton*, 49–50.
61 *Morning Chronicle*, 18 March 1850: 5
62 Ibid., 8 April 1850: 5.
63 Leonore Davidoff and Catherine Hall, *Family Fortunes: Men and Women of the English Middle Class 1780–1850* (London: Hutchinson Educational, 1987); Stena Nenadic, 'Middle-Rank Consumers and Domestic Culture in Edinburgh and Glasgow 1720–1840', *Past and Present* 145 (1994): 122–56.
64 K. Theodore Hoppen, *The Mid-Victorian Generation 1846–1886* (Oxford: Clarendon Press, 1998): 336. See also Thad Logan, *The Victorian Parlour: A Cultural Study* (Cambridge: Cambridge University Press, 2001).
65 J. A. Banks, *Prosperity and Parenthood: A Study of Family Planning among the Victorian Middle Classes* (London: Routledge and Kegan Paul, 1954).
66 Davidoff and Hall, *Family Fortunes*, 387; Cohen, *Household Gods*; Jane Hamlett, *Material Relations: Domestic Interiors and Middle-Class Families in England, 1850–1910* (Manchester: Manchester University Press, 2010).
67 Neil Armstrong, *Christmas in Nineteenth-Century England* (Manchester: Manchester University Press, 2010): 147–50.
68 See K. D. Brown, *The British Toy Business: A History Since 1700* (London: Hambledon Press, 1996).
69 Armstrong, *Christmas in Nineteenth-Century England*, 151–2, 162–4. Note also J. A. R. Pimlott, *The Englishman's Christmas: A Social History* (Hassocks, UK: Harvester Press, 1978); Mark Connolly, *Christmas: A Social History* (London: I. B. Tauris, 1999); Martin Johnes, *Christmas and the British: A Modern History* (London: Bloomsbury Academic, 2016).

70 See my monograph *Wanting and Having: Popular Politics and Liberal Consumerism in England, 1830–70* (Manchester: Manchester University Press, 2015): 191–4, *passim*; '"The Age of Veneer": Charles Dickens and the Antinomies of Victorian Consumer Culture', *Dickens Quarterly* 32, no. 3 (2015): 217–34.
71 'Shopping in London', *The Living Age*, 8 June 1844: 250–1.
72 'Shopping Without Money', *The Leisure Hour*, 18 February 1865: 110.
73 'Physiology of London Life', *Bentley's Miscellany* 16 (1844): 286.
74 Hazlitt, 'On Fashion', in Cook (ed.), *William Hazlitt*, 148–54.
75 Alison Adburgham, *Shops and Shopping, 1800–1914* (London: Faber & Faber, 1964): 115. On the popularity of cotton goods from the eighteenth century onwards, see Hoh-Cheung Mui and Lorna H. Mui, *Shops and Shopkeeping in Eighteenth-Century England* (London: Routledge, 1989): 236–7; Beverly Lemire, *Fashion's Favourite: The Cotton Trade and the Consumer in Britain, 1660–1800* (Oxford: Oxford University Press, 1991).
76 'Directions to Ladies for Shopping', *Punch, or the London Charivari* 7 (1844): 142. See also 'The Lady Shopping', *London Saturday Journal*, 21 August 1841: 86; 'The Science of Shopping', *Examiner*, 29 November 1856: 755–6.
77 *Going out a Shopping – Happy Moments* (London: 1850); Whitlock, *Crime, Gender and Consumer Culture*, 107.
78 Margot Finn, 'Women, Consumption and Coverture in England, c. 1760–1860', *Historical Journal* 39, no. 3 (1996): 703–22; Sarah Stickney Ellis, *The Wives of England: Their Relative Duties, Domestic Influence, and Social Obligations* (London: Fisher, Son, 1843): 206–11.
79 *Struggle*, 91 (1843): 2.
80 'A Word on Shopcraft', *Ainsworth's Magazine* 14 (1848): 115; *Northern Star*, 12 August 1848: 3. See also 'Modern Shopping', *The London Review*, 18 March 1865: 294–5.
81 Trollope, *The Struggles of Brown*, 138–50.
82 Whitlock, *Crime, Gender and Consumer Culture*, 129–42, passim.
83 Krista Lysack, *Come Buy, Come Buy: Shopping and the Culture of Consumption in Victorian Women's Writing* (Athens: Ohio University Press, 2008): 8.
84 'A Day's Shopping', *Saturday Review*, 2 June 1860: 708.

Chapter 3

1 See Sidney Mintz, *Sweetness and Power: The Place of Sugar in Modern History* (New York: Penguin Books, 1986); Joanna de Groot, 'Metropolitan Desires and Colonial Connections: Reflections on Consumption and Empire', in Catherine Hall and Sonya Rose (eds), *At Home with the Empire: Metropolitan Culture and the Imperial World* (Cambridge: Cambridge University Press, 2006).
2 William Allen, *The Duty of Abstaining from the Use of West India Produce* (London: T. W. Hawkins, 1792): 7; Charlotte Sussman, *Consuming*

Anxieties: Consumer Protest, Gender, and British Slavery, 1713–1833 (Stanford: Stanford University Press, 2000): 40.

3 Clare Midgley, *Women against Slavery: The British Campaigns, 1780–1870* (London: Routledge, 1992): 35–40, 60–2.

4 Asa Briggs, 'Middle-Class Consciousness in English Politics, 1780–1846', *Past and Present* 9 (1956): 68, 71. This view still has much to recommend it, notwithstanding Dror Wahrman's sophistry in *Imagining the Middle Class: The Political Representation of Class in Britain, c. 1780–1840* (Cambridge: Cambridge University Press, 1995): 268–72.

5 Thomas Perronet Thompson, *Catechism on the Corn Laws*, 14th edn (London: Robert Heward, 1829): 42–3; Michael J. Turner, '"The Bonaparte of Free Trade" and the Anti-Corn Law League', *Historical Journal* 41, no. 4 (1998): 1013–15.

6 See my monograph and article: *Wanting and Having: Popular Politics and Liberal Consumerism in England, 1830–70* (Manchester: Manchester University Press, 2015): 148–52; 'Exclusive Dealing in the Chartist Movement', *Labour History Review* 74, no. 1 (2009): 90–110.

7 G. M. Trevelyan, *The Life of John Bright* (London: Constable, 1913): 60.

8 Norman McCord, *The Anti-Corn Law League, 1838–1846*, 2nd edn (London: Allen & Unwin, 1968): 34–54.

9 Gurney, *Wanting and Having*, 1–2, 31–4; Anthony Howe, *Free Trade and Liberal England, 1846–1946* (Oxford: Clarendon Press, 1997): 5–6, 30.

10 Paul Pickering and Alex Tyrrell, *The People's Bread: A History of the Anti-Corn Law League* (London: Leicester University Press, 2000): 144.

11 Thomas Wemyss Reid, *The Life, Letters and Friendships of Richard Monckton Milnes, First Lord Houghton*, 3rd edn (London: Cassell, 1891): Vol. I, 436.

12 *Manchester Times*, 17 January 1846: 6; J. A. Hobson, *Richard Cobden: The International Man* (London: Unwin, 1918).

13 *The Times*, 15 January 1840: 3.

14 Deborah A. Logan, *Harriet Martineau, Victorian Imperialism, and the Civilizing Mission* (Burlington, VT: Ashgate, 2010): 99–105. See also David Todd, 'John Bowring and the Global Dissemination of Free Trade', *Historical Journal* 51, no. 2 (2008): 373–97.

15 McCord points out that O'Connell's support for free trade made it possible for the League to forge an alliance with the Manchester Irish against the Chartists in *The Anti-Corn Law League*, 99–103.

16 George Kitson Clark, 'Hunger and Politics in 1842', *Journal of Modern History* 25, no. 4 (1953): 366.

17 Gurney, *Wanting and Having*, 29, 39–42; '"Rejoicing in Potatoes": The Politics of Consumption in England During the "Hungry Forties"', *Past and Present* 203 (2009): 99–136.

18 William Field, *A Lecture on the Provision Laws, Chiefly Considered as a Moral and Religious Question* (London: Edward Foden, 1842): 29–30.

19 Alexander Harvey, *The Influence of the Provision Laws on Trade, Wages, and Society* (Glasgow: G. Brookman, 1843): 4, 17. See also W. R. Greg, *Not Overproduction but Deficient Consumption, the Source of Our Sufferings* (London: Henry Hooper, 1842): 27; Alon Kadish, 'Free Trade and High Wages: the Economics of the Anti-Corn Law League', in Andrew Marrison

(ed.), *Free Trade and Its Reception 1815–1960* (London: Routledge, 1998): 24–5.

20 Gurney, *Wanting and Having*, 48; Wahrman, *Imagining the Middle Class*, 409–10.

21 Pickering and Tyrrell, *The People's Bread*, 144–5.

22 Anthony Howe, 'Free Trade and its Enemies', in Martin Hewitt (ed.), *The Victorian World* (London: Routledge, 2012); Frank Trentmann, *Free Trade Nation: Commerce, Consumption, and Civil Society in Modern Britain* (Oxford: Oxford University Press, 2008). For a proper discussion see Chapter 6.

23 Simon Morgan, 'Material Culture and the Politics of Personality in Early Victorian England', *Journal of Victorian Culture* 17, no. 2 (2012): 127–46.

24 *Douglas Jerrold's Shilling Magazine*, June 1845: 517; Gurney, *Wanting and Having*, 223–37; '"The Sublime of the Bazaar": A Moment in the Making of a Consumer Culture in Mid-Victorian England', *Journal of Social History* 40, no. 2 (2006): 385–405.

25 For protectionist arguments see Anna Gambles, *Protection and Politics: Conservative Economic Discourse, 1815–1852* (Woodbridge: Royal Historical Society, 1999).

26 Gurney, *Wanting and Having*, 19, 107, 132–4.

27 George Henry Smith, *The Rights of Rich and Poor: Just Taxation; Abolition of all Duties on the Necessaries of Life; and of all Restrictions on Trade, Commerce, Manufactures, Agriculture; and on all Professions* (London: J. R. Williams, 1862): 6; W. N. Calkins, 'A Victorian Free Trade Lobby', *Economic History Review* 13, no. 1 (1960): 90–104.

28 Gurney, *Wanting and Having*, 311–12.

29 *The Times*, 31 December 1859: 6.

30 Jennifer Tann, 'Co-operative Corn Milling: Self Help During the Grain Crises of the Napoleonic Wars', *Agricultural History Review* 28, no. 1 (1980): 45–57; Joshua Bamfield, 'Consumer-Owned Community Flour and Bread Societies in the Eighteenth and Early Nineteenth Centuries', *Business History* 40, no. 4 (1998): 16–36.

31 Benjamin Jones, *Co-operative Production* (Oxford: Clarendon Press, 1894): 173–4.

32 E. P. Thompson, 'The Moral Economy of the English Crowd in the Eighteenth Century', *Past and Present* 50 (1971): 136.

33 Jones, *Co-operative Production*, 170–2. See also G. J. Holyoake, *Self-Help a Hundred Years Ago* (London: Swan Sonnenschein, 1888): 66–72.

34 Noel Thompson, *Social Opulence and Private Restraint. The Consumer in British Socialist Thought Since 1800* (Oxford: Oxford University Press, 2015): 14–25.

35 *New Moral World*, 3 May 1835: 186.

36 Thompson, *Social Opulence and Private Restraint*, 32–9.

37 G. D. H. Cole, *A Century of Co-operation* (Manchester: Co-operative Union, 1945): 24–6; Andy Durr, 'William King of Brighton: Co-operation's Prophet?' in Stephen Yeo (ed.), *New Views of Co-operation* (London: Routledge, 1988): 10–26.

38 Gurney, *Wanting and Having*, 11–16, 65–104.

39 Valerie Johnston, *Diets in Workhouses and Prisons, 1835–1895* (New York: Garland, 1985); Nadja Durbach, 'Roast Beef, the New Poor Law, and the British Nation, 1834–63', *Journal of British Studies* 52, no. 4 (2013): 963–89.
40 Nicholas Edsall, *The Anti-Poor Law Movement, 1834–44* (Manchester: Manchester University Press, 1971); John Knott, *Popular Opposition to the 1834 Poor Law* (London: Croom Helm, 1986).
41 John Foster, *Class Struggle and the Industrial Revolution* (London: Methuen, 1977): 53–4; Gurney, *Wanting and Having*, 148–9.
42 *Poor Man's Guardian*, 28 September 1833: 315; 26 October 1833: 346.
43 Dorothy Thompson (ed.), *The Early Chartists* (London: Macmillan, 1971): 194–5; Gurney, *Wanting and Having*, 159–62.
44 *Northern Liberator*, 21 September 1839: 3; Malcolm Chase, *Chartism: A New History* (Manchester: Manchester University Press, 2007): 62–3, 146–7; Gurney, *Wanting and Having*, 164.
45 Robert Lowery, *Address to the Fathers and Mothers, Sons and Daughters, of the Working Classes, on the System of Exclusive Dealing, and the Formation of Joint Stock Provision Companies, Shewing how the People may Free Themselves from Oppression*(1839), in Brian Harrison and Patricia Hollis (eds), *Robert Lowery, Radical and Chartist* (London: Europa, 1979), 202.
46 *Northern Liberator*, 26 October 1839: 6; Gurney, *Wanting and Having*, 167–8.
47 Timothy Alborn, *Conceiving Companies: Joint-Stock Politics in Victorian England* (London: Routledge, 1998); Donna Loftus, 'Capital and Community: Limited Liability and Attempts to Democratize the Market in Mid-Nineteenth-Century England', *Victorian Studies* 45, no. 1 (2001): 93–120; James Taylor, *Creating Capitalism: Joint-Stock Enterprise in British Politics and Culture, 1800–1870* (Woodbridge: Royal Historical Society, 2006).
48 See my article, 'The Democratic Idiom: Languages of Democracy in the Chartist Movement', *Journal of Modern History* 86, no. 3 (2014): 566–602.
49 Charles Parker, *The Life and Letters of Sir James Graham* (London: John Murray, 1907): Vol. I, 323.
50 Gurney, *Wanting and Having*, 43–7; Mick Jenkins, *The General Strike of 1842* (London: Lawrence & Wishart, 1980), 93–5.
51 Gurney, *Wanting and Having*, 52; Jenkins, *The General Strike*, 236; Gareth Stedman Jones, 'The Language of Chartism', in James Epstein and Dorothy Thompson (eds), *The Chartist Experience: Studies in Working-Class Radicalism and Culture, 1830–60* (London: Macmillan, 1982), 51–2.
52 Catherine Webb (ed.), *Industrial Co-operation: The Story of a Peaceful Revolution* (Manchester: Co-operative Union, 1904), 68–9; Martin Purvis, 'Co-operative Retailing in England, 1835–1850: Developments Beyond Rochdale', *Northern History* 22 (1986): 198–215; Robin Thornes, 'Change and Continuity in the Development of Co-operation, 1827–44', in Yeo (ed.), *New Views of Co-operation*, 27–51.
53 John K. Walton, 'Revisiting the Rochdale Pioneers', *Labour History Review* 80, no. 3 (2015): 215–48.
54 Gurney, *Wanting and Having*, 172–3.
55 *Notes to the People*, 7 February 1852.
56 Gurney, *Wanting and Having*, 43–4.

57 Colin Matthew, 'Disraeli, Gladstone, and the Politics of Mid-Victorian Budgets', *Historical Journal* 22, no. 3 (1979): 615–43.
58 Eugenio Biagini, 'Popular Liberals, Gladstonian Finance, and the Debate on Taxation, 1860–1874', in Eugenio Biagini and Alastair Reid (eds), *Currents of Radicalism: Popular Radicalism, Organised Labour and Party Politics in Britain, 1850–1914* (Cambridge: Cambridge University Press, 1991); Gurney, *Wanting and Having*, 257–9.
59 W. L. Burn, *The Age of Equipoise: A Study of the Mid-Victorian Generation* (London: George Allen & Unwin, 1964); Martin Hewitt (ed.), *An Age of Equipoise? Reassessing Mid-Victorian Britain* (Aldershot: Ashgate, 2000).
60 John Burnett, *Plenty and Want: A Social History of Diet in England from 1815 to the Present Day* (London: Penguin Books, 1968): 240–48; Arthur Hassall, *Food and its Adulterations: Comprising the Reports of the Analytical Sanitary Commission of 'The Lancet' for the Years 1851 to 1854* (London: Longman, Brown, Green, and Longmans, 1855); P. J. Atkins, 'Sophistication Detected: Or, the Adulteration of the Milk Supply, 1850–1914', *Social History* 16, no. 3 (1991): 317–39; S. D. Smith, 'Coffee, Microscopy, and *The Lancet*'s Analytical Sanitary Commission', *Social History of Medicine* 14, no. 2 (2001): 171–97.
61 'The English Thugs', *Chambers's Journal of Popular Literature, Science and Arts*, 5 May 1855: 273.
62 Karl Marx, *Capital: A Critique of Political Economy. Volume I: The Process of Capitalist Production* (Harmondsworth: Penguin Books, 1976): 232.
63 Burnett, *Plenty and Want*, 248–60; Gurney, *Wanting and Having*, 308–9.
64 Bill Lancaster, *The Department Store: A Social History* (London: Leicester University Press, 1995): 132–4.
65 *The Mirror of Literature, Amusement, and Instruction*, 9 May 1846: 303–4; *Chambers's Edinburgh Journal*, 7 May 1853: 297.
66 *The Times*, 25 April 1856: 9.
67 *London Review*, 1 September 1866: 230.
68 Deborah Cohen, *Household Gods: The British and their Possessions* (New Haven, CT: Yale University Press, 2006).
69 Peter N. Stearns, 'Stages of Consumerism: Recent Work on the Issues of Periodization', *Journal of Modern History* 69, no. 1 (1997): 116.
70 Reginia Gagnier overestimates Jevons's influence in her otherwise stimulating study, *The Insatiability of Human Wants: Economics and Aesthetics in Market Society* (Chicago: Chicago University Press, 2000). Useful studies of Jevons and Marshall are Sandra Peart, *The Economics of W. S. Jevons* (London: Routledge, 1996); David Reisman, *Alfred Marshall's Mission* (Basingstoke: Macmillan, 1990).
71 See Judith Stoddart, *Ruskin's Culture Wars: 'Fors Clavigera' and the Crisis of Victorian Liberalism* (Charlottesville: University of Virginia Press,1998); David Craig, *John Ruskin and the Ethics of Consumption* (Charlottesville: University of Virginia Press, 2006); Gill Cockram, *Ruskin and Social Reform: Ethics and Economics in the Victorian Age* (London: I. B. Tauris, 2007); Stuart Eagles, *After Ruskin: The Social and Political Legacies of a Victorian Prophet, 1870–1920* (Oxford: Oxford University Press, 2011).
72 Owen Jones, *On the True and the False in the Decorative Arts: Lectures Delivered at Marlborough House, June 1852* (1863).

73 Cohen, *Household Gods*, 21–4; Lara Kriegel, *Grand Designs: Labor, Empire, and the Museum in Victorian Culture* (Durham: Duke University Press, 2007): 126–59.
74 'The Fashion of Furniture', *Cornhill Magazine* 9, no. 51 (1864): 337.
75 Charles Eastlake, *Hints on Household Taste in Furniture, Upholstery and Other Details* (London: Longmans, Green, 1868): vii; Asa Briggs, *Victorian Things* (Harmondsworth: Penguin, 1990): 226, passim.
76 Philip N. Backstrom, *Christian Socialism and Co-operation in Victorian England* (London: Croom Helm, 1974): 45–6, 68; Peter Gurney, *Co-operative Culture and the Politics of Consumption in England, 1870–1930* (Manchester: Manchester University Press, 1996): 16–17, 94.
77 Martin Purvis, 'Stocking the Store: Co-operative Retailers in North-East England and Systems of Wholesale Supply circa 1860–77', *Business History* 40, no. 4 (1998): 55–78; John F. Wilson, Anthony Webster and Rachael Vorberg-Rugh, *Building Co-operation: A Business History of the Co-operative Group, 1863–2013* (Oxford: Oxford University Press, 2013): 66–72.
78 Daniel Stone, *The Rochdale Co-operative Societies: A Study for Working Men* (Manchester: Abel Heywood, 1861): 5. The last clause is a swipe against secret oaths used by trade societies.
79 The classic early articulation of this view was by Sidney Pollard, 'Nineteenth-Century Co-operation: From Community Building to Shopkeeping', in Asa Briggs and John Saville (eds), *Essays in Labour History* (London: Macmillan, 1960): 74–112.
80 Walton, 'Revisiting the Rochdale Pioneers', 216–22.
81 *Transactions of the National Association for the Promotion of Social Science* (London: John W. Parker, 1872): 454. On this body see Lawrence Goldman, *Science, Reform, and Politics in Victorian Britain: The Social Science Association, 1857–1886* (Cambridge: Cambridge University Press, 2002).
82 Julia Hood and B. S. Yamey, 'The Middle-Class Co-operative Retailing Societies in London, 1864–1900', *Oxford Economic Papers* 9, no. 3 (1957): 309–22.
83 Arthur Arnold, *The History of the Cotton Famine* (London: Saunders, Otley, 1864): 36; W. O. Henderson, *The Lancashire Cotton Famine 1861–1865* (Manchester: Manchester University Press, 1934): 95–8; Gurney, *Wanting and Having*, 264–70.
84 Michael Rose, 'Rochdale Man and the Stalybridge Riot: The Relief and Control of the Unemployed during the Lancashire Cotton Famine', in A. P. Donajgrodzki (ed.), *Social Control in Nineteenth Century Britain* (London: Croom Helm, 1977); Gurney, *Wanting and Having*, 270–88; G. D. H. Cole, *A Century of Co-operation*, 188.

Chapter 4

1 Henry Sampson, *A History of Advertising* (London: Chatto and Windus, 1874): 1, 25–9.
2 George Gissing, *In the Year of Jubilee* (London: J. M. Dent, 1994): 52–3, 63.
3 Robert Giffen, *The Progress of the Working Classes in the Last Half Century* (London: George Bell and Sons, 1884): 8–9, 13, 16–7.

4 Alun Howkins, *Reshaping Rural England: A Social History, 1850–1925* (London: Harper Collins Academic, 1991); Gareth Stedman Jones, *Outcast London: A Study in the Relationship Between Classes in Victorian Society* (Oxford: Clarendon Press, 1971); Sheila Blackburn, *A Fair Day's Wage for a Fair Day's Work? Sweated Labour and the Origins of Minimum Wage Legislation in Britain* (London: Routledge, 2007); David Englander and Rosemary O'Day (eds), *Retrieved Riches: Social Investigation in Britain, 1840–1914* (Aldershot: Scolar Press, 1995).

5 Joseph Arch, *Free Trade Versus Protection or Fair Trade, Weighed in the Balance and Found Wanting*, 4th edn (Coventry: Curtis and Beamish, 1884): 13, 44–6; Annie Besant, 'The Future of the Workers in England', *Our Corner* 10 (1887): 21.

6 E. S. Turner, *The Shocking History of Advertising!* (London: Michael Joseph, 1952): 87.

7 Brian Lewis, *So Clean: Lord Leverhulme, Soap and Civilization* (Manchester: Manchester University Press, 2008): 65–6; Roy Church, 'Advertising Consumer Goods in Nineteenth Century Britain: Reinterpretations', *Economic History Review* 53, no. 4 (2000): 635; Robert Fitzgerald, *Rowntree and the Marketing Revolution 1862–1969* (Cambridge: Cambridge University Press, 1995): 28, 91–2.

8 Matthew Hilton, *Smoking in British Popular Culture 1800–2000: Perfect Pleasures* (Manchester: Manchester University Press, 2000): 83.

9 T. R. Nevett, *Advertising in Britain: A History* (London: Heinemann on behalf of the History of Advertising Trust, 1982): 71.

10 Lewis, *So Clean*, 59–60.

11 Diana and Geoffrey Hindley, *Advertising in Victorian England, 1837–1901* (London: Wayland, 1972): 74–5; John Hewitt, 'Designing the Poster in England, 1890–1914', *Early Popular Visual Culture* 5, no. 1 (2007): 57–8.

12 John Thomson and Adolph Smith, *Street Life in London* (London: Sampson Low, 1877): 69.

13 G. W. Goodall, *Advertising: A Study of Modern Business Power* (London: Constable, 1914): 35–7; D. and G. Hindley, *Advertising in Victorian England*, 101; T. R. Nevett, *Advertising in Britain*, 93–7.

14 Goodall, *Advertising*, 3; Nevett, *Advertising in Britain*, 70–1; 78; Michael J. Winstanley, *The Shopkeeper's World 1830–1914* (Manchester: Manchester University Press, 1983): 155.

15 Goodall, *Advertising*, 13–14.

16 Hulda Friederichs, *The Life of Sir George Newnes* (London: Hodder & Stoughton, 1911): 80–95; S. J. Taylor, *The Great Outsiders: Northcliffe, Rothermere and the 'Daily Mail'* (London: Weidenfeld & Nicolson, 1998): 7.

17 Turner, *The Shocking History of Advertising!*, 150, 154–5; Frank Presbrey, *The History and Development of Advertising* (New York: Doubleday, Doran, 1929): 102–3.

18 W. Teignmouth Shore, 'The Craft of the Advertiser', *Fortnightly Review* 81, no. 482 (1907): 307.

19 Hilton, *Smoking in British Popular Culture*, 92.

20 Presbrey, *The History and Development of Advertising*, 98–9; Turner, *The Shocking History of Advertising!*, 106–8; D. and G. Hindley, *Advertising*

in Victorian England, 43–4; Nevett, *Advertising in Britain*, 87–8; Lewis, *So Clean*, 65.

21 'Artistic Advertising', *Magazine of Art* 12, no. 1 (1889): 426; Presbrey, *The History and Development of Advertising*, 100.

22 Hewitt, 'Designing the Poster in England', 58, 65–7.

23 *Reynolds's News*, 27 January 1884.

24 *Pall Mall Gazette*, 6 November 1889.

25 *Speaker*, 10 April 1897: 396–7; Peter T. Marsh, *Joseph Chamberlain: Entrepreneur in Politics* (New Haven, CT: Yale University Press, 1994): xi, 643.

26 Graham Wallas, *Human Nature in Politics* (London: Transaction, 1981): 108–10; Martin J. Wiener, *Between Two Worlds: The Political Thought of Graham Wallas* (Oxford: Clarendon Press, 1971): 94–5.

27 Goodall, *Advertising*, 53; James Thompson, '"Pictorial Lies"? – Posters and Politics in Britain c. 1880–1914', *Past and Present* 197 (2007): 177–210.

28 Nicholas Hiley, 'Sir Hedley Le Bas and the Origins of Domestic Propaganda in Britain, 1914–1917', *European Journal of Marketing* 21, no. 8 (1987): 30–46; Jim Aulich and John Hewitt, *Seduction or Instruction? First World War Posters in Britain and Europe* (Manchester: Manchester University Press, 2007); *Daily Mail*, 19 April 1915: 4.

29 Raymond Williams, 'Advertising: the Magic System', in *Problems in Materialism and Culture* (London: Verso, 1980): 179.

30 See J. A. Hobson, *The Evolution of Modern Capitalism: A Study of Machine Production* (London: Walter Scott, 1894); D. H. Macgregor, *Industrial Combination* (London: George Bell and Sons, 1906); Leslie Hannah, *The Rise of the Corporate Economy* (London: Methuen, 1976).

31 T. A. B. Corley, 'Competition and the Growth of Advertising in the US and Britain, 1880–1914', *Business and Economic History* 17 (1988): 155. For more on US developments see Susan Strasser, *Satisfaction Guaranteed: The Making of the American Mass Market* (Washington, DC: Smithsonian Institution Press, 1989); Richard S. Tedlow, *New and Improved: The Story of Mass Marketing in America* (New York: Basic Books, 1990).

32 John Mercer, 'A Mark of Distinction: Branding and Trade Mark Law in the UK from the 1860s', *Business History* 52, no. 1 (2010): 17–23.

33 Lewis, *So Clean*, 61; Mercer, 'A Mark of Distinction', 29–30.

34 Ibid., 25–6.

35 Turner, *The Shocking History of Advertising!*, 90; D. and G. Hindley, *Advertising in Victorian England*, 46.

36 Williams, 'Advertising: the Magic System', 178; Turner, *The Shocking History of Advertising!*, 91.

37 Nevett, *Advertising in Britain*, 100; Stefan Schwarzkopf, 'Consumer Communication as Commodity: British Advertising Agencies and the Global Market for Advertising, 1780–1980', in Erica Rappaport, Mark J. Crowley and Sandra Trudgen Dawson (eds), *Consuming Behaviours: Identity, Politics and Pleasure in Twentieth-Century Britain* (London: Bloomsbury Academic, 2015): 124–8.

38 Nevett, *Advertising in Britain*, 102; Church, 'Advertising Consumer Goods', 642; Lewis, *So Clean*, 70.

39 Nevett, *Advertising in Britain*, 103, 105.

40 William Stead Jr., *The Art of Advertising: Its Theory and Practice Fully Described* (London: T. B. Browne, 1899): 51; D. and G. Hindley, *Advertising in Victorian England*, 38.
41 Stead, *The Art of Advertising*, 76, 78.
42 Lewis, *So Clean*, 61–2.
43 Nevett, *Advertising in Britain*, 74. Other soap makers were big advertisers, especially Pears that spent between £100,000 and £130,000 per annum after Thomas Barratt took over in 1875. Turner, *The Shocking History of Advertising!*, 89–90.
44 Lori Anne Loeb, *Consuming Angels: Advertising and Victorian Women* (New York: Oxford University Press, 1994): 44.
45 Ibid., 115.
46 Charles Wilson, *The History of Unilever: A Study in Economic Growth and Social Change* (London: Cassell, 1954): Vol. 1, 21, citing a letter from Lever to John Cheshire, 13 June 1909. Lever may have been adapting from Scott, who wrote that when he thought about Ivory Soap, 'a halo of spotless elegance envelops it, and I do not think of it merely as a prosaic chunk of fat and alkali'. Walter Dill Scott, *The Psychology of Advertising: A Simple Exposition of the Principles of Psychology in Their Relation to Successful Advertising*, 2nd edn (Boston: Small, Maynard, 1910): 193.
47 Robert Opie, *Rule Britannia: Trading on the British Image* (London: Viking, 1985), 8.
48 Thomas Richards, *The Commodity Culture of Victorian England: Advertising and Spectacle, 1851–1914* (London, Verso, 1990): 73–118.
49 Anne McClintock, *Imperial Leather: Race, Gender, and Sexuality in the Colonial Contest* (London: Routledge, 1994); Anandi Ramamurthy, *Imperial Persuaders: Images of Africa and Asia in British Advertising* (Manchester: Manchester University Press, 2003), 24–62.
50 *Longman's Magazine* 13, no. 75 (1889): 228; D. and G. Hindley, *Advertising in Victorian England*, 97–9.
51 Nevett, *Advertising in Britain*, 98; D. and G. Hindley, *Advertising in Victorian England*, 119.
52 John MacKenzie, *Propaganda and Empire: The Manipulation of British Public Opinion, 1880–1960* (Manchester: Manchester University Press, 1984) argued for the success of imperial propaganda, including advertising; alternatively, Bernard Porter in *The Absent-Minded Imperialists: Empire, Society, and Culture in Britain* (Oxford: Oxford University Press, 2004) maintained that it was largely the ideology of ruling elites.
53 John Morgan Richards, *With John Bull and Jonathan* (London: T. Werner Laurie, 1905), 47; Nevett, *Advertising in Britain*, 84.
54 D. and G. Hindley, *Advertising in Victorian England*, 57–8; *Standard*, 24 April 1899: 4.
55 Nevett, *Advertising in Britain*, 76–83; D. and G. Hindley, *Advertising in Victorian England*, 60–2.
56 George Binney Dibblee, *The Newspaper* (London: Williams & Norgate, 1913): 115.
57 Turner, *The Shocking History of Advertising!*, 146–9; B. W. E. Alford, *W. D. & H. O. Wills and the Development of the UK Tobacco Industry 1786–1965* (London: Methuen, 1973); Maurice Corina, *Trust in Tobacco: The*

Anglo-American Struggle for Power (London: Joseph, 1975); Hilton, *Smoking in British Popular Culture*, 86–7.

58 Wilson, *The History of Unilever*, 72–88; W. P. Jolly, *Lord Leverhulme. A Biography* (London: Constable, 1976), 38–57; Peter Gurney, *Co-operative Culture and the Politics of Consumption in England, 1870–1930* (Manchester: Manchester University Press, 1996): 204–7.

59 See James Taylor, 'Written in the Skies: Advertising, Technology, and Modernity in Britain since 1885', *Journal of British Studies* 55, no. 4 (2016): 750–80.

60 *Standard*, 2 May 1890: 3; 3 May 1890: 3; 5 May 1890: 3.

61 Cyril Sheldon, *A History of Poster Advertising* (London: Chapman and Hall, 1937), 56–65; Turner, *The Shocking History of Advertising!*, 100; Nevett, *Advertising in Britain*, 122–3; Tracey C. Davis, 'Sex in Public Places: The Zaeo Aquarium Scandal and the Victorian Moral Majority', *Theatre History Studies* 10 (1990): 1–13.

62 *The Times*, 22 November 1892: 11; 24 November 1892: 9–10.

63 *Reynolds's News*, 4 December 1892: 2.

64 *Sala's Journal*, 3 December 1892, cited by Terry Nevett, 'The Scapa Society: The First Organised Reaction against Advertising', *Media, Culture and Society* 3, no. 2 (1981): 184.

65 Ibid., 179–83; Turner, *The Shocking History of Advertising!*, 112–15.

66 Richardson Evans, *The Age of Disfigurement* (London: Remington, 1893): 10–1, 19, 51. On the limited nature of SCAPA's critique see also Evan's history of the organization, *An Account of the Scapa Society* (London: Constable, 1926): 9; and Paul Readman, 'Landscape Preservation, "Advertising Disfigurement", and English National Identity c. 1890–1914', *Rural History* 12, no. 1 (2001): 72.

67 Richardson Evans, 'Advertising as a Trespass on the Public', *Nineteenth Century* 37, no. 220 (1895): 973.

68 Peter Gould, *Early Green Politics: Back to Nature, Back to the Land, and Socialism in Britain, 1880–1900* (Brighton: Harvester, 1988); Chris Waters, *British Socialists and the Politics of Popular Culture, 1884–1914* (Manchester: Manchester University Press, 1990).

69 Turner, *The Shocking History of Advertising!*, 119–20.

70 Readman, 'Landscape Preservation', 65. The quotation is from a letter that was sent to Evans.

71 Nevett, 'The Scapa Society', 186–7.

72 *Review of Reviews* June 1895: 525; February 1911: 149.

73 Ibid., March 1914: 252 (a puff for an advertising agent); May 1914: 421 (a puff for an advertising manager); June 1914: 453–5 (a general puff). The article 'Is Advertising Fair Play?' by Thomas Russell, president of the Incorporated Society of Advertisement Consultants, in *Daily Express*, 4 July 1914: 4, is an excellent example of this symbiotic trend.

74 Turner, *The Shocking History of Advertising!*, 103–4; Nevett, *Advertising in Britain*, 134–6.

75 Lori Loeb, 'Doctors and Patent Medicines in Modern Britain: Professionalism and Consumerism', *Albion* 33, no. 3 (2001): 411.

76 Ibid., 414.

77 H. G. Wells, *Tono-Bungay* (London: Penguin Books, 2005): 136–7.

78 Ibid., 159.
79 David C. Smith, *H. G. Wells: Desperately Mortal. A Biography* (New Haven, CT: Yale University Press, 1988): 43–4, 98, 129–30.
80 Wells, *Tono-Bungay*, 381.
81 Thomas Richards, *The Imperial Archive: Knowledge and the Fantasy of Empire* (London: Verso, 1993): 88–104; Benita Parry, *Postcolonial Studies. A Materialist Critique* (London: Routledge, 2004): 148–61.
82 *Saturday Review*, 21 September 1912: 359–61.
83 *Report on the Select Committee on Patent Medicines* (London: HMSO, 1914): x, xxvii-xxviii, 95–8, 270–1.
84 Turner, *The Shocking History of Advertising!*, 172–6; Loeb, 'Doctors and Patent Medicines in Modern Britain', 404–7, 415–8, 422.

Chapter 5

1 *Graphic*, 3 August 1872: 98; Erika Diane Rappaport, *Shopping for Pleasure: Women in the Making of London's West End* (Princeton: Princeton University Press, 2000): 38.
2 Richard S. Lambert, *The Universal Provider: A Study of William Whiteley and the Rise of the London Department Store* (London: Harrap, 1938): 77, 85–6; Rappaport, *Shopping for Pleasure*, 16–17.
3 Ibid., 39–41.
4 See for example Lambert, *The Universal Provider*; H. D. Willcock (ed.), *Brown's of Chester: Portrait of a Shop* (London: Lindsay Drummond, 1947); Alison Adburgham, *Shops and Shopping 1800–1914* (London: Faber & Faber, 1964); Reginald Pound, *The Fenwick Story* (London: Fenwick Ltd, 1972); Maurice Corina, *Fine Silks and Oak Counters: Debenhams 1778–1978* (London: Hutchinson, 1978); Gordon Honeycombe, *Selfridges. Seventy-Five Years. The Story of the Store 1909–1984* (London: Park Lane Press, 1984).
5 Michael B. Miller, *The Bon Marché: Bourgeois Culture and the Department Store, 1869–1920* (Princeton: Princeton University Press, 1981). Note also Asa Briggs's early groundbreaking work, *Friends of the People: The Centenary History of Lewis's* (London: B. T. Batsford, 1956).
6 Useful studies of the wider impact include Hrant Pasdermadjian, *The Department Store: Its Origins, Evolution and Economics* (London: Newman Books, 1954); Rosalind Williams, *Dream Worlds: Mass Consumption in Late Nineteenth-Century France* (Berkeley: University of California Press, 1982); William Leach, *Land of Desire: Merchants, Power, and the Rise of a New American Culture* (New York: Vintage Books, 1993); Geoffrey Crossick and Serge Jaumain (eds), *Cathedrals of Consumption: The European Department Store, 1850–1939* (Aldershot: Ashgate, 1998).
7 J. B. Jefferys, *Retail Trading in Britain, 1850–1950: A Study of Trends in Retailing with Special Reference to the Development of Co-operative, Multiple Shop and Department Store Methods of Trading* (Cambridge: Cambridge University Press, 1954): 24–30.

8 See H. Gordon Selfridge, *The Romance of Commerce* (London: John Lane, 1918), which constructed a typically inflated historical genealogy for department store bosses.
9 Rachel Bowlby, *Just Looking: Consumer Culture in Dreiser, Gissing and Zola* (London: Methuen, 1985).
10 William Leach, 'Transformations in a Culture of Consumption: Women and Department Stores', *Journal of American History* 71, no. 2 (1984): 342. See also Bill Lancaster, *The Department Store. A Social History* (London: Leicester University Press, 1995): 174–5; Rappaport, *Shopping for Pleasure*, 13.
11 Émile Zola, *The Ladies' Paradise* (Oxford: Oxford University Press, 1995): 76–7, 83–4, 315.
12 *The Bookman* 9, no. 49 (1895): 30. The novel was serialized in the *London Journal* in 1883.
13 Cited in *Belfast News-Letter*, 16 June 1888: 8.
14 Lambert, *The Universal Provider*, 46–9, 60–1, 68–9, 80–3; Rappaport, *Shopping for Pleasure*, 19–27.
15 Cited by Lambert, *The Universal Provider*, 79.
16 Ibid., 215; Lancaster, *The Department Store*, 50–1.
17 Lambert, *The Universal Provider*, 16–21. Rappaport suggests that this story was part of Whiteley's self-promoted mythology in *Shopping for Pleasure*, 27–8.
18 Lady Jeune, 'The Ethics of Shopping', *Fortnightly Review* 57, no. 337 (1895): 124.
19 *Birmingham Daily Post*, 23 September 1885: 5.
20 Leach, *Land of Desire*, 31, 60, 68–9, 86–7.
21 Honeycombe, *Selfridges*, 9–12, 36; Rappaport, *Shopping for Pleasure*, 142, 150–1, 154–7; Lancaster, *The Department Store*, 61–80.
22 Briggs, *Friends of the People*, 30, 38–9, 45–6, 122.
23 Ibid, 65, 80–8; *Birmingham Daily Post*, 23 September 1885: 5.
24 Michael Moss and Alison Turton, *A Legend of Retailing: House of Fraser* (London: Weidenfeld and Nicolson, 1989), 50, 54–60.
25 Lancaster, *The Department Store*, 31–6.
26 Moss and Turton, *A Legend of Retailing*, 36, 75; Lambert, *The Universal Provider*, 87.
27 Briggs, *Friends of the People*, 57–8, 69–70; *Manchester Times*, 26 November 1881: 8.
28 Honeycombe, *Selfridges*, 39.
29 Zola, *The Ladies' Paradise*, 254, 394.
30 C. Wright Mills, *White Collar: The American Middle Classes* (New York: Oxford University Press, 1951): 168–9, cited by Briggs, *Friends of the People*, 170.
31 Judith Walkowitz, 'Going Public: Shopping, Street Harassment, and Streetwalking in Late Victorian London', *Representations* 62 (1998): 1–30.
32 Christopher Breward, 'Femininity and Consumption: The Problem of the Late Nineteenth-Century Fashion Journal', *Journal of Design History* 7, no. 2 (1994): 71, 87.
33 Rappaport, *Shopping for Pleasure*, 111–22; Margaret Beetham, *A Magazine of Her Own? Domesticity and Desire in the Woman's Magazine, 1800–1914* (London: Routledge, 1996): 122; Janet Wolff, 'The Invisible *Flâneuse*: Women

and the Literature of Modernity', *Theory, Culture and Society* 2, no. 3 (1985): 37–46.

34 Lancaster, *The Department Store*, 23; 41; Moss and Turton, *A Legend of Retailing*, 80; J. H. Porter, 'The Development of a Provincial Department Store 1870–1939', *Business History* 13, no. 1 (1971): 64–71. For smaller stores in the United States see Vicki Howard, *From Main Street to Mall: The Rise and Fall of the American Department Store* (Philadelphia: University of Pennsylvania Press, 2015).

35 Neil Armstrong, *Christmas in Nineteenth-Century England* (Manchester: Manchester University Press, 2010): 140; Lady Jeune, 'The Ethics of Shopping', 127–8; Christopher P. Hosgood, 'Mrs Pooter's Purchase: Lower-Middle-Class Consumerism and the Sales, 1870–1914', in Alan Kidd and David Nicholls (eds), *Gender, Civic Culture and Consumerism: Middle-Class Identity in Britain, 1800–1940* (Manchester: Manchester University Press, 1999): 150–5.

36 Cited in Lambert, *The Universal Provider*, 125.

37 For a discussion of these links see Mariana Valverde, 'The Love of Finery: Fashion and the Fallen Woman in Nineteenth-Century Social Discourse', *Victorian Studies* 32, no. 2 (1989): 168–88.

38 Rappaport, *Shopping for Pleasure*, 30–3; Lambert, *The Universal Provider*, 73.

39 Lori Anne Loeb, *Consuming Angels: Advertising and Victorian Women* (Oxford: Oxford University Press, 1994), 33–4, *passim*.

40 Patricia O'Brien, 'The Kleptomania Diagnosis: Bourgeois Women and Theft in Late Nineteenth-Century France', *Journal of Social History* 17, no. 1 (1983): 65–77; Tammy Whitlock, 'Gender, Medicine, and Consumer Culture in Victorian England: Creating the Kleptomaniac', *Albion* 31, no. 3 (1999): 413–37. For the American experience see Elaine Abelson, *When Ladies Go A-Thieving: Middle-Class Shoplifters in the Victorian Department Store* (New York: Oxford University Press, 1989).

41 'Thieves and Thieving', *Cornhill Magazine* 2, no. 9 (1860): 340.

42 Tammy C. Whitlock, *Crime, Gender and Consumer Culture in Nineteenth Century England* (Aldershot: Ashgate, 2005): 130–8; William M. Meier, 'Going on the Hoist: Women, Work, and Shoplifting in London, ca. 1890–1940', *Journal of British Studies* 50, no. 2 (2011): 426–7.

43 Lambert, *The Universal Provider*, 126–9.

44 Margot Finn, 'Women, Consumption, and Coverture in England, ca. 1760–1860', *Historical Journal* 39, no. 3 (1996): 703–22; *The Character of Credit: Personal Debt in English Culture, 1740–1914* (Cambridge: Cambridge University Press, 2003).

45 Rappaport, *Shopping for Pleasure*, 49, 56, 59–61, 63, 70–1. Wives were not made fully responsible for their debts until 1935.

46 *English Illustrated Magazine* 89 (1910): 429.

47 Krista Lysack, *Come Buy, Come Buy: Shopping and the Culture of Consumption in Victorian Women's Writing* (Athens: Ohio University Press, 2008): 58.

48 Lancaster, *The Department Store*, 125; Adburgham, *Shops and Shopping*, 236; Lee Holcombe, *Victorian Ladies at Work: Middle-Class Working Women in England and Wales, 1850–1914* (Hamden, CT: Archon Books, 1973). For the US experience see Susan Porter Benson, *Counter Cultures: Saleswomen,*

Managers, and Customers in American Department Stores, 1890–1940 (Urbana: University of Illinois Press, 1988).

49 Thomas Sutherst, *Death and Disease Behind the Counter* (London: Kegan Paul, 1884): 19; Lambert, *The Universal Provider*, 136–48; Christopher P. Hosgood, '"Mercantile Monasteries": Shops, Shop Assistants, and Shop Life in Late-Victorian and Edwardian Britain', *Journal of British Studies* 38, no. 3 (1999): 322–52. For the French experience see Theresa McBride, '"A Woman's World": Department Stores and the Evolution of Women's Employment', *French Historical Studies* 10, no. 4 (1978): 664–83.

50 Lady Jeune, 'The Ethics of Shopping', 128–9.

51 Ibid., 130–1; Isabella O. Ford, *Women's Wages and the Conditions under Which They Are Earned* (London: Wm Reeves, 1893): 15–17.

52 W. T. Stead, *If Christ Came to Chicago!* (Chicago: Laird & Lee, 1894): 234, 244; Lancaster, *The Department Store*, 179–82; Judith Walkowitz, *City of Dreadful Delight: Narratives of Sexual Danger in Late-Victorian London* (London: Virago Press, 1992).

53 Lancaster, *The Department Store*, 142; Lise Sanders, *Consuming Fantasies: Labor, Leisure, and the London Shopgirl, 1880–1920* (Columbus: Ohio State University Press, 2006): 42–53, *passim*. Two accessible studies are Pamela Horn, *Behind the Counter: Shop Lives from Market Stall to Supermarket* (Stroud: Sutton, 2006); Pamela Cox and Annabel Hobley, *Shopgirls: The True Story of Life Behind the Counter* (London: Hutchinson, 2014).

54 Christopher Breward, *The Hidden Consumer: Masculinities, Fashion and City Life 1860–1914* (Manchester: Manchester University Press, 1999), ch. 2, *passim*. See also Laura Ugolini, *Men and Menswear: Sartorial Consumption in Britain, 1880–1939* (Aldershot: Ashgate, 2007).

55 F. W. Burgess, *The Practical Retail Draper: A Complete Guide for the Drapery and Allied Trades*, Vol. IV, (London: Virtue, 1912): 23–4, cited in Breward, *The Hidden Consumer*, 116, 167.

56 Briggs, *Friends of the People*, 68, 74; Lambert, *The Universal Provider*, 69; Rappaport, *Shopping for Pleasure*, 171.

57 Brent Shannon, *The Cut of His Coat: Men, Dress, and Consumer Culture in Britain, 1860–1914* (Athens: Ohio University Press, 2006), 44, 64–74; Lancaster, *The Department Store*, 183.

58 *Pall Mall Gazette*, 9 February 1886: 8; *Morning Post*, 10 February 1886: 5.

59 Briggs, *Friends of the People*, 67, 129–30.

60 Corina, *Fine Silks and Oak Counters*, 71.

61 Lambert, *The Universal Provider*, 150–4, 210–1, 222.

62 Moss and Turton, *A Legend of Retailing*, 81–2, 93–5; Lambert, *The Universal Provider*, 239.

63 Ibid., 263–4.

64 *Pall Mall Gazette*, 20 June 1887: 13.

65 Lambert, *The Universal Provider*, 122–4, 196, 230–1, 235; Honeycombe, *Selfridges*, 39–40.

66 *Daily News*, 23 June 1897: 7.

67 Moss and Turton, *A Legend of Retailing*, 76; Julia Hood and B. S. Yamey, 'The Middle-Class Co-operative Retailing Societies in London, 1864–1900', *Oxford Economic Papers* 9, no. 3 (1957): 309–22.

68 *Yesterday's Shopping: The Army & Navy Stores Catalogue, 1907; a Facsimile of the Army & Navy Co-operative Society's 1907 Issue of Rules of the Society and Price List of Articles Sold at the Stores* (Newton Abbot: David & Charles, 1969): 272–94, 627–67, 1235.
69 See John Plotz, *Portable Property: Victorian Culture on the Move* (Princeton: Princeton University Press, 2008).
70 *The Times*, 16 March 1909: 9; *Daily Express*, 4 October 1909: 5; Moss and Turton, *A Legend of Retailing*, 95.
71 *Justice*, 20 March 1909: 1; 26 June 1909: 1.
72 Moss and Turton, *A Legend of Retailing*, 100; *Daily Express*, 7 January 1911: 1; 23 March 1911: 7; 27 March 1911: 1.
73 Honeycombe, *Selfridges*, 44; Moss and Turton, *A Legend of Retailing*, 108.
74 *Daily Mail*, 12 May 1911: 10. See also 18 May 1911, 10. On the 'thingness' of empire see Catherine Hall and Sonya O. Rose (eds), *At Home with the Empire: Metropolitan Culture and the Imperial World* (Cambridge: Cambridge University Press, 2006); Plotz, *Portable Property*; Erika Rappaport, 'Imperial Possessions, Cultural Histories, and the Material Turn: Response', *Victorian Studies* 50, no. 2 (2008): 289–96.
75 On the Festival of Empire see my essay, 'An Appropriated Space: The Great Exhibition, the Crystal Palace and the Working Class', in Louise Purbrick (ed.), *The Great Exhibition of 1851: New Interdisciplinary Essays* (Manchester: Manchester University Press, 2001), 138; and Daniel Gorman, *The Emergence of International Society in the 1920s* (Cambridge: Cambridge University Press, 2012): 150–5.
76 Georg Simmel, 'Fashion', *International Quarterly* 10 (1904): 130–55, reprinted in *American Journal of Sociology* 62, no. 6 (1957): 541–58; Elizabeth Wilson, *Adorned in Dreams: Fashion and Modernity* (London: Virago, 1985): 108–14; Kathy Peiss, *Hope in a Jar: The Making of America's Beauty Culture* (New York: Metropolitan Books, 1998).
77 Lancaster, *The Department Store*, 190–2; Rappaport, *Shopping for Pleasure*, 167, 170.
78 Deborah Cohen, *Household Gods: The British and Their Possessions* (New Haven, CT: Yale University Press, 2006), 105–8, 115.
79 Lancaster, *The Department Store*, 192; Mica Nava, 'Modernity's Disavowal. Women, the City and the Department Store', in Mica Nava and Alan O'Shea (eds), *Modern Times: Reflections on a Century of English Modernity* (London: Routledge, 1996): 55; Sanders, *Consuming Fantasies*, 77; and for the American experience Margaret Finnegan, *Selling Suffrage: Consumer Culture and Votes for Women* (New York: Columbia University Press, 1999).
80 Rappaport, *Shopping for Pleasure*, 220; Lisa Tickner, *The Spectacle of Women. Imagery of the Suffrage Campaign 1907–14* (London: Chatto & Windus, 1987): 142.
81 *Daily Mirror*, 15 March 1912: 5; Rappaport, *Shopping for Pleasure*, 215–7.
82 John Mercer, 'Shopping for Suffrage: the Campaign Shops of the Women's Social and Political Union', *Women's History Review* 18, no. 2 (2009): 293–309.
83 Roger Fulford, *Votes for Women: The Story of a Struggle* (London: Faber & Faber, 1957): 254.

84 See Jill Liddington and Jill Norris, *One Hand Tied behind Us: The Rise of the Women's Suffrage Movement* (London: Virago, 1978); Jill Liddington, *The Life and Times of a Respectable Rebel: Selina Cooper, 1864–1946* (London: Virago, 1984).

85 Teresa Billington Greig, *The Consumer in Revolt* (London: Stephen Swift, 1912); Matthew Hilton, *Consumerism in Twentieth Century Britain* (Cambridge: Cambridge University Press, 2003): 45–6.

Chapter 6

1 'Memories of Seventy Years, by Mrs Layton', in Margaret Llewelyn Davies (ed.), *Life As We Have Known It by Co-operative Working Women* (London: Virago, 1977): 14, 21–2.

2 The best history of the Guild is Gillian Scott, *Feminism and the Politics of Working Women: The Women's Co-operative Guild, 1880s to the Second World War* (London: UCL Press, 1998). See also Jean Gaffin and David Thoms, *Caring and Sharing: The Centenary History of the Co-operative Women's Guild* (Manchester: Co-operative Union, 1983); Barbara J. Blaszak, *The Matriarchs of England's Co-operative Movement: A Study in Gender Politics and Female Leadership, 1883–1921* (Westport, CT: Greenwood Press, 2000).

3 'Memories of Seventy Years, by Mrs Layton', 38–40, 46, 49, 50–2.

4 Karen Hunt, 'Negotiating the Boundaries of the Domestic: British Socialist Women and the Politics of Consumption', *Women's History Review* 9, no. 2 (2000): 389–410.

5 Two very different works that share this general approach are John Foster, *Class Struggle and the Industrial Revolution* (London: Weidenfeld & Nicolson, 1974) and Trygve Tholfsen, *Working-Class Radicalism in Mid-Victorian England* (London: Croom Helm, 1976). Other historians accorded workers a more independent outlook, including Robert Q. Gray, *The Labour Aristocracy in Victorian Edinburgh* (Oxford: Clarendon Press, 1976) and Geoffrey Crossick, *An Artisan Elite in Victorian Society: Kentish London 1840–1880* (London: Croom Helm, 1978).

6 Thomas Cooper, *The Life of Thomas Cooper* (Leicester: Leicester University Press, 1971): 393.

7 Samuel Smiles, *Thrift; or, How to Get on in the World* (Detroit: Rose-Belford, 1878): 104.

8 Ian Gazeley, 'The Cost of Living for Urban Workers in Late Victorian and Edwardian Britain', *Economic History Review* 42, no. 2 (1989): 214. See also Ian Gazeley and Andrew Newell, 'Poverty in Edwardian Britain', *Economic History Review* 64, no. 1 (2011): 52–71.

9 G. J. Holyoake, *The Policy of Commercial Co-operation as Respects Including the Consumer* (London: Trübner, 1873): 7. Holyoake later sided with those elements in the movement that included Christian Socialists, who sought to further the interest of workers as producers through profit-sharing, as against Mitchell and the CWS who put consumption first. For an account of the struggle that backs the profit-sharers see Philip N. Backstrom,

Christian Socialism and Co-operation in Victorian England (London: Croom Helm, 1974).

10 G. D. H. Cole, *A Century of Co-operation* (Manchester: Co-operative Union, 1945): 371; Peter Gurney, *Co-operative Culture and the Politics of Consumption in England, 1870–1930* (Manchester: Manchester University Press, 1996): 18–19; Martin Purvis, 'The Development of Co-operative Retailing in England and Wales, 1851–1901: A Geographical Study', *Journal of Historical Geography* 16, no. 3 (1990): 314–31.

11 Catherine Webb (ed.), *Industrial Co-operation: The Story of a Peaceful Revolution* (Manchester: Co-operative Union, 1904): 204; Cole, *A Century of Co-operation*, 202–3.

12 Victoria Kelley, 'The Equitable Consumer: Shopping at the Co-op in Manchester', *Journal of Design History* 11, no. 4 (1998): 299–301; Michael French and Jim Phillips, 'Sophisticates or Dupes? Attitudes toward Food Consumers in Edwardian Britain', *Enterprise & Society* 4, no. 3 (2003): 442–70; John F. Wilson, Anthony Webster and Rachael Vorberg-Rugh, *Building Co-operation: A Business History of the Co-operative Group, 1863–2013* (Oxford: Oxford University Press, 2013): 83.

13 Ibid., 65–6.

14 Percy Redfern, *The Story of the CWS* (Manchester: Co-operative Wholesale Society, 1913): 418–19; *The New History of the CWS* (London: J. M. Dent, 1938): 532–3; Wilson, Webster and Vorberg-Rugh, *Building Co-operation*, 94–5, 132–3.

15 H. D. Lloyd, *Labour Co-partnership* (New York: Harper Brothers, 1898): 148; *Co-operative News*, 7 April 1877: 162.

16 Abraham Greenwood, *The Educational Department of the Rochdale Equitable Pioneers' Society Limited* (Manchester: Co-operative Printing Society, 1877); Fred Hall, *The Co-ordination and Extension of Co-operative Education* (Manchester: Co-operative Union, 1914): 21.

17 *Wheatsheaf*, November 1907: 88; *Labour Co-partnership*, September 1897: 152–3.

18 See Gurney, *Co-operative Culture*, chapters 4 and 5. For studies of other national movements see Ellen Furlough and Carl Strikwerda (eds), *Consumers Against Capitalism? Consumer cooperation in Europe, North America, and Japan, 1840–1990* (Lanham, MD: Rowman & Littlefield, 1999).

19 *Co-operative News*, 3 August 1878: 503.

20 *Co-operative Congress Report* (Manchester: Co-op Printing Society, 1892): 6–8. The address is reproduced in Gurney, *Co-operative Culture*, 250–8.

21 J. B. Jefferys, *Retail Trading in Britain, 1850–1950: A Study of Trends in Retailing with Special Reference to the Development of Co-operative, Multiple Shop and Department Store Methods of Trading* (Cambridge: Cambridge University Press, 1954): 22.

22 Peter Mathias, *Retailing Revolution: A History of Multiple Retailing in the Food Trades Based upon the Allied Suppliers Group of Companies* (London: Longmans, 1967): 41–54, 96–104.

23 Mathias, *Retailing Revolution*, 104–8; Thomas J. Lipton, *Leaves from the Lipton Logs* (London: Hitchinson, 1931).

24 Jefferys, *Retail Trading in Britain*, 29. Diversity is stressed by Michael J. Winstanley in *The Shopkeeper's World 1830–1914* (Manchester: Manchester University Press, 1983).

25 Christopher P. Hosgood, 'The "Pigmies of Commerce" and the Working-Class Community: Small Shopkeepers in England, 1870–1914', *Journal of Social History* 22, no. 3 (1989): 439–60.

26 See W. H. Fraser, *The Coming of the Mass Market, 1850–1914* (London: Macmillan, 1981): 85–93; Melanie Tebbutt, *Making Ends Meet: Pawnbroking and Working-Class Credit* (Leicester: Leicester University Press, 1983); Sean O'Connell, *Credit and Community: Working-Class Debt in the UK Since 1880* (Oxford: Oxford University Press, 2009): 55–9. The Provident and other check traders issued checks to customers on credit that were redeemable at participating stores, charging high rates of interest for the service.

27 Paul Johnson underestimates the role of credit in the co-operative movement in his otherwise useful study, *Saving and Spending: The Working-Class Economy in Britain, 1870–1939* (Oxford: Clarendon Press, 1985).

28 Geoffrey Crossick, 'Shopkeepers and the State in Britain, 1870–1914', in Geoffrey Crossick and Heinz-Gerhard Haupt (eds), *Shopkeepers and Master Artisans in Nineteenth Century Europe* (London: Methuen, 1984); Winstanley, *The Shopkeeper's World*, 83–8, 99–103; Christopher P. Hosgood, 'A "Brave and Daring Folk"? Shopkeepers and Trade Associational Life in Victorian and Edwardian England', *Journal of Social History* 26, no. 2 (1992): 285–308; Gurney, *Co-operative Culture*, 199–202.

29 Benjamin H. Brown, *The Tariff Reform Movement in Great Britain, 1881–1895* (New York: AMS Press, 1966): 12, 16.

30 Cole, *A Century of Co-operation*, 95, 188; *Blackburn Standard*, 9 November 1878: 3; 12 April 1879: 8; 19 April 1879: 3; 5 October 1889: 6; *Pall Mall Gazette*, 1 May 1876: 4.

31 William Farrer Ecroyd, *The Policy of Self-Help: Suggestions towards the Consolidation of the Empire and the Defence of Its Industries and Commerce* (London: Hamilton, Adams, 1879): 3–4, 18; Brown, *Tariff Reform Movement*, 64–5, 89; Sydney H. Zebel, 'Fair Trade: An English Reaction to the Breakdown of the Cobden Treaty System', *Journal of Modern History* 12, no. 2 (1940): 169.

32 Robert Boyd, *British Agriculture and Industries at Stake: A Working Man's Question* (Manchester: John Heywood, 1888): 30–1, 74–6, 101. See also *Fair Trade*, 4 December 1885: 63; Carl Johannes Fuchs, *The Trade Policy of Great Britain and Her Colonies Since 1860* (London: Macmillan, 1905): 182.

33 Ecroyd, *The Policy of Self-Help*, 5–6, 21–2; William Farrer Ecroyd, *Fair-Trade* (London: National Fair-Trade League, 1882): 4, 7–8.

34 *Reynolds's Newspaper*, 31 July 1881: 3; 14 August 1881: 3; 28 August 1881: 2; 11 September 1881: 3.

35 Brown, *Tariff Reform Movement*, 62–3; J. L. Garvin, *The Life of Joseph Chamberlain* (London: Macmillan, 1933): Vol. 2, 121–2.

36 Brown, *Tariff Reform Movement*, 67–71; Zebel, 'Fair Trade', 177–8, 180; Janet Robb, *The Primrose League 1883–1906* (New York: AMS Press, 1968): 149, 151.

37 E. H. H. Green, *The Crisis of Conservatism: The Politics, Economics and Ideology of the British Conservative Party, 1880–1914* (London: Routledge, 1995): 33.

38 *National Review* 11, no. 65 (1888): 720. For criticism of free trade from trade unionists see *Reynolds's Newspaper*, 9 September 1888: 5; *Fair Trade*, 7 September 1888: 712–13.
39 Patrick Joyce, *Visions of the People: Industrial England and the Question of Class 1848–1914* (Cambridge: Cambridge University Press, 1991): 89–90.
40 Cited by E. P. Thompson, 'Homage to Tom Maguire', in *Persons and Polemics* (London: Merlin, 1994): 32.
41 Ross McKibbin, 'Why Was there No Marxism in Great Britain?', *English Historical Review* 99, no. 391 (1984): 322–3; Pat Thane, 'The Working-Class and State "Welfare" in Britain, 1880–1914', *Historical Journal* 27, no. 4 (1984): 877–900.
42 *Fair Trade*, 2 March 1888: 282–3; Brown, *Tariff Reform Movement*, 30; David Howell, *British Workers and the Independent Labour Party, 1888–1906* (Manchester: Manchester University Press, 1983): 377.
43 *Justice*, 9 July 1887: 2; 30 March 1889: 1; 13 March 1909: 2; 10 April 1909: 6.
44 See Frank Trentmann, 'Wealth versus Welfare: The British Left between Free Trade and National Political Economy before the First World War', *Historical Research* 70, no. 171 (1997): 70, 96. Trentmann spins the evidence differently in his detailed study, *Free Trade Nation: Commerce, Consumption, and Civil Society in Modern Britain* (Oxford: Oxford University Press, 2008).
45 *The New Review* 7, no. 39 (1892): 148–9, 151; *The Platform*, 28 February 1909, cited by Trentmann, 'Wealth versus Welfare', 85.
46 Gavan Duffy in *Labour Leader*, 19 December 1903: 406.
47 Paul Thompson, *The Work of William Morris* (London: Heinemann, 1967); Peter Stansky, *Redesigning the World: William Morris, the 1880's, and the Arts and Crafts* (Princeton: Princeton University Press, 1985). For sharp criticism of the Arts and Crafts movement as a form of elite consumerism see J. A. Hobson, *Veblen* (New York: Kelly, 1963): 100–1.
48 'The Future of the Workers in England', *Our Corner* 10, July 1887: 21.
49 John Burns, *Brains Better than Bets or Beer* (London: Clarion Press, 1902): 12.
50 Robert Blatchford, *Merrie England: A Series of Letters on the Labour Problem* (London: Journeyman Press, 1977): 4–5, 7–8; Noel Thompson, *Social Opulence and Private Restraint. The Consumer in British Socialist Thought since 1800* (Oxford: Oxford University Press, 2015): 43–73.
51 Charles Booth, *Old Age Pensions and the Aged Poor: A Proposal* (London: Macmillan, 1899): 6; Asa Briggs, *Social Thought and Social Action: A Study of the Work of Seebohm Rowntree* (London: Longmans, 1961); E. P. Hennock, 'The Measurement of Urban Poverty: From the Metropolis to the Nation, 1880–1920', *Economic History Review* 40, no. 4 (1987): 208–27; Rosemary O'Day and David Englander, *Mr Charles Booth's Inquiry: Life and Labour of the People in London Reconsidered* (London: Hambledon Press, 1993).
52 See Stefan Collini, *Liberalism and Sociology: L.T. Hobhouse and Political Argument in England, 1880–1914* (Cambridge: Cambridge University Press, 1979).
53 Marc Brodie, '"You Could Not Get Any Person to Be Trusted except the State": Poorer Workers' Loss of Faith in Voluntarism in Late 19th Century Britain', *Journal of Social History* 47, no. 4 (2014): 1071–95.

54 *Contemporary Review* 69 (1896): 488–9, 495.
55 Ibid., 67 (1895): 747, 751–4, 758; Matthew Hilton, *Consumerism in Twentieth Century Britain: The Search for a Historical Movement* (Cambridge: Cambridge University Press, 2003): 88–90. Also deeply influenced by Ruskin, like many socialists, Hobson looked for an improvement in the tastes of those working-class consumers who had experienced material progress. On this theme see his essay, 'Over-Specialism in Work and Life', *Saint George* 1, no. 4 (1898): 187–201; and Thompson, *Social Opulence and Private Restraint*, 90–1.
56 Martin Daunton, *Trusting Leviathan: The Politics of Taxation in Britain, 1799–1914* (Cambridge: Cambridge University Press, 2001): 302, 316; *Wealth and Welfare: An Economic and Social History of Britain, 1851–1951* (Oxford: Oxford University Press, 2007): 211; Frank Trentmann, 'The Transformation of Fiscal Reform: Reciprocity, Modernization, and the Fiscal Debate within the Business Community in Early Twentieth-Century Britain', *Historical Journal* 39, no. 4 (1996): 1005–48.
57 Erica Rappaport, 'Consumption', in Philippa Levine and John Marriott (eds), *Ashgate Research Companion to Modern Imperial Histories* (Farnham: Ashgate, 2012): 343–58.
58 Peter T. Marsh, *Joseph Chamberlain: Entrepreneur in Politics* (New Haven, CT: Yale University Press, 1994), 304, 408, 428, 550.
59 Thomas Henry Farrer, *The Neo-Protection Scheme of the Right Hon. Joseph Chamberlain, Secretary of State for the Colonies* (London: Cassell, 1896); Marsh, *Joseph Chamberlain*, 585, 608.
60 See Duncan Bell, *The Idea of Greater Britain: Empire and the Future of World Order, 1860–1900* (Princeton: Princeton University Press, 2007).
61 *Speaker*, 10 April 1897: 396–7.
62 Stefan Collini, *Public Moralists: Political Thought and Intellectual Life in Britain, 1850–1930* (Oxford: Clarendon Press, 1993).
63 See James Thompson, *British Political Culture and the Idea of 'Public Opinion', 1867–1914* (Cambridge: Cambridge University Press, 2013).
64 Joseph Chamberlain, *Imperial Union and Tariff Reform* (London: Grant Richards, 1903): 64–5, 98–9; E. H. H. Green, 'Radical Conservatism: The Electoral Genesis of Tariff Reform', *Historical Journal* 28, no. 3 (1985): 667–92; *The Crisis of Conservatism*.
65 Chamberlain, *Imperial Union and Tariff Reform*, 78–9, 81, 130–1, 133–5, 168, 178–82; *Saturday Review*, 31 October 1903: 536–7; Marsh, *Joseph Chamberlain*, 587–8.
66 *Daily Mail*, 5 November 1903: 5. Trentmann downplays the impact of Chamberlain's stunt in *Free Trade Nation*, 89–91.
67 *Daily Mail*, 2 October 1903: 7; 7 October 1903: 4. The result, unsurprisingly, was a resounding victory for protection.
68 Anthony Howe, *Free Trade and Liberal England, 1846–1946* (Oxford: Clarendon Press, 1997): 231.
69 Trentmann, *Free Trade Nation*, 81–5, *passim*.
70 Carl Johannes Fuchs, *The Trade Policy of Great Britain*, 204; Zebel, 'Fair Trade', 184–5.
71 Alan Sykes, *Tariff Reform in British Politics, 1903–1913* (Oxford: Clarendon Press, 1979); Andrew S. Thompson, 'Tariff Reform: An Imperial Strategy, 1903–1913', *Historical Journal* 40, no. 4 (1997): 1033–54.

72 Dilwyn Porter, 'The Unionist Tariff Reformers 1903–1914', PhD thesis, University of Manchester (1976): 258.

73 Kenneth D. Brown, 'The Trade Union Tariff Reform Association, 1904–1913', *Journal of British Studies* 9, no. 2 (1970): 149–50; Alan Sykes, 'Radical Conservatism and the Working Classes in Edwardian England: The Case of the Workers' Defence Union', *English Historical Review* 113, no. 454 (1998): 1182.

74 David A. Thackeray, 'The Crisis of the Tariff Reform League and the Division of "Radical Conservatism", c. 1913–1922', *History* 91, no. 301 (2006): 49, 61.

75 *Daily Express*, 15 October 1903: 6.

76 David A. Thackeray, 'Home and Politics: Women and Conservative Activism in Early Twentieth-Century Britain', *Journal of British Studies* 49, no. 4, (2010): 826, 830, 833; 'Rethinking the Edwardian Crisis of Conservatism', *Historical Journal* 54, no. 1 (2011): 191–213; *Conservatism for the Democratic Age: Conservative Cultures and the Challenge of Mass Politics in Early Twentieth Century England* (Manchester: Manchester University Press, 2013).

77 Thane, 'The Working Class and State "Welfare" in Britain', 879, 892; Gurney, *Co-operative Culture*, 185.

78 The budget proposed a graduated income tax rising from 9d. to 1s. in the pound on incomes below £2,000 per annum and 1s. 2d. for those above; taxation of unearned income at the same rate; a super-tax of 6d. in the pound on all incomes over £5,000 per annum; increases in death duties, land valuation and land duties; and increased tax on luxuries like tobacco, whisky, petrol and automobiles. Daunton, *Trusting Leviathan*, 361.

79 Cited by H. V. Emy, 'The Impact of Financial Policy on English Party Politics before 1914', *Historical Journal* 15, no. 1 (1972): 121.

80 W. S. Churchill, *Liberalism and the Social Problem* (London: Hodder & Stoughton, 1909): 362–4. Churchill appropriated the concept of a 'National Minimum' from Fabian socialists like Sidney Webb. Daunton, *Wealth and Welfare*, 471.

81 Bruce K. Murray, 'The Politics of the "People's Budget"', *Historical Journal* 16, no. 3 (1973): 557, 569; *The People's Budget 1909–10: Lloyd George and Liberal Politics* (Oxford: Clarendon Press, 1980).

82 Robert Tressell, *The Ragged Trousered Philanthropists* (London: Panther Books, 1965), 541. On the role of visual art see James Thompson, '"Pictorial Lies"? – Posters and Politics in Britain c.1880–1914', *Past and Present* 197 (2007): 177–210.

83 Stephen Reynolds and Bob and Tom Woolley, *Seems So! A Working-Class View of Politics* (London: Macmillan, 1911): 10.

84 Gurney, *Co-operative Culture*, 208–13; Hilton, *Consumerism*, 53–78.

85 On the general impact of the war see Avner Offer, *The First World War: An Agrarian Interpretation* (Oxford: Clarendon Press, 1989).

86 Anthony J. Coles, 'The Moral Economy of the Crowd: Some Twentieth-Century Food Riots', *Journal of British Studies* 18, no. 1 (1978): 157–76.

87 Gurney, *Co-operative Culture*, 214; Mary Hilson, *Political Change and the Rise of Labour in Comparative Perspective: Britain and Sweden, 1890–1920* (Lund: Nordic Academic, 2006); Belinda Davis, *Home Fires Burning: Food, Politics, and Everyday Life in World War I Berlin* (Chapel

Hill: University of North Carolina Press, 2000); Tyler Stovall, *Paris and the Spirit of 1919: Consumer Struggles, Transnationalism, and Revolution* (Cambridge: Cambridge University Press, 2012).

88 Sidney Pollard, 'The Foundation of the Co-operative Party', in Asa Briggs and John Saville (eds), *Essays in Labour History 1886–1923* (London: Macmillan, 1971); Tony Adams, 'The Formation of the Co-operative Party Reconsidered', *International Review of Social History* 32, no. 1 (1987): 48–68.

89 G. D. H. Cole, *A History of the Labour Party from 1914* (London: Routledge & Kegan Paul, 1948): 53, cited by Geoffrey W. Rhodes, *Co-operative-Labour Relations, 1900–1962* (Loughborough: Co-operative Union, 1962): 19.

Chapter 7

1 George Orwell, *The Road to Wigan Pier* (London: Penguin Books, 1962): 16–17.

2 Peter Scott, *Triumph of the South: A Regional Economic History of Early Twentieth Century Britain* (Aldershot: Ashgate, 2007).

3 Orwell, *The Road to Wigan Pier*, 79–81. Useful critical studies are Raymond Williams, *Orwell* (London: Fontana, 1971); Alok Rai, *Orwell and the Politics of Despair* (Cambridge: Cambridge University Press, 1988); Robert Colls, *George Orwell: English Rebel* (Oxford: Oxford University Press, 2013).

4 J. B. Priestley, *English Journey* (London: William Heinemann, 1934): 401.

5 Ibid., 405; John Baxendale, *Priestley's England: J. B. Priestley and English Culture* (Manchester: Manchester University Press, 2007): 129–30; Roger Fagge, *The Vision of J. B. Priestley* (London: Continuum, 2012).

6 Sue Bowden, 'The New Consumerism', in Paul Johnson (ed.), *Twentieth-Century Britain: Economic, Social, and Cultural Change* (London: Longman, 1994).

7 Charles Loch Mowat, *Britain between the Wars, 1918–1940* (London: Methuen, 1968): 451–2; John Stevenson and Chris Cook, *The Slump: Society and Politics during the Depression* (London: Quartet Books, 1979): 16; Ian Gazeley and Andrew Newell, 'The End of Destitution: Evidence from Urban British Working Households 1904–37', *Oxford Economic Papers* 64, no. 1 (2012): 80–102.

8 Mowat, *Britain between the Wars*, 455; Sue Bowden and Avner Offer, 'Household Appliances and the Use of Time: The United States and Britain Since the 1920s', *Economic History Review* 47, no. 4 (1994): 725–48; Michael French, 'Commercials, Careers, and Culture: Travelling Salesmen in Britain, 1890s–1930s', *Economic History Review* 58, no. 2 (2005): 352–77.

9 B. Seebohm Rowntree, *Poverty and Progress: A Second Social Survey of York* (London: Longmans, 1941): 173.

10 J. B. Jefferys, *Retail Trading in Britain, 1850–1950: A Study of Trends in Retailing with Special Reference to the Development of Co-operative, Multiple*

Shop and Department Store Methods of Trading (Cambridge: Cambridge University Press, 1954): 69–70.

11 Andrew Godley, 'Foreign Multinationals and Innovation in British Retailing, 1850–1962', *Business History* 45, no. 1 (2003): 86.

12 Rowntree, *Poverty and Progress*, 218.

13 Bill Lancaster, *The Department Store: A Social History* (London: Leicester University Press, 1995): 85–6; Charles Wilson, *First with the News: The History of W. H. Smith 1792–1972* (London: Cape, 1985); S. D. Chapman, *Jesse Boot of Boots the Chemists: A Study in Business History* (London: Hodder & Stoughton, 1974); Bridget Williams, *The Best Butter in the World: A History of Sainsbury's* (London: Ebury Press, 1994): 74.

14 Stevenson and Cook, *The Slump*, 15; Goronwy Rees, *St Michael: A History of Marks and Spencer* (London: Weidenfeld & Nicolson, 1969); Rachel Worth, *Fashion for the People: A History of Clothing at Marks & Spencer* (Oxford: Berg, 2007).

15 *The Times*, 26 May 1936: 24.

16 Michael Moss and Alison Turton, *A Legend of Retailing: House of Fraser* (London: Weidenfeld and Nicolson, 1989): 123–4, 131–2; Asa Briggs, *Friends of the People: The Centenary History of Lewis's* (London: B. T. Batsford, 1956): 185–90.

17 Peter Scott and James Walker, 'Advertising, Promotion, and the Competitive Advantage of Interwar British Department Stores', *Economic History Review* 63, no. 4 (2010): 1105–28; Jefferys, *Retail Trading in Britain*, 59; Lancaster, *The Department Store*, 103.

18 Moss and Turton, *A Legend of Retailing*, 153; Maurice Corina, *Fine Silks and Oak Counters: Debenhams 1778–1978* (London: Hutchinson, 1978): 117–18; Lancaster, *The Department Store*, 96–7; Susan Lomax, 'The Department Store and the Creation of the Spectacle 1880–1940', PhD thesis, University of Essex (2005).

19 Briggs, *Friends of the People*, 140, 153–4.

20 Lancaster, *The Department Store*, 90–2, 119–21; Moss and Turton, *A Legend of Retailing*, 126–30; Corina, *Fine Silks and Oak Counters*, 84–5.

21 Briggs, *Friends of the People*, 140–50, 165; Lancaster, *The Department Store*, 148–9, 151.

22 Nicholas Hiley, 'Sir Hedley Le Bas and the Origins of Domestic Propaganda in Britain 1914–1917', *European Journal of Marketing* 21, no. 8 (1987): 42, citing Russell's essay, 'Government by Propaganda' (1924).

23 Brian Lewis, *So Clean: Lord Leverhulme, Soap and Civilization* (Manchester: Manchester University Press, 2008): 71, 86.

24 *Daily Express*, 12 July 1924: 9; 15 July 1924: 1, 7.

25 Sir Charles Higham, *Advertising: Its Use and Abuse* (London: Butterworth, 1931): 229.

26 Ethel Mannin, *Sounding Brass* (London: Jarrolds, 1937): 231–43. George Orwell poured scorn on the advertising copywriter in *Keep the Aspidistra Flying* (1936). A more positive view of the industry was presented by the crime writer Dorothy L. Sayers in *Murder Must Advertise: A Detective Story* (London: Victor Gollancz, 1933). Sayers had worked for Benson's in the 1920s.

27 Denys Thompson, *Voice of Civilisation: An Enquiry into Advertising* (London: Muller, 1943): 9; Lewis, *So Clean*, 82–4; Stuart Ewan, *Captains of Consciousness: Advertising and the Social Roots of the Consumer Culture* (New York: Basic Books, 2001): 35–9.

28 Higham, *Advertising*, 45; 'The Profession of Advertising', *The Times*, 13 February 1925: 8; Matthew Thomson, *Psychological Subjects: Identity, Culture, and Health in Twentieth-Century Britain* (Oxford: Oxford University Press, 2006): 155–7.

29 Stefan Schwarzkopf, 'Discovering the Consumer. Market Research, Product Innovation, and the Creation of Brand Loyalty in Britain and the United States in the Interwar Years', *Journal of Macromarketing* 29, no. 1 (2009): 13–4; John Mercer, 'A Mark of Distinction: Branding and Trade Mark Law in the UK from the 1860s', *Business History* 52, no. 1 (2010): 33.

30 John Hewitt, 'Posters of Distinction: Art, Advertising and the London, Midland, and Scottish Railways', *Design Issues* 16, no. 1 (2000): 16–35; 'The "Nature" and "Art" of Shell Advertising in the Early 1930s', *Journal of Design History* 5, no. 2 (1992): 121–39.

31 Deirdre Beddoe, *Back to Home and Duty: Women between the Wars 1918–1939* (London: Pandora: 1989); Billie Melman, *Women and the Popular Imagination in the Twenties: Flappers and Nymphs* (Basingstoke: Macmillan, 1988).

32 Leonore Davidoff, 'The Family in Britain', in F. M. L. Thompson (ed.), *The Cambridge Social History of Britain, 1750–1950. Volume 2. People and their Environment* (Cambridge: Cambridge University Press, 1990): 118.

33 Cynthia White, *Women's Magazines, 1693–1968* (London: Michael Joseph, 1970); Martin Pugh, *Women and the Women's Movement in Britain, 1914–1959* (Basingstoke: Macmillan, 1992): 209–17; Jill Greenfield and Chris Reid, 'Women's Magazines and the Commercial Orchestration of Femininity in the 1930s', *Media History* 4, no. 2 (1998): 161–74; Judy Giles, *The Parlour and the Suburb: Domestic Identities, Class, Femininity and Modernity* (Oxford: Berg, 2004): 117–29.

34 Alison Light, *Forever England: Femininity, Literature and Conservatism between the Wars* (London: Routledge, 1991).

35 Adrian Bingham, *Gender, Modernity, and the Popular Press in Inter-War Britain* (Oxford: Oxford University Press, 2004); John Carey, *The Intellectuals and the Masses: Pride and Prejudice among the Literary Intelligentsia, 1880–1939* (London: Faber & Faber, 1992): 8.

36 Wareham Smith, *Spilt Ink: Autobiography* (London: Ernest Benn, 1932): 66–78; *Daily Mail*, 9 October 1908: 4.

37 Peter Scott, *The Making of the Modern British Home: The Suburban Semi and Family Life between the Wars* (Oxford: Oxford University Press, 2013): 45–6, 99–108, 153–74.

38 Deborah S. Ryan, '"All the World and Her Husband": The *Daily Mail* Ideal Home Exhibition 1908–39', in Maggie Andrews and Mary M. Talbot (eds), *All the World and Her Husband: Women in Twentieth-Century Consumer Culture* (London: Cassell, 2000): 15–18; Deborah S. Ryan, *The Ideal Home through the 20th Century* (London: Hazar, 1997); Giles, *The Parlour and the Suburb*, 109–11; *Daily Mail*, 17 April 1935: 6, 11.

39 Peter Gurney (ed.), *Bolton Working-Class Life in the 1930s: A Mass-Observation Anthology* (Brighton: Mass-Observation Archive, 1988): 6.
40 Selina Todd, *Young Women, Work, and Family in England, 1918–1950* (Oxford: Oxford University Press, 2005); Miriam Glucksmann, *Women Assemble: Women Workers and the New Industries in Inter-War Britain* (London: Routledge, 1990).
41 David Fowler, *The First Teenagers: The Lifestyle of Young Wage-Earners in Interwar Britain* (London: Woburn Press, 1995): 116–31; Jeffrey Richards, *The Age of the Dream Palace: Cinema and Society in Britain, 1930–1939* (London: Routledge & Kegan Paul, 1984).
42 John Hilton, *Rich Man, Poor Man* (London: Allen & Unwin, 1944): 121.
43 Jeffrey Richards and Dorothy Sheridan (eds), *Mass-Observation at the Movies* (London: Routledge & Kegan Paul, 1987): 34; Fowler, *The First Teenagers*, 132.
44 Richards and Sheridan (eds), *Mass-Observation at the Movies*, 110.
45 Briggs, *Friends of the People*, 157–8.
46 Cited in my article, 'Co-operation and the "New Consumerism" in Inter-War England', *Business History* 54, no. 6 (2012): 914.
47 Fowler, *The First Teenagers*, 101.
48 Katrina Honeyman, 'Style Monotony and the Business of Fashion: The Marketing of Menswear in Inter-War England', *Textile History* 34, no. 2 (2003): 171–91; *Well Suited: A History of the Leeds Clothing Industry, 1850–1990* (Oxford: Oxford University Press, 2000), chapter 3.
49 Laura Ugolini, *Men and Menswear: Sartorial Consumption in Britain 1880–1939* (Aldershot: Ashgate, 2007): 108–24; Joanna Bourke, 'The Great Male Renunciation: Men's Dress Reform in Inter-War Britain', *Journal of Design History* 9, no. 1 (1996): 23–33.
50 Jill Greenfield, Sean O'Connell and Chris Reid, 'Fashioning Masculinity: *Men Only*, Consumption and the Development of Marketing in the 1930s', *Twentieth Century British History* 10, no. 4 (1999): 457–76; Justin Bengry, 'Courting the Pink Pound: *Men Only* and the Queer Consumer, 1935–39', *History Workshop Journal* 68 (2009): 123–48.
51 Stephanie Ward, 'The Means Test and the Unemployed in South Wales and the North-East of England, 1931–1939', *Labour History Review* 73, no. 1 (2008): 118; Albert Paul, *Hard Work and No Consideration: 51 Years as a Carpenter-Joiner 1917–1968* (Brighton: Queenspark Books, 1981): 22–5.
52 Walter Brierley, *Means Test Man* (London: Methuen, 1935): 17–18, 74.
53 Michael T. Saler, *The Avant-Garde in Interwar England: Medieval Modernism and the London Underground* (Oxford: Oxford University Press, 2001): 99–102.
54 *Education for the Consumer* (London: Council for Art and Industry, 1935): 7–8; Saler, *The Avant-Garde in Interwar England*, 138–47.
55 *The Working Class Home: Its Furnishing and Equipment* (London: Council for Art and Industry, 1937): 42.
56 Stephen Constantine, 'Bringing the Empire Alive: The Empire Marketing Board and Imperial Propaganda, 1926–33', in John MacKenzie (ed.), *Imperialism and Popular Culture* (Manchester: Manchester University Press, 1986); *Buy and Build: The Advertising Posters of the Empire Marketing Board* (London: HMSO, 1986).

57 *Selfridge's Decorations for the Coronation* (London: Selfridge's, 1937); Andrew S. Thompson, *The Empire Strikes Back? The Impact of Imperialism on Britain from the Mid-Nineteenth Century* (London: Routledge, 2014): 185–6.
58 Reginald Pound, *Selfridge: A Biography* (London: Heinemann, 1960): 238–40; Humphrey Jennings and Charles Madge (eds), *May the Twelfth: Mass-Observation Day-Surveys, 1937* (London: Faber & Faber, 1937): 99, 114–5, 120, 149.
59 David Thackeray, 'From Prudent Housewife to Empire Shopper: Appeals to the Female Voter, 1918–28', in Julie Gottlieb and Richard Toye (eds), *The Aftermath of Suffrage: Women, Gender, and Politics in Britain, 1918–1945* (Basingstoke: Palgrave Macmillan, 2013): 45.
60 Percy Redfern, *The New History of the CWS* (London: J. M. Dent, 1938): 379.
61 Thackeray, 'From Prudent Housewife to Empire Shopper', 45; Peter Gurney, *Co-operative Culture and the Politics of Consumption in England, 1870–1930* (Manchester: Manchester University Press, 1996): 221.
62 Ibid., 224–5; Matthew Hilton, *Consumerism in Twentieth-Century Britain: The Search for a Historical Movement* (Cambridge: Cambridge University Press, 2003): 117–22.
63 Moss and Turton, *A Legend of Retailing*, 130–5; Corina, *Fine Silks and Oak Counters*, 94–105; *The Times*, 21 January, 1936: 10.
64 Gurney, *Co-operative Culture*, 222–3.
65 Charles Wilson, *The History of Unilever: A Study in Economic Growth and Change* (London: Cassell, 1954); Peter Mathias, *Retailing Revolution: A History of Multiple Retailing in the Food Trades Based upon the Allied Suppliers Group of Companies* (London: Longmans, 1967).
66 Hermann Levy, *Monopolies, Cartels and Trusts in British Industry* (London: Macmillan, 1927); *Retail Trade Associations: A New Form of Monopolist Organisation in Britain* (London: Kegan Paul, 1942).
67 Sydney R. Elliott, *England Cradle of Co-operation* (London: Faber, 1937): 13–17, 85–6.
68 Arnold Bonner, *British Co-operation: The History, Principles, and Organisation of the British Co-operative Movement* (Manchester: Co-operative Union, 1961): 169; Redfern, *The New History of the CWS*, 319–22, 343–7.
69 For a fuller discussion of the themes in this section see my article '"The Curse of the Co-ops": Co-operation, the Mass Press and the Market in Interwar Britain', *English Historical Review* 130, no. 546 (2015): 1479–512.
70 See Jonathan Morris, *The Political Economy of Shopkeeping in Milan, 1886–1922* (Cambridge: Cambridge University Press, 1993).
71 Neil Killingback, 'Limits to Mutuality: Economic and Political Attacks on Co-operation', in Stephen Yeo (ed.), *New Views of Co-operation* (London, Routledge, 1988).
72 Thomas F. Carbery, *Consumers in Politics: A History and General Review of the Co-operative Party* (Manchester: Manchester University Press, 1969): 38.
73 G. D. H. Cole, *A Century of Co-operation* (Manchester: Co-operative Union, 1945): 372.
74 Kevin Manton, 'The Labour Party and Retail Distribution, 1919–1951', *Labour History Review* 73, no. 3 (2008): 269–86.

75 Peter Scott, 'Mr Drage, Mr Everyman, and the Creation of a Mass Market for Domestic Furniture in Interwar Britain', *Economic History Review* 62, no. 4 (2009): 802–27.
76 Sean O'Connell, *Credit and Community: Working-Class Debt in the UK since 1880* (Oxford: Oxford University Press, 2009): 211–4; Peter Scott, 'The Twilight World of Interwar British Hire Purchase', *Past and Present* 177 (2002): 195–225.
77 Aylmer Vallance, *Hire-Purchase* (London: Thomas Nelson & Sons, 1939): 50, 59–62, 71–81; Avram Taylor, *Working-Class Credit and Community Since 1918* (Basingstoke: Palgrave Macmillan, 2002).
78 Paula Bartley, *Ellen Wilkinson: From Red Suffragist to Government Minister* (London: Pluto Press, 2014): 96–7; Matt Perry, *'Red Ellen' Wilkinson: Her Ideas, Movements and World* (Manchester: Manchester University Press, 2014).
79 See Dominic Wring, *The Politics of Marketing the Labour Party* (Basingstoke: Palgrave Macmillan, 2005): 29.
80 On this see my articles, 'Co-operation and the "New Consumerism"', 909; and '"The Curse of the Co-ops"', 1495, fn. 57.
81 See J. M. Keynes, *The General Theory of Employment, Interest and Money* (London: Macmillan, 1936), chapter 23.
82 W. H. Hutt, *Economists and the Public: A Study of Competition and Opinion* (New Brunswick: Transaction, 1990): 261–2, 311, *passim*. The influential right-wing economist, Friedrich Hayek, had argued that socialism and the 'sovereignty of the consumer' were fundamentally opposed in *Collectivist Economic Planning: Critical Studies on the Possibilities of Socialism* (London: Routledge, 1935).

Chapter 8

1 Ina Zweiniger-Bargielowska, *Austerity in Britain: Rationing, Controls, and Consumption, 1939–1955* (Oxford: Oxford University Press, 2000): 10–1; Robert Mackay, *Half the Battle: Civilian Morale in Britain during the Second World War* (Manchester: Manchester University Press, 2002): 109, 111, 114.
2 Angus Calder, *The People's War: Britain 1939–45* (London: Pimlico, 1992): 71–2; Zweiniger-Bargielowska, *Austerity in Britain*, 12–16, 19–23; Mackay, *Half the Battle*, 53, 113, 198–9.
3 Calder, *The People's War*, 276, 377–9; Zweiniger-Bargielowska, *Austerity in Britain*, 19–23, 48–9; Mackay, *Half the Battle*, 113, 199; Geoffrey Field, *Blood, Sweat, and Toil: Remaking the British Working Class, 1939–1945* (Oxford: Oxford University Press, 2011): 133.
4 Richard Farmer, *The Food Companions: Cinema and Consumption in Wartime Britain, 1939–45* (Manchester: Manchester University Press, 2011): 20–3.
5 Mackay, *Half the Battle*, 197.
6 See the letter from Churchill to Woolton dated 14 July 1940, cited in Roy Jenkins, *Churchill* (London: Macmillan, 2001): 628; Field, *Blood, Sweat, and Toil*, 323, 330.

7 Calder, *The People's War*, 381–4; Zweiniger-Bargielowska, *Austerity in Britain*, 80, 148; Farmer, *The Food Companions*, 21–30; Asa Briggs, *Friends of the People: The Centenary History of Lewis's* (London: B. T. Batsford, 1956): 199.
8 Sir Thomas G. Jones, *The Unbroken Front: Ministry of Food, 1916–1944* (London: Everybody's Books, 1944): 164–5.
9 Calder, *The People's War*, 405; Mackay, *Half the Battle*, 198–200; Field, *Blood, Sweat, and Toil*, 132; James Vernon, *Hunger: A Modern History* (Cambridge, MA: Harvard University Press, 2006): 187–90.
10 Zweiniger-Bargielowska, *Austerity in Britain*, 66; Mackay, *Half the Battle*, 10–11, 201–2; Field, *Blood, Sweat, and Toil*, 134.
11 Sir William Richardson, *The CWS in War and Peace 1938–1976* (Manchester: Co-operative Wholesale Society, 1977): 58–60, 100–1, 125–8, *passim.*
12 Gillian Scott overlooks the guild's role in making rationing a success in *Feminism and the Politics of Working Women: The Women's Co-operative Guild, 1880s to the Second World War* (London: UCL Press, 1998).
13 George Darling, *The Politics of Food* (London: Labour Book Service, 1941): 3, 27, 40, 67–8, 85, 90.
14 *How Britain Was Fed in War Time. Food Control 1939–1945* (London: HMSO, 1946): 21; David Clampin, *Advertising and Propaganda in World War Two: Cultural Identity and the Blitz Spirit* (London: I. B. Tauris, 2014).
15 *Parliamentary Debates* (House of Commons), 8 July 1941, Vol. 373, cc. 82, 91–2; Lori Loeb, 'Doctors and Patent Medicines in Modern Britain: Professionalism and Consumerism', *Albion* 33, no. 3 (2001): 410–11.
16 Karl Mannheim, *Man and Society in an Age of Reconstruction* (London: Kegan Paul, 1940): 347–8.
17 Denys Thompson, *Voice of Civilisation: An Enquiry into Advertising* (London: Muller, 1943): 163.
18 An early debunking was Steven Fielding, Peter Thompson and Nick Tiratsoo, *England Arise! The Labour Party and Popular Politics in 1940s Britain* (Manchester: Manchester University Press, 1995), which stressed that working-class 'apathy' was more important than solidarity. Geoffrey Field effectively rebuts this argument in *Blood, Sweat, and Toil*, 128, 282, 342, 361, 369–70, 380.
19 Edward Smithies, *The Black Economy in England since 1914* (Dublin: Gill and Macmillan, 1984): 84.
20 Field, *Blood, Sweat, and Toil*, 135; Zweiniger-Bargielowska, *Austerity in Britain*, 157; Donald Thomas, *An Underworld at War: Spivs, Deserters, Racketeers and Civilians in the Second World War* (London: John Murray, 2003).
21 Mark Roodhouse, *Black Market Britain, 1939–1955* (Oxford: Oxford University Press, 2013): 253–63.
22 Calder, *The People's War*, 405.
23 David Kynaston, *Austerity Britain, 1945–51* (London: Bloomsbury, 2007); 117–18; Ina Zweiniger-Bargielowska, 'Bread Rationing in Britain, July 1946–July 1948', *Twentieth Century British History* 4, no. 1 (1993): 57–85.
24 James Hinton, 'Militant Housewives: The British Housewives' League and the Attlee Government', *History Workshop Journal* 38 (1994): 128–56.

25 For cinematic representations of the black market during the war and immediately after see Farmer, *The Food Companions*, 148–84; Robert Murphy, *Realism and Tinsel: Cinema and Society in Britain, 1939–49* (London: Routledge, 1989): 146–67.
26 Pearson Phillips, 'The New Look', in Michael Sissons and Philip French (eds), *Age of Austerity 1945–51* (Harmondsworth: Penguin Books, 1964): 147–50; Harry Hopkins, *The New Look: A Social History of the Forties and Fifties* (London: Secker & Warburg, 1964): 95–104; Elizabeth Wilson, *Adorned in Dreams: Fashion and Modernity* (London: Virago, 1985): 225–6; Carolyn Steedman, *Landscape for a Good Woman: A Story of Two Lives* (London: Virago, 1986): 121.
27 'A Briton's Faith in Britain's Future', *New York Times*, 31 August 1947: 5.
28 Briggs, *Friends of the People*, 204–9; Michael Moss and Alison Turton, *A Legend of Retailing: House of Fraser* (London: Weidenfeld and Nicolson, 1989): 166–7.
29 Henry Irving, 'The Birth of a Politician: Harold Wilson and the Bonfires of Controls, 1948–9', *Twentieth Century British History* 25, no. 1 (2014): 87–107.
30 *Daily Express*, 27 November 1947: 2; 4 December 1947: 1; *The Times*, 16 December 1947: 2; Farmer, *The Food Companions*, 19.
31 Ina Zweiniger-Bargielowska, 'Rationing, Austerity and the Conservative Party Recovery after 1945', *Historical Journal* 37, no. 1 (1994): 173–97; Hinton, 'Militant Housewives', 129–30.
32 Maurice Corina, *Fine Silks and Oak Counters: Debenhams 1778–1978* (London: Hutchinson, 1978), 140; Briggs, *Friends of the People*, 211.
33 Frank Mort and Peter Thompson, 'Retailing, Commercial Culture and Masculinity in 1950s Britain: The Case of Montague Burton, the "Tailor of Taste"', *History Workshop Journal* 38 (1994): 110, 114.
34 Sean O'Connell, *Credit and Community: Working-Class Debt in the UK Since 1880* (Oxford: Oxford University Press, 2009), 73, 82, 120, *passim*; Richard Coopey, Sean O'Connell, and Dilwyn Porter, *Mail Order Retailing in Britain: A Business and Social History* (Oxford: Oxford University Press, 2005); Arnold Bonner, *British Co-operation: The History, Principles, and Organisation of the British Co-operative Movement* (Manchester: Co-operative Union, 1961), 248, 253; Liz McFall, *Devising Consumption: Cultural Economies of Insurance, Credit and Spending* (London: Routledge, 2015).
35 Barbara Usherwood, '"Mrs Housewife and Her Grocer": The Advent of Self-Service Food Shopping in Britain', in Maggie Andrews and Mary Talbot (eds), *All the World and Her Husband: Women in Twentieth-Century Consumer Culture* (London: Cassell, 2000): 113–30.
36 Dawn Nell, Simon Phillips, Andrew Alexander and Gareth Shaw, 'Helping Yourself: Self-Service Grocery Retailing and Shoplifting in Britain, c. 1950–75', *Cultural and Social History* 8, no. 3 (2011): 373–4, 376, 381–2. For the American experience see Tracey Deutsch, *Building a Housewife's Paradise: Gender, Politics, and American Grocery Stores in the Twentieth Century* (Chapel Hill: University of North Carolina Press, 2010).
37 F. P. Bishop, *The Ethics of Advertising* (London: Robert Hale, 1949): 46, 78, 116. See also Bishop's earlier work, *The Economics of Advertising* (London: Robert Hale, 1944).

38 For the United States see Gary Cross, *An All-Consuming Century: Why Commercialism Won in Modern America* (New York: Columbia University Press, 2000): 88–143; Lizabeth Cohen, *A Consumers' Republic: The Politics of Mass Consumption in Post-War America* (New York: Knopf, 2003): 114–29; for Germany see David Crewe (ed.), *Consuming Germany in the Cold War* (Oxford: Berg, 2003): 1–19; Erica Carter, *How German Is She? Post-War West German Reconstruction and the Consuming Woman* (Ann Arbor: University of Michigan Press, 1997); Jan Logemann, *Trams or Tailfins? Public and Private Prosperity in Postwar West Germany and the United States* (Chicago: University of Chicago Press, 2012); and for East Germany see Mark Landsman, *Dictatorship and Demand: The Politics of Consumerism in East Germany* (Cambridge, MA: Harvard University Press, 2005). More generally see Victoria De Grazia, *Irresistible Empire: America's Advance through Twentieth-Century Europe* (Cambridge, MA: Harvard University Press, 2005); Sheryl Kroen, 'Renegotiating the Social Contract in Post-War Europe: The American Marshall Plan and Consumer Democracy', in John Brewer and Frank Trentmann (eds), *Consuming Cultures, Global Perspectives* (Oxford: Berg, 2006).

39 Bill Lancaster, *The Department Store: A Social History* (London: Leicester University Press, 1995): 151. The book written by John Spedan Lewis outlining his scheme was titled *Fairer Shares: A Possible Advance in Civilisation and Perhaps the Only Alternative to Communism* (London: Staples Press, 1954).

40 Terry Nevett, 'The Scapa Society: The First Organised Reaction Against Advertising', *Media, Culture and Society* 3, no. 2 (1981): 187; *The Times*, 17 June 1955: 9.

41 Stefan Schwarzkopf, 'They Do It with Mirrors: Advertising and British Cold War Consumer Politics', *Contemporary British History* 19, no. 2 (2005): 140–3.

42 G. D. H. Cole, *The British Co-operative Movement in a Socialist Society* (London: George, Allen & Unwin, 1951): 13–14; Bonner, *British Co-operation*; 251, 253, 259; Johnston Birchall, *Co-op: The People's Business* (Manchester: Manchester University Press, 1994): 142–6.

43 Cole, *The British Co-operative Movement*, 41–2; *A Century of Co-operation* (Manchester: Co-operative Union, 1945): 398–9; Mary Stott, *Forgetting's No Excuse* (London: Virago, 1989): 33.

44 Jonathan Woodham, 'An Episode in Post-Utility Design Management: The Council of Industrial Design and the Co-operative Wholesale Society', in Judy Attfield (ed.), *Utility Reassessed: The Role of Ethics in the Practice of Good Design* (Manchester: Manchester University Press, 1999): 39–57; Lesley Whitworth, 'Promoting Product Quality: The Co-op and the Council of Industrial Design', in Lawrence Black and Nicole Robertson (eds), *Consumerism and the Co-operative Movement in Modern British History* (Manchester: Manchester University Press, 2009): 174–96.

45 See my article, 'The Battle of the Consumer in Postwar Britain', *Journal of Modern History* 77, no. 4 (2005): 964–9.

46 *Daily Express*, 2 May 1953: 2.

47 Labour attitudes are explored in Lawrence Black, *The Political Culture of the Left in Affluent Britain, 1951–64* (Basingstoke: Palgrave Macmillan, 2003).

48 *The Times*, 2 May 1953: 3.
49 Lord Woolton, *The Memoirs of the Rt. Hon. The Earl of Woolton* (London: Cassell, 1959): 392; H. H. Wilson, *Pressure Group: The Campaign for Commercial Television* (London: Secker & Warburg, 1961): 80–2, 94–5; Hopkins, *The New Look*, 406–7.
50 Tory attitudes are explored in Mark Jarvis, *Conservative Governments, Morality and Social Change in Affluent Britain, 1957–64* (Manchester: Manchester University Press, 2005).
51 Gurney, 'The Battle of the Consumer in Postwar Britain', 969–72; Hopkins, *The New Look*, 405.
52 T. R. Nevett, *Advertising in Britain: A History* (London: Heinemann on behalf of the History of Advertising Trust, 1982): 177; Sean Nixon, *Hard Sell: Advertising, Affluence and Transatlantic Relations, c. 1951–69* (Manchester: Manchester University Press, 2013): 20–5, 97, 114, 145–51; Stefan Schwarzkopf, '"A Moment of Triumph in the History of the Free Mind"? British and American Advertising Agencies' Responses to the Introduction of Commercial Television in the United Kingdom', in Michael Bailey (ed.), *Narrating Media History* (London: Routledge, 2009).
53 Schwarzkopf, 'They Do It with Mirrors', 137–9; Stefan Schwarzkopf and Rainer Gries (eds), *Ernest Dichter and Motivation Research: New Perspectives on the Making of Post-War Consumer Culture* (Basingstoke: Palgrave Macmillan, 2010); Nixon, *Hard Sell*, 167–9.
54 Frank Mort, 'The Commercial Domain: Advertising and the Cultural Management of Demand' in Becky Conekin, Frank Mort and Chris Waters (eds), *Moments of Modernity: Reconstructing Britain, 1945–1964* (London: Rivers Oram, 1999); Nixon, *Hard Sell*, 43–59, 72–4.
55 See Harry Henry, *Motivation Research: Its Practice and Uses for Advertising, Marketing, and Other Business Purposes* (London: Crosby Lockwood & Son, 1958). Henry had been head of consumer research at McCann-Erickson and published this comprehensive guide in order to refute Packard's overblown claims.
56 Charles Wilson, *Unilever 1945–1965: Challenge and Response in the Post-War Industrial Revolution* (London: Cassell, 1968): 101; Brian Henry (ed.), *British Television Advertising: The First 30 Years* (London: Century Benham, 1986); Nixon, *Hard Sell*, 22, 74–87, 127–35, 156–7.
57 *The Times*, 22 July 1957: 4. Macmillan went on to express anxiety about whether the good times would last and warned of the dangers of inflation.
58 Peter Clarke, *Hope and Glory: Britain 1900–2000* (London: Penguin, 2004): 254–5.
59 Victor Montagu, (Lord Hinchingbrooke), *Parliamentary Debates* (House of Commons), 21 May 1962, Vol. 660, cc. 56–7. Anthony Crosland went on to ridicule Montagu.
60 Richard Hoggart, *The Uses of Literacy* (Harmondsworth: Penguin Books, 1958): 169, 248–50. Unsurprisingly perhaps, Hoggart was particularly scathing about the enervating effects of television on the 'passive' majority: 'nightly, dead from the eyes downwards, they would be able to link on to the Great Mother. They might spend their days fixing a dozen screws on each of a hundred TV sets, but their nights could be passed sitting in front of one. The eyes would register but not connect to the nerves, the heart, and the

brain' (189). The classic study of subcultures is Stuart Hall and Tony Jefferson (eds), *Resistance through Rituals: Youth Subcultures in Post-War Britain* (London: Hutchinson, 1975). See also Bill Osgerby, *Youth in Britain Since 1945* (Oxford: Blackwell, 1998).

61 Mark Abrams, *The Teenage Consumer* (London: London Press Exchange, 1959); *Daily Mail*, 13 December 1962: 8.

62 Ibid., 21 May 1954: 7. See also W. H. Greenleaf, *The British Political Tradition. Vol. 2. The Ideological Heritage* (London: Routledge, 2003): 322–3.

63 Richard Cockett, *Thinking the Unthinkable: Think-Tanks and the Economic Counter-Revolution, 1931–1983* (London: Harper Collins, 1994): 162–3; See also Daniel Stedman Jones, *Masters of the Universe: Hayek, Friedman, and the Birth of Neoliberal Politics* (Princeton: Princeton University Press, 2012): 148–9.

64 Cited in John Gloag, *Advertising in Modern Life* (London: Heinemann, 1959): 6.

65 Ralph Harris and Arthur Seldon, *Advertising in a Free Society* (London: Institute of Economic Affairs, 1959): 63, 110. See also Gloag, *Advertising in Modern Life*, 1.

66 Steven Fielding, 'Activists against "Affluence": Labour Party Culture During the "Golden Age", circa 1950–1970', *Journal of British Studies* 40, no. 2 (2001): 247, 251.

67 C. A. R. Crosland, *The Future of Socialism* (London: Jonathan Cape, 1956): 112, 278–94; James E. Cronin, *New Labour's Pasts: The Labour Party and Its Discontents* (Harlow: Pearson, 2004): 56–8.

68 Joe Moran, 'Mass-Observation, Market Research, and the Birth of the Focus Group, 1937–1997', *Journal of British Studies* 47, no. 3 (2008): 840–3.

69 Noel Thompson, *Social Opulence and Private Restraint: The Consumer in British Socialist Thought since 1800* (Oxford: Oxford University Press, 2015): 124–6; C. A. R. Crosland, *A Social-Democratic Britain* (1971), reprinted in Dick Leonard (ed.), *Socialism Now, and Other Essays* (London: Cape, 1974): 79; David Reisman, *Crosland's Future: Opportunity and Outcome* (Basingstoke: Macmillan, 1997): 145; Catherine Ellis, 'Total Abstinence and a Good Filing-System? Anthony Crosland and the Affluent Society', in Lawrence Black and Hugh Pemberton (eds), *An Affluent Society? Britain's Post-War 'Golden Age' Revisited* (Aldershot: Ashgate, 2004): 69–84.

70 Kevin Jefferys, *Anthony Crosland: A New Biography* (London: Richard Cohen, 1999): 178; Bernard Donoughue and G. W. Jones, *Herbert Morrison: Portrait of a Politician* (London: Weidenfeld and Nicolson, 1973): 31, 57; Martin Francis, 'The Labour Party: Modernisation and the Politics of Restraint', in Conekin, Mort and Waters (eds), *Moments of Modernity*: 168–70; 'Tears, Tantrums, and Bared Teeth: The Emotional Economy of Three Conservative Prime Ministers, 1951–1963', *Journal of British Studies* 41, no. 3 (2002): 354–87.

71 Harris and Seldon, *Advertising in a Free Society*, 112.

72 Matthew Hilton, 'The Fable of the Sheep, or, Private Virtues, Public Vices: The Consumer Revolution of the Twentieth Century', *Past and Present* 171 (2002): 233; Kate Bradley, '"All Human Life Is There": The John Hilton Bureau of the *News of the World* and Advising the Public, 1942–1969', *English Historical Review* 129, no. 539 (2014): 904–5; London School of

Economics, Peter Shore Papers, B/57: 'The Speaker's Handbook of Data on the Subject of Value for Money in Consumer Goods'.

73 Nixon, *Hard Sell*, 171–5, 191; Richard Hoggart, 'Where Is It All Leading Us?', in Alexander Wilson (ed.), *Advertising and the Community* (Manchester: Manchester University Press, 1968): 50–4.

74 Nicholas Kaldor and Rodney Silverman, *A Statistical Analysis of Advertising Expenditure and of the Revenue of the Press* (Cambridge: Cambridge University Press, 1948); Nicholas Kaldor, 'The Economic Aspects of Advertising', *Review of Economic Studies* 18, no. 1 (1950–51): 1–27; Noel Thompson, 'Socialist Political Economy in the Age of Affluence: The Reception of J. K. Galbraith by the British Left in the 1950s and 1960s', *Twentieth Century British History* 21, no. 1 (2010): 50–79.

75 Francis Noel-Baker, 'The Role of the Consumer Organisations', in Wilson (ed.), *Advertising and the Community*, 150–2; Schwarzkopf, 'They do it With Mirrors', 136–7.

76 Matthew Hilton, *Consumerism in Twentieth-Century Britain: The Search for a Historical Movement* (Cambridge: Cambridge University Press, 2003): 100–5; 'The Fable of the Sheep', 239; Irving, 'The Birth of a Politician', 105; Nixon, *Hard Sell*, 175–7; Elaine Burton, *The Battle of the Consumer* (London: Labour Party, 1955), 26–7.

77 Asa Briggs, *Michael Young: Social Entrepreneur* (Basingstoke: Palgrave, 2001): 96; Robert Millar, *The Affluent Sheep: A Profile of the British Consumer* (London: Longmans, 1963): 164–5.

78 Alan Aldridge, 'The Construction of Rational Consumption in *Which?* Magazine: The More Blobs the Better', *Sociology* 28, no. 4 (1994): 899–912; Chris Beauchamp, 'Getting *Your Money's Worth*: American Models for the Remaking of the Consumer Interest in Britain, 1930s–1960s', in Mark Bevir and Frank Trentmann (eds), *Critiques of Capital in Modern Britain and America: Transatlantic Exchanges 1800 to the Present Day* (Basingstoke: Palgrave Macmillan, 2002): 127–50; Matthew Hilton, 'The Female Consumer and the Politics of Consumption in Twentieth-Century Britain', *Historical Journal* 45, no. 1 (2002): 126; 'The Fable of the Sheep', 230.

79 In his pamphlet, *The Chipped White Cups of Dover* (London: Unit 2, 1960). Note also Young's essay, 'Anthony Crosland and Socialism', in Dick Leonard (ed.), *Crosland and New Labour* (Basingstoke: Macmillan, 1999): 49–53.

80 Hilton, *Consumerism in Twentieth-Century Britain*, 210, 212–14; Lawrence Black, '*Which?*Craft in Post-War Britain: The Consumers' Association and the Politics of Affluence', *Albion* 36, no. 1 (2004): 52–82; Gurney, 'The Battle of the Consumer in Postwar Britain', 979–80.

81 *Co-operative Independent Commission Report* (Manchester: Co-operative Union, 1958): 19; Lawrence Black, '"Trying to Sell a Parcel of Politics with a Parcel of Groceries": The Co-operative Independent Commission (CIC) and Consumerism in Post-War Britain', in Black and Robertson (eds), *Consumerism and the Co-operative Movement*, 33–50.

82 Peter Gurney (ed.), *Co-operation and Consumerism in Interwar England: Transcripts of Interviews with Co-operative Society Members from Lancashire and Yorkshire*, UK Data Archive, University of Essex (2012): 17.

83 G. N. Ostergaard and A. H. Halsey, *Power in Co-operatives: A Study of the Internal Politics of British Retail Societies* (Oxford: Basil Blackwell, 1965): 233–4.

84 John K. Walton, 'The Post-War Decline of the British Retail Co-operative Movement: Nature, Causes and Consequences', in Black and Robertson (eds), *Consumerism and the Co-operative Movement*, 26, citing John Attfield, *With Light of Knowledge: A Hundred Years of Education in the Royal Arsenal Co-operative Society, 1877–1977* (London: Journeyman Press, 1981): 63, 73.

85 See Richard Cockett, 'The Party, Publicity, and the Media', in Anthony Seldon and Stuart Ball (eds), *Conservative Century: The Conservative Party Since 1900* (Oxford: Oxford University Press, 1994); John Ramsden, *The Age of Churchill and Eden, 1940–1957* (London: Longman, 1995); Black, *Political Culture of the Left*, 155–87; Brian Girvan, 'Affluence, Conservatism and Political Competition in Britain and the United States, 1945–64', in Black and Pemberton (eds), *An Affluent Society?*, 15–33.

86 *New Statesman and Nation*, 1 November 1958: 1. The concept of 'Admass' was introduced by Priestley after his visit to the United States in 1954, and represented an attempt to grasp the homogenizing effects and colonizing tendencies of consumer culture. For further discussion see Black, *Political Culture of the Left*, 87–8; John Baxendale, *Priestley's England: J. B. Priestley and English Culture* (Manchester: Manchester University Press, 2007): 176–80, passim.

87 *New Statesman and Nation*, 11 June 1960: 866; Thompson, *Social Opulence and Private Restraint*, 130–3.

88 Dominic Wring, *The Politics of Marketing the Labour Party* (Basingstoke: Palgrave Macmillan, 2005): 66–71.

89 Helen Mercer, *Constructing a Competitive Order: The Hidden History of British Anti-Trust Policy* (Cambridge: Cambridge University Press, 1995): 135, *passim*; Gurney, 'The Battle of the Consumer in Postwar Britain', 973–4.

90 *Daily Mirror*, 26 November 1963: 8; 17 January 1964: 4; Maurice Corina, *Pile It High, Sell It Cheap* (London: Weidenfeld and Nicolson, 1971): 34; Richard Findley, 'The Conservative Party and Defeat: The Significance of Resale Price Maintenance for the General Election of 1964', *Twentieth Century British History* 12, no. 3 (2001): 327–53.

91 *Daily Mirror*, 29 May 1964: 25.

92 Nixon, *Hard Sell*, 151–3.

93 Raymond Williams, 'Advertising the Magic System', *New Left Review* 4 (1960): 27–32. An expanded version of the essay was later published in *Problems in Materialism and Culture* (London: Verso, 1980).

94 E. P. Thompson, 'Revolution Again! Or Shut Your Ears and Run', *New Left Review* 6 (1960): 18–31. See also E. P. Thompson (ed.), *Out of Apathy* (London: New Left Books, 1960); Madeleine Davis, 'Arguing Affluence: New Left Contributions to the Socialist Debate 1957–63', *Twentieth Century British History* 23, no. 4 (2012): 496–528.

95 John Goldthorpe, Frank Bechhofer, David Lockwood and Jennifer Platt, *The Affluent Worker: Political Attitudes and Behaviour* (Cambridge: Cambridge University Press, 1968); Nick Tiratsoo, 'Popular Politics, Affluence and the Labour Party in the 1950s', in Anthony Gorst, Lewis Johnman and W. Scott Lucas (eds), *Contemporary British History 1931–1961* (London: Pinter, 1991); Mike Savage, 'Working-Class Identities in the 1960s: Revisiting the Affluent Worker Study', *Sociology* 39, no. 5 (2005): 929–46; Jon Lawrence, 'Class, "Affluence" and the Study of Everyday Life in Britain, c. 1930–64', *Cultural and Social History* 10, no. 2 (2013): 273–99.

Chapter 9

1 Rachel Bowlby, *Carried Away: The Invention of Modern Shopping* (London: Faber, 2000): 6–7; Matthew Hilton, 'The Female Consumer and the Politics of Consumption in Twentieth-Century Britain', *Historical Journal* 45, no. 1 (2002): 103–28.

2 Daniel Miller, 'Consumption as the Vanguard of History', in Daniel Miller (ed.), *Acknowledging Consumption: A Review of New Studies* (London: Routledge, 1995).

3 Stephen Marglin and Juliet Schor (eds), *The Golden Age of Capitalism* (Oxford: Clarendon Press, 1990): vi, 23–4, 49–50; Eric Hobsbawm, *Age of Extremes: The Short Twentieth Century 1914–1991* (London: Abacus, 1995): 257–86. Hobsbawm provides a fascinating personal account in his autobiography, *Interesting Times: A Twentieth-Century Life* (London: Allen Lane, 2002): 222–4.

4 Jim Tomlinson, 'The Politics of Declinism', in Lawrence Black, Hugh Pemberton and Pat Thane (eds), *Reassessing 1970s Britain* (Manchester: Manchester University Press, 2015): 45–6; Peter Clarke, *Hope and Glory: Britain 1900–2000* (London: Penguin, 2004): 351–2.

5 *Daily Express*, 9 February 1974: 2; *Daily Mail*, 16 February 1974: 1.

6 Andrew Taylor, *The NUM and British Politics. Vol. 2: 1969–1995* (Aldershot: Ashgate, 2005): 94–102; Clarke, *Hope and Glory*, 337–9.

7 Jim Tomlinson, 'Inventing "Decline": The Falling Behind of the British Economy in the Postwar Years', *Economic History Review* 49, no. 4 (1996): 734–60; 'De-industrialization Not Decline: A New Meta-Narrative for Post-war British History', *Twentieth Century British History* 27, no. 1 (2016): 76–99.

8 Avner Offer, 'British Manual Workers: From Producers to Consumers, c. 1950–2000', *Contemporary British History* 22, no. 4 (2008): 537–71; 'Consumption and Affluence', in Roderick Floud, Jane Humphries and Paul Johnson (eds), *Cambridge Economic History of Modern Britain*, Vol. 2 (Cambridge: Cambridge University Press, 2014).

9 A useful critique is Julia Swindells and Lisa Jardine, *What's Left? Women in Culture and the Labour Movement* (London: Routledge, 1989).

10 Leigh Sparks, 'The Rise and Fall of Mass Marketing? Food Retailing in Great Britain since 1960', in Richard Tedlow and Geoffrey Jones (eds), *The Rise and Fall of Mass Marketing* (London: Routledge, 2015): 61–4.

11 S. R. Bowlby, 'Planning for Women to Shop in Postwar Britain', *Environment and Planning D: Society and Space* 2, no. 2 (1984): 185–6.

12 Leigh Sparks, 'Consumer Co-operation in the United Kingdom 1945–93: Review and Prospects', *Journal of Co-operative Studies* 79 (1994): 15–20.

13 Bill Lancaster, *The Department Store: A Social History* (London: Leicester University Press, 1995): 198, 204.

14 Sparks, 'The Rise and Fall of Mass Marketing?', 66–70; Edward Higgs, *Identifying the English: A History of Personal Identification, 1500 to the Present* (London: Continuum, 2011): 182–6.

15 Jonathan Zeitlin, 'The Clothing Industry in Transition', *Textile History* 19, no. 2 (1988): 211–38.

16 Sean Nixon, *Hard Looks: Masculinities, Spectatorship and Contemporary Consumption* (London: UCL Press, 1996): 56–9.
17 Peter Townsend, *Poverty in the United Kingdom: A Survey of Household Resources and Standards of Living* (Harmondsworth: Penguin Books, 1979).
18 John F. Wilson, Anthony Webster and Rachael Vorberg-Rugh, *Building Co-operation: A Business History of the Co-operative Group, 1863–2013* (Oxford: Oxford University Press, 2013): 149, passim.
19 Sparks, 'Consumer Co-operation in the United Kingdom', 21–7, 53–4.
20 Peter Gurney (ed.), *Co-operation and Consumerism in Interwar England: Transcripts of Interviews with Co-operative Society Members from Lancashire and Yorkshire*, UK Data Archive, University of Essex (2012): 38. In Yorkshire dialect 'clemmed' usually means very hungry but it can also mean cold.
21 Matthew Hilton, 'The Fable of the Sheep, or, Private Virtues, Public Vices: The Consumer Revolution of the Twentieth Century', *Past and Present* 171 (2002): 244, 249; *Consumerism in Twentieth-Century Britain: The Search for a Historical Movement* (Cambridge: Cambridge University Press, 2003).
22 *Daily Express*, 15 January 1968: 7; 6 March 1968: 9; 25 February 1969: 7; 14 January 1970: 8; 3 December 1973: 13.
23 Peter Shapely, 'Tenants Arise! Consumerism, Tenants and the Challenge to Council Authority in Manchester, 1968–92', *Social History* 31, no. 1 (2006): 60–78; *The Politics of Housing: Power, Consumers and Urban Culture* (Manchester: Manchester University Press, 2007).
24 *Spare Rib*, July 1978: 18–19. Judith Williamson's important text, *Decoding Advertisements: Ideology and Meaning in Advertising* (London: Marion Boyars, 1978), was part of this feminist critique.
25 Matthew Worley, 'Punk, Politics and British (Fan)zines, 1976–84: "While the World Was Dying, Did You Wonder Why?"', *History Workshop Journal* 79, no. 1 (2015): 92; Frank Cartledge, 'Distress to Impress? Local Punk Fashion and Commodity Exchange', in Roger Sabin (ed.), *Punk Rock, So What? The Cultural Legacy of Punk* (London: Routledge, 1999): 145.
26 Roland Wymer, *Derek Jarman* (Manchester: Manchester University Press, 2005): 54–69.
27 Matthew Worley, 'Shot by Both Sides: Punk, Politics and the End of "Consensus"', *Contemporary British History* 26, no. 3, (2012): 345. See also Jon Savage, *England's Dreaming: Sex Pistols and Punk Rock* (London: Faber, 2005).
28 See Keith Gildart, 'The Antithesis of Humankind: Exploring Responses to the Sex Pistols Anarchy Tour 1976', *Cultural and Social History* 10, no. 1 (2013): 129–49; Lawrence Black, *Redefining British Politics: Culture, Consumerism and Participation, 1954–70* (Basingstoke: Palgrave Macmillan, 2010).
29 *Daily Mirror*, 18 April 1988: 14–15.
30 Ibid., 21 May 1988: 2; Gavin Schaffer, 'Fighting Thatcher with Comedy: What to Do When There Is No Alternative', *Journal of British Studies* 55, no. 2 (2016): 385.
31 J. M. Keynes, 'Economic Possibilities for Our Grandchildren' (1930), in *Essays in Persuasion* (Basingstoke: Palgrave Macmillan, 2010): 326. For earlier views see Matthew Hilton, 'The Legacy of Luxury: Moralities of

Consumption Since the 18th Century', *Journal of Consumer Culture* 4, no. 1 (2004): 101–23.

32 See Christopher Payne, *The Consumer, Credit and Neoliberalism: Governing the Modern Economy* (Abingdon: Routledge, 2012).

33 *Sunday Express*, 23 November 1975.

34 Ibid., 25 March 1975.

35 David Cannadine, 'Apocalypse When? British Politicians and British "Decline" in the Twentieth Century', in Peter Clarke and Clive Trebilcock (eds), *Understanding Decline: Perceptions and Realities of British Economic Performance* (Cambridge: Cambridge University Press, 1997).

36 Catherine Needham, *The Reform of Public Services Under New Labour: Narratives of Consumerism* (Basingstoke: Palgrave Macmillan, 2007): 53–6; Hilton, 'The Fable of the Sheep', 250–3.

37 Richard Cockett, *Thinking the Unthinkable: Think-Tanks and the Economic Counter-Revolution, 1931–1983* (London: Harper Collins, 1994): 204–7, 236–8, 266; Daniel Stedman Jones, *Masters of the Universe: Hayek, Friedman, and the Birth of Neoliberal Politics* (Princeton: Princeton University Press, 2012): 161–2.

38 Ralph Harris and Arthur Seldon, *Over-Ruled on Welfare: The Increasing Desire for Choice in Education and Medicine and Its Frustration by 'Representative' Government* (London: Institute of Economic Affairs, 1979). A later study in 1987 reported an apparent shift of opinion back to raising taxes to pay for better state services, though the majority were found to be still in favour of greater choice and private provision. Ralph Harris and Arthur Seldon, *Welfare without the State: A Quarter-Century of Suppressed Public Choice* (London: Institute of Economic Affairs, 1987).

39 For examples see *Daily Mail*, 22 July 1963: 7; 23 October 1965: 12; 28 June 1979: 6.

40 Colin Hay, 'Narrating Crisis: The Discursive Construction of the "Winter of Discontent"', *Sociology* 30, no. 2 (1996): 253–77. See also Tara Martin López, *The Winter of Discontent: Myth, Memory, and History* (Liverpool: Liverpool University Press, 2014).

41 John Shepherd, *Crisis? What Crisis? The Callaghan Government and the British 'Winter of Discontent'* (Manchester: Manchester University Press, 2013): 130–2.

42 *Parliamentary Debates*, House of Commons, fifth series, 28 March 1979, vol. 965, cols. 465–7; Shepherd, *Crisis?*, 153–5.

43 For important contemporary analyses see Stuart Hall's essays, 'The Great Moving Right Show' and 'The Culture Gap' in Stuart Hall (ed.), *The Hard Road to Renewal: Thatcherism and the Crisis of the Left* (London: Verso, 1988).

44 Matthew Francis, '"A Crusade to Enfranchise the Many": Thatcherism and the "Property-Owning Democracy"', *Twentieth Century British History* 23, no. 2 (2012): 276–9, 283, 288–90, 294–6. See also Stedman Jones, *Masters of the Universe*, 308–15; Colin Jones and Alan Murie, *The Right to Buy: Analysis and Evaluation of a Housing Policy* (Oxford: Blackwell, 2006).

45 *Daily Express*, 18 May 1979: 1; 9 January 1986: 1–2.

46 Ibid., 12 October 1982: 6; 5 February 1986: 26–7.

47 Offer, 'British Manual Workers', 549.

48 Amy Edwards, '"Manufacturing Capitalists": The Wider Share Ownership Council and the Problem of "Popular Capitalism", 1958–92', *Twentieth Century British History* 27, no. 1 (2016): 101–10.
49 Francis, '"A Crusade to Enfranchise the Many"', 290–4.
50 Edwards, '"Manufacturing Capitalists"', 117–20, 123.
51 Alex Mold, 'Making the Patient-Consumer in Margaret Thatcher's Britain', *Historical Journal* 54, no. 2 (2011): 509–28; *Making the Patient–Consumer: Patient Organisations and Health Consumerism in Britain* (Manchester: Manchester University Press, 2015).
52 Nixon, *Hard Looks*, 77–8; Frank Mort, *Cultures of Consumption: Masculinities and Social Space in Late Twentieth-Century Britain* (London: Routledge, 1996): 91–2; Douglas West, 'Multinational Competition in the British Advertising Agency Business, 1936–1987', *Business History Review* 62, no. 3 (1987): 467–501.
53 Nixon, *Hard Looks*, 79–89, 116–19; Mort, *Cultures of Consumption*, 8–10, 100, *passim*. See also Sean Nixon, *Advertising Cultures: Gender, Commerce, Creativity* (London: Sage, 2003); Paul Joblin, *Advertising Menswear: Masculinity and Fashion in the British Media Since 1945* (London: Bloomsbury, 2014).
54 Martin Jacques and Francis Mulhern (eds), *The Forward March of Labour Halted?* (London: Verso, 1981): 18.
55 Ibid., 176.
56 Bob Jessop, Kevin Bonnett, Simon Bromley and Tom Ling, 'Authoritarian Populism, Two Nations, and Thatcherism', *New Left Review* 147 (1984): 53.
57 See Hall's essay, 'The Culture Gap', in *The Hard Road to Renewal.*
58 *Marxism Today*, January 1987: 18–23.
59 Charles Leadbeater, *The Politics of Prosperity* (London: Fabian Society, 1987): 6–7; Noel Thompson, *Left in the Wilderness: The Political Economy of Democratic Socialism since 1979* (Cheshum: Acumen, 2002): 23.
60 *Marxism Today*, October 1988: 14–19.
61 Frank Mort and Nicholas Green, 'You've Never Had It So Good – Again', *Marxism Today*, May 1988: 30–3. Mort later published a somewhat different version of this article as 'The Politics of Consumption', in Stuart Hall and Martin Jacques (eds), *New Times: The Changing Face of Politics in the 1990s* (London: Verso, 1989).
62 Martin Smith, *The Consumer Case for Socialism* (London: Fabian Society, 1986): 10, 13–15, 23.
63 Bryan Gould, *Socialism and Freedom* (Basingstoke: Macmillan, 1985): 73, 103–5. Mort and Green praised Gould in their *Marxism Today* article, though the reference was cut from Mort's chapter.
64 Bryan Gould, *A Future for Socialism* (London: Cape, 1989): 169–71.
65 Noel Thompson, *Left in the Wilderness*, 20–4, 109.
66 See Laura Beers, *Your Britain: Media and the Making of the Labour Party* (Cambridge, MA: Harvard University Press, 2010).
67 James E. Cronin, *New Labour's Pasts: The Labour Party and Its Discontents* (Harlow: Pearson, 2004): 279–82; Dominic Wring, *The Politics of Marketing the Labour Party* (Basingstoke: Palgrave Macmillan, 2005): 89, 90–4, 101–7.
68 'Still A Question of Hegemony', *New Left Review* 181 (1990): 119.

69 Wring, *The Politics of Marketing the Labour Party*, 94; 'The Long And The Short About Labour's Red Rose', *Daily Telegraph*, 26 June 2001: 20. Apparently, Kinnock quibbled over the length of the stem.
70 *Daily Mail*, 17 June 1987: 32; 18 April 1989: 26; 22 May 1990: 4.
71 Ibid., 2 October 1986: 8.
72 Margaret Scammell, 'Political Marketing: Lessons for Political Science', *Political Studies* 47, no. 4 (1999): 733–4.
73 Including the father of a later Labour leader, Ralph Miliband, in his seminal work, *Parliamentary Socialism: A Study in the Politics of Labour* (London: Allen & Unwin, 1961).
74 Cronin, *New Labour's Pasts*, 383–7; Wring, *The Politics of Marketing the Labour Party*, 134–8.
75 Margaret Scammell, *Consumer Democracy: The Marketing of Politics* (Cambridge: Cambridge University Press, 2014): 78.
76 Wring, *The Politics of Marketing the Labour Party*, 145–7.
77 Tony Blair, *The Third Way. New Politics for the New Century* (London: Fabian Society, 1998): 7; Needham, *The Reform of Public Services Under New Labour*, 92–5.
78 Cronin, *New Labour's Pasts*, 424–30; Anthony Giddens, *The Third Way: The Renewal of Social Democracy* (Cambridge: Polity Press, 1998).
79 *Guardian*, 30 April 1998: 10.
80 *Modern Markets: Confident Consumers. The Government's Consumer White Paper*, Cm 4410 (London: HMSO, 1999): 4. The words are of Stephen Byers, secretary of state for trade and industry, in the foreword to the paper.
81 John Wilson, Anthony Webster and Rachael Vorberg-Rugh, 'The Co-operative Movement in Britain: From Crisis to "Renaissance," 1950–2010', *Enterprise and Society* 14, no. 2 (2013): 291–4. Regan avoided imprisonment and typically went on to have a successful career as a financier and polar explorer. For more detail of the failed takeover see John F. Wilson, 'Co-operativism Meets City Ethics: The 1997 Lanica Takeover Bid for CWS', in Anthony Webster, Alison Brown, David Stewart, Linda Shaw and John K. Walton (eds), *The Hidden Alternative: Co-operative Values, Past, Present and Future* (Manchester: Manchester University Press, 2011).

Epilogue

1 Catherine Needham, *The Reform of Public Services under New Labour: Narratives of Consumerism* (Basingstoke: Palgrave Macmillan, 2007): 64.
2 Mark Bevir, *New Labour: A Critique* (London: Routledge, 2005): 81.
3 Tony Blair, *The Courage of Our Convictions: Why Reform of the Public Services is the Route to Social Justice* (London: Fabian Society, 2002): 2; Needham, *The Reform of Public Services under New Labour*, 97.
4 Blair, *The Courage of Our Convictions*, 5, 19–20, 30.
5 John Clarke, 'Dissolving the Public Realm? The Logics and Limits of Neoliberalism', *Journal of Social Policy* 33, no. 1 (2004): 42; Needham, *The Reform of Public Services under New Labour*, 77.

6 Eric Shaw, 'The Consumer and New Labour: The Consumer as King?', in Richard Simmons, Martin Powell and Ian Greener (eds), *The Consumer in Public Services: Choice, Values and Difference* (Bristol: Policy Press, 2009): 19.
7 Ibid, 24; Daniel Stedman Jones, *Masters of the Universe: Hayek, Friedman, and the Birth of Neoliberal Politics* (Princeton: Princeton University Press, 2014): 126–32.
8 David Miliband, 'Choice and Voice in Personalised Learning', in *Personalising Education* (Paris: Organisation for Economic Co-operation and Development, 2006): 24–5. Charles Leadbeater also contributed a chapter on personalized learning to this collection. Miliband's interest in Hirschman can be traced back to when he was employed as a researcher by the left think-tank, the Institute for Public Policy Research, in the early 1990s. See David Miliband, *Markets, Politics and Education: Beyond the Education Reform Act* (London: Institute for Public Policy Research, 1991): 13–14. Albert Hirschman's work is titled *Exit, Voice, and Loyalty; Responses to Decline in Firms, Organizations, and States* (Cambridge, MA: Harvard University Press, 1970).
9 Madeleine Arnot, *Educating the Gendered Citizen: Sociological Engagements with National and Global Political Agendas* (London: Routledge, 2009): 202–7.
10 Needham, *The Reform of Public Services under New Labour*, 73–5; Shaw, 'The Consumer and New Labour', 31–4.
11 Margaret Scammell, *Consumer Democracy: The Marketing of Politics* (Cambridge: Cambridge University Press, 2014): 74–81.
12 See the report commissioned by English Heritage, *The Changing Face of the High Street: Decline and Revival. A Review of Retail and Town Centre Issues in Historic Areas* (2013). Available online: https://content.historicengland.org.uk/images-books/publications/changing-face-high-street-decline-revival/773_130604_final_retail_and_town_centre.pdf/ (accessed 31 July 2016).
13 Mary Portas, *The Portas Review: An Independent Review into the Future of Our High Streets* (2011): 8. Available online: https://www.gov.uk/government/uploads/system/uploads/attachment_data/file/6292/2081646.pdf (accessed 31 July 2016); http://www.maryportas.com/about-mary/ (accessed 31 July 2016).
14 Neil Doherty and Fiona Ellis-Chadwick, 'Internet Retailing: The Past, the Present and the Future', *International Journal of Retail & Distribution Management* 38, nos. 11/12 (2010): 943–65.
15 *Guardian*, 26 February 2016. Available online: https://0-www-nexis-com.serlib0.essex.ac.uk/results/enhdocview.do?docLinkInd=true&ersKey=23_T24447532999&format=GNBFI&startDocNo=0&resultsUrlKey=0_T24447560809&backKey=20_T24447560810&csi=138620&docNo=1 (accessed 31 July 2016); https://www.trusselltrust.org/what-we-do/ (accessed 31 July 2016).
16 Frank Trentmann, *Free Trade Nation: Commerce, Consumption, and Civil Society in Modern Britain* (Oxford: Oxford University Press, 2008): 354; T. W. Zeiler, *Free Trade, Free World: The Advent of GATT* (Chapel Hill: University of North Carolina Press, 1999).
17 Matthew Hilton, James McKay, Nicholas Crowson, and Jean-François Mouhot, *The Politics of Expertise: How NGOs Shaped Modern Britain* (Oxford: Oxford University Press, 2013); Matthew Hilton, 'Politics is Ordinary: Non-governmental Organizations and Political Participation

in Contemporary Britain', *Twentieth Century British History* 22, no. 2 (2011): 230–68; Lawrence Black, *Redefining British Politics: Culture, Consumerism and Participation, 1954–70* (Basingstoke: Palgrave Macmillan, 2010).

18 *The Fairtrade Foundation. Annual Report and Financial Statements. For the Year Ended 31 December 2014*, 3. Available online: http://www.fairtrade.org.uk/~/media/fairtradeuk/what%20is%20fairtrade/documents/annual%20impact%20reports/2014%20final%20signed%20accounts.ashx (accessed 31 July 2016).

19 Matthew Anderson, *A History of Fair Trade in Contemporary Britain: From Civil Society Campaigns to Corporate Compliance* (Basingstoke: Palgrave Macmillan, 2015): 5; Kathryn Wheeler, *Fair Trade and the Citizen-Consumer: Shopping for Justice?* (Basingstoke: Palgrave Macmillan, 2012): 36–40.

20 Quoted in Anderson, *A History of Fair Trade in Contemporary Britain*, 5.

21 *Observer*, 26 February 2006: 39. Lamb referred to 'mainstreaming' as a 'revolution of consciousness' in this article. In a later essay titled, 'The Impact of Fairtrade', in John Bowes (ed.), *The Fair Trade Revolution* (London: Pluto, 2011): 36, she widened her definition somewhat: 'You do not need a PhD in trade policy, you only need to buy your Fairtrade tea and biscuits, and to chat about it at the school gate, to play your part in creating positive change.' See also Lamb's relentlessly cheery, *Fighting the Banana Wars and Other Fairtrade Battles: How We Took On The Corporate Giants To Change The World* (London: Rider, 2008).

22 Anderson, *A History of Fair Trade in Contemporary Britain*, 126–7; Wheeler, *Fair Trade and the Citizen–Consumer*, 42–5, 55–8; Tehila Sasson, 'Milking the Third World? Humanitarianism, Capitalism, and the Moral Economy of the Nestlé Boycott', *American Historical Review* 121, no. 4 (2016): 1196–224.

23 One of the best studies is Daniel Jaffee, *Brewing Justice: Fair Trade Coffee, Sustainability, and Survival* (Berkeley: University of California Press, 2007). For an uncritical assessment, see Alex Nicholls and Charlotte Opal, *Fair Trade: Market Driven Ethical Consumption* (London: Sage, 2005).

24 *Guardian*, 24 July 2007: 27; Wheeler, *Fair Trade and the Citizen–Consumer*, 64–5, 112–13.

25 Michael K. Goodman, 'The Mirror of Consumption: Celebritization, Developmental Consumption and the Shifting Cultural Politics of Fair Trade', *Geoforum* 41, no. 1 (2010): 104–16.

26 Laura Raynolds, Douglas Murray and John Wilkinson (eds), *Fair Trade: The Challenges of Transforming Globalization* (London: Routledge, 2007): 103; Bob Doherty, Iain A. Davies and Sophi Tranchell, 'Where Now For Fair Trade?', *Business History* 55, no. 2 (2012): 161–89; Anderson, *A History of Fair Trade in Contemporary Britain*, 128–9.

27 John Wilson, Anthony Webster and Rachael Vorberg-Rugh, 'The Co-operative Movement in Britain: From Crisis to "Renaissance", 1950–2010', *Enterprise and Society* 14, no. 2 (2013): 290–1; Anderson, *A History of Fair Trade in Contemporary Britain*, 80–3. The Co-op Bank – on which the purported 'renaissance' was built – nearly collapsed due to mismanagement in 2013 and was taken over by US hedge funds, with the Co-op Group reduced to the position of a minority shareholder. The group subsequently reviewed its

governance, though it seems unlikely that tighter control at the centre will rejuvenate participation by consumers from below.

28 Ibid., 19, 146; Wheeler, *Fair Trade and the Citizen–Consumer*, 188–9; Clive Barnett, Paul Cloke, Nick Clarke and Alice Malpass, *Globalizing Responsibility: The Political Rationalities of Ethical Consumption* (Chichester: Wiley-Blackwell, 2011): 22.

29 Wheeler, *Fair Trade and the Citizen–Consumer*, 41.

30 See Philip Gould, *Early Green Politics: Back to Nature, Back to the Land, and Socialism in Britain, 1880–1900* (Brighton: Harvester, 1988); Noel Thompson, *Social Opulence and Private Restraint: The Consumer in British Socialist Thought Since 1800* (Oxford: Oxford University Press, 2015): 181–4. Historians have yet to explore environmental change in modern Britain in sufficient depth but see Bill Luckin, *Pollution and Control: A Social History of the Thames in the Nineteenth Century* (Bristol: Hilger, 1986); *Death and Survival in Urban Britain. Disease, Pollution and Environment, 1800–1950* (London: I. B. Tauris, 2015); Stephen Mosley, *The Chimney of the World: A History of Smoke Pollution in Victorian and Edwardian Manchester* (Abingdon: Routledge, 2008).

31 See Naomi Klein, *No Logo* (London: Flamingo, 2000); George Monbiot, *The Captive State: The Corporate Takeover of Britain* (London: Macmillan, 2000).

32 Michele Micheletti and Dietlind Stolle, *Political Consumerism: Global Responsibility in Action* (Cambridge: Cambridge University Press, 2013).

33 Anderson, *A History of Fair Trade in Contemporary Britain*, 114–6; Matthew Hilton, *Consumerism in Twentieth-Century Britain. The Search for a Historical Movement* (2003): 317–28; Robert Harrison, Terry Newholm, Deirdre Shaw (eds), *The Ethical Consumer* (London: Sage, 2005); Robert Harrison (ed.), *People over Capital: The Co-operative Alternative to Capitalism* (Oxford: New Internationalist, 2013); George Monbiot, *How Did We Get into This Mess? Politics, Equality, Nature* (London: Verso, 2016).

34 See Avner Offer, *The Challenge of Affluence: Self-Control and Well-Being in the United States and Britain Since 1950* (Oxford: Oxford University Press, 2007); Kate Soper, 'Rethinking the "Good Life": The Consumer as Citizen', *Capitalism, Nature, Socialism* 15, no. 3 (2004): 111–16; '"Alternative Hedonism" and the Citizen Consumer', in Frank Trentmann and Kate Soper (eds), *Citizenship and Consumption* (Basingstoke: Palgrave Macmillan, 2008).

35 *The Economist*, 9 December 2006: 11.

36 *Guardian*, 6 September 1989; 4 July 1990; 23 July 1991.

37 Ibid., 5 September 1995; *Daily Telegraph*, 3 January 2004; *New Ambitions for Our Country: A New Contract for Welfare* (London: HMSO, 1998): 16.

38 Ruth Lister, 'Investing in the Citizen–Workers of the Future: Transformations in Citizenship and the State under New Labour', *Social Policy and Administration* 37, no. 5 (2003): 439.

39 Dennis Potter, *The Glittering Coffin* (London: Victor Gollancz, 1960): 13.

SELECT BIBLIOGRAPHY

Chapter 1

Baudrillard, J., *The Consumer Society: Myths and Structures* (1970. Thousand Oaks, CA: Sage, 1998).

Douglas, M. and Isherwood, B., *The World of Goods: Towards an Anthropology of Consumption* (London: Allen Lane, 1979).

Fine, B. and Leopold, E., *The World of Consumption* (London: Routledge, 1993).

Lang, T. and Gabriel, Y., *The Unmanageable Consumer* (London: Sage, 1995).

Mandeville, B., *The Fable of the Bees: Or, Private Vices, Publick Benefits* (1714. Harmondsworth: Penguin Books, 1970).

Marx, K., *Capital: A Critique of Political Economy. Volume I* (1867. Harmondsworth: Penguin Books, 1976).

McKendrick, N., Brewer, J. and Plumb, J. H., *The Birth of a Consumer Society: The Commercialization of Eighteenth-Century England* (London: Europa Publications, 1982).

Slater, D., *Consumer Culture and Modernity* (Oxford: Polity Press, 1997).

Thompson, E. P., 'The Moral Economy of the English Crowd in the Eighteenth Century', *Past and Present* 50 (1971).

Trentmann, F. (ed.), *The Oxford Handbook of the History of Consumption* (Oxford: Oxford University Press, 2012).

Veblen, T., *The Theory of the Leisure Class: An Economic Study in the Evolution of Institutions* (New York: Macmillan, 1899).

Williams, R., *Keywords: A Vocabulary of Culture and Society* (London: Fontana, 1983).

Chapter 2

Ablett, W. H., *Reminiscences of an Old Draper* (London: S. Low, Marston, Searle & Rivington, 1876).

Adburgham, A., *Shops and Shopping, 1800–1914* (London: Faber & Faber, 1964).

Alexander, D., *Retailing in England during the Industrial Revolution* (London: Athlone Press, 1970).

Burnett, J., *Plenty and Want: A Social History of Diet in England from 1815 to the Present Day* (London: Penguin Books, 1966).

Cohen, D., *Household Gods: The British and Their Possessions* (New Haven, CT: Yale University Press, 2006).

Davidoff, L. and Hall, C., *Family Fortunes: Men and Women of the English Middle Class 1780–1850* (London: Hutchinson Educational, 1987).

Finn, M., *The Character of Credit: Personal Debt in English Culture, 1740–1914* (Cambridge: Cambridge University Press, 2003).
Fraser, W. H., *The Coming of the Mass Market, 1850–1914* (London: Macmillan, 1981).
Jefferys, J. B., *Retail Trading in Britain, 1850–1950* (Cambridge: Cambridge University Press, 1954).
Mitchell, I., *Tradition and Innovation in English Retailing, 1700 to 1850: Narratives of Consumption* (Farnham: Ashgate, 2014).
Scola, R., *Feeding the Victorian City: The Food Supply of Manchester, 1770–1870* (Manchester: Manchester University Press, 1992).
Trollope, A., *The Struggles of Brown, Jones and Robinson: By One of the Firm* (1862. London: Penguin Books, 1993).

Chapter 3

Alborn, T., *Conceiving Companies: Joint-Stock Politics in Victorian England* (London: Routledge, 1998).
Backstrom, P. N., *Christian Socialism and Co-operation in Victorian England* (London: Croom Helm, 1974).
Bamfield, J., 'Consumer-Owned Community Flour and Bread Societies in the Eighteenth and Early Nineteenth Centuries', *Business History* 40, no. 4 (1998).
Chase, M., *Chartism: A New History* (Manchester: Manchester University Press, 2007).
Gurney, P., *Wanting and Having: Popular Politics and Liberal Consumerism in England, 1830–70* (Manchester: Manchester University Press, 2015).
Matthew, C., 'Disraeli, Gladstone, and the Politics of Mid-Victorian Budgets', *Historical Journal* 22, no. 3 (1979).
Midgley, C., *Women against Slavery: The British Campaigns, 1780–1870* (London: Routledge, 1992).
Pickering, P. and Tyrrell, A., *The People's Bread: A History of the Anti-Corn Law League* (London: Leicester University Press, 2000).
Pollard, S., 'Nineteenth-Century Co-operation: From Community Building to Shopkeeping', in Asa Briggs and John Saville (eds), *Essays in Labour History* (London: Macmillan, 1960).
Purvis, M., 'Co-operative Retailing in England, 1835–1850: Developments beyond Rochdale', *Northern History*, 22 (1986).
Sussman, C., *Consuming Anxieties: Consumer Protest, Gender, and British Slavery, 1713–1833* (Stanford: Stanford University Press, 2000).
Thompson, N., *Social Opulence and Private Restraint: The Consumer in British Socialist Thought since 1800* (Oxford: Oxford University Press, 2015).

Chapter 4

Church, R., 'Advertising Consumer Goods in Nineteenth Century Britain: Reinterpretations', *Economic History Review* 53, no. 4 (2000).

Gissing, G., *In the Year of Jubilee* (1894. London: J. M. Dent, 1994).
Hindley, D. and Hindley, G., *Advertising in Victorian England, 1837–1901* (London: Wayland, 1972).
Loeb, L. A., *Consuming Angels: Advertising and Victorian Women* (New York: Oxford University Press, 1994).
Mercer, J., 'A Mark of Distinction: Branding and Trade Mark law in the UK from the 1860s', *Business History* 52, no. 1 (2010).
Nevett, T. R., *Advertising in Britain: A History* (London: Heinemann, 1982).
Ramamurthy, A., *Imperial Persuaders: Images of Africa and Asia in British Advertising* (Manchester: Manchester University Press, 2003).
Readman, P., 'Landscape Preservation, "Advertising Disfigurement", and English National Identity c. 1890–1914', *Rural History* 12, no. 1 (2001).
Richards, T., *The Commodity Culture of Victorian England: Advertising and Spectacle, 1851–1914* (London: Verso, 1990).
Turner, E. S., *The Shocking History of Advertising!* (London: Michael Joseph, 1952).
Wells, H. G., *Tono-Bungay* (1909. London: Penguin Books, 2005).
Williams, R., 'Advertising: the Magic System', in *Problems in Materialism and Culture* (London: Verso, 1980).

Chapter 5

Adburgham, A., *Shops and Shopping 1800–1914* (London: Faber & Faber, 1964).
Billington Greig, T., *The Consumer in Revolt* (London: Stephen Swift, 1912).
Breward, C., *The Hidden Consumer: Masculinities, Fashion and City Life 1860–1914* (Manchester: Manchester University Press, 1999).
Briggs, A., *Friends of the People: The Centenary History of Lewis's* (London: B. T. Batsford, 1956).
Crossick, G. and Jaumain, S. (eds), *Cathedrals of Consumption: The European Department Store, 1850–1939* (Aldershot: Ashgate, 1998).
Hosgood, C. P., 'Mrs Pooter's Purchase: Lower-Middle-Class Consumerism and the Sales, 1870–1914', in Alan Kidd and David Nicholls (eds), *Gender, Civic Culture and Consumerism: Middle-Class Identity in Britain, 1800–1940* (Manchester: Manchester University Press, 1999).
Lancaster, B., *The Department Store: A Social History* (Leicester: Leicester University Press, 1995).
Moss, M. and Turton, A., *A Legend of Retailing: House of Fraser* (London: Weidenfeld and Nicolson, 1989).
Rappaport, E. D., *Shopping for Pleasure: Women in the Making of London's West End* (Princeton: Princeton University Press, 2000).
Sanders, L., *Consuming Fantasies: Labor, Leisure, and the London Shopgirl, 1880–1920* (Columbus: Ohio State University Press, 2006).
Whitlock, T. C., *Crime, Gender and Consumer Culture in Nineteenth Century England* (Aldershot: Ashgate, 2005).
Zola, E., *The Ladies' Paradise* (1883. Oxford: Oxford University Press, 1995).

Chapter 6

Daunton, M., *Trusting Leviathan: The Politics of Taxation in Britain, 1799–1914* (Cambridge: Cambridge University Press, 2001).

Davies, M. L. (ed.), *Life As We Have Known It by Co-operative Working Women* (1931. London: Verso, 1977).

Gurney, P., *Co-operative Culture and the Politics of Consumption in England, 1870–1930* (Manchester: Manchester University Press, 1996).

Howe, A., *Free Trade and Liberal England, 1846–1946* (Oxford: Clarendon Press, 1997).

Hunt, K., 'Negotiating the Boundaries of the Domestic: British Socialist Women and the Politics of Consumption', *Women's History Review* 9, no. 2 (2000).

Mathias, P., *Retailing Revolution: A History of Multiple Retailing in the Food Trades Based upon the Allied Suppliers Group of Companies* (London: Longmans, 1967).

O'Connell, S., *Credit and Community: Working-Class Debt in the UK since 1880* (Oxford: Oxford University Press, 2009).

Scott, G., *Feminism and the Politics of Working Women. The Women's Co-operative Guild, 1880s to the Second World War* (London: UCL Press, 1998).

Thackeray, D. A., *Conservatism for the Democratic Age: Conservative Cultures and the Challenge of Mass Politics in Early Twentieth Century England* (Manchester: Manchester University Press, 2013).

Trentmann, F., *Free Trade Nation: Commerce, Consumption, and Civil Society in Modern Britain* (Oxford: Oxford University Press, 2008).

Wilson, J. F., Webster, A. and Vorberg-Rugh, R., *Building Co-operation: A Business History of the Co-operative Group, 1863–2013* (Oxford: Oxford University Press, 2013).

Winstanley, M. J., *The Shopkeeper's World 1830–1914* (Manchester: Manchester University Press, 1983).

Chapter 7

Bengry, J., 'Courting the Pink Pound: *Men Only* and the Queer Consumer, 1935–39', *History Workshop Journal* 68 (2009).

Bowden, S., 'The New Consumerism', in P. Johnson (ed.), *Twentieth-Century Britain: Economic, Social, and Cultural Change* (London: Longman, 1994).

Fowler, D., *The First Teenagers: The Lifestyle of Young Wage-Earners in Interwar Britain* (London: Woburn Press, 1995).

Honeyman, K., 'Style Monotony and the Business of Fashion: The Marketing of Menswear in Inter-war England', *Textile History* 34, no. 2 (2003).

Giles, J., *The Parlour and the Suburb: Domestic Identities, Class, Femininity and Modernity* (Oxford: Berg, 2004).

Gurney, P., '"The Curse of the Co-ops": Co-operation, the Mass Press and the Market in Interwar Britain', *English Historical Review* 130, no. 546 (2015).

Hewitt, J., 'The "Nature" and "Art" of Shell Advertising in the Early 1930s', *Journal of Design History* 5, no. 2 (1992).

Mannin, E., *Sounding Brass* (1925. London: Jarrolds, 1937).

Priestley, J. B., *English Journey* (London: William Heinemann, 1934).
Schwarzkopf, S., 'Discovering the Consumer. Market Research, Product Innovation, and the Creation of Brand Loyalty in Britain and the United States in the Interwar Years', *Journal of Macromarketing* 29, no. 1 (2009).
Scott, P., *The Making of the Modern British Home: The Suburban Semi and Family Life Between the Wars* (Oxford: Oxford University Press, 2013).
Worth, R., *Fashion for the People: A History of Clothing at Marks & Spencer* (Oxford: Berg, 2007).

Chapter 8

Black, L., *The Political Culture of the Left in Affluent Britain, 1951–64* (Basingstoke: Palgrave Macmillan, 2003).
Black, L., *Redefining British Politics: Culture, Consumerism and Participation, 1954–70* (Basingstoke: Palgrave Macmillan, 2010).
Gurney, P., 'The Battle of the Consumer in Postwar Britain', *Journal of Modern History* 77, no. 4 (2005).
Hilton, M., *Consumerism in Twentieth-Century Britain: The Search for a Historical Movement* (Cambridge: Cambridge University Press, 2003).
Hinton, J., 'Militant Housewives: The British Housewives' League and the Attlee Government', *History Workshop Journal* 38 (1994).
Mort, F. and Thompson, P., 'Retailing, Commercial Culture and Masculinity in 1950s Britain: The case of Montague Burton, the "Tailor of Taste"', *History Workshop Journal* 38 (1994).
Nell, D., Phillips, S., Alexander, A. and Shaw, G., 'Helping Yourself: Self-Service Grocery Retailing and Shoplifting in Britain, c. 1950–75', *Cultural and Social History* 8, no. 3 (2011).
Nixon, S., *Hard Sell: Advertising, Affluence and Transatlantic Relations, c. 1951–69* (Manchester: Manchester University Press, 2013).
Roodhouse, M., *Black Market Britain, 1939–1955* (Oxford: Oxford University Press, 2013).
Schwarzkopf, S., 'They Do It with Mirrors: Advertising and British Cold War Consumer Politics', *Contemporary British History* 19, no. 2 (2005).
Vernon, J., *Hunger: A Modern History* (Harvard, MA: Harvard University Press, 2006).
Zweiniger-Bargielowska, I., *Austerity in Britain: Rationing, Controls, and Consumption, 1939–1955* (Oxford: Oxford University Press, 2000).

Chapter 9

Bowlby, R., *Carried Away: The Invention of Modern Shopping* (London: Faber, 2000).
Edwards, A., '"Manufacturing Capitalists": The Wider Share Ownership Council and the Problem of "Popular Capitalism", 1958–92', *Twentieth Century British History* 27, no. 1 (2016).
Francis, M., '"A Crusade to Enfranchise the Many": Thatcherism and the

"Property-Owning Democracy"', *Twentieth Century British History* 23, no. 2 (2012).
Hall, S. and Jacques, M. (eds), *New Times: The Changing Face of Politics in the 1990s* (London: Verso, 1989).
Mold, A., *Making the Patient-Consumer: Patient Organisations and Health Consumerism in Britain* (Manchester: Manchester University Press, 2015).
Mort, F., *Cultures of Consumption: Masculinities and Social Space in Late Twentieth-Century Britain* (London: Routledge, 1996).
Needham, C., *The Reform of Public Services under New Labour: Narratives of Consumerism* (Basingstoke: Palgrave Macmillan, 2007).
Nixon, S., *Hard Looks: Masculinities, Spectatorship and Contemporary Consumption* (London: UCL Press, 1996).
Offer, A., 'British Manual Workers: From Producers to Consumers, c. 1950–2000', *Contemporary British History* 22, no. 4 (2008).
Shapely, P., 'Tenants Arise! Consumerism, Tenants and the Challenge to Council Authority in Manchester, 1968–92', *Social History* 31, no. 1 (2006).
Sparks, L., 'The Rise and Fall of Mass Marketing? Food Retailing in Great Britain since 1960', in Richard Tedlow and Geoffrey Jones (eds), *The Rise and Fall of Mass Marketing* (1993. London: Routledge, 2015).
Thompson, N., *Left in the Wilderness: The Political Economy of Democratic Socialism since 1979* (Cheshum: Acumen, 2002).

Epilogue

Anderson, M., *A History of Fair Trade in Contemporary Britain: From Civil Society Campaigns to Corporate Compliance* (Basingstoke: Palgrave Macmillan, 2015).
Hilton, M., McKay, J., Crowson, N. and Mouhot, J. F., *The Politics of Expertise: How NGOs Shaped Modern Britain* (Oxford: Oxford University Press, 2013).
Jaffee, D., *Brewing Justice: Fair Trade Coffee, Sustainability, and Survival* (Berkeley: University of California Press, 2007).
Offer, A., *The Challenge of Affluence: Self-Control and Well-Being in the United States and Britain since 1950* (Oxford: Oxford University Press, 2007).
Scammell, M., *Consumer Democracy: The Marketing of Politics* (Cambridge: Cambridge University Press, 2014).
Wheeler, K., *Fair Trade and the Citizen-Consumer: Shopping for Justice?* (Basingstoke: Palgrave Macmillan, 2012).

INDEX

Ablett, William 21–2, 24, 39
Abrams, Mark 171, 173, 177
adulteration 56–7, 83–5
Adulteration of Foods Act (1860) 56–7
advertising
  agencies 32, 74–5, 143, 192
  colonizing art 70–1
  colonizing politics 71–2, 175–7
  commercial television 167–9
  criticism of 80–5, 142, 161, 178, 184–5
  and domesticity 75–6
  and empire 76–7
  and the Great Exhibition 28
  growth of 30–3, 65–70, 141–3, 166
  and the mass press 69, 77–8
  and monopoly 72–5, 78–80, 174
  and showmanship 115
Advertising Association 142, 167
Advertising Convention 142–3
Advertisements Regulation Act (1907) 81–2
affluence 169–74, 176, 178, 204
America 3, 15, 73–4, 78, 88, 137, 142, 161, 165
American influence 67, 79, 90, 115, 136
Americanization 90, 168, 170–1, 173
Anti-Corn Law League 15, 39, 42–7, 123–4, 204
Anti-Corn Law Operative Associations 43, 46
anxieties 1–2, 7, 32–3, 38–9, 55–60, 94–8 (*see also* shoplifting)
arcades 23

Babbage, Charles 28–9
Baldwin, Stanley 150, 153
Barnum, P. T. 68, 115
Bath 9, 23
Baudrillard, Jean 7–8
bazaars 23, 38
Bell, Laura 96–7
Benson, S. H. 76–8, 155
Besant, Annie 66–7, 120
Bevan, Aneurin 167, 172
Binns 94, 138
Birmingham 26, 35–6, 91, 175, 184
black market 161–2
Blackpool 63, 136, 140, 181
Blair, Tony 197–200, 201–3
Blatchford, Robert 121, 207
Board of Trade 66, 147, 157, 163, 167, 177
Boase, Massimi, Pollitt 196–7
Bobby's 92, 94
Bon Marché, Brixton 94, 140
Bonfire of Controls 163, 167
Booth, Charles 66, 121
Bovril 67, 73, 74, 76
boycotts 41–2, 51, 116, 151 (*see also* exclusive dealing)
Bowley, A. L. 110–11
branding 30, 67, 73–4, 196–7, 203
Bright, John 42, 47–8, 53, 56, 57, 59, 61, 119, 123
Brighton 23, 50, 89
British Home Stores 137, 203
British Housewives' League 162
British Restaurants 159
Budgets (*see also* taxation)
  1842 55
  1853 55
  1860 55–6
Bull Ring Shopping Centre 177–8
Burns, John 120–1, 127, 130
Burton, Elaine 165, 173–4
Burton's 147, 164, 182

Cadbury's 25, 67, 74, 177
Cardiff 95, 138

Carlyle, Thomas 30, 32, 44
Chamberlain, Joseph 72, 118, 123–5
Chamberlain, Neville 153, 158
Chartism 35, 39, 51–5, 204
check traders 116, 164 (*see also* Provident Clothing Supply Co Limited)
Chester 9, 92
Chicago 88, 90
China 15, 172
Christian Socialists 55, 58, 111, 119
Christmas 36, 50
Churchill, Randolph 71, 118
Churchill, Winston 129, 158
cinema 145–6
citizen-consumer 2, 208
City of London 1, 21, 103, 123, 187, 192–3, 199
Civil Service Supply Association 60
Cobden, Richard 15, 42–3, 45–7, 56, 59, 61, 119
Cobden Club 118, 123, 124–5
Cold War 134, 165, 169, 172
Colman's 30, 71, 74
colonial goods 11, 15, 41–2, 112 (*see also* empire)
commercial television 167–8
commodity fetishism 5–6, 28
Conservatives
  and advertising 71–2, 161, 163, 167–8, 187–8, 192
  and consumer interest 55, 149–50, 153, 158, 162, 169–72, 181, 183, 187–92
  and protectionism 117, 124
Conservative Central Office 168, 171
Conservative Party 16–17, 116, 118, 133, 155, 163, 172, 177, 180, 192
conspicuous consumption 6
consumer
  choice 2, 155, 163–4, 172–3, 181, 187–95, 198, 201–2, 206
  culture 2–5, 14, 28, 212 n.13
  definition of 2–3, 28–9, 179
  expenditure 66, 110, 135–7, 157, 169–70, 187, 190
  protection 48, 83, 154–5, 168, 174–5, 183
  society 2–3
  sovereignty 17, 155, 173, 181, 202, 209
Consumer Council 131, 152, 174, 183
consumerism 2–3
Consumers' Association 174, 179, 183, 188, 191, 199, 204
Co-operative Independent Commission 175
co-operative mills *see* Hull Anti-Mill Society
co-operative movement 59–60, 109–14, 130, 134, 166–7, 175, 182–3, 199–200, 206
Co-operative Party 131, 152, 154
Co-operative Union 111, 152
Co-operative Wholesale Society 59, 111–12, 148–9, 152, 160, 167, 183, 199
Cornhill Magazine 58, 95–6
Corn Laws 42–3
costermongers *see* street traders
Cotton Famine 60–1, 110
Council for Art and Industry 147–8
Council of Industrial Design 165, 167
coverture 38–9, 96–7
credit 2, 27, 39, 97, 116, 154–5, 164 (*see also* debt)
Crosland, Anthony 172–3, 175, 177–8
Cruikshank, George 28, 36, 38
Crystal Palace 28, 90, 103–4, 113

Daily Express 3, 69, 84, 91, 103, 127, 163, 168, 190
Daily Mail 69, 72, 83, 92, 103, 124, 171, 180
Daily Mirror 79–80, 106, 168, 178, 186
Daily Telegraph 69, 89
Darling, George 160, 168
Debenham's 97–8, 100, 140, 150, 164, 182–3
debt 2, 27, 38, 64, 96–7 (*see also* credit)
deindustrialization 180–1
democratic consumerism 16–17, 64
department stores (*see also* fashion; shopping; shops)
  amalgamation/rationalization 140–1, 150, 164
  cause of anxieties, 38, 64, 87, 94–8
  decline of 182, 203

as dream worlds 16, 28, 92–3, 146
and empire 101–4
and feminism 104–7
and labour 98–9, 100–1
metropolitan 89–91
origins 19, 21, 23, 47, 88–9
provincial 91–2, 146
suburban 138–40
Dichter, E. 168–9
Dickens, Charles 30, 36, 51, 57, 58
Dickens and Jones 101, 140
direct mailing 31, 68
display 7, 24, 28, 35, 47, 90, 91, 93, 140
domesticity 75–6, 143–5
Drage's 133, 154

empire 76, 84, 101–4, 117, 123, 125, 148–9 (*see also* colonial goods)
emporia 23–4, 38
English Illustrated Magazine 97–8
Evans, Richardson 81
exclusive dealing 42, 51, 52, 54–5, 204 (*see also* boycotts)

Fabian socialists 72, 83, 194
fair trade 16, 117–19, 124, 127, 204–7
Fair Trade Foundation 204–7
fashion (*see also* department stores; shopping; shops)
consciousness 8, 10, 37, 58–9, 94
economic stimulus 9, 13, 94
magazines 9, 27, 37, 93
men's 21, 99–100
middle-class formation 35–7, 41, 47
as seduction 88–9, 104
female consumers (*see also* male consumers)
gendered practices of 6, 35–6, 88–9, 92–3, 104–5, 116, 143–6
as gullible 27, 38, 94
as political shoppers 41–2, 51, 106–7, 109–10
meaning of goods for 10–11
Festival of Empire 103–4
Financial Reform Association 47–8
Food Council 150, 152
France 15, 73, 96
Fraser's 91, 101, 140, 185
free trade
after 1850 59, 64, 71, 117–20, 125, 208
before 1850 15–16, 20, 39, 43–8, 53, 55

Gaitskell, Hugh 172, 175, 177
Galbraith, J. K. 3, 7, 134, 174
Gaskell, Elizabeth 25–6, 34
general elections
1847 54
1880 118
1885 118
1906 127, 130
1910 72, 129–30
1924 150
1951 164
1959 176
1974 180, 188
1979 187–8, 192
1997 197–8
general strike 45–6, 53
Germany 15, 204
Gissing, George 65–6
Gladstone, William 55, 61, 118, 123
Glasgow 23, 35, 91, 101, 140
Gould, Bryan 195–6
Gould, Philip 196–7
Great Exhibition 28, 58, 90

Haldane, Richard 102–3, 129
Hall, Stuart 193–4
Harmsworth, Alfred 69, 77, 78, 80, 91, 124, 144
Harris, Ralph 172–3
Harrods 92, 98, 101–3, 138, 140, 148
Harvey, Nichols & Co. 22, 103, 140, 182
Hattersley, Roy 197, 202
Hayek, Friedrich 163, 165, 180
Hazlitt, William 21, 37, 94
Heath, Edward 177, 180, 189
Higham, Charles 72, 141, 142–3
Hire Purchase Act (1938) 154–5
Hobson, J. A. 122, 155
Hoggart, Richard 170–1, 173, 178
Holloway, Thomas 30, 67
Holyoake, G. J. 50, 60, 111
Home and Colonial Stores 114, 137, 151
Howell's 94, 138

Hull Anti-Mill Society 48–9
Hutt, William 155, 163

Ideal Home Exhibition 144–5
imperial consumerism 16–17, 64, 84, 103, 123, 155
Incorporated Society of Advertisment Consultants 82, 143
Independent Labour Party 120, 129
India 75, 172
Industrial and Provident Societies Acts
 1852 52, 59
 1862 59
inflation 179–80
Institute of Economic Affairs 134, 172, 188

J. Walter Thompson 143, 168–9, 192
John Lewis Partnership 140, 141, 165
John Player's 67, 74, 78
Jones, Ernest 55, 119, 208

Kendal Milne 23, 98, 140
Keynes, J. M. 13, 155, 187
Kinnock, Neil 186, 196–7
kleptomania *see* shoplifting

Labour (*see also* Labour Party; New Labour; socialism)
 and advertising 163, 167
 asceticism162, 167–8, 172
 and consumer interest 149–50, 152–3, 173–4, 180–1, 194–5
Labour Party 134, 154, 162, 181, 183, 193, 197 (*see also* Labour; New Labour; socialism)
 and market research 177, 195–6
Lady Jeune 90, 98–9
Lancaster 10, 53
Layton, Mrs 109–10
Le Bas, Hedley 72, 141
Leadbeater, Charles 194–5
Leeds 140, 146–7, 183
Leicester 140, 149
Lever, W. H. 67, 70, 74, 78–9, 112, 141
Lewis, David 91–2, 99–100
Lewis's 91, 140–1, 146, 164, 182
liberal consumerism 16, 55–6, 59–60, 64, 116–17, 122–3
Liberals
 and advertising 72
 and consumer interest 17, 84, 149, 153
 and free trade 55, 120, 125–6, 128–9
Liberal Party 71, 116, 118, 122, 125, 128–9
Liberty's 106, 120
Lipton, Thomas 68, 112, 115
Lipton's 88, 114–15, 137, 151
Littlewoods 137, 164
Liverpool 9, 91, 137, 184, 189
London
 and advertising 31–3, 142, 166, 169
 department stores 105, 138, 141
 riots 1, 203
 shopping centre 5, 8–9, 11, 14, 21–4, 47, 138
 street traders 27, 33–4
Ludlow, J. M. 59, 111
luxury 7–8, 10–11, 13–14, 23–4, 35, 118, 121, 136–8, 158, 162 (*see also* restraint)

Macmillan, Harold 169–71
mail order 7, 100, 102, 164
male consumers 99–100, 147, 192 (*see also* female consumers)
Manchester 1, 23, 25–7, 44, 47, 91–2, 100, 140, 184–5
Mandelson, Peter 196, 198
Mandeville, B. 13, 155
Margate 63, 92, 94
market research 143, 171, 177, 195, 203
markets 26, 33–4
Marks & Spencer 115, 138–9, 182–3, 203
Married Women's Property Acts
 1870 96
 1882 97
Marshall, Alfred 58, 111
Marshall and Snelgrove 89, 91, 100, 101, 106, 140
Marshall Field's 88, 90
Martin, Kingsley 176, 208
Martineau, Harriet 28, 45
Marx, Karl 5–6, 55, 57, 208
Marxism Today 194–5
Mass-Observation 145, 157, 159, 161–2

McKendrick, Neil 8–9
Merthyr Tydfil 14, 34–5
middle-class consumers 15, 19–20, 27, 35–6, 41–8, 206 (*see also* working-class consumers)
Mill, J. S. 58, 59
Millais, John 70, 81
Ministry of Food 131, 157–8, 160
Miss Selfridge 1, 182
Mitchell, J. T. W. 59, 111, 113
Monbiot, George 206–7
monopolies 73, 150, 153, 167
moral economy 12, 49, 53, 131, 162
Morison, James 30, 32
Morning Chronicle 34–5, 47
Morris, William 81, 120, 207
Morrison, Herbert 168, 172
Moses and Son 27, 30

National Consumer Council 183–4, 191, 194, 199, 202
National Government 153, 155
National Union of Women's Suffrage Societies 106–7
neo-liberalism 17, 182, 188–91, 201–2, 216 n.58
New Labour 134, 197–200, 201–3, 208 (*see also* Labour; Labour Party; socialism)
New Poor Law 50–1, 61
New Times 194–5
New York 88, 141
New York Times 162–3
Newcastle 24, 26, 52, 105
News of the World 170, 173
newspapers *see under* press
Noel-Baker, Francis 173–4
Northern Star 39, 51

O'Brien, Bronterre 51, 119
O'Connell, Daniel 44–5
One Nation Group 171–2
Orwell, George 135, 145, 149
Owen, Robert 49–50
Owenism 49–50, 51, 54, 172

Packard, Vince 3, 169
Pall Mall Gazette 71, 99–101
Paris 23, 59, 88, 162
patent medicines 30, 67, 69, 82–5, 160–1
patriotism 76, 78
Pears soap 70–1, 74, 76, 80, 192
Pearson, Arthur 69, 77, 91, 127
pedlars *see under* Scotch drapers
Peel, Robert 46, 55
Peter Robinson 91, 98, 153
Pick, Frank 147–8
plate glass 24, 37
Poor Law Ammendment Act (1834) 50–1
posters 30–1, 68, 70–1, 75, 82, 124
press 31–2, 69
Priestley, J. B. 136, 162–3, 176
profiteering 130–1, 134, 149–51
prostitutes 37, 94, 97, 99
protectionism 42–3, 45, 47, 117–19, 123–5, 127–8 (*see also* tariff reform)
Provident Clothing Supply Co Limited 116, 164 (*see also* check traders)
Punch 28, 38

Quaker Oats Company 67, 81
Quarterly Review 30, 45
Queen Victoria 27, 53, 76, 101, 115

rationing 130–1, 157–60, 161–2
Reform Acts
  1832 42, 51
  1867 61
  1884 118
Resale Price Mechanism 177–8
restraint 49, 120, 129, 157 (*see also* luxury)
retailing revolution 63, 114–15
Reynolds's Newspaper 48, 80, 118, 152
Right to Buy 190
Rochdale Society of Equitable Pioneers 54, 59–60, 113
Rowntree, Joseph 66, 121, 137–8
Royal Commission on Food Prices 150, 152
Ruskin, John 58, 120

Sainsbury's 114, 137, 165, 181
Sala, G. A. 80, 100
Salford 25, 186
Salisbury, Lord 71, 118

sandwichmen 30, 68
Scotch drapers 9, 19, 27
Scotland 45, 52–3, 59, 103, 115–16, 163
Scott, Walter Dill 76, 142
second-hand goods 27
Seldon, Arthur 172–3, 188
self-service 164–5
Selfridge, Gordon 88, 90–2, 104–6, 149, 150
Selfridge's 91, 94–5, 100, 102–6, 140
sexuality 37, 92–3, 94, 99
Shackleton, Elizabeth 10–11
Sheffield 25–6, 91, 184
shoplifting 39, 95–8, 165 (*see also* anxieties)
shopping (*see also* department stores; fashion; shops)
  changing meanings of 1–2, 11, 20, 37, 181–2, 194, 203
  dangers of 38–9, 60, 64, 94, 100
  experience of 21–6, 33–7, 68, 87–8, 90–1, 94, 98, 140, 165, 178
  as political action 46–7, 51, 101, 205, 208
shopkeepers 115–16, 177, 181–2
shops 25–6, 34–5 (*see also* department stores; fashion; shopping)
sky signs 68, 80
Smith, Adam 8–9, 12, 13, 42
Smith, Martin 194–5
Smith, Wareham 69, 144
Social Democratic Federation 103, 119–20
social emulation 6–7, 8, 10
socialism 119–21, 153 (*see also* Labour; Labour Party; New Labour)
Society for Checking the Abuses of Public Advertising 81–2, 143, 166
Soviet Union 3, 149
spectacle 24, 28, 37, 47, 90
standard of living 13–14, 66, 121–2, 129–30, 137
street traders 27, 33–4
Sunderland 94, 101, 138
Sunlight soap 67, 74, 75–6
supermarkets 164–5, 181
Swan and Edgar 38, 89, 106, 140

tariff reform 64, 72, 119, 124–5, 127–30 (*see also* protectionism)
taste reform 58–9, 70, 147–8
taxation 43, 48, 55–6, 69, 81, 118, 123–4, 130 (*see also* budgets)
teddy boys 170–1
teenagers 145, 170–1
Tesco 165, 177, 181, 204
Thatcher, Margaret 134, 186–90, 201
Thatcherism 187, 189, 191, 193–4
The Economist 180, 208
The Times 4, 31, 48, 50, 69, 80, 171, 180
Thompson, E. P. 12, 178
Trollope, Anthony 24, 39

underconsumption 13, 46, 122, 155
Unilever 143, 150–1, 167, 169, 172
United Kingdom Billposters' Association 31, 80

Veblen, Thorstein 6–7, 8, 10

Wales 26, 159
W. D. & H. O. Wills 67, 78
Wedgwood, Josiah 9, 41
Wells, H. G. 83–4
Whiteley, William 72, 123
Whiteley's 22, 87, 89–90, 92, 94, 96–7, 99–101, 140, 150
Wilkinson, Ellen 154–5
Wilson, Harold 163, 177–8, 180, 195
Winter of Discontent 188–9
Women's Co-operative Guild 107, 109–10, 125, 160, 162, 166
Women's Social and Political Union 106–7
Women's Unionist and Tariff Reform Association 128
Woolton, Lord 158–60, 163
Woolworths 136–7, 203
working-class consumers 3, 4, 19–20, 25–6, 27, 33–4, 48–55 (*see also* middle-class consumers)

York 48, 137
Young, Michael 174, 183–4, 191

Zola, Émile 89, 92, 104